# The Illustrated Encyclopedia of
# Māori Myth and Legend

Margaret Orbell is the author of seven other
books on Māori tradition, literature and belief,
including *The Natural World of the Māori;
Hawaiki: A new approach to Māori tradition;*
and *Traditional Māori Stories*. Until recently
Associate-Professor of Māori at the University
of Canterbury in Christchurch, New Zealand,
she is now a full-time writer.

# The Illustrated Encyclopedia of
# Māori Myth
# and
# Legend

## Margaret Orbell

CANTERBURY UNIVERSITY PRESS

First published in 1995 by
CANTERBURY UNIVERSITY PRESS
University of Canterbury
Private Bag 4800
Christchurch 8001, New Zealand

Reprinted 1996, 1999 and 2003

Designed by Richard King
Typeset in Palatino by Orca Publishing Services Ltd, Christchurch
Printed in China through Colorcraft Ltd, Hong Kong

ISBN 0-908812-45-0 (cased)
ISBN 0-908812-47-7 (limpbound)

*Front cover:* A painting of Hinemoa by June Northcroft Grant, of Te Arawa
and Ngāti Tūwharetoa. Hinemoa holds the gourds that helped her
to swim across Lake Rotorua to her lover Tūtānekai on Mokoia Island.
On her right is the flute that Tūtānekai played; on her left
is Matuatonga, the atua on Mokoia Island that ensured the
fertility of the kūmara in the Rotorua region.

*Back cover:* Te Pāea (Guide Sophia), photographed in the porch of
the Rotorua meeting house Raura beside the figure of Kurangaituku.

# Contents

# Acknowledgements

My main debt is to the Māori authorities of the nineteenth and twentieth centuries who recorded their traditions and songs for later generations. There were a multitude of these people, from every part of the country; some are named elsewhere in this book.

I owe much to those who introduced me to Māori literature, most especially Arapeta Awatere, Wiremu Parker and Beth Ranapia.

I am much indebted also to the Pākehā writers and students of tradition who preserved and sometimes published Māori writings, and at the same time recorded their own experiences and interpretations. While much of this early Pākehā literature is now dated in various ways, it remains important.

More recently, in the 1950s, a Danish historian of religion, J. Prytz Johansen, developed an approach based upon the close, comparative reading of Māori writings. Johansen's methods and his insights into the myths have been a major influence upon my work.

For many years at the University of Canterbury I taught courses in Māori mythology. To the students who attended these classes, asked questions, showed interest and contributed ideas, my heartfelt thanks.

In the making of this book I am much indebted to all of the persons and institutions that are named in the photographic credits. My special thanks go to Sandra Parkkali for the drawings she has done for the book, June Northcroft Grant, Ailsa Smith, John Perry and Andrew Warner of the Rotorua Museum of Art and History Te Whare Taonga o Te Arawa, Eva Yokum of the Museum of New Zealand Te Papa Tongarewa, Roger Neich of the Auckland Museum Te Papa Whakahiku, David Woodings of Te Awamutu District Museum, Jos of Jos's Photography, Whakatāne, and Duncan Shaw-Brown, Merilyn Hooper and Barbara Cotrell of the University of Canterbury's Audio-Visual Aids Department.

John Hearnshaw of the University of Canterbury kindly corrected the entries on stars and planets. If errors remain, the fault is mine.

The publisher at Canterbury University Press, Mike Bradstock, and the book's editor and designer, Richard King, have been endlessly patient and given excellent advice.

I am grateful too to Gordon Walters, Alexa Walters and David Walters for being so supportive and tolerant.

*Margaret Orbell*

# Introduction

The ancestors of the Māori were fishermen and farmers who made their way from Southeast Asia to islands just north of New Guinea, moved on eventually to Fiji and then, some time before 1000 BC, sailed across the wide ocean to Tonga, Sāmoa and islands nearby. They were the first humans to settle in this region. During the next thousand years their cultures and languages acquired the character that has come to be known as Polynesian.

About two thousand years ago, Samoan explorers set out across the vast ocean lying to the east. Here the islands are much more scattered and generally smaller, volcanic islands and coral atolls dotted over enormous expanses of water, yet nearly all were eventually settled, from Hawai'i in the north to Easter Island in the east. Finally, about a thousand years ago, one or more expeditions from the Society Islands, the Cooks or Tubuai (the Australs) reached Aotearoa (New Zealand) in the far south. It was the last habitable region of the world to be settled by humans.

All these expeditions set out laden with plants such as coconut, breadfruit, banana, paper mulberry, pandanus, taro, yam, gourd and often kūmara, together sometimes with dogs, pigs, edible rats and fowls. Especially careful organisation was necessary because the islands with which the explorers were familiar, while very rich in seafood, had no large land animals and, often, relatively few plant resources. Nor could they be sure that they would be able to return to their former homes for further supplies: although trading voyages took place in many cases between island groups, this might happen at rare intervals or not at all. They were well prepared for a self-reliant existence in a highly specialised tropical environment.

In Aotearoa, however, the explorers discovered something entirely unexpected. Moving out of the tropics they found a much larger and colder archipelago, greatly varied in its landscapes, soils and climate. A fragment of an ancient continent, Aotearoa had been thrust up into hills and mountains and very slowly, over many millions of years, pushed into the Pacific. It had been isolated from the rest of the world for some eighty million years, from before the period when mammals evolved, so its animals and dense forests had evolved differently from those elsewhere. Most obviously, the country was full of birds. Many had become weak fliers or flightless and some of these, in particular the moa, were extraordinarily large.

The new settlers soon found that their bountiful coconut, breadfruit and banana trees could not grow in this climate. Other crop plants were only marginally viable; even the kūmara, the sweet potato, could be grown only with much effort and under highly favourable conditions. Their only introduced animals, furthermore, were dogs and rats. But for the first few centuries the immigrants must in many ways have led a fairly easy existence, a small number of people in a country full of game. Moa and other birds were very plentiful, seals and sea lions lay on the shore, whales beached themselves from time to time, the fishing was excellent, there were plenty of shellfish, the rivers and wetlands were full of eels.

The much colder climate and more pronounced seasonal rhythms required immediate adjustment, especially as regards clothing and housing. The paper mulberry tree now grew only in the warmest places, and it was in any case much too cold for garments of bark cloth. Fortunately there was the flax plant, abundant and widespread in wetlands, with stiff tough leaves up to three metres long; this became the essential material for garments, baskets, mats, cordage and much else. In the forests there were excellent timber trees, in particular the tōtara, for use in smaller, solid houses and long narrow waka [canoes].

On the eastern plains of the South Island, where moa were most common, the population grew rapidly. The archaeological evidence shows that great numbers of moa were caught in this region, with hunting reaching a peak at about the beginning of the fourteenth century. After this the slow-breeding moa became more difficult to find, and by the sixteenth century a moa was a rare catch. They disappeared soon afterwards, along with the great eagle that had preyed upon them.

Meanwhile most of the Māori population had shifted to the North Island, with its warmer climate. People were now dependent mainly upon fish, shellfish and fernroot, although as well they hunted pigeon, kākā and other birds, gathered a variety of plant foods and, where possible, cultivated more kūmara than before. Coastal regions with good agricultural land were especially prized, and inevitably were increasingly fought over. In the early fifteenth century, communities in these coveted districts began building pā, forts with elaborate ditch-and-bank defences topped with massive palisades. Usually they did not live in these throughout the year but moved around their lands engaged in seasonal tasks. The pā were refuges when danger threatened and ceremonial centres for meetings and the reception of visitors.

Since these peoples were now living permanently in the one area and their pā provided relative safety, their buildings became more ambitious. Stone tools for woodworking and other purposes – especially tools of basalt, argillite and obsidian – had always been greatly valued and traded over long distances; now, at some point, apparently, in the fifteenth or sixteenth century, another important material became available when new ways of working greenstone (nephrite jade) led to greater use being made of this always scarce resource. Treasured greenstone chisels made possible the remarkable development of wood sculpture which took place at this time.

Further population growth in the North Island led to the full exploitation of the rugged interior and regions with poorer soils, but the populous districts remained mainly in the northern and coastal regions of the island. As elsewhere in Polynesia, the social system was based on the principle of kinship. Extended families, or whānau, varied in size and composition but were led by a man who, if he were of good birth, would be termed a rangatira. Such a man might have two or more wives; the higher his rank (and therefore the more substantial his assets), the larger his family was likely to be. Some of his married sons or daughters might be living with him, probably in houses fairly close to his own.

In addition a large household would probably have some slaves, usually female, and these might also be wives of the rangatira.

A number of closely related whānau made up a larger descent group known as a hapū. These varied greatly in size. Small, related hapū formed sections of larger hapū, and for some purposes these would come together into still larger hapū. It all depended upon the circumstances: some tasks or events would concern only a small descent group, while others would involve a larger number of people. The construction and use of a large seine net required many people's labour, so would bring together a number of small hapū; such a communal undertaking was efficient economically and served to reinforce social ties. A military threat from outside would probably unite even fairly distantly related hapū, which on other occasions might have their differences.*

It was generally not possible, in the hilly terrain and with the available technology and resources, for a single ruler to seize control of a large area. In this situation the flexibility of Māori social organisation allowed related hapū to form and reform their alliances as the constantly changing circumstances required. Since the marriages of people of rank were political events, further flexibility came from marriage practices that permitted either the man or the woman to move to live with the family of their spouse.

Another consequence was that even minor rangatira, while acknowledging their superiors in rank and status, in many circumstances were able to act independently of them. Despite their keen awareness of hierarchical distinctions, free men generally possessed a forceful, proud and independent manner. Successful warriors, especially, knew their own worth.

This being so, the leading rangatira of a hapū was dependent upon the approval of his fellow rangatira and had to persuade rather than order them to a course of action. Leaders in particular had to be masters of oratory, though others spoke as well; public affairs were passionately debated, and complex rhetorical songs became a major art form.

At every level, hapū are named after the ancestor (usually but not always male) from whom its members trace descent. This ancestral name, sometimes in shortened form, is preceded by the

---

* In the late nineteenth and the twentieth centuries, in very different political circumstances, large groupings of related hapū came to be known as iwi, or 'tribes', while the word hapū came to be translated as 'sub-tribe'. Before this time, the word iwi was used only when speaking of, or addressing, the *members* of hapū (large or small).

Above: *The high palisades of Waitahanui Pā, with out-ward-facing ancestral figures. This pā by Lake Taupō, at the mouth of the Tongariro River, was one of the main strong-holds of Ngāti Tūwharetoa until the introduction of muskets in the 1820s.*

*When not on hilltops, pā were generally on headlands, river banks or islands. Motuopuhi Pā on Lake Rotoaira (below) was surrounded on three sides by water and protected by a double palisade, with deep trenches and high embank-ments.*

appellation Ngāti, or a similar expression; thus Ngāti Maru are descendants of the early ancestor Maru-tūahu (spouses from outside this descent group being excluded from membership). Within the region, especially, the name Ngāti Maru often referred to Ngāti Maru 'proper' [tūturu], a senior and relatively small hapū, but for some purposes related hapū associated themselves with this descent group and all were spoken of collectively as Ngāti Maru. This practice still continues.

In this book, hapū are referred to as peoples or as descent groups.

## Polynesian tradition

All societies possess collections of narratives which explain the past, and therefore the present. The myths of the Māori attribute the origins of the world and its inhabitants mostly to the achievements of powerful early ancestors, whose stories were carefully memorised and passed from one generation to the next. The sources of many of these stories can be traced back two thousand years to the time when the Samoan explorers sailed out into the eastern ocean, taking with them their ancestral myths.

Some of these narratives were retained in Eastern Polynesia, in variant forms; thus there are many islands in the region, including Aotearoa's northern island, which are said to have been fished up by a trickster hero named Māui. The handsome Tāwhaki, the great warrior Whakatau, Rata the voyager, and Hina and Tinirau are other Māori figures with names and stories related to ones still known in Sāmoa.

In addition, new myths developed in Eastern Polynesia. Some are widespread in the region, so must have evolved while all the migrants were still in the one place; afterwards, as further expeditions set out, the new stories must have gone with them. A number of figures in these myths have names that show them to have originated as personifications. Among them, in Māori tradition, are Rangi [Sky], Papa [Foundation], Tāne [Male] and Tū, whose name, literally 'Upright', refers to the way in which he asserts himself as a warrior.

At the same time, memories of a former home were transformed into myth. Savai'i, the name of the largest Samoan island, now became the name of a land with supernatural associations. As the centuries passed, and the descendants of the first migrants spread out through the region, this name Savai'i changed with the local languages, becoming Hawaiki in Aotearoa, Havai'i in the Marquesas, Havaiki in the Tuamotus, Avaiki in the Cooks. In all but two instances, these names were assigned in religious tradition to an island which might be regarded as a place of origin and was always a place to which some persons, at least, made their way after death. This homeland lay towards the setting sun, or sometimes the rising sun; in some accounts it is in the sky, or under the water.

One of the exceptions is the island of Hawai'i in the Hawaiian group. Here an actual island received this name because it is the site of two spectacular volcanoes which were regarded as manifestations of supernatural power and homes of the gods. The other exception is an island in the Society Islands, now known as Ra'iatea but formerly Havai'i, which is an extinct volcano with a deep crater that was believed to be the entrance to the underworld. Again this island was thought to be the home of the gods.

It is remarkable that the development of Polynesian thought can be traced in such detail through so much space and time, and that the ancient myths – to the Polynesians, their early history – should have been retained so tenaciously. Names, especially, along with certain events and relationships, were faithfully passed from one generation to the next. Exposed to no outside influences, much given to historical discussion and debate, the learned men of Eastern Polynesia treasured and elaborated their traditions.

One circumstance remained more or less constant throughout the region. Apart from the pigs, dogs and rats they sometimes took on their migrations, Polynesians were acquainted only with fish and other sea creatures, birds, and small creatures such as lizards. All of these had roles in their beliefs and traditions; pigs and dogs were significant when present, individuals or families were often believed to have animal guardians such as sharks or birds, and reptiles were feared so much that there are stories about giant reptiles. In reality, however, the migrants encountered no large land animals other than the flightless moa in Aotearoa – where there were also, in the trees above, enormous eagles that preyed upon the moa. Both of these birds must have entered Māori mythology, since their existence had to be explained, but only traces of such beliefs survived after they became extinct.

Since large animals could not be held responsible for early events, as in many other mythologies, the humans assumed even more significance. As well as revealing the powers and roles of males and females, they often bring about the existence of natural phenomena and other life forms. Accounts of their adventures acquired narrative force and sophistication, and often an elaboration of detail. Long genealogies revealed them to be early ancestors of high-ranking men and women. On some islands, choral songs celebrated their exploits. Generally they were important in ritual.

In each archipelago the inhabitants shaped their inherited traditions in their own way, changing not only the details but the narrative style, the social world depicted and, to some extent, the myths' wider significance. Partly this happened because of differing environments. Volcanic islands such as those of the Hawaiian group, having rich soil and being relatively large, produced highly stratified and ceremonious societies, and their myths reflect this. Tiny coral atolls had simpler societies and different storytelling conventions.

Explorers reached Aotearoa from the southern Cook Islands, the Society Islands or Tubuai, or perhaps from more than one of these. The traditions of the Cooks and the Societies are fairly well known, and in some instances there are close parallels with Māori ones. Nevertheless the Māori myths, like their culture and society in general, became distinctively their own.

## Māori myths and legends

Traditions from different parts of Aotearoa have a general similarity, despite their differences. Since everything in the world was alive, and all living things were related, there was no distinction of the kind found in Western thought between nature and culture. The natural world and human society were inseparable from the beginning because the sky, Rangi, is the first male and the earth, Papa, the first female. It follows that human males are like the sky and human females like the earth.

These first parents have a number of children, who in most versions are all sons. One of the sons is always Tāne [Male], who brings the world into existence by separating his parents and after-wards – in most accounts – fathers human beings. The other sons often include Tangaroa, father of sea creatures; Tū, the first warrior; Rongo, father of the kūmara; Haumia, father of fernroot; and Tāwhirimātea, father of the winds. Sometimes there are others as well.

In some regions, many of these are regarded as Tāne's sons rather than his brothers, but this makes little difference; either way, humans and other life forms are bound by the indissoluble ties of kinship. Tāne is often said to have fathered

trees and birds before making a woman from the soil of Hawaiki and becoming the progenitor of human beings, and humans as a consequence are especially close to life forms that belong to the land.

Between them, these earliest ancestors and their immediate descendants determine the charac-teristic behaviour [tikanga] of natural phenomena, men and women, and other life forms. Some of them also satisfy human needs, as when the trickster hero Māui acquires fire and pulls up the fish that becomes Aotea (the North Island). Succeeding generations, who are exclusively human, become rather more specialised in their activities, introducing to the world such practices as tattooing and weaving.

Further down the genealogies we come to the men and women who leave their homes in Hawaiki to sail to Aotearoa and become ancestors of the peoples now living in different parts of the country. Traditions telling of such voyages exist in every region. Even those who trace descent in part from ancestors, such as Toi, who had always lived in Aotearoa, acknowledge other ancestors of mana whose origin was in Hawaiki.

These ancestors sailed on vessels such as *Te Arawa, Tainui, Tākitimu, Māmari, Horouta, Toko-maru*, and many more. During the voyage they displayed remarkable powers, overcoming many dangers, and on their arrival they introduced valuable resources such as the kūmara and the karaka tree. They then explored the country, establishing territorial boundaries, placing in the hills and on the shore the mauri that ensured fertility, and creating landmarks. In the south, for instance, Rākaihaitū, captain of the *Uruao*, dug out a number of lakes that the country needed. In the north, the powerful tohunga Ngātoro-i-rangi introduced the volcanic fires still to be found there.

In such cases the interaction of the tradition and the landmark reinforced belief: while the myth explained the existence of the landmark, the presence of this landmark confirmed the truth of the myth. The existence of the fiery crater in Ngāuruhoe was explained by the story that Ngātoro-i-rangi, having reached the mountain's snowy summit, called to his sisters back in Ha-waiki and told them to bring fire to warm him. At the same time, the fire on the mountain showed this tradition to be correct and was a most powerful sign of the mana of Ngātoro-i-rangi.

Tapu landmarks often take the form of sig-nificantly shaped stones and rocky outcrops. Many are associated with the ancestors who sailed from Hawaiki and the waka in which they came, for it was believed that nearly all of these vessels afterwards turned to stone – becoming, usually, reefs by the shore, unchanging presences that convey powerful messages concerning the people's origins and rights of possession.

After telling of the voyage to Aotearoa and the definitive acts that occurred subsequently, the traditions of each people trace through the genealogies the famous ancestors who founded descent groups, defended their lands against outsiders, avenged defeats and, often, made politically significant marriages that ensured their people's wellbeing. There are, as well, plenty of accounts of men and women who stubbornly chose for themselves the lives they would lead. Some of these are love stories, and sometimes they end happily.

These narratives concerning more recent times can generally be described as legends rather than myths, in that they contain much that is historically accurate. Certainly these ancestors, especially those belonging to the first generations to live in Aotearoa, are occasionally said to be giants, or to perform prodigious feats of one kind and another; but even so, their names and those of their relatives must generally have belonged to actual persons and many of the events with which they are associated must in fact have occurred. Naturally enough, the traditions of neighbouring peoples are often at variance, as when they give differing accounts of the outcomes of battles in which the two sides had engaged, but there is much corroboration as well. A tremendous amount of historical information is available, especially for the last few centuries.

While stories telling of encounters with supernatural beings such as taniwha, fairies [patupaiarehe] and giant reptiles are often set in the distant past, human involvement with them continued. Most taniwha had a relationship with one particular people, who made them offerings; fairies were seen on misty hills or in dreams, and again might have a relationship with humans; even reptiles, in the form of the small geckos that were so dreaded, might be employed in sorcery or made guardians of buried treasure. Traditions relating to these beings were part of a complex body of belief and practice.

## Ritual and song

Intricate and often surprising uses were made of myths in ritual, song, proverbial sayings [whakataukī] and oratory. The poles or props [toko], for instance, with which Tāne, in the beginning, separated Rangi the sky and Papa the earth, were

sometimes identified with small poles placed upright at the tūāhu, the shrine where the tohunga communicated with the gods – so that by implication the tūāhu became a microcosm, a miniature version of the world, and its poles safeguarded the order that Tāne had brought to the world.

Similarly, on the east coast the work song [tewha] sung by the sons of Rangi and Papa when separating their parents, and the form of scaffolding they used – known as a toko-Rangi or 'prop up Rangi' – were employed by men building the palisade of a pā, hauling up its heavy posts. By re-enacting in this way the event that had brought the world into being, the workers put to their own use the immense power [mana] possessed, because of their origin, by this chant and scaffolding. The workers' identification with the sons of sky and earth – the first workmen – gave great dignity to their task. And the posts in the palisades that were to defend their stronghold acquired a special significance through their identification with the posts that supported the sky.

On the west coast, a different chant was believed to have been used by Tāne when he separated Rangi and Papa, propping them apart with tall trees. This chant, known as a toko, was employed in ritual when a marriage had ended but the husband or wife was still suffering from love. In this context, a tohunga's performance of the chant re-enacted the first separation and identified the husband with Rangi and the wife with Papa. The separation of these two people became the separation of sky and earth, and just as inevitable.

Some such usages were ancient, while others came into existence as required. People responded to significant events with eloquent speech – ritual chants, songs and oratory – and in so doing they thought, for much of the time, in terms of images and events from the past. In songs known as oriori, sung over infants, the child's origin in Hawaiki might be celebrated and distinguished ancestors would be mentioned. In waiata tangi – passionate, allusive laments for the dead – the poets spoke of the early generations who had created precedents and shown what must be done.

Faced with disaster, men and women looked to the past for explanations and took upon themselves the roles that had been established for them. Māui, Hine-nui-te-pō or Whiro might be blamed for the existence of death. The wairua of the person who had died would be sung out of the body, sent on the journey northwards to Te

*Successful orators possessed a mastery of tradition and song.*
*A speaker in the far north in 1827.*

Rēinga or told to assume Tāwhaki's role and rise up to the sky. For a death in battle there might be mention of Apakura, who wept constantly and urged revenge. Like Whakatau, to whom she had appealed, the warriors related to the fallen rangatira would accept this sacred duty.

Nor were songs sung only in the circumstances that first occasioned them. Later they were sung whenever it was appropriate to express or contemplate the ideas they contained. In oratory, both songs and ritual chants were often adapted to new circumstances. Some songs were sung at night around fires, especially when there was a full moon. Old people, especially, used to sing during the night, or in the early morning before rising.

Māori songs move rapidly from one allusion to another, usually with only brief passages of narration. The poets depended upon the understanding of highly informed listeners, and this they generally had. At the same time their songs played an important part in the preservation of tradition. Certain mythical figures, for instance, seem to have been known in many parts of the country only from brief references in songs. Miru, whose home is in the underworld, appears in myths on the west coast and in the far north of the North Island, but elsewhere is mentioned only in songs.

## Representations of gods and ancestors

Māori ritual sites were generally small and inconspicuous, hidden away in wild places. Often they were natural features in the landscape, as with the sacred spring or pool [wai tapu] near every village. Perhaps the most important were tūāhu, where gods [atua] were invoked, offerings were made and many ceremonies performed. These shrines often took the form of a naturally occurring hillock or a small pile of stones, together with a fence, small upright poles and, sometimes, unworked upright stones that might represent certain gods. In other regions, the god (such as Maru) or early ancestor (Tāne, Tangaroa, Tū, Tāwhirimātea or Rongo) who had been summoned by the tohunga might enter a small wooden image [taumata atua] placed upright at the tūāhu.

Sacred stones, whether unworked or carved, were immutable and eternal presences. Very small stones, believed to have been brought from Hawaiki, were employed by tohunga. Mauri, which contained and guarded the vitality and mana of a resource or other entity, often took the form of stones, sometimes quite small and either unworked or simply shaped. The existence in the landscape of extraordinarily shaped rocks is often, as we have seen, explained by myths associating them with early ancestors.

It is perhaps for this reason – because of the inherent powers possessed by significant stones – that stone figures, while possessing great expressive force, are sometimes only slightly carved. Treasured possessions of greenstone, such as tiki, were laboriously shaped and polished, along with stone adzes and chisels. But ancestors and other kin who conferred and guarded fertility, such as

*In Te Tokanganui-a-Noho, a meeting house opened in 1873 which still stands at Te Kūiti, ancestors (like saints in a medieval church) are depicted with objects relating to their histories. Tama-te-kapua has his stilts, and his enemies' house is shown. Māui has the sun in his noose, and holds the whip with which he slowed its progress; below are the pigeon into which he turned, and the waka in which he fished up the land of Aotearoa. Whakaotirangi holds the little kete in which she saved her seed kūmara, and the cord with which she tied it; the stars must be those that bring the kūmara harvest in the autumn.*

Horoirangi in the Rotorua district and Rongo and others who protected kūmara gardens, needed only to have their powers made visible. Because of this they could be carved from materials that would otherwise have been difficult to work with the available technology.

The situation was very different with woodworking, especially when greenstone chisels began to become available. For the houses and storehouses of rangatira, the gateways of pā, large waka, and numerous small objects such as treasure boxes [waka huia], the material mainly employed was tōtara wood. This could be readily split and worked, and would take fine detail.

In the sculptural style that developed as a consequence, human figures are sometimes three-dimensional but are more often depicted in bas-relief, on the timbers of houses and other structures and on small objects. Figures are generally wide and shallow, defined largely by the exuberantly inventive patterns that swirl and circle on their surface. Body parts, especially the head, are freely interpreted – though some heads have features realistic enough to bear the patterns of facial tattoo [moko]. Stylised heads and profile

heads proliferate, with smaller figures super-imposed on larger figures, grasping one another, dissolving into pattern, forming highly sophisticated compositions.

Most of these carved structures and objects were associated in one way or another with high-ranking people or with the status of the community as a whole, so were tapu – sacred, under religious restriction – to a greater or lesser degree. Usually they were painted with red ochre, though some were polychrome. While detailed information about the figures' significance is often lacking, it is known that they generally represent ancestors. While some are early, such as Māui, most are the relatively recent ancestors who protect and advise (or when necessary, punish) their living descendants.

Until the nineteenth century, the house of a rangatira and his family was very small by present standards, with a low door and a single window alongside. These thick-walled houses were built to provide warmth in winter, and were typically about two metres high, two and a half to three metres in width and three to five metres in length. The interiors were used largely for sleeping, and then only on winter nights. During the day people often worked in the porch, and in hot weather they generally slept in the open or under light shelters. Since no food could be taken inside, meals were eaten in the open, or in the porch on wet days.

Carved figures in these early houses were mostly on the outside timbers. They were not merely depictions of departed relatives; instead, in some sense, they were the relatives themselves, and their splendour revealed their power. On the façade and the porch walls they guarded their descendants and revealed these persons' ancestry and mana. It was especially important for the threshold to be protected from sorcery [mākutu], and this role they performed in carved lintels over the door, and often the window. Inside the house, an especially significant ancestor formed the lower part of the central pillar [pou-toko-manawa] that supported the ridgepole. Here as elsewhere the ancestor was part of the very structure of the building, sheltering its occupants.

On storehouses and treasure boxes, in particular, carved ancestors are sometimes sexually joined. This is clearly appropriate for ancestors, to whose powers of fertility their descendants owe their existence. Their embraces speak of the abundance within, and at the same time they ensure that plenitude. For this reason, too, the bargeboards of many storehouses depict stylised whales – these being symbolic of abundance.

*Tapu storehouses (pātaka) held treasured possessions of rangatira. This building in the far north is supported by an ancestral figure and guarded by a lizard. On the façade, two pairs of embracing ancestors ensure an abundance within.*

## Consequences of Pākehā colonisation

At the time of the earliest substantial contact with Pākehā, late in the eighteenth century, the Māori population was perhaps about a hundred thousand. Their lives were soon affected by the acquisition of new resources and technology (potatoes and other plants, pigs, metal tools, later muskets), and new diseases such as measles to which they had no inherited immunity. Sailors, sealers, whalers, traders and assorted adventurers began to visit Aotearoa. Missionaries arrived in 1815, speeding technological change, eventually introducing a knowledge of reading and writing and a new religion. The realisation that other, different peoples existed elsewhere was unsettling in itself.

By the 1820s, Māori life and thought were rapidly changing. The new technology had led to an arms race; there had been increased fighting, and much social disruption as people struggled to earn money for the new weapons. In the far north especially, new experiences and economic opportunities were in complex ways undermining the authority of rangatira and tohunga. Perhaps most important of all were the effects of the introduced diseases – a historical accident which no-one at the time understood. Terrible epidemics ravaged the country, yet the Pākehā did not die.

People were exhausted, no longer able to rely upon their own sources of power. The Pākehā god was clearly very powerful, since he protected his people from illness and gave them so much, but he could not be introduced into the Māori religious system as readily as others had been in the past. The multitudinous ancestors and atua of Māori belief, who had brought the world into being and controlled it, had no part to play in Christianity as the Pākehā understood it.

Another difficulty was that the Pākehā claimed that only their god was tapu. The complex interplay of tapu and noa, sacred and profane, which had ordered all Māori activities and experience of the world, had no counterpart in Pākehā thought.

Yet tapu observances in the north were diminishing and the intricately harmonious world view was in fact changing. A sudden change came in the late 1820s, when the missionaries printed sections of the Bible in translation and taught Māori people to read. They learnt very rapidly, and studied the scriptures with intense interest. Christianity offered new hope, and the Bible provided absorbing histories, sometimes similar to their own; like them, they were full of incidents that established precedents for later times. By the mid-1840s, two-thirds of the Māori population were attending Christian services.

But the missionaries, of course, did not succeed in turning them into Christians like themselves. Instead, Māori people became Māori Christians. Although tapu observances became less extensive, they did not disappear (and still exist today). Many rituals involving ancestors and atua fell into disuse, some through missionary pressure and some in any case through social change (war gods such as Maru, and myths such as that of Whakatau, were no longer needed when traditional warfare came to an end). Much, gradually, was lost. But a veneration for ancestors, early and recent, has remained, and often there is still a sense of kinship with the natural world.

Fortunately, some Māori religious traditions were regarded by both Māori and missionaries as historical narratives, so were not thought to

conflict with Christian belief. This was true, for instance, of myths relating to the voyages from Hawaiki.

Aotearoa had become a British colony in 1840, with a treaty signed with many of the principal rangatira. Pākehā colonists arrived after this in ever-increasing numbers, a great many more than could have been envisaged, nearly all seeking land. The unprincipled actions of the colonists' government led to war in the 1860s, as Māori peoples in different parts of the country sought to retain their lands and their independence. Afterwards there were massive land confiscations by the Government, and continuing loss of land in other ways. And there was still much illness. It took time for the Māori population to acquire a degree of immunity to introduced diseases; by the end of the century their numbers had declined to just over forty thousand. But this was the turning point. After this the population steadily increased.

Through all the vicissitudes of Māori life in the nineteenth and twentieth centuries there has been a continuity of thought and feeling, a tradition that is still evolving. Two areas of innovation can be mentioned here. One concerns the architecture and art of the later nineteenth century. The other is the written literature created by Māori authorities who recorded their traditional narratives and songs.

## Meeting houses and their art

In earlier times, as we have seen, the houses of rangatira were small and nearly all woodcarvings were on the exterior; large-scale meetings took place in the open, often on the marae in front of the house. In the early nineteenth century these houses became rather bigger, although immediately after the acceptance of Christianity much energy went into the building of churches. Then in the late 1850s, as Māori people felt a new need to affirm their identity and mana in the face of the Pākehā invasion, they began to build houses a great deal larger than before. These buildings are meeting houses, carved often on the interior walls as well as the exterior, designed to accommodate parties of visitors and to allow meetings to be held inside them (although the marae remains the most important area for social ritual and oratory).

There are hundreds of meeting houses in Aotearoa, large and small, some recently constructed and others dating back to the last decades of the nineteenth century. Generally a house bears the name of an ancestor from whom the com-

*By the 1870s, painted figures and scenes were appearing on meeting houses. On this house at Mangakuta Pā, near Masterton, Māui catches his fish on one bargeboard, and the names of two of his brothers, apparently with the same fish, are on the other.*

munity who own it trace their descent. Inside the house they shelter within the embrace of this ancestor, in the company of other ancestors carved upon the walls.

By the 1870s, some carvers were introducing into their work new elements of realism. Often these take the form of a possession associated with an ancestor's exploit, as when Māui is depicted with his fish, Tūtānekai with his flute, Whakaotirangi with her basket of kūmara, Pāoa with his dog, Maniapoto with his cave. In earlier carvings an ancestral figure might hold a mere, but if there were other distinguishing marks they did not involve realism of this kind and cannot now be recognised.

Also in the 1870s, paintings of a new kind – decorative detail, symbolic figures, scenes from the past – began to occupy small spaces in houses. These combine Western influence with patterns based on traditional painted ones [kōwhaiwhai]. Sometimes an entire house is painted in this manner.

The work of present-day Māori artists, whether in meeting houses or art galleries, often draws upon these different traditions, reinterpreting and extending them.

## Nineteenth-century writers

When Māori people acquired a knowledge of reading and writing, they began at once to make extensive use of it in letters and records of all kinds. From the mid-1840s, people with a knowledge of tradition were writing down, or occasionally dictating, mythic narratives, recent histories, accounts of cultural practices and the words of songs of all kinds. They continued to do this throughout the latter part of the nineteenth century and into the early years of the twentieth century.

Sometimes the traditions were recorded and passed down within a family. In many cases, though, such documents resulted from an association between a Māori authority and an interested Pākehā, and these records have generally ended up in public libraries. A few of the early missionaries, notably Richard Taylor and J. F. H. Wohlers, were serious students of tradition. George Grey, who in 1845 became governor of the colony, was frustrated to find that he could not understand letters written by rangatira who made reference to mythology and quoted from

*Like many of his contemporaries, Matiaha Tiramōrehu of Ngāi Tahu (d. 1881) received a traditional education, later became a Christian, but nevertheless recorded his knowledge of tradition for later generations. A portrait painted in 1849, a year after he had written an important account of South Island mythology.*

medium. Less specialised writers also recorded valuable songs and stories. Women seem not to have been consulted very much by Pākehā students of tradition; perhaps, too, these Pākehā men were less likely to note the source of information when it had been provided by a woman. Yet one form of women's literature is well recorded. Māori men wrote down, in all, hundreds of songs by women poets.

The extent to which Pākehā students of tradition requested and preserved manuscripts by Māori writers is still not generally appreciated. Some Pākehā made little or no acknowledgement in their books and articles; others, such as Elsdon Best in his book *Tūhoe*, acknowledged assistance but did not make it clear that this assistance in some cases had been given in written form. These documents now require editing and translation that are in accord with modern standards, and publication in full. A few such books have recently been published, and more must follow.

This is not all. Numerous Māori-language periodicals appeared during the same period the manuscripts were produced; among other things they contain a great deal relating to traditional matters, and their contents are now being

*Māori-language periodicals record a great deal of discussion and debate on matters of tradition. One of the most important in this respect, as in others, is Te Puke ki Hikurangi, founded in 1897 by Hamuera Tamahau Mahupuku, a leading rangatira of Ngāti Kahungunu in the Wairarapa.*

songs, so he determined to study the oral tradition and make a collection of manuscripts. He did this very successfully, largely because his position gave him, in these early years, a high status among leading rangatira; also, he was able to make use of government interpreters, some of them young Pākehā men who had grown up in missionary establishments and were more or less bilingual. Two of these officials, John White and C. O. B. Davis, went on to publish major works of their own; like other Pākehā, they give eye-witness accounts of social and religious activities that most Māori authors took for granted so did not describe.

Many of the Māori writers were rangatira whose education had included the intensive study of religious tradition and song, and who now, aware of rapid changes, wanted to preserve their peoples' histories in this powerful new explored. Valuable accounts by Māori writers are in the early issues of the *Journal of the Polynesian Society*, which began publication in 1892; much here requires re-editing and reinterpretation. Then there are the land court records, which contain few Māori-language texts but an immense amount of information concerning traditional history.

This vast collection of documents is unusual, when compared to records existing elsewhere, in its sheer size. There must be few if any comparable peoples whose early writings are so prolific.

Also, bodies of oral tradition have frequently been recorded some generations after a people's initial acquisition of literacy, at a time when the introduction of this skill, along with associated

*In the 1870s, when he was an old man, the great Ngāti Porou tohunga Mohi Ruatapu wrote traditional histories for three persons of high rank, in each case tracing his or her descent from earliest times to the present. These people were Rōpata Wahawaha (right); Herewaka (below), daughter of Tama-i-whakanehua-i-te-rangi; and Hēnare Pōtae. The last two are known to have been related to Mohi; Rōpata was probably also a relative. Mohi's manuscripts are now in public libraries and those relating to Rōpata and Herewaka have recently been published, with translations.*

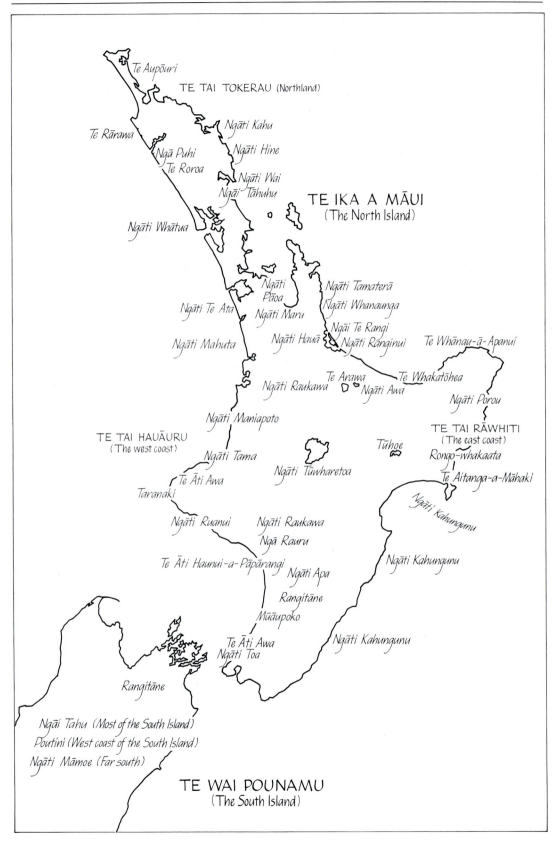

Te Aupōuri

TE TAI TOKERAU (Northland)

Ngāti Kahu

Te Rārawa

Ngāti Hine

Ngā Puhi
Te Roroa

Ngāti Wai
Ngāi-Tāhuhu

TE IKA A MĀUI
(The North Island)

Ngāti Whātua

Ngāti Pāoa

Ngāti Te Ata

Ngāti Maru

Ngāti Tamaterā
Ngāti Whanaunga

Ngāti Mahuta

Ngāti Hauā

Ngāi Te Rangi
Ngāti Ranginui

Te Whānau-ā-Apanui

Ngāti Raukawa

Te Arawa

Te Whakatōhea

Ngāti Awa

Ngāti Porou

Ngāti Maniapoto

TE TAI HAUĀURU
(The west coast)

TE TAI RĀWHITI
(The east coast)

Tūhoe

Rongo-whakaata

Ngāti Tama

Ngāti Tūwharetoa

Te Aitanga-a-Māhaki

Te Āti Awa

Taranaki

Ngāti Kahungunu

Ngāti Ruanui

Ngāti Raukawa
Ngā Rauru

Te Āti Haunui-a-Pāpārangi

Ngāti Apa

Ngāti Kahungunu

Rangitāne

Mūaupoko

Te Āti Awa
Ngāti Toa

Ngāti Kahungunu

Rangitāne

Ngāi Tahu (Most of the South Island)
Poutini (West coast of the South Island)
Ngāti Māmoe (Far south)

TE WAI POUNAMU
(The South Island)

circumstances, has already led to substantial change in their thought and religion; this happened, for instance, with Greek and Irish mythologies. The situation in Aotearoa was different. Because Māori and Pākehā were acting together in creating and preserving these records, the first of them were made very soon after the culture began to change, and we have as a consequence much more information than usual about the original significance of these traditions.

## The scope of this book

Information bearing upon the meanings of the myths is, in fact, so extensive – their functions in ritual, songs and oratory, the ways in which their images resonate elsewhere in the culture – that in the present work it is not possible to discuss these matters systematically and at length: it would amount to another book. They are discussed briefly, as opportunity offers. More

Left: *The Māori peoples of Aotearoa, as at 1840. Numerous other peoples are not shown, for lack of space. Te Arawa (the Arawa Confederation of Tribes) includes, among others, Ngāti Pikiao, Tūhourangi, Ngāti Rangiwewehi, Ngāti Uenuku-kōpako, Ngāti Whakaue, and Ngāti Tūwharetoa. The Tainui Confederation of Tribes includes the peoples of the Waikato and Hauraki regions.*

generally, however, an acquaintance with these areas lies behind the interpretations offered. The present writer began some thirty years ago with an interest in the songs, and found that this led to the myths.

An interest in Māori myths leads to an investigation of the relationship between Māori and other Polynesian mythologies. Here again this book provides some information but is far from comprehensive.

Māori tradition is such a large and diverse field that even the narratives, the accounts of mythical and historical people, cannot be covered comprehensively. Every region has endless stories of its own, along with others that differ in subtle ways from those told elsewhere. This book is intended as an introduction and makes no claim to be definitive. In particular, accounts of the exploits of relatively recent ancestors, the founders of descent groups, are so numerous that they could not be fully represented. Only histories that are regionally based can deal adequately with so much material; a number of these are available, and more will undoubtedly be written.

The Māori writers who are mentioned and portrayed are a representative few of the multitude of people who in one way and another – orally, also – have left Aotearoa its great heritage of tradition.

## A note on the language

In nearly all cases, Māori words do not change their form in the plural. This usage has been retained in the present work in the case of Māori words that have been adopted into New Zealand English. Macrons (for example, ā, ē) indicate long vowels. Square brackets enclose translations of names; parentheses enclose present-day place-names

## Glossary

Terms which are also the subject of an encyclopedia entry are indicated by an asterisk *.

atua*: spirit, god
haka: dance, song occompanying a dance
hine: often the first element in a woman's name
kete: basket
mana*: influence, prestige, power
marae: ceremonial space in front of a house
mauri*: life principle, source of vitality, protector of mana
mere: short, flat striking weapon of greenstone
noa: profane, everyday, without restriction
ngārara: reptile (gecko or tuatara)
pā: fortress
Pākehā: person of European descent

patu: short, flat, striking weapon
poupou: upright slab in wall of house
puhi: high-ranking girl who was cherished and carefully guarded before marriage
rangatira: chief, person of high rank
taiaha: long, two-handed weapon with blade at one end and point at the other
taniwha*: spirit living, usually, in the sea or inland waters
tapu*: sacred, under religious restriction
te: the singular definite article; often the first element in the name of a person or place
tipua*: being with supernatural powers
tohunga*: priest, expert
tūāhu*: shrine
wairua*: soul, spirit
waka: canoe, ship

# The Encyclopedia

## Aituā
### Evil Fate

The word aituā means 'disaster, fate'. Often it becomes a personification, so that orators and poets speak of Aituā, or Fate. Who, they ask, can withstand the strong hand of Aituā?

On the west coast of the North Island, poets speak of Aituā as the captain of a fine vessel, the *Karamū-rau-riki*, which after a death comes to convey the wairua to the homeland of Hawaiki.

## Ancestors
### Source and substance of the world

Ancestors were regarded as the substance of their descendants, their very being. This was more than a close bond, it was a continuity of existence. On the one hand, it was believed that individuals had participated in the lives of their ancestors, so that their own lives went backward in time to early events. An orator describing an early event in his people's history might speak, quite explicitly, as though he himself had been present at the scene. At the same time, it was taken for granted that people behave as they do because of the presence within them of their ancestors, both early and recent; that people owe their identity as well as their existence to the men and women who have preceded them. These two ideas were inseparable. People were present in their ancestors, and their ancestors were present in them.

Everything in the world has life, and all are descended from the first parents, Rangi the sky and Papa the earth. Because of this common descent all life forms belong to the one kinship group, and all can be spoken of as persons [tāngata]. Human beings are related to the trees and birds, and more distantly to other life forms such as sand on the beach and mist on the hills.

The earliest ancestors make up the world (they are the sky, earth, ocean, plants and so on), yet some are human beings as well. Rangi and Papa are not only sky and earth, they are the first man and woman, and accordingly they establish the basic natures of men and women, showing that men are like the sky and women like the earth. Tāne [Male], who gives the world its basic structure and fathers the birds, plants and humans, provides a further precedent for human males.

The first of the ancestors who follow – women

*Tall ancestral figures formed an integral part of the palisades of pā, declaring the identity of those within and challenging the enemy. This ancestor is from Puketōtara, a Rangitāne stronghold in the lower Manawatū.*

25

such as Hine-ahu-one and Hine-te-iwaiwa, men such as Māui and Tāwhaki – are, most of them, exclusively human. These people live, it is often said, in Hawaiki. Sometimes they shape and order the world in various ways. Always their activities provide precedents for human circumstances and behaviour.

From these early generations the genealogists trace lines of descent down through the men and women who sail from Hawaiki to Aotearoa, explore the new land and make it ready for their descendants. When the recital continues to the present, forty or fifty ancestors may separate a living person from Rangi and Papa.

Early ancestors whose descendants took the form of resources – food and materials – provided their human relatives with appropriate assistance, as when Tangaroa provided fish, Tāne gave birds, and Rongo ensured good kūmara harvests. Before a resource was utilised it was necessary, therefore, that an offering should be made to the ancestor concerned. Because fish were Tangaroa, the first fish caught on a fishing expedition had its head bumped against the gunwale before being dropped back into the sea with the words, 'This is for you, Tangaroa' [Ki a koe, e Tangaroa]. The first bird caught in the forest was laid at the foot of a tree with equivalent words addressed to Tāne.

On an especially significant occasion a longer ritual would be performed, as at a kūmara harvest, or when a large tree such as a tōtara was to be felled. If this ritual were not carried out correctly there was bound to be misfortune of some kind.

Early ancestors who had established patterns of behaviour, correct ways of doing things, also provided assistance within their sphere of action, as when Hine-te-iwaiwa helped women in childbirth and Tū and Whiro assisted warriors in battle. When a descendant was in need of assistance, a ritual chant [karakia] would name the ancestor concerned, in this way identifying ancestor and descendant and allowing the descendant to re-enact the events (the episode in a myth) which had established the procedures to be followed on such an occasion. Sometimes this chant gained much of its mana by quoting a passage from a chant that had been recited initially by an ancestor during his adventures.

Ancestors whose names occur rather later in the genealogies may also, in the accounts of their lives (in myths), establish precedents for later times and recite ritual chants which are employed by their descendants. This is especially important in the case of those who made the voyage from Hawaiki and afterwards explored the new land of Aotearoa.

More recent ancestors had a rather different role. Belonging as they did to the same immediate kinship group as their descendants, these ancestors had a continuing interest in their behaviour and welfare. Since persons of mana had inherited their powers from them, they watched vigilantly to ensure that these descendants observed the restrictions as regards tapu which accompanied this status. They might also communicate with their relatives in various ways, and warn of coming danger. While they were generally spoken of as men and women [tāngata, wāhine] and as ancestors [tīpuna or tūpuna], when their wairua [souls] visited their descendants they were referred to as atua [spirits, gods].

## Aoraki
### A man who became a mountain

Aoraki (Mount Cook) is the highest mountain in Aotearoa. A myth explains that this mountain was once a man, one of the sons of Raki the sky (in the South Island the sky is Raki, rather than Rangi as in the north).

When Raki married Papa, the earth, these first parents already had children from other unions. Some of Raki's sons came down from the sky to inspect his new wife and visit her children. Among them were Aoraki and his younger brothers Rakiroa, Rakirua and Rarakiroa, who arrived in an immense waka known as Te Waka-a-Aoraki [Aoraki's waka].

Down below they found Papa lying in the ocean, a huge body of land consisting mostly of Hawaiki. The voyagers sailed right around her, then set off to discover other countries. But wherever they went they found only the ocean.

They attempted to return to the sky, but disaster overtook them, for their ritual chant was performed incorrectly and the vessel began to sink. As this happened it turned to stone and earth, and it heeled over, leaving the western side much higher than the eastern.

The four men climbed to the higher side and turned into mountains. Aoraki, the eldest, is the tallest peak. The others stand nearby. The English name of Rakiroa is Mount Dampier, that of Rakirua is Mount Teichelmann, and that of Rarakiroa is the Silberhorn. Their ship is now the South Island.

Some time later a man named Tū-te-raki-whānoa prepared the land for human habitation. Inspecting the vessel, he found much to be done. To the north-east the carved prow had fallen and shattered to pieces, forming inlets and islands (known now as the Marlborough Sounds). These he left as they were. But on the east coast he heaped up Banks Peninsula, with its productive harbours, and he sent off an assistant, Marokura, to form the Kaikōura Peninsula. On the west coast he chopped out openings with his great adze to let the sea flow into the land, especially in the south-west. He also planted vegetation to make the island beautiful.

Tū-te-rakiwhānoa was believed to visit the east coast occasionally with Takaroa (whose name is equivalent to the North Island Tangaroa). When these two beings appeared as whales in estuaries and river mouths, people were awestruck and recognised their presence as an important omen.

According to this southern story, the famous Māui who fished up Te Ika a Māui (the North Island) was a descendant of Aoraki. Māui's task, in this tradition, was to sail around the waka that Aoraki had left and make it safe for people to land on. His own vessel, *Māhunui*, turned to stone and now rests on a high ridge behind Mount Peel.

Others explain Aoraki's presence differently, saying he was a member of the crew of *Āraiteuru* and that after it was wrecked he turned to stone along with his companions. And many people claim the entire South Island is Māui's waka.

## *Aotea*

### A west coast waka

Turi and his people set out on this vessel because of Uenuku. When this great man seized their land at Awarua, they fought and won a war against him. But Uenuku's younger brother was killed in the fighting, and in revenge he afterwards murdered Turi's son Pōtiki-roroa.

Turi in his turn killed Uenuku's son Hawe-pōtiki, then cooked the boy's body. He concealed a small piece of flesh in cooked kūmara, and in the course of a ceremonial presentation he offered the kūmara to Uenuku, who unknowingly ate his own son's flesh. Soon afterwards he discovered the terrible truth.

That night Turi's wife Rongorongo, to quiet her crying baby, went out from their house (named Rangiātea). Outside Uenuku's house, she overheard him chanting a song predicting death. When she returned and sang this song to Turi, he knew that Uenuku intended to destroy them and their people. And he knew that if they stayed in Hawaiki, Uenuku would win in the end.

Having learnt about Aotearoa from the recently returned explorer Kupe, Turi determined to set out for this new land. So he sent Rongorongo to ask her father Toto for the *Aotea*, and the old

man gave it to them. The return present was a treasured cloak sewn from the skins of eight dogs.

Turi now made his preparations. On board the waka he stowed seed kūmara (under the special care of Rongorongo), seeds of the karaka tree, and other plants as well. He brought birds – the pūkeko and the kākāriki – and rats to liberate in the forests, and as well he brought the caterpillars of the sphinx moth, which feed upon kūmara plants. His ship brought so many things that it is known proverbially as '*Aotea* utanga rau' [the heavily laden *Aotea*]. Other possessions, such as the taro, were brought on waka that accompanied the *Aotea*.

*The kernels of karaka berries were a much-appreciated food, and in coastal regions the trees were planted in groves. A number of waka, among them the* Aotea, *are said in different traditions to have brought seeds of the karaka from Hawaiki.*

Some people say that one of these vessels, the *Kurahaupō*, was wrecked on the way, and that the ship's captain Ruatea then transferred to the *Aotea* with his crew. This, they claim, was the real reason why the *Aotea* was heavily laden.

The tohunga on board are often said to have included Tuau, whom Turi had tricked into coming, and Kauika. As well there was a man named Tapō. Before long Tapō behaved insolently towards Turi and was thrown into the ocean. But when he swam fearlessly after the ship, shouting that the voyage would not succeed without him, it became clear that he was under the protection of the god Maru and the people took him back on board. From this time on their main god was Maru and his tohunga was Tapō.

During the voyage the waka put in at an island, Rangitahua (or some say Mōtiwatiwa). There the vessel was refitted and a dog was sacrificed to Maru with a request for a safe passage. This was granted.

But first there was trouble, because of Potoru. Some say this man came on the *Aotea*, others that he captained the *Ririno*, which accompanied it. Potoru saw the sacrificed dog at the tūāhu and he ate it, although he knew it was for Maru. Having broken tapu in this terrible way, he went mad.

As a consequence he urged upon Turi a course that nearly took them to disaster. Turi had directed the bow of the *Aotea* towards the rising sun, following Kupe's instructions, but Potoru now argued that they should sail instead towards the setting sun. For a while Turi listened, and the ship was caught in strong currents going down into the mouth of Te Parata, the monster at the edge of the ocean. Then when water was pouring in and it seemed that all was lost, Turi recited a chant that brought the waka up from the depths. He seized his bailer, recited another chant and bailed the water from the vessel, then with a third chant he hastened the progress of the *Aotea*

*Hetaraka Tautahi, a leading rangatira of Ngā Rauru in southern Taranaki, in 1900 dictated a detailed account of the voyage of the* Aotea. *Hetaraka traced his descent back twenty-three generations to Turi, captain of the* Aotea.

and brought it to land, near a harbour known now as the Aotea. There it can be seen, turned to stone under the water.

As for Potoru, those who assert he was on the *Aotea* tell us that in the end Turi threw him into the ocean. Of those who believe he came on *Ririno,* some say his waka was lost in the mouth of Te Parata and others claim it was wrecked far in the south, on Ōtamaiea (Boulder Bank).

After going ashore, Turi and his crew set out southwards to find their new home. On the way Turi named all the rivers they passed, and planted seeds of the karaka tree. Finally they came to Pātea in southern Taranaki. Kupe had told Turi of this place, and as a sign he had left a post standing at Rangitāwhi, on the south headland of the Pātea River.

There Turi built a pā named Rangitāwhi, and erected a tūāhu named Rangitaka and a house of learning, Matangirei. Not far away, on a piece of land known as Hekeheke-i-papa, his wife Rongorongo planted the eight kūmara she had brought from Hawaiki – and when autumn came, they harvested eight hundred basketsful.

Turi and Rongorongo had a son, Tūranga-i-mua, and a daughter, Tāne-roroa, who were born in Hawaiki. A second son, Tūtaua-whānau-moana [Tūtaua born on the ocean], was born on the voyage, and in Aotearoa they had another son, Tonga-pōtiki. In his old age Turi went away. No-one knows where he died; some say he returned to Hawaiki on a taniwha.

After Turi's death, dissension arose when Tāne-roroa, having married a man named Uenga-puanake (from the *Tākitimu* migration), became pregnant and craved dog meat. Her husband secretly killed and cooked a dog belonging to her brother Tūranga-i-mua, but the theft was discovered. So the woman and her husband crossed the river and lived on the north bank, where their son Ruanui became the founding ancestor of the people of Ngāti Ruanui, while the descendants of the sons continued to live on the south bank and became known as Ngā Rauru.

Descent from *Aotea* is claimed as well by many peoples to the south, among them Te Āti Haunui-ā-Pāpārangi in the Whanganui region, Ngāti Apa in the Rangitīkei district, and sections of Mūāupoko.

## Aotearoa
### Traditionally, the North Island

In earlier times one of the names given the North Island was Aotea. Since this name can be understood as meaning 'white, or clear', 'cloud, or day', in a general way it must have been felt to be propitious. Aotearoa, or 'Long Aotea', is a related name for the North Island which has been in use since the nineteenth century, and perhaps before this in some regions.

The name Aotearoa is sometimes explained as meaning 'Land of the long white cloud' and is said to have had its origin in the voyage of the explorer Kupe, when he and his wife Hine-te-apa-rangi glimpsed clouds resting upon high hills in the far distance and realised that they had discovered a new land. This tradition was known to some peoples, though not all. It evolved as a way of explaining the meaning of a name that was already in existence.

Another story is that since Aotea is the traditional name of Great Barrier Island, the North Island, being so much larger, became known as Aotearoa.

There are other applications of this ancient name Aotea. The ancestral waka of this name is well known (see the previous entry). In some traditions in the far north, Aotea is a region in Te Rēinga, the underworld.

In the twentieth century the name Aotearoa came to refer, often, to the entire country, south as well as north. (It is used in this way in the present work.) In this sense Aotearoa sometimes refers to the land as it was before the arrival of Europeans, but increasingly it is being employed as well as a present-day alternative to the name New Zealand (which is the English version of a Dutch name given the country after the visit of a seventeenth-century sea captain). This usage is certain to become increasingly popular.

# Apakura
### The woman who urged revenge

When someone was killed, it was the sacred duty of the male relatives to obtain revenge. The women's role was to lament the dead and incite the men to undertake this task.

The main mythical figure who set the pattern for women in this respect was Apakura. The murdered man is nearly always Tū-whakararo, her husband (or sometimes eldest son). Usually he has been treacherously slain by Apakura's own brothers. Forced to choose between her kin and her husband (or son), she very properly seeks revenge for this crime.

She weeps constantly, singing her lament, as she seeks out her youngest son, Whakatau. She appeals to him to avenge the death of Tū-whakararo, and he does so.

Poets speaking of Apakura's lament liken it to

When the King Movement [Te Kīngitanga] opposed British troops in 1863 in the Waikato, this red silk flag was one of those that named the land for which they were fighting. It was sewn in the Hūnua Ranges by a young woman, Hēni Te Kiri Karamū, who had joined a military force there.

the endless weeping of the waves on the shore. It is said, too, that her voice can be heard in the sound of the sea.

# Apanui-waipapa
### Ancestor of Te Whānau-ā-Apanui

Te Whānau-ā-Apanui, a people whose lands on the east coast extend from a point north of Tōrere to a landmark east of Cape Runaway, take their name from Apanui-waipapa.

This man lived at Whāngārā with his eight children. He was killed by his uncle Hauiti, but his children escaped and migrated to Maraenui, at the mouth of the Mōtū River. According to one account, the sons knew they would be pursued and sent word to an Arawa relative, Turirangi. He came to their assistance and fought and killed Hauiti on the beach at Maraenui.

The young men were so grateful that they gave Turirangi their sister Rongomai-hua-tahi. From this union came Apanui-ringa-mutu. He married Kahukura-mihi-ata, a descendant of the Tūranga ancestor Ruapani, and their son was Tūkākī. He in turn had three notable sons, Te Ehutu, Kaiaio and Tamahae. Kaiaio was famous for his skill and industry in horticulture. Tamahae, the youngest, was the greatest and most feared of the warriors of his people.

# Āraiteuru
### A taniwha at Hokianga

This female taniwha is sometimes said to have arrived from the homeland of Hawaiki before the *Māmari*, and sometimes to have escorted this waka during its voyage. Others say it was the *Tākitimu* that she accompanied and guided.

Āraiteuru was pregnant when she arrived,

and soon gave birth to eleven sons. Each of them set off on a journey of exploration, digging a trench with his nose as he went, and together they created the many branches of the Hokianga Harbour.

Some of these taniwha still live with their mother, while others have dens elsewhere. One, Ōhopa, was so enraged by the number of rocks he encountered that he acquired a deep hatred of every living thing and terrorised people living near the Panguru mountains. Another, Waihou, burrowed far inland, formed Lake Ōmāpere by lashing his tail about and made it his home.

Āraiteuru lives in a cave on the south head of the Hokianga Harbour, where heavy surf breaks across the bar. She is a guardian of the region, but in former times she might also, when angry, raise storms and wreck vessels on the bar. The leading tohunga of the Hokianga people was believed to have the power to command the taniwha to send heavy seas or to calm the ocean.

Close to her home, high up in the cliff on the south side of the heads, is a cave where down through the ages the bones of the people in the region were laid to rest. Āraiteuru must have been regarded as their guardian.

A companion, a taniwha known as Niwa (or Niniwa, Niua or Tauneri), lives by the north head of the harbour.

*At Hokianga in the 1830s, the powerful tohunga Te Waenga was the medium [kaupapa] of the taniwha Āraiteuru.*

# Āraiteuru
## A petrified cargo and crew

The *Āraiteuru* arrived from the homeland of Hawaiki and made its way southwards. Its entire crew turned into mountains, hills and pillars of rock.

As the waka sailed down the east coast of the South Island, several of the men on board plunged into the sea, swam ashore and became mountains. Among them are Tapuae-o-Uenuku in the Inland Kaikoura Range, Tawera (Torlesse, inland from Christchurch) and Te Kiekie (Somers, in from Ashburton).

A violent gale swept the vessel onward as far as Matakaea (Shag Point), near Waihemo (Palmerston). There it was wrecked, and it turned into a reef along with the captain, Hipo. The cargo was swept ashore at Moeraki, where large numbers of spherical and elongated boulders are the petrified eel pots, gourds and kūmara that the vessel was carrying.

*Āraiteuru* had been hurled to destruction by three great waves followed by a cross-wave. These waves also turned to stone. Their English names are Old Man Range, Raggedy Range, Rough Range and Horse Range.

When the crew struggled ashore they were very cold, so they set out that same night to look for firewood. It was only to be found in the far south, at the mouth of the Matau (the Clutha River). A woman named Puke-tapu made her way there and came back with a bundle of sticks, though some of these slipped down and grew into forests. At Waihemo she was overtaken by daylight and became a conical hill known as Puketapu.

One man, Kai-tangata, had brought painting materials with him, and when the sun rose he became a hill bearing deposits of red ochre which stands near the present town of Kaitangata. As for Pakihiwi-tahi [One shoulder], who had carried the whetstones, he fell as he left the wreck and broke his right arm, and he is now a lopsided hill between the sea and Waihemo.

More than a hundred and fifty mountains and .ranges in the South Island are said to have been people who arrived on *Āraiteuru* and turned to stone. Some went south, some inland and others far to the north, where they became the highest peaks in the land. Among them are Horokau (Mount Tasman), Kakiroa (Sefton) and Aoraki (Cook). Aoraki is sometimes said to have been a small boy who was being carried on a relative's shoulders, so was taller than everyone else when the sun rose and he became a mountain.

*Large round boulders on the coast at Moeraki, along with elongated ones, were believed to be kūmara, gourds and eel-pots that had been brought from Hawaiki on the Āraiteuru, then turned to stone when the vessel was wrecked.*

# Atua

## Unseen powers

There are two main categories of beings, supernatural ones [atua] and people [tāngata]. People are not only the humans we know now, but also the earliest figures in the genealogies. Rangi, Papa and their first descendants (those who constitute the world, shape it, or act as role models for humans now) are all generally spoken of as persons. Humans, that is, are only one kind of people; there are others who are different.

In the same way, there are different kinds of supernatural beings. This word atua can be translated as 'god, spirit', though the word 'god' would be misleading if it led to the assumption that worship was involved. There was no worship of atua, no ceremonies simply to praise them. Māori had contact with their atua and made them offerings on occasions such as the presentation of first-fruits, and when they had a specific need for communication and assistance.

Every family of rank had a relationship with the wairua of recent ancestors (and children who had died), who visited them as atua. One Pākehā inquirer was told that if you dream you 'see an atua hovering around or over you, then know that it is probably the wairua ... of a dead relative, your father maybe, or your child, which has come to warn you of impending danger. That spirit has come to abide with you as an apa, and you are the kaupapa or medium of that apa.' It was explained further that 'the apa hau was a

company of spirits of the dead, which spirits were represented in the living world by some living relative, who was the medium ... through which [they] communicated with, and acted as guardians of, their yet living relatives'.

Offerings were made to these atua. Sometimes a small basket of food would be placed on the branch of a tree near the tapu grove that held the body of a deceased relative. If a small bird were seen eating this food, it would be known that the spirit had accepted the offering and would help his or her descendants.

Since a person possessed of mana had inherited this quality from ancestors, the ancestral spirits watched vigilantly to ensure that he or she respected the restrictions relating to tapu which this high status involved. If they broke these rules, even accidentally, the spirits might punish them with illness. But ancestral spirits, and the spirits of children who had lived with their family before death, were generally believed to cause only the milder forms of disease. The worst forms were caused by the spirits of dead infants [atua kahukahu], who had never known their relatives and so attacked them without compunction.

Tohunga always had powerful guardian spirits; two such men are on record as explaining that their atua was located in their forehead. A tohunga's atua might take possession of him and speak through him, especially when predicting the future. Sometimes they might be sent to attack human beings, or other atua.

Atua could enter a person's body because they themselves were generally bodiless. They might also pass into the body of a green gecko, a bird or an insect, or into the wind, a cloud, the sun's rays. In appropriate circumstances such manifestations revealed the presence of an atua, and ritual

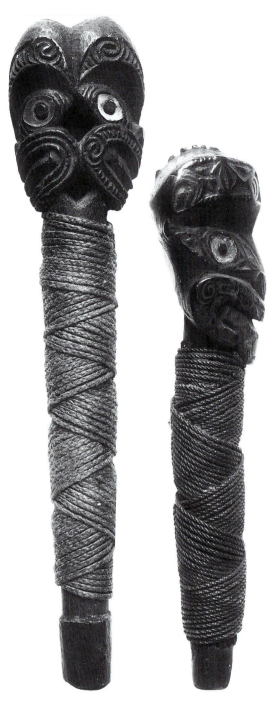

*In some regions a tohunga wishing to communicate with an atua would ritually compel it to enter a small, ceremonially bound figure [taumata atua or tiki wānanga] placed upright at the tūāhu; sometimes, too, this was done with persons such as Rongo and Tāwhirimātea who represented natural phenomena and were not generally termed atua. These two figures from Ngāti Ruanui are thought to represent Rongo (the double-headed one on the left) and either Tangaroa or Maru.*

chants asking for assistance might be recited. People would seek perhaps a favourable wind, fine weather, healing, or success in war.

For large issues, especially success in war, there were also the atua who had been brought from Hawaiki: Uenuku, Maru, Kahukura and many others. Offerings were made to small figures of these gods, or other objects representing them. Since related peoples often had the same war god (who had been brought on their ancestral waka from Hawaiki), peoples who formed alliances in times of war would probably all acknowledge the one atua.

Any inexplicable object or occurrence might be thought to indicate the presence of an atua; European watches and compasses were at first understood in this way. The word atua was also sometimes used of fairies [patupaiarehe], although unlike most atua these did have bodies. Taniwha, too, were occasionally spoken of as atua.

The European missionaries chose to translate their word 'god' with this term atua. Perhaps as a consequence, early ancestors such as Tāne and Tangaroa (whose descendants are birds, plants, fish and other life forms) are now often referred to as atua. In early Māori-language writings, however, this usage is very rare. Generally such figures were regarded as people [tāngata].

## Atua kahukahu
### Malignant spirits

While the wairua of people who had died in childhood would sometimes return to advise their parents, the wairua of aborted foetuses and stillborn children were potentially ill-disposed towards the living. They owed no loyalty to their relatives, for they had never known them, nor had they had performed over them the ritual that declared their identity and dedicated them to their future life. Indeed they might well resent the fact that they had been deprived of life.

To prevent such a wairua from afflicting people with illness and perhaps killing them, it was necessary to bury the body with appropriate rituals and offerings to the atua. Occasionally this was not done, or the ceremony was not successful, and the wairua turned into a dangerous atua kahukahu.

The Tūhoe people in the eighteenth century possessed a war god [atua mō te riri] that had its origin in such an atua kahukahu. First this spirit entered a green gecko, then a man named Uhia made it offerings and became its medium. For a long time this atua, now named Te Rehu-o-Tainui, was successful in its prophecies and the warriors

# Ancestors

A1

The artist George French Angas, who in 1844 sketched this massive column
at Raroera Pā in the southern Waikato, was told that the lower figure was
Māui (see pages 114–17). The woman portrayed above Māui may be his
mother Taranga, or possibly Hine-nui-te-pō, who overcame him in the end.
The figures may have indicated the presence of a tapu area.

A2

*Above:* Ancestors, a husband and wife, carved in a traditional manner in 1908 on the facade of Uruika, a Ngāti Pikiao meeting house on the southern shore of Lake Rotoiti.

*Right:* These two ancestral figures originally supported a central pillar [pou-toko-manawa] in an old house on the shore of Lake Taupō. They are now in the Otago Museum.

PANIA
OF THE REEF

AN OLD MAORI LEGEND
TELLS HOW PANIA, LURED
BY THE SIREN VOICES OF
THE SEA PEOPLE SWAM OUT
TO MEET THEM WHEN SHE
ENDEAVOURED TO RETURN TO
HER LOVER SHE WAS TRANS
FORMED INTO THE REEF
WHICH NOW LIES BEYOND
THE NAPIER BREAKWATER

*Right:* A view of the ceiling of Rangiātea, a noble church built in 1851 by the Māori people of Ōtaki. Traditionally the name Rangiātea belongs to an ancestral homeland, also to the house of learning of the high god Io. Some houses of learning also bore this ancient name.

*Left:* On the Napier foreshore there sits the bronze figure of Pānia, who came from the ocean to visit her human husband (see page 132).

*Below:* The meeting house Apumoana, named after the founding ancestor of Ngāti Apumoana and reopened in 1988 in Rotorua. The tekoteko, the highest figure, is Apumoana himself; on the pillar below are his six brothers and his sister (see pages 148–50). On one bargeboard Māui pulls up his fish; on the other is Muturangi's Octopus, encountered by Kupe when he discovered Aotearoa. Other ancestors stand in the porch and the interior. The dining hall of the marae is named after Apumoana's wife Te Aowhēoro.

A5

A7

Pikiao, founding ancestor of Ngāti Pikiao (see page 138), in the porch of Te Takinga, a pātaka [storehouse] carved in the 1820s and now in the Museum of New Zealand Te Papa Tongarewa.

Hākirirangi, who in Tākitimu tradition brought the kūmara to Aotearoa and showed how it should be cultivated (see page 44). A painting in Rongopai, a meeting house at Waituhi near Gisborne.

A8

The ancestor Pukaki holds his two sons; his wife was formerly depicted beneath, but the lower part of the sculpture has decayed and only her legs remain. This ancient figure, now two metres high, belonged to Pukaki's descendants (Ngāti Pukaki, a section of Ngāti Whakaue by Lake Rotorua) and probably stood originally over the gateway of a pā. It is now in the Auckland Museum Te Papa Whakahiku.

Taniwha are depicted in some regions as marakihau, with tails and long tubular tongues. This marakihau is Ureia, a taniwha of the Hauraki peoples (see page 238). He stands in Hotunui, a meeting house opened near Thames in 1878 and now in the Auckland Museum Te Papa Whakahiku.

see page 238

of Tūhoe were triumphant. Later the atua lost its powers and the people were defeated.

## Atutahi
### The first-born star

This is Canopus, second brightest of the visible stars. When Tāne, creating the world, was about to throw his basket of stars into the sky, Atutahi clung to the outside of the basket so that he would be the first-born and could therefore, because of the tapu of high rank, stay aloof from the common horde. The basket of stars became Te Mangō-roa (the Milky Way) and Atutahi still hangs outside, remaining apart.

Being the first-born, and so bright, he is the lord [ariki] of the stars of the year. He was one of the stars thought to make food plants fertile in the fields and forests, and ceremonial offerings of food were made to him. Other forms of his name are Autahi and Aotahi.

In poetry and oratory, a man of rank might be honoured by being spoken of as Atutahi.

## Awa-nui-ā-rangi
### Son of a celestial father

Two distant but related peoples, Ngāti Awa in the southern Bay of Plenty and Te Āti Awa in northern Taranaki, trace their origins to an ancestor, Awa-nui-ā-rangi, whose father came down from the sky.

In the Bay of Plenty story, a girl was sent to draw water from a stream. As she stooped to fill her gourd, a blaze of light shone around her. She could see nobody, but a shadow of a man fell upon the shining water. She felt his arms about her, and he told her, 'If you have a boy, let him be named after the great river [awa nui] of light on which I came down to you.'

And so Awa-nui-ā-rangi [Great river of sky] received his name. His father is sometimes an atua named Tamarau, sometimes Tama-i-waho, sometimes even Rangi the sky himself. His mother is often Te Kura and her earthly husband the famous Toi, though sometimes he is a descendant of Tōroa, captain of the *Mātaatua*.

In Taranaki, Awa-nui-ā-rangi's father is Tamarau-te-heketanga-ā-rangi [Tamarau who came down from the sky]. Again the boy is associated with Toi, often as his grandson. He lives in Hawaiki and has among his descendants Turi, captain of the *Aotea*.

This time a woman named Rongoueroa (or Rongouaroa) went to a stream to wash her son. There was no light, but she saw the man's re-

flection on the water and found him standing behind her. Again she was instructed that when she bore her child she was to call him after the 'awa nui' that had brought her lover down to the earth; although in this case the 'awa nui' was not a river of light but a powerful [nui] chant of the kind known as an awa.

## Birds
### Winged children of Tāne

The early ancestor Tāne [Male] is usually regarded as the creator of birds, along with other life forms that belong to the land. In some accounts he goes searching for a human female, and instead meets other kinds of women. He couples with them and they produce the different kinds of birds – as when Parauri [Dark] gives birth to the tūī and Haere-awaawa [Go through hollows] the weka. Tāne then creates the trees and other plants, providing birds with their food and their homes.

*The name of the weka's mother, Haere-awaawa, refers to this bird's habit of skulking through hidden hollows.*

Since there was believed to be a continuity of existence between ancestors and their descendants, birds could individually and collectively be spoken of as Tāne. They are the form that he takes.

But the myths vary. Sometimes the origin of forest birds is Punaweko and that of seabirds is Hurumanu. Small birds are said by some to owe their origin to Tāne-te-hokahoka.

People were often spoken of as birds, and the image was generally complimentary. Recognising them as their distant kin, all the more aware of their presence because of the absence of large land animals, dependent upon them for much of the food they most enjoyed, wearing their plumes in their hair and treasuring cloaks covered with their feathers, people thought about birds a great

*After Tāne took to wife Moe-tāhuna, whose name means 'Sleep on mudbank', she gave birth to the grey duck.*

deal. Often they identified themselves with them.

The singing of birds at dawn was regarded as a sign and celebration of the triumph of light over darkness, and the chiming chorus of bellbirds in particular was associated with oratory, the power of speech. A good singer or graceful speaker might be praised as 'like a bellbird pealing at daybreak' [he rite ki te kōpara e kō nei i te ata].

Most kinds of birds had a particular character assigned to them. The pigeon is quiet and peaceful, the kākā clamorous and active, and individuals might be likened to either bird. Brave warriors were 'flapping birds' and 'stubborn birds'. Rangatira could be spoken of as harrier hawks, because this bird was associated with victory in battle. An early writer remarks that 'for a hawk to fly over the heads of those who are settling the affairs of war, is a certain assurance of success in whatever they undertake'.

With their power of flight, birds have a freedom and unpredictability of movement similar to that possessed by supernatural beings. When the wairua of the dead visited their descendants, they sometimes took the form of a small bird.

## Birth

### Entrance to the world

Ceremonial feasting and much rejoicing greeted the news that a woman of rank was pregnant, especially when she was expecting her first child.

Gifts of food were brought, in particular the foods she might crave at this time.

Before the baby's birth a small temporary house was built for the mother, since the rules of tapu did not allow a birth (or a death) to occur inside a permanent building. She lived with an attendant in this house, in a tapu state, until the time came for the baby to be born. Relatives were usually with her during the birth. Women gave birth in a kneeling position, often with an attendant facing them.

Childbirth and everything connected with it were under the care of Hine-te-iwaiwa and Hine-kōrako. When Hine-te-iwaiwa, in the beginning, experienced a difficult birth, a ritual chant hastened her son's arrival. Since that time this chant has often been recited to assist a woman in this situation.

The term for the placenta is whenua, a word that also means 'land'. The whenua was taken by the mother or a close relative to a secret place already chosen and ready to receive it, and was buried there. In this way the land that had sustained the child within the woman was brought together with the land that sustains people during their lives. The umbilical cord was also disposed of carefully. It might be placed in a tapu hollow tree or else buried, perhaps at the foot of a boundary post to show the child's claim to this land.

After a baby's cord has been tied and severed, it takes seven or eight days for the end of the cord to fall away. When this final separation from the cord had taken place, a ceremony known as the

*Makereti of Te Arawa (1872–1930). Her book* The Old-time Maori *has valuable descriptions of women's lives, with much relating to marriage and children.*

tohi [separation] ritual was performed by a tohunga to mark the child's entry to this world and proclaim his or her identity and future life. This required the presence of the parents as well as the child.

The conception of a child, and its growth within the mother, was a re-enactment of the occasion when the creator Tāne had made the first human by shaping her from the soil of Hawaiki. Every human male was in a way identified with Tāne, for the word tāne is the ordinary term for a husband or lover; it means simply 'male'. Since men were thought to be the active agents in the generation of children, every man who fathered a child was repeating Tāne's action. Mourning the deaths of his sons, a poet recalls this:

> Nāku pea koutou koi tiki atu
> Ki Hawaiki ahu mai ai,
> Ka tupu koutou hei tāngata.

> It was I who fetched you
> From Hawaiki, forming you here
> So you grew to be people.

Every child was formed by the father in the homeland of Hawaiki. And the mother's womb, by implication at least, was identified with the soil of Hawaiki.

# Death
## The soul's journey

Death, like birth, was a transition that could not take place inside a house if people were to continue living there. When a person of rank became ill, a temporary shelter would be erected for them. At the approach of death the person might speak and sing a farewell, giving advice for the future.

It was thought fitting to die when there was an ebbing tide, and the person might ask about the state of the tide. Often a special food would be requested and brought as a last meal, or water would be carried from a favourite spring or stream.

*Sketched in 1844 in the Taupō region, this figure is described as a 'raised stand for supporting tapued articles consecrated to the dead'. Often a gourd of water and a small dish of food, sustenance for the wairua when it came at night, were left on a high place near a tomb.*

35

The rituals performed at the funeral [tangi-hanga] varied from one region to another, as did the treatment of the body afterwards. The person would sit or lie in state surrounded by weeping relatives while parties of mourners arrived, wept, and spoke and sang their farewells. Laments for the dead [waiata tangi] are among the highest achievements of the great Māori poetic tradition. These songs mourned and praised the person who had died, and sent their wairua on the journey it now must make. Usually the wairua was thought to travel to Te Rēinga in the far north, but persons of rank were sometimes believed to rise up to the sky. Ritual chants as well as laments eased the passage of the wairua.

After a year or two, when the body had decomposed, the bones were often disinterred and prepared with solemn ritual for their final resting place. Usually the bones of relatives lay together through the generations, often in a hidden cave, sometimes in a hollow tree or other repository. These places were intensely tapu and could be approached only by a tohunga of rank, along with any others he might instruct to accompany him. When possible, people migrating to a new home took with them the bones of their ancestors.

After death, people lived on in their descendants. In many cases, too, their wairua continued to guide and advise them.

It was sometimes claimed that if it were not for women, men would have lived forever like the stars in the sky. But women have the power to give birth, and the introduction of new life implies that death must follow. A woman therefore, Hine-nui-te-pō [Great woman the night], was held mainly responsible for the existence of death (although there was also the evil Whiro).

As well, however, there are the myths of Tura and Tiki. Both of these men are associated, in different ways, with the production of children. And it is interesting that here too the introduction of new life was believed to have brought with it the unforeseen consequences of physical decay (with Tura) and death (with Tiki). In each case the logic is the same.

## Dogs
### Close companions

Polynesian dogs had been brought all the way from Southeast Asia. Black, brown or whitish, long-bodied and short-legged, with pointed muzzles, pricked ears and bushy tails, they did not bark but howled. In tropical Polynesia they were often treated with affection but were reared mainly to be eaten, as meat was scarce. They were not used for hunting and were generally quiet creatures.

But Aotearoa was found to be full of big flightless birds, and the settlers' dogs regained their ancient role as hunting companions. Some species of moa must have been hunted with dogs, and when the moa disappeared there were still kiwi and kākāpō to track through the forest at night.

*Women mourners at a tangi, drawn by Dennis Turner in about 1960.*

In the colder climate, dogs' fur became valuable. Elegantly striped and checked cloaks of dogskin were now the most prized of garments, worn on important occasions by high-ranking men. In winter a dogskin cape might be worn inside out, for warmth. In battle it was a shield against spears.

Dogs were favourite items at feasts, and they were fed to the gods at rituals marking major events such as that accompanying the tattooing of a person of rank. Yet despite their value they were never common, perhaps because they had now to be fed largely on fish and fernroot rather than the abundant vegetable foods of the tropical islands.

Since people and dogs lived closely together (and dogs, apart from humans, were the only land mammals other than bats and the introduced rats), it is not surprising that the myths accord dogs a special status in their origin and final fate. Unlike other creatures, they have as their first ancestor a man, Irawaru, and when they die they go to the underworld just as humans do, though by a different path. An early writer records a northern belief that the wairua of men and women on their way to the underworld sing a last song of farewell before leaping down, and that the wairua of dogs howl a chorus at the end of each verse.

But this closeness to humans led to implicit comparisons, and so to an emphasis upon the dogs' low status. In songs, proverbs and oratory they were a useful source of perjorative metaphor: warriors could be spoken of as dogs, but only apparently when they were the enemy. Proverbially dogs were lazy, always skulking by the fire, cowardly, greedy, and indiscriminate in eating and mating. Their ancestor Irawaru had after all been greatly demeaned by being turned into a dog by the trickster Māui.

Numerous legends tell of a rangatira who was exceedingly fond of his pet dog. Usually in these stories the animal is lured away by an enemy and killed and eaten. This grave insult leads to war and sometimes a migration.

In myths, an ancestor's dog could be transformed into a rock or cliff – which was still to be seen and bore witness, therefore, to the truth of the story. Such landmarks remained dogs, and could be dangerous. The western shore of Lake Taupō was haunted by two dogs, in the form of cliffs, which might be heard howling on misty days. If a man in a waka were stupid enough to call to them as to a dog ('Moi, moi'), they would be insulted and send a storm to destroy him.

Demonic figures occasionally own packs of

*Two early representations of dogs in Te Wai Pounamu (the South Island). Above: A reconstructed rock drawing and (below) a wooden image, eight centimetres high, from a coastal cave near Christchurch.*

ferocious dogs. In Tūhoe belief, Tama-i-waho and his dogs attack heroes who dare to ascend to the skies. In the interior of the South Island, the dog-headed monster Kōpūwai hunted with a pack of two-headed dogs.

In a few stories, an enormous dog living alone in its lair devours humans who come too close. Usually, though, such a dog did once have a master. Some kind of association with humans is nearly always present.

*The earth, Papa, is her children's home.*
*A drawing by Wilhelm Dittmer.*

# Earth

## The mother

The earth is female, as the sky is male, and while the sky is sacred [tapu], the earth in general is everyday, ordinary, profane [noa]. She has to be, because this is where life goes on. Fertility and decay, life, death and more life are what the earth produces. And since people are part of the world, there is no essential difference between the fertility of the earth and that of human women.

The earth was understood in terms of human experience, and the experiences and roles of women were understood in terms of the earth. So the first woman, Papa, was the earth.

When Tāne decided to make a wife from the sand (some say soil) of Hawaiki, he went, it is often said, to 'the sands at Kurawaka' [te one i Kurawaka] – and this place is the mons veneris of Papa herself. So while it was Tāne who created Hine-ahu-one, he achieved this by going to the source of Papa's fertility. Hawaiki, as the origin of life, is necessarily associated with Papa's life-giving powers.

Later came Hine-nui-te-pō [Great woman the night], who brought death into the world. Inevitably the main responsibility for death is assigned in tradition to women, since life implies eventual death, and they give life. And again the earth comes into this, because Hine-nui-te-pō belongs with Night [Te Pō], which is part of the earth, or perhaps beneath it (there is an ambiguity here). Yet the role of Hine-nui-te-pō is complex

and may be differently interpreted: she does after all care for her descendants at the ends of their lives. And while Papa has hidden within her the Night and those who are now down there, new life keeps coming from the earth and from human women.

# Fairies

## Spirit people

Handsome, uncanny people, known usually as patupaiarehe or tūrehu, lived on hilltops and other remote places. Their houses and pā were built from swirling mist, and the fairies themselves were usually glimpsed on misty, overcast days. Most of the time they were visible only to tohunga with visionary powers [matakite], though others could hear them.

Fairies were atua, but not the usual kind, because they possessed bodies, whereas most atua were bodiless (and so could enter the bodies of humans or animals). Like humans the fairies hunted and fished, wove garments, sang, danced and made love, but there were differences. Their skins were pale and their hair was light in colour. Being atua they were highly tapu, so they ate only raw food; they greatly feared cooked food, steam from ovens, fire, even ashes. Perhaps because of their tapu, they were not tattooed. (Some Māori tohunga were not tattooed, it being thought dangerous to shed their blood.) There are occasional accounts of battles between fairy peoples, but warfare seems not to have been common.

Any human struck by a fairy fell as if dead, but soon recovered.

Most of the stories about fairies tell how they sought humans as lovers. The men were expert flute players and the sound of their music, heard in the hills, greatly excited human women, who were always susceptible to the music of the flute. Sometimes a fairy and a human would meet in the forest, or a fairy would visit a human in a house at night. Fairy men and women both did this.

Erotic dreams could be explained in this way, and a further proof was the occasional birth of an albino child, whose pale skin, fair hair and inability to stand the sunlight were obviously inherited from a fairy father. The writer Makereti (see page 35), born in 1872, tells of an albino girl she knew as a child who always spoke of her father as an atua and a tūrehu, and used to hold conversations with this unseen father in the night – 'a thing which terrified me'.

Despite this evidence of the fairies' attentions, in poetic metaphor fairies appear as illusory or 'pretend' lovers. This is in accord with the shifting and ambiguous nature of their relationship with humans, not least where nocturnal visits were concerned. Though erotic dreams are real enough in one way, in another way they are illusory. It was only in stories about people living elsewhere

*The presence of remarkable landmarks was sometimes attributed to the actions of fairies. Some said that Rangitoto Island once stood at Karekare in the Waitakere Ranges, then was lifted up, leaving cliffs behind, by a fairy tohunga who objected to its blocking his view. The tohunga strode across the ranges with his burden, intending to carry it out beyond the Hauraki Gulf, but the winter water was cold so he dropped it quite close to the shore.*

that a beautiful fairy might be tricked into remaining in the house after daybreak, to be seen by all. One's own fairies were not to be caught.

Sometimes the fairies support the human order to some extent, even punishing those who break tapu restrictions; some writers speak of them as the spirits of ancestors, though without naming the ancestors concerned. One reason for such associations was that the fairies often lived on the peaks of sacred mountains. Indeed, the powerful tohunga Ngātoro-i-rangi is sometimes said to have placed the fairies in the hills upon his arrival from Hawaiki. In some regions, generations of tohunga had a long-established relationship with the fairies on their people's mountain.

But often the fairies were believed to have been living in the land before the arrival of the first humans and to have been displaced by them. Generally they are rivals of human beings, or at the very least a race of strangers who live apart. There was a feeling that the products of the land really belonged to them, and placatory offerings might be made by fishermen or men digging fernroot.

In many places, humans were thought to have gained a knowledge of plaiting and weaving techniques from the fairies, usually by tricking them into continuing their work until the sun rose, so that they fled the light and left behind their nets or weaving. Sometimes they were believed to have taught humans to play the flute. Their songs differed from human ones in that 'a peculiar thing about them was that they had to be memorized one line at a time. Although the whole song was heard, the listener could only remember one line; the rest faded from his memory.'

Māori fairies, while taking different forms, are

*Many mountains, such as Pirongia, were famous haunts of the fairies.*

uncanny people who exist at the margins of human experience, in dreams and wild places. They occupy an intermediate, ambiguous position between the human and spirit worlds and were felt to be sometimes dangerous, sometimes attractive. Beliefs about them explained much that needed to be explained and provided satisfying scope for the imagination.

These beings have sufficient in common with fairies in other traditions to justify the use of this word 'fairy', although each tradition is naturally quite distinct. In Britain, too, one of the main things fairies do is make love to human men and women, in reported 'reality' and in dreams. Just as the presence of the Māori fairies provided an explanation for the birth of albino children, the British fairies' habit of replacing human children with changelings explained why some children were different from usual.

The words patupaiarehe and tūrehu seem generally to have been used in different regions to refer to the same beings, although occasionally both terms were employed in the one district to refer to rather different kinds of fairies (in one region in the far north, tūrehu were more dangerous than patupaiarehe). The word tūrehu refers to the fact that they could only be dimly seen. Other terms occasionally used are karitehe, kōrakorako (with reference to their pale skins) and Tahurangi, an honorific term sometimes used as a personification.

As well there are other beings, in particular maero, who are more like ogres than fairies.

## Fernroot
### A reliable food

Fernroot is not a root but the rhizome of the bracken fern. In good soil this plant grows to three metres in height and has starchy rhizomes up to forty-five centimetres in length. Some of the best fernroot came from land that was lying fallow after kūmara had grown on it for a couple of seasons. Such plants were productive and needed almost no attention; there was virtually no risk of crop failure, and dried fernroot would keep for years. So though fernroot was liked much less than kūmara, it was a staple food in many areas.

Before use the dried rhizomes were soaked in water, roasted in embers, scraped, then pounded with a wooden mallet on a smooth stone. Only the starchy part was eaten, the fibres being rejected. Often there was a relish of dried fish or shellfish.

Fernroot was proverbially reliable as a source of food. Perhaps because of this, and because it was firmly rooted and considered a strengthening food, it was believed that a small piece of fernroot worn around the neck would protect the wearer from minor afflictions such as headaches. And since fernroot was regarded as a food suitable for warriors and others engaged in arduous pursuits, it was frequently associated with warfare. In ritual it was opposed to the kūmara, which belonged with peace and festivity, and it had always to be stored separately from the kūmara.

The parent of fernroot is generally Haumia, a son (sometimes grandson) of Rangi and Papa. Since fernroot was so readily cultivated, the only myths relating to it are those concerning its origin. There are no complex stories telling of its subsequent acquisition by humans, as there are for the kūmara.

## Fish
### Tangaroa's children

The early ancestor Tangaroa, whose realm is the sea, is the parent of fish and other sea creatures. In some traditions, though, certain fish are assigned other parents, as when sharks are regarded as the children of Punga (or some say Takaaho). Whales and other marine mammals are also often the children of Punga.

Orators and poets spoke of many kinds of fish and other sea creatures as possessing distinctive qualities. Whales, especially sperm whales, were thought to be like rangatira, so high-ranking men could be likened to them. As well, whales were associated with rich food and abundance, since those stranded on the shore presented their finders with enormous quantities of meat and oil. For this reason they were depicted in some parts of the country on the carved façades of storehouses.

Warriors could be compared to sharks, also to the small yellow-eyed mullet that leap so vigorously. Other creatures had more specialised roles in metaphor. In inland waters, for instance, some species of kōkopu have beautiful markings, so an admired object might be described as 'mottled like a kōkopu'.

More generally, fish in Māori symbolic thought have the special role of being caught and put to use; this was the very reason for their existence. Because of this, people who had been defeated in warfare were frequently spoken of as fish. The land itself had been a fish, brought up from the depths by Māui and made a home for human

*The giant kōkopu, whose darkish body is covered with golden spots and lines. These markings were much admired.*

*Human beings, the children of Tāne, attack Tangaroa's children in many cunning ways. A large fish hook, perhaps for shark, formed from a twig that had been bent while growing then tipped with serrated albatross bone.*

beings. The much-treasured greenstone was another resource which had been a fish – and which had swum all the way from Hawaiki, followed by its owner Ngahue.

## Gourds
### A treasured plant

Some young gourds were eaten as vegetables, and the rest were left to mature for use as containers. They were trained into the shapes required, their spongy contents were removed, and they were dried and hardened in the sun and beside fires. Small gourds became containers for scented oils, red ochre and other substances, larger ones sliced in half were dishes and bowls, some had a hole bored by the neck and held water, and a few large ones stored preserved birds.

In the far south, where gourds would not grow, containers for water and preserved birds were made from bull kelp, which flourishes on the coast there.

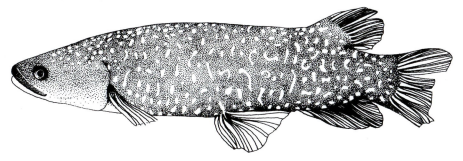

*Gourd plants were often trained up the side of a building, as on this house sketched in the Tauranga region in 1839.*

Pū-tē-hue is in some regions the parent of the gourd. On the east coast, a myth tells how a man named Māia introduced gourds from Hawaiki.

# Greenstone
## Ngahue's fish

Greenstone, or jade, was obtainable only in the South Island, in a few remote, rugged places on the west coast and to a lesser extent in Fiordland and Central Otago. Being extremely hard and tough it was very difficult to work, until a new technique of abrasive cutting was developed some five hundred years ago. This was most laborious but gave workmen precise control over their materials.

From that time greenstone adzes and chisels were used extensively in woodworking, and much finer carving became possible. Pieces of greenstone were the most precious of trade commodities, carried over mountain passes to the east and north, taken across the dangerous waters of Raukawa (Cook Strait), passed from one community to the next until they reached the most distant parts of the country.

Greenstone was treasured for its beauty, hardness and indestructibility: though the generations

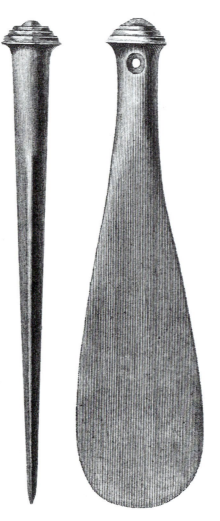

*Patiently and skilfully shaped from slabs of greenstone, mere were highly formidable and greatly treasured weapons owned by leading rangatira. A mere taken to England in the late eighteenth century.*

came and went, it lasted forever. Pendants that had been worn by departed relatives were venerated because of their associations with the dead, and kinsfolk wept over them and sang laments. As well there were endless stories about the magical properties of treasured pieces.

Even on the west coast of the South Island, by the Arahura Valley, greenstone of high quality was most difficult to find. Boulders and pieces of stone lay hidden in riverbeds and along beaches, and it was said that they were caught like fish. If a man who sought greenstone dreamt he was sleeping with a beautiful woman, this was a sign that he would discover a fine piece. Next morning he would know where to go. At the right place he would enter the water, and the greenstone would be lying there. He would noose his fish and pull it to the shore, and afterwards it would turn to stone.

For this reason the South Island is known as Te Wai Pounamu [The waters of greenstone].

Several myths explain the origin of greenstone. In one of the best known, greenstone was a fish named Poutini that swam from Hawaiki to its present location in Aotearoa. This fish was the pet of a man named Ngahue.

## Hakawau

### A tohunga who fought evil

When Hakawau was young and knew no magic, a girl he loved, named Rona, was kidnapped by atua at the command of Pāka, an old sorcerer who wanted her as a wife. Pāka lived on the Rangitoto Range near the headwaters of the Waipā River. Rona's relatives raised an army and attempted to rescue her, but Pāka's atua killed them all.

Knowing that Pāka could be conquered only through ritual powers, Hakawau left his home at Kāwhia and travelled to the distant Urewera Mountains to visit his uncle, a powerful tohunga. His uncle taught him potent chants that enabled him to summon and command his own spirits.

On his return, Hakawau set out for Rangitoto with a few carefully chosen warriors. They approached Pāka's pā with no attempt at concealment. Outside the walls Hakawau could see, though his companions could not, Pāka's atua waiting to destroy them. He sent out his own army of spirits, and it was Pāka's spirits that were overcome.

At once the mana of Rangitoto was gone. Pāka offered no further resistance and was found cowering inside a house. Hakawau allowed him to live, shamed and disgraced. He restored Rona

*The atua of the sorcerers Puarata and Tautohito, owners of the talking head, are overcome by atua sent against them by Hakawau. A drawing by Russell Clark.*

to her relatives, and soon afterwards she married Hakawau.

On another occasion Hakawau overcame two sorcerers, Puarata and Tautohito, whose pā was at Puke-tapu, near the south head of the Manukau Harbour. These men possessed a carved head with terrible powers, a vessel for powerful atua. When armies or travellers approached, these spirits would inform the head and it would shout with a voice so loud that the strangers would perish. Soon the bones of many men lay on that path, and people living in distant places knew of the head and dreaded it.

Hakawau resolved to test the strength of this head. With a single servant he made his way northwards from Kāwhia, repeating as he went chants to ward off the attacks of enemy spirits and collect his own spirits around him. After crossing the Waikato River they passed the bodies of those the head had destroyed, and they expected death at every moment.

But they continued on, and when Hakawau came within sight of the enemy pā he sent his atua forward to attack those that kept watch over it. The spirits on both sides engaged in battle, and

Hakawau's spirits were triumphant.

The enemy watchmen saw the two men and ran to Puarata. He at once addressed the head: 'People are here, two of them!'

But the head had been deserted by Puarata's spirits and could no longer lift up its voice. It made only a low, wailing sound.

The two men continued on. At the palisades of the pā, Hakawau asserted his mana by climbing the walls rather than passing through the gateway that was common to all. They rested in a house and were offered food, but they would not eat and soon left. As Hakawau was going out of the house, he struck the threshold. By the time they left the pā behind, every person in that house was dead.

## Hākirirangi
### A skilled horticulturalist

In the Tūranga (Gisborne) district, this woman is usually said to have come from Hawaiki to Aotearoa on the *Tākitimu*, bringing with her a basket containing seed tubers of the kūmara. Some say she was the leading female tohunga on the waka, and that her duties included the ritual removal of excess tapu from the male tohunga when they landed; she did this by standing on the bulwarks while they left the vessel by passing under her thighs.

At Tūranga she planted her kūmara and established the proper procedures for growing them; she worked diligently, and her plants yielded heavy crops. One of her plantations, named Manawarū, was at Muriwai. The other, Āraiteuru, gave its name to the present Te Ārai.

Some of the people in this region associate Hākirirangi with the *Horouta* rather than the *Tākitimu*, and some call her Hine-hākirirangi. All agree in honouring her as the person who brought the kūmara and showed how it should be grown.

## Hākuturi
### Guardians of the forest

It was the task of the Multitude of the Hākuturi [te Tini o te Hākuturi] to protect the forests in Hawaiki and avenge any desecration of their tapu. When Rata felled a tree without performing the proper ritual, the Hākuturi punished him by making the tree stand upright again. Afterwards, though, in a single night they adzed the tree into a waka for him. In carving the ship they were assisted by the spiders.

Some say too that Rua (or Rua-te-pupuke), the first man to learn and teach woodcarving, was taught this art by the Hākuturi.

These forest guardians seem generally to have been regarded as birds; one writer calls them the children of Tāne. It seems that they could be thought, sometimes at least, to inhabit the forests of Aotearoa as well as Hawaiki.

When the hull of *Tākitimu* had been adzed and its owners were hauling it down to the coast, they were assisted by the Hākuturi – who in this case were certain kinds of birds such as pigeons, kākā and saddlebacks. Each kind had a rope of its own, so that all the pigeons, for instance, pulled on the same rope. When the ropes were cut by enemies, the birds flew on together. And that is why these kinds of birds still fly in flocks today.

## Hani and Puna
### Sacred stones at Kāwhia

The final resting-place of the *Tainui*, after its voyage from Hawaiki, was near Maketū on the Kāwhia Harbour. The waka lies under the soil, turned to stone, with two limestone pillars marking the positions of the prow and stern. Some say these tapu pillars are themselves the prow and sternpost, others that they were placed there by the ship's captain, Hoturoa, and the tohunga, Raka-taura.

Raka-taura's pillar is the prow, which stands at the higher, inland end of the waka. Its name is Hani, or Hani-whakarere-tāngata [Hani who destroys people], and its power is that of the warrior spirit, the capacity to destroy human beings. Hoturoa's stone on the seaward side is the sternpost Puna, or Puna-whakatupu-tāngata [Spring that makes people increase]. This has the power of fertility, including the ability to create human beings. At the start of a fishing season, the first fish caught would be placed beside Puna as an offering.

On a low hill above these pillars Hoturoa set up a tūāhu, and nearby he established a house of learning. Both of these were known as Te Ahurei.

In a different account, drawn from the esoteric lore of the Tainui peoples as it existed in the late nineteenth century and subsequently, Hani is the male essence and Puna the female essence. At the beginning of time these two were apart, and they sought constantly to unite. They passed separately through the Bespaced Heavens, then merged at last in the high god Io. Until this time, Io was not fully evolved. When male and female entered him, he assumed his final form; and he has within him therefore the powers of both male and female.

As well as merging with Io, Hani and Puna are present in Io's sacred shrine [ahurewa], which is located at the centre of creation. Here they remain distinct, kept apart by Te Tumu [The foundation, or post].

Later, when Rangi the sky and Papa the earth made their appearance, Hani and Puna came together on the bosom of Papa. There they found the one place where they could be together. On Papa they brought forth the creatures that live in the sea, those that live in fresh water and those that live on the land. They also created two sacred beings, Tiki-āhua and Tiki-apoa, who were the first to be formed in the likeness of human beings.

These activities disturbed Rangi and Papa as they lay sleeping. Awakened in this way by Hani, Rangi himself, though a male, gave birth to children, and so then did Papa. Afterwards the sky and earth together produced more children.

This account by the scholar Pei Te Hurinui does not mention the two stone pillars at Maketū, although he certainly knew of their existence. He may have taken for granted a relationship between these pillars and the Hani and Puna whose early activities he describes.

The name Hani may be associated with the word hani, one of the terms used of a taiaha –

*A meeting house at Waimana belonging to people who trace descent from Hape, or Hape-ki-tuarangi. The name of the house, Te Tatau-o-Hape-ki-tuarangi [The door of Hape-ki-tuarangi], indicates that its door is always open to visitors.*

because this was a favourite weapon of high-ranking warriors.

# Hape
## An early inhabitant

Some trace Hape's ancestry to Toi, who was here in the beginning, and others to Māui himself, who fished up the land then went to live on it. Other accounts have him arriving from Hawaiki on the *Rangi-mātoru*, bringing the kūmara. It is agreed that he lived at Ōhiwa, where the harbour provides rich resources of shellfish, sharks and other seafood, and that he was the founding ancestor of a people known, because of their early origin, as Te Hapū Oneone [The People of the Soil]. They belong mostly to Ōhiwa and to the Waimana and Rūātoki valleys.

Hape is often said to have come from Hawaiki in search of greenstone. He arrived soon after Ngahue had set out on a similar quest, and after living for a while at Ōhiwa he set off on a long journey to Te Wai Pounamu (the South Island). There he found greenstone, and there he finally died.

Back at Ōhiwa, Hape's sons Rawaho and Tamarau had discovered that their kūmara crops no longer flourished, because their father had taken with him the mauri that contained the mana of the kūmara. So the two brothers set off in pursuit, seeking the mauri. After many adventures they found themselves in Te Wai Pounamu,

standing before the tapu house where their father lay dead.

The story now becomes an account of the rivalry between these two. Rawaho was the elder, and he was a tohunga; furthermore his birth had been miraculous, for he had been born from an armpit. But now, as he recited lengthy chants before entering his father's house, he waited too long. His younger brother recited shorter chants and entered first.

Inside, Tamarau found Hape's desiccated body. Following an ancient ritual, he closed his teeth upon Hape's ear and at once inherited his father's powers. He was now an atua. Tamarau possessed himself of the two belts that contained the mauri of the kūmara (in the form of a piece of stalk from a kūmara plant), and he took as well his father's wairua, present in hair from the head. Leaving the house, he informed his elder brother that it was too late for him to inherit their father's powers.

Rawaho now entered the house, but he could only greet his father with a hongi, the pressing of noses.

On the return journey Tamarau revealed that he now possessed the power of flight. Back at Ōhiwa he showed kindness towards Rawaho, presenting him with the mauri of the kūmara so that his crops did well. He himself lived at Kawekawe, though he flew from place to place and sometimes up to the sky. He became the atua of his descendants and protected them in times of war. Sometimes he appeared as a bird, a pūkeko. If anyone approached his home at Kawekawe he would dart away in the form of a meteor.

A different story about Hape is told by the Arawa peoples. They say that in the early times their ancestor Ngātoro-i-rangi, a great tohunga, confronted Hape at Taupō while both men were travelling separately through the region. Ngātoro-i-rangi suspected that Hape was there to claim land for himself and his descendants, so to assert his own claim he began the ascent of Mount Ngāuruhoe. Looking back he saw Hape climbing up behind him, and he called upon his gods to destroy his rival. They sent sleet and snow, and Hape perished in the storm.

## Hāpōpō
### Always a loser

Hāpōpō is a minor figure who turns up in several myths. Always he trusts to appearances and is deceived.

In a story from Ngāti Porou, the great Uenuku and his son Whatiua are leading an army against their enemy Wheta. Hāpōpō is Wheta's ally, and a party of men led by Whatiua surround his house under cover of darkness. The warriors can hear Hāpōpō, inside, anxiously asking his atua whether the enemy are on their way. The god reassures Hāpōpō that he is entirely safe, that no attack will come. But soon afterwards Hāpōpō is attacked and killed. As he dies, he reproaches his 'lying, deceitful' god in words that have become proverbial [He atua kahurakiraki, waiho te raru i a Hāpōpō].

Another myth has Hāpōpō as one of the crew of the *Tainui* on its voyage from Hawaiki. As the vessel is about to reach the shore, Hāpōpō sees the glowing flowers of the pōhutukawa and rātā trees and thinks them treasures. Believing he will no longer need the precious red plume he has brought with him, he tosses it into the water. By the time he discovers the truth, his plume is gone.

## Hatupatu
### An Arawa hero

After arriving from Hawaiki on *Te Arawa*, Hatupatu settled with his relatives on Mokoia Island in Lake Rotorua. He was the youngest son, and his three brothers treated him badly.

On a bird-hunting expedition into the interior, two of the brothers, Hānui and Hāroa, ate the good birds themselves and gave Hatupatu only the lean, tough ones. After this had gone on for a long time, the boy planned mischief. One day when his brothers were gone and he was left as usual to watch their belongings, he ate up all the birds they had preserved in gourds and bark containers. Then he trampled the path and disturbed everything in the camp so it would look as if a war party had come. He wounded himself in a couple of places, and lay there covered in blood.

Hatupatu's brothers believed his story. But they continued to ill-treat him, he kept on stealing the potted birds, and they became suspicious. They hid, caught him in the act, killed him, and buried him in the heap of feathers they had plucked from their birds. Then they went back home and told their parents they did not know what had happened to him.

The parents, suspecting murder, sent out an atua in the form of a blowfly. The spirit found the place where Hatupatu lay buried, and with a chant it brought him back to life.

When Hatupatu went on through the forest, he came across a giant woman in the form of a bird, with wings and beak, who was spearing birds for herself. This woman, Kurangaituku, imprisoned him in her cave. Eventually he escaped, taking her fine cloaks and her taiaha, and ran towards his home on Mokoia Island.

She followed and was about to overtake him, but he recited a chant and hid inside a rock. Later he went on again. By the time he reached the hot springs at Whakarewarewa, she was once more close behind. But Hatupatu, knowing

*Having escaped from Kurangaituku, Hatupatu swims under the water to his home on Mokoia Island. A carving by Tene Waitere on the window panel of Nuku Te Apiapi.*

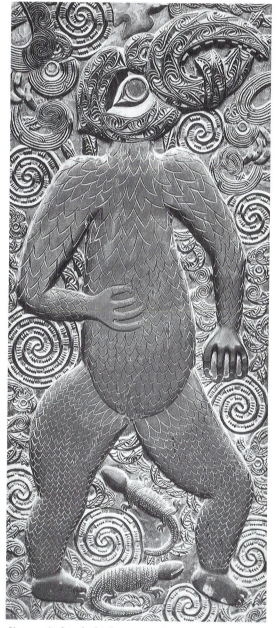

*Kurangaituku, the bird-woman who captured Hatupatu, depicted with her pet birds and tuatara. A figure carved by Tene Waitere on the door of Nuku Te Apiapi, a Rotorua meeting house opened in 1906.*

the springs to be dangerous, jumped right across. Kurangaituku tried to wade through and was burnt to death.

Then Hatupatu dived into Lake Rotorua and swam underwater to his island home. When his three brothers learnt of his presence and came to fight him, they found he was no longer a boy but a fearsome warrior. He overcame his brothers and allowed them to live.

Their father then addressed the defeated brothers, telling them that instead of this disgraceful behaviour they should be seeking revenge for the destruction of their ancestral waka, *Te Arawa*. After its voyage from Hawaiki the vessel had been beached at Maketū, and there it had been burnt by Raumati, an enemy from Tauranga. As yet no revenge had been taken.

Shamed by this reproach, the brothers prepared for war. Meanwhile, their father secretly taught Hatupatu the tattoo marks and other signs by which he would be able to recognise Raumati in battle.

When the war party set out in their waka, Hatupatu remained behind. Afterwards he dived into the lake, taking with him thirty red feather cloaks; in the deepest place he stopped for a meal of freshwater mussels, then he emerged from the water and made his way overland. The brothers and their army, when they reached their camp that evening, found Hatupatu there ahead of them, spreading out his cloaks to dry. Next day the brothers proceeded on, and Hatupatu again swam underwater and reached their destination before them.

When they came to Maketū, and the warriors were ranged in divisions, the jealous brothers did not place any men under Hatupatu's command. Because of this insult he went off to sleep on his own among some bushes. And then he had an idea. He tied the bushes into bundles with vines and draped his fine cloaks around them, making them look like a band of warriors.

Early next morning the rangatira in the brothers' camp rose to encourage their men with warlike speeches, while their hidden enemies watched this performance. When all had finished, Hatupatu rose in his turn and addressed his bundles in their cloaks. He made many speeches, each time dressing himself differently, so that it seemed that this division was led by many valorous rangatira. Seeing this, the other side dreaded Hatupatu and his bushes more than his brothers' divisions.

When battle commenced, the cowardly brothers and their men soon ran away. As they fled, pursued by enemy warriors, Hatupatu seized his opportunity. He fought and killed two important rangatira, one of them Raumati himself, and the enemy, seeing their leaders fall, turned and fled.

Afterwards, when the brothers had returned to Mokoia, Hatupatu revealed to his father that it was he who had killed Raumati and avenged the burning of *Te Arawa*. From this time on, Hatupatu's rank and mana were greater than those of his brothers.

Near Ātiamuri, an extraordinary rock standing beside the road is said to be the one inside which Hatupatu hid from Kurangaituku. A deep hole shows where the rock opened to receive him, and marks on the outside are scratches made by Kurangaituku's fingernails. This rock is a tipua, a tapu entity with special powers. Offerings of twigs are still made to it.

# Hau
### Breath, wind, life

In traditional belief there are in a person's body two presences, a wairua and a hau, which can both be described as souls. The wairua leaves the body during sleep and also after death, though it continues to exist. The hau is always present in the living body, then disappears at death.

This word hau is the usual term for breath, but since breath is life, it also has a more general significance. Furthermore, it was believed by

extension that a hau was possessed by an entire people, and by such valued possessions and resources as a pā, a house, a forest, the ocean. In each case its hau was the life and vitality of the entity concerned. It was preserved and protected by being ritually located within a mauri, a highly tapu object that was carefully hidden from enemies who might wish to attack it.

As well, hau is the standard term for wind. Again there was the concept of a living force; the wind was the counterpart of a human's breath. In some situations a wind represented, or foretokened, the presence of a person who was living in the direction from which it came. And a light breeze might be thought to indicate the presence of a spirit.

# Hau and Wairaka
### A runaway wife

Soon after his arrival from Hawaiki, the early ancestor Hau set out to find his wife Wairaka, who had disappeared. Some say she had been abducted by two slaves, Kiwi and Weka, others that she had run off with a man named Wheku.

Travelling south from Whanganui, he crossed many rivers and named each of them according to an experience he had there. For instance, finding a large river he feared he could not cross, he called it Manawatū [Nervous heart].

On the wild coast by Pukerua Bay, Hau found Wairaka and killed her two companions. He ordered his wife into the sea to collect shellfish, then with a chant he turned her to stone. (She is still there now, a large rock accessible at low tide.) Afterwards he continued his journey of exploration and finally reached Lake Wairarapa.

Hau's full name is Hau-pipi. Generally he is believed to have arrived on the *Aotea* and to have lived with others of the crew at Pātea before losing his wife and setting out to find her. The Whanganui peoples (Te Āti Haunui-a-Pāpārangi) often trace descent from him, as do people in the Rangitīkei region, and his story provides explanations for the names of many rivers and other landmarks.

# Hauāuru
### The strong west wind

At Tāmaki (Auckland) the west wind, Hauāuru, once coveted Wairaka, the wife of Tamatea-te-rā, who lived in the volcanic peaks in the region. In Tamatea's absence he played soft tunes in the forest trees, winning Wairaka with his music, then he took her south with him.

Tamatea returned, found his wife gone and traced her at last to Arahura, the greenstone valley in Te Wai Pounamu (the South Island). Wairaka was sitting by the water while Hauāuru was away searching for greenstone in the rivers.

Tamatea told her to collect shellfish for his dinner, but she knew her infidelity would be punished and she chose to drown. She is now a rock, a solitary pillar known as Wairaka, off the coast near Westport. Back at Tāmaki her name is recalled, for the Māori name of Mount Albert is Ōwairaka [Wairaka's place].

This story must be related in some way to the one in the previous entry.

# Haumapūhia
### Creator of Lake Waikaremoana

Haumapūhia was the daughter (some say the son) of Māhu, who lived in the Urewera Mountains long ago. One day he told her to draw water from a spring, she refused to go, and in a rage he thrust her under the water. Instead of drowning, she turned into a taniwha.

Struggling to escape, she formed the great arms of Lake Waikaremoana. Then she heard the sea far to the south, and attempted to reach it. She forced her way down at Te Whāngaromanga [The place of disappearance], forming as she did so the underground channel which is the only outlet from the lake, but as she came back up she was overtaken by daylight and turned to stone.

She lay there groaning, and her father, who

*Lake Waikaremoana in the Urewera Mountains, formed as Haumapūhia struggled to escape.*

had gone off to the ocean, heard the sound and knew it was his child. So he sent her fish to eat, stocking the lake with lamprey and kōkopu, and also shellfish, which can be seen today embedded in cliffs in the region.

Haumapūhia still lies there as a rock, face downward and moaning in the rushing waters. She is a tipua stone, with special powers. Passers-by generally treated such tapu stones with great respect, reciting a ritual chant and leaving an offering of leaves or grass. Once, though, two young men interfered with Haumapūhia by pulling off some of the water weed that forms her rippling hair. They were punished with a heavy rainstorm, and many thought them fortunate to escape with their lives.

# Haumia
### Origin of fernroot

Fernroot, the starchy rhizome of the bracken fern, was dug in early summer then dried and stored for the winter, when other food was often scarce. Though not liked nearly as much as kūmara, it was much valued for the relative ease with which it could be obtained and stored.

Usually it is is Haumia who is the fernroot, or father of the fernroot. The Arawa peoples regarded him as one of the sons of Rangi and Papa, the first parents, and said that when these sons fought among themselves in the beginning, Haumia was attacked with others by his brother Tāwhirimātea, the wind. He tried to hide in the ground, but his hair stuck out and he was found by the warrior Tū (who here represents human beings). Tū dragged Haumia from the ground

and devoured him, having first recited the chant that made it safe to do so. And ever since this time, human beings have eaten their relative Haumia.

In the southern Bay of Plenty and parts of the east coast, Haumia is a son of Tāne and grandson of Rangi and Papa. He is sometimes considered to be the bones and flesh of Papa, the earth, who provides food in this way for human beings because they are her children. It is also said that Haumia grew from the back of his father Rangi, and that because of this he is a hardy plant that grows on cold hills and needs no sun.

The young bracken fronds that shoot up in spring are known as mōkehu – or personified, Mōkehu. These are Haumia's children. Mosquitoes and sandflies, since they often live in bracken, are children of Mōkehu and grandchildren of Haumia.

## Haumia
### A taniwha at Manukau

This taniwha was a powerful atua of the Waikato peoples, and regularly communicated with tohunga who were his mediums. His home was in the Manukau Harbour.

On one occasion Haumia informed his tohunga that Ureia, the taniwha of the neighbouring Hauraki peoples, must be killed, and that he himself would entice Ureia to the Manukau. So he visited Ureia at Hauraki, then suggested a return visit: a feast had been prepared, he said, and there were gifts as well. Ureia, deceived, accepted the invitation.

At Manukau, Haumia's people had placed an enormous noose across the entrance to the harbour, and on each side great numbers of men stood ready to pull on the ropes. As the tohunga at the tūāhu recited their chants, Haumia led Ureia straight into the snare. Ureia fought hard but at last was overcome.

This treachery did not go unrevenged. Armies from Hauraki attacked the peoples of Tāmaki, Manukau and Waikato, and some were driven from their homes.

## Haumia-whakatere-taniwha
### A courageous confrontation

At Kāwhia many generations ago, a man named Haumia owned a kūmara plantation on a cliff overlooking the sea. Year after year his crops were destroyed by extraordinarily high waves which reared right up over the cliff. In the end he climbed down the cliff and discovered an im-

mense taniwha living in a cave. This taniwha, whose name was Rapanui, had sent the waves that caused the damage.

Haumia bravely overcame Rapanui and was henceforth known as Haumia-whakatere-taniwha [Haumia who makes taniwha swim away]. Some say he killed the monster, others that he persuaded him to swim north to feed on the fish in the plentiful waters of the Manukau Harbour, then in his absence blocked the entrance to his cave; when the taniwha returned, he had to look elsewhere for a place to live. And Haumia-whakatere-taniwha has been taken as their name by Haumia's descendants.

## Hautapu
### A meeting with a fairy

Hunting takahē with his dog on the heights of Mount Tākitimu in the far south, Hautapu met a beautiful woman named Kaiheraki. When asked about her people, she said she had no relatives. Her mother was the mountain on which she lived.

Hautapu knew then that she was a fairy [patupaiarehe], and that if he took her as his wife she might keep him on the mountain for ever. But he was a tohunga, with a knowledge of the rituals by which this danger could be averted. A sacred fire had to be kindled, and a small portion of food cooked in a special oven. This food would destroy Kaiheraki's tapu and make it safe to marry her.

The ritual kindling of fire required the presence of a man and a woman; while the man rapidly twirled the upper part of the fire-plough, the woman placed her foot upon the lower part. So Hautapu now showed Kaiheraki what to do. He turned his stick vigorously in the groove, the dust began to smoke, and soon there was a little flame. The woman cried out in fear, being unused to fire. Then a spark fell on her foot and it started to bleed, because this is what fire does to these people.

She ran, he caught her, and again they began to make fire together. Then for a moment his attention was diverted and she fled into the forest. The mist came down and he knew he would never find her.

But Kaiheraki is still on her mountain, and on misty days her giant figure can be seen striding along the ridges.

## Hawaiki
### The homeland in the east

This mythical land is best known as the country from which, in numerous traditions, the ancestors of the different peoples make the voyage to

Aotearoa. Sometimes the crew of a waka set out because they have been involved in warfare, or will be if they stay; generally in such cases they have quarrelled with the great rangatira Uenuku, who always wins in the end. In other accounts no motivation is given, or needed.

Nearly all the peoples of Aotearoa have a tradition of such a voyage, or else an ancestor who came by other means, perhaps riding on a piece of pumice or the back of a whale. Even when a people trace descent to an ancestor who was in the country in the beginning (such as Māui or Toi), they often celebrate as well their descent from an ancestor or ancestors who arrived from Hawaiki. Many important early marriages, we are told, occurred between the immigrants from Hawaiki and the people of the land [tāngata whenua] whom they found living here.

These accounts of astonishing voyages – great dangers overcome through the power of ritual chant, struggles for supremacy between rangatira and tohunga, vessels which subsequently turn to stone, long journeys undertaken by leading men to establish landmarks and claim territory in the new land – can be recognised as myths when they are considered in the context of other beliefs about Hawaiki.

In the southern Bay of Plenty, immediately beyond Whakaari (White Island), three small tapu rocks were regarded as a kind of halfway point for people travelling between Hawaiki and the ordinary, human land of Aotearoa (or Aotea, as the North Island was often known). The name of these rocks, Paepae-Aotea, means 'Threshold of Aotea'. Their English name is the Volkner Rocks.

Shining cuckoos, which migrate each autumn to the Solomon Islands and the Bismarck Archipelago, were believed to spend the winter in Hawaiki. They returned as messengers of Mahuru [Spring] to remind people that it was time to dig the fields.

Since the sun rises in the east, and so do the stars that bring the changing seasons with their food resources, it is not surprising that this direction was associated in Māori thought with life, fertility and success. This was not metaphor but reality, the way things were. It is for this reason that Hawaiki was generally said to lie in the direction of the rising sun.

In the beginning, human life itself was created in Hawaiki, because the first human being was shaped from the soil of Hawaiki by Tāne (or sometimes Tiki). Many other myths are set there, and it is the source of many valued resources. The kūmara, for instance, the most highly valued of food plants, grows wild in Hawaiki, untouched by human hands. Whales and fish come from a spring in the ocean near Hawaiki. Certain birds, such as the kākā and the shining cuckoo, fly backwards and forwards between Hawaiki and Aotearoa. Rats, some say, swam from Hawaiki in a long chain, each holding in its mouth the tail of the rat in front. Greenstone swam from Hawaiki in the form of a fish. Even volcanic fire was brought from there.

When the ancestors arrived in their waka, they brought with them many treasured plants and birds, also important atua and ritual objects such as mauri. In one way and another, Hawaiki was the ultimate source of the mana of all of these. The crops flourished, the gods exerted their powers, the mauri ensured the continuing fertility of the resources they protected, because of their origin in Hawaiki.

This continuing relationship between Hawaiki and the people of Aotearoa was expressed in ritual. To gain access to Hawaiki, certain ceremonies were performed while facing the rising sun. Rituals to ensure a person's health and welfare might be performed at dawn, with the tohunga stretching an arm towards the sun. To ensure a good kūmara crop, the tubers were placed in the ground as the planters faced the east.

There are several accounts, apparently historical, of people setting out from Aotearoa to sail back to Hawaiki; the best known of these expeditions was led from the east coast by Pahiko, after his people suffered a defeat. On these occasions the ship's course was, naturally, directed towards the rising sun.

It was often thought that after death many wairua were able to return to the homeland of Hawaiki. Sometimes, as from East Cape, this journey was believed to be made in an eastward direction. In other regions an orator at a funeral might tell the deceased person to travel northwards, or to follow the setting sun to Hawaiki (since the west, on such occasions, was associated with death). This did not involve any sense of geographical contradiction.

In as far as Hawaiki is the source of life and fertility, a homeland to which many return after death, it can be regarded as a paradisial land. But so many different events occur there, it is the source of so much, that its nature differs from one myth to another. In a sense, events there encompass the whole of human experience.

## Hawaiki-rangi
### The house with four doors

In the southernmost regions of the North Island, there was a belief that after death a person's wairua often makes its way to a distant place, Te Hono-i-wairua [The meeting of wairua], which is located in the far land of Irihia. There, it was sometimes said, the wairua enters a house, Hawaiki-rangi [Sky Hawaiki], which stands on the summit of a mountain. Its four doors face east, west, south and north.

According to a Whanganui poet of the early eighteenth century, three of these doors lead down to Night. Down there are the regions known as Te Muriwaihou and Rarohenga, and Hine-tītama (whose other name is Hine-nui-te-pō) is there, the woman who receives her descendants at the end of their lives. Night is the destination of many wairua:

E toru te tatau ki Te Pō-kākarauri,
Ki Te Pō-tiwhatiwha, ki Te Pō-ka-wheau-atu,
Ki Te Muriwaihou, ki Rarohenga,
Ki a Hine-tītama, e pūtiki mai rā
I te kāpunipuni o ngā wairua.

Three doors lead to Dark-night,
Black-night, Night-forever,
To Te Muriwaihou and Rarohenga,
And Hine-tītama, who brings the wairua together
In their gathering-place.

But the fourth door leads upwards to the sky. In the earliest times the great Tāne passed through that door, climbed the raised-up centre, and reached the highest of the skies. It was believed that some wairua could follow him.

In a late account associated with beliefs about the high god Io, the wairua approach the house from the directions in which they lived during their lives: 'when people die they each return by their own wind, to their own door'. Within Hawaiki-rangi, some pass through the eastern door and mount to the sky, while others go down through the southern door.

Another name for the house is Hawaiki-nui [Great Hawaiki]. In some traditions there is no house, and all the wairua go down Tāheke-roa [Long descent] to Te Muriwaihou and Rarohenga. Sometimes they are taken below by the evil Whiro, who lost a battle with Tāne and now lives down there with Rūaumoko and others.

## Hei
### An Arawa ancestor

This man was an uncle of Tama-te-kapua, captain of Te Arawa on its voyage from Hawaiki. When the ship had just arrived and was coasting south, several of its leading men claimed land for their descendants by identifying a landmark on the shore with some part of their body. While they were passing Whitianga on the eastern shore of Te Paeroa-o-Toi (the Coromandel Peninsula), Hei named a prominent rock after the curve of his nose (Te Kūraetanga-o-te-ihu-o-Hei). In this way he laid claim to the coastline in that locality.

Later he went there to live. His descendants intermarried with the ancient peoples in the region, and became known as Ngāti Hei. A wide, productive harbour there (its English name is Mercury Bay) was called Te Whanga-nui-o-Hei [Hei's great harbour].

Hei's son Waitaha settled in the Tauranga area, and his descendants remained there.

## Hikurangi
### A sacred mountain

It was believed in some regions that when the hero Māui was pulling up the fish that became the North Island, the first part of the fish that rose

*In some myths, Te Puke ki Hikurangi [Mount Hikurangi] becomes a place of refuge for people threatened by a great flood. For this reason its name was given in 1897 to a Māori-language periodical published by H. T. Mahupuku as a way of proposing political and economic solutions to the severe difficulties facing most Māori people at the time. On the masthead of the paper the mountain rises above a peaceful island.*

through the water was a mountain named Hikurangi. This was therefore the first part of the land that the light fell upon.

In another myth, the story of Paikea and Ruatapu who were living in Hawaiki, Paikea is about to travel to Aotearoa when he is warned by his demonic brother Ruatapu that at a certain time he will arrive at Paikea's new home in the form of high waves breaking upon the shore, and that the people must then run to Mount Hikurangi to escape the flood. And when these great waves come, the crowds upon Hikurangi survive the disaster.

In both these myths, then, Hikurangi rises above the ocean (which is a nonhuman realm associated with danger and destruction). In both stories it is a sacred mountain of great power, in the first because of its primacy and the light that falls upon it, in the second because it is a place of refuge and survival.

As well as existing in mythology, the name Hikurangi was given in reality to a number of prominent hills and mountains in different parts of the country. The best known is Hikurangi on the east coast, the tapu mountain of the people of Ngāti Porou. They believed that their mountain was the first land fished up by Māui, and that his waka was still up there on the summit, turned to stone. At dawn the sun lights up this high peak while all around is in darkness – and this event

repeats the first occasion on which the sun shone upon Hikurangi as it rose above the waters.

Almost certainly, some of the other mountains called Hikurangi were similarly identified with the mythic mountain, but little is known about this.

## Hina
### Māui's sister, or wife

Hina (or Hina-uri or occasionally Hine) is sometimes the sister of the trickster hero Māui, and sometimes his wife. As his sister she marries a man named Irawaru, and a quarrel between the two brothers-in-law ends with Māui turning Irawaru into the first dog. Occasionally Hina is so upset at this that she throws herself into the sea and swims for many days before finding Tinirau on his island and marrying him.

When Hina is Māui's wife rather than sister, she has an encounter while bathing with Tuna [Eel], who seduces her. Learning of this, Māui digs a channel, places ten waka skids inside it and entices Tuna to visit Hina. When Tuna comes up over the skids, Māui chops him to pieces.

Similar events occur in traditions from other parts of Polynesia. In stories about Hina and Tinirau (or persons with equivalent names), Hina is a 'good wife' and a positive role model; in stories about Hina and the eel, her dangerous sexuality has to be controlled.

In Aotearoa, however, it is usually Hine-te-iwaiwa rather than Hina who marries Tinirau and is the positive role model (as is apparent from the fact that ritual chants relating to women usually if not always refer to Hine-te-iwaiwa). Nevertheless, Hina continued in some ways to represent women in general.

# Hine-ahu-one
## The woman shaped from sand

In some regions, such as the east coast and the Urewera, it is said that the creator Tāne, son of Rangi the sky and Papa the earth, went looking for a human woman and eventually decided he would have to make one himself. So he went to the beach and modelled a woman from sand (some say from mud). According to some, the place he chose for this purpose was the mons veneris of his mother, Papa, which is known as 'the sands at Kurawaka' [te one i Kurawaka].

Tāne formed arms, legs, a body, head, and sexual parts, reciting as he did so a ritual chant. He breathed life into his woman, and called her Hine-ahu-one [Woman shaped from sand] – or some say Hine-hau-one.

Then Tāne tried out this woman he had made. According to Mohi Ruatapu of Ngāti Porou, Tāne first thrust his penis against her head, and that is why people sweat. Then he tried her eyeballs, and that is how people acquired pupils in their eyes. He thrust against the nose, and that is why there is mucus. Then her mouth – saliva comes from that. All these things are from Tāne's penis. Then he thrust against her front, and behold, he lived with a woman. She bore him a daughter, whom he took to wife as well.

It is sometimes thought that this myth must have been influenced by the biblical story in which God creates Adam in his own image from earth. In fact it is unrelated.

# Hine-hopu
## Ancestor of Ngāti Pikiao

Between Lakes Rotoiti and Rotoehu there was a well-known track, called Hine-hopu's Path [Te Ara o Hine-hopu], where waka were portaged. When a Ngā Puhi force under the command of Hongi Hika invaded the region in 1823, they took their own waka with much difficulty up a river from the coast near Maketū, through Lake Rotoehu, then over this portage. They were then able to sail straight through to Lake Rotorua. There they attacked and took Mokoia Island, where the people of Te Arawa had sought refuge. Te Arawa put up a strong resistance but it was an unequal fight, since all of Ngā Puhi were armed with muskets while Te Arawa had only a single gun.

Because of these events, Hine-hopu's Path is now generally known as Hongi's Track. A road has replaced the path. Beside this road there is a tapu tree, a matai, which is known now as Hine-hopu's Wishing Tree. Many visitors pay this tipua

tree the tribute of a green twig, then ask for its assistance by making a wish.

When Hine-hopu was a baby her mother hid her from enemies by this tree, and it was there, when she grew up, that she met the man she was to marry. To mark their meeting, she called upon her ancestors to endow the tree with spiritual powers.

Hine-hopu's husband was Pikiao, son of Tama-kari and grandson of an earlier Pikiao. Their descendants became the people of Ngāti Pikiao, who belong to the Lake Rotoiti district. The veneration shown to Hine-hopu's tree down through the generations, and the naming of the path by which it stands, are evidence of the importance accorded this woman by her descendants.

# Hine-i-tapeka
## Underground fire

Fire in general comes from Mahuika, and is her possession. But volcanic fire, the fire that burns under the earth, was sometimes thought to belong to Mahuika's sister, Hine-i-tapeka. The charred tree trunks embedded in the vast pumice deposits on the Kaingaroa Plains were attributed to her activities.

# Hine-kōrako
## The pale rainbow

The luminous halo often seen around the moon was regarded as Hine-kōrako [Pale woman]. Sometimes she took the form of a pale rainbow, and sometimes she was identified with the moon itself. Along with Hine-te-iwaiwa she assisted women in childbirth.

During the voyage from Hawaiki of the *Tākitimu*, Hine-kōrako stood before the vessel each night as a lunar rainbow and Kahukura guided it each day in the shape of the rainbow visible by day. Because these two atua had guided and protected *Tākitimu*, they were appealed to in later times by deep-sea voyagers.

At Waiapu, Hine-kōrako's name was Tū-kō-rako. She was thought by some to be a daughter of Tangaroa.

# Hine-kōrako
## A female taniwha

The original inhabitants of Te Rēinga on the Wairoa River, and rugged Mount Whakapunake nearby, were a race of taniwha. After some generations a female taniwha, Hine-kōrako, fell in love with a human man, Tāne-kino. They married and had a son, whom they named Taurenga, but Hine-kōrako abandoned her husband and child when some of his relatives made insulting remarks about her ancestry. She went to live under the spectacular Te Rēinga waterfall, and she is still there today.

Two present-day peoples in the Te Rēinga region, Ngāti Hinehika and Ngāti Pōhatu, trace their descent from Tāne-kino and Hine-kōrako. And their taniwha ancestor assists them when they appeal to her. On one occasion the river was in flood and some people in a waka were being swept towards the falls. An old man called aloud to Hine-kōrako, and just in time the waka stood still. Then it began to move slowly upstream and the people were saved.

The name Hine-kōrako belongs in Tākitimu tradition to the lunar rainbow and in the present story there seems to be an association with the rainbow visible at Te Rēinga Falls. See the previous entry.

## Hinemoa and Tūtānekai
### Famous lovers

Tūtānekai, who lived many generations ago on Mokoia Island in Lake Rotorua, was of high rank but illegitimate birth. His mother was Rangiuru, wife of the leading rangatira Whakaue, but his father was Tūwharetoa, a rangatira from Kawerau who had visited the island during Whakaue's absence. Whakaue forgave his wife, reared the boy as his own son and grew very fond of him. Nevertheless, Tūtānekai had to contend with the jealous animosity of his three elder half-brothers.

Every year the people living around Lakes Rotorua and Rotoiti gathered for some days at Ōwhata, on the eastern shore of the lake, to discuss issues of importance. At these meetings the young men would gaze from a distance at the beautiful Hinemoa, high-ranking daughter of two great rangatira, Te Umu-karia and his wife Hine-maru. This girl had been made a puhi at birth; she was tapu, set apart, and lived in a special house with female attendants. Many men had sought to marry her, among them Whakaue's elder sons, but her people had not yet chosen a husband for her.

Like his brothers Tūtānekai was in love with Hinemoa, although he did not imagine that she would return his love. But Tūtānekai was a handsome man and a fine dancer and athlete, and soon Hinemoa fell in love with him. Glances were exchanged, then messages.

They did not tell their relatives, because Hine-moa's people would not have accepted such a marriage and Tūtānekai's brothers would have strenuously objected. When the meeting ended, Whakaue and his sons returned to Mokoia. Tūtānekai told his father that he wanted Hinemoa and that his love was returned. He built himself a platform [atamira] on a rise behind his father's house, and every evening he and his friend Tiki sat there and played their flutes.

In the still air their music floated across to Ōwhata, four kilometres away, and Hinemoa knew it came from Tūtānekai. Every evening she sat listening by the shore on the great rock Iriiri-kapua, wanting so much to go to him. But her people by now were suspicious, and every evening they dragged up their waka so that she could not paddle across to Mokoia.

One night she could stand it no longer, and despite the distance she made up her mind to swim. She found six gourds in a cookhouse, rested for a while on Iriiri-kapua, then took off her clothes and entered the water, three empty gourds tied together under each arm. It was getting dark, but the sound of the flutes told her the way to go. After a while she came to a post, known as Hine-whata, to which her father tied his fishing nets. She rested there, then swam on, still guided by the flutes.

At last she reached Mokoia and found Wai-kimihia, a warm pool near the shore; she knew that Tūtānekai's home was on the slope above. She was shivering with cold, so she got into the pool to warm herself. As well she was shivering with shame, wondering what Tūtānekai would think about what she had done and ashamed to be without clothes.

Just then it happened that Tūtānekai felt thirsty and sent his slave with a gourd to draw water. On the way back, the slave had to pass the pool where Hinemoa sat. She asked in a gruff voice, 'Who is the water for?'

The slave told her, 'Tūtānekai.'

Hinemoa asked for the gourd, drank from it, then broke it. He asked why she had done this, but she gave no answer. So he went and told his master, and was sent back again. Again Hinemoa took the gourd, drank, and broke it.

When the slave returned the second time, Tūtānekai was furious at the insult. He put on fine cloaks, took his mere and went forward to fight this stranger who had infringed his tapu.

At the pool's edge he called out, but Hinemoa hid under a ledge of rock. Tūtānekai felt around the edge, found her and pulled her out, saying, 'Who is this?'

She told him, 'It's me, Tūtānekai.'

Tūtānekai said, 'But who are you?'

'It's me – Hinemoa.'

Tūtānekai led her from the pool and saw how beautiful she was. He placed one of his cloaks around her, and they went to his house and slept together. This, in those days, signified marriage.

At daybreak everyone was up and working, but Tūtānekai did not appear. His father wondered if he was ill and sent someone to see. The messenger slid aside the shutter on the window and saw four legs inside, not two. He rushed back and told what he had seen, he was sent again, and this time he recognised Hinemoa.

When he shouted his news, the elder brothers would not believe it. But then Tūtānekai came out of his house with Hinemoa beside him. At the

same time, across the lake, several large waka were seen approaching from Ōwhata. They knew it was Te Umu-karia and they expected war, but instead the two peoples made peace and there was much rejoicing. Tūtānekai's elder brothers were the only ones who continued to resent the marriage.

As for Hinemoa and Tūtānekai, they lived together happily and had many distinguished descendants.

## Hine-mokemoke
### A lonely singer

Long ago, men fishing off Matakaoa Point, near Wharekāhika (Hicks Bay), used to hear strange

*Hinemoa and Tūtānekai above a gateway at Whakarewarewa,*
*near Rotorua, carved in the early years of the twentieth century.*

*Shell trumpets were blown to assemble people on special occasions and announce visitors. This one has a toggle of bird skin.*

songs coming up from under the water. Then one day some fishermen pulled up their anchor and found a pūpū-tara [trumpet shell] clinging to it. This shell had been singing the songs they had heard.

The shell was fitted with a mouthpiece and was named Hine-mokemoke [Lonely woman]. It was regarded as a tipua, a being with uncanny powers, and was used as a trumpet for many years.

# Hine-nui-te-pō
## The woman who brought death

Although they told different stories about her, nearly everyone knew Hine-nui-te-pō [Great woman the night] as the woman who brought death into the world. In some regions it was believed that after Tāne married his daughter Hine-tītama and she discovered her father's identity, she was greatly shamed and rushed down to the underworld. There, it was often said, her name changed to Hine-nui-te-pō. Tāne followed and begged her to return, but she told him to go back to the world and rear up their offspring. She would remain below to receive them when they died.

It was also believed that the trickster hero Māui, after performing many marvellous deeds, determined to overcome death by conquering Hine-nui-te-pō. Although warned not to do so, he approached her as she lay sleeping, intending to enter her body by the path through which children enter this world. But the little birds that accompanied him laughed when they saw Māui's head and shoulders disappear inside the great woman's vagina, and their laughter woke her. She brought her legs together, and Māui was crushed to death.

The details vary. Sometimes Māui, fishing up the land, angers Hine-nui-te-pō when his hook catches in the bargeboard of her house under the ocean, and draws her house up too. In a Mātaatua tradition, Māui discovers that Hine-nui-te-pō has taken Tuna [Eel] as a lover, so he kills Tuna. In retaliation, Hine-nui-te-pō sends the mosquito against him; the mosquito takes a drop of blood from Māui's forehead, and Hine-nui-te-pō's sorcery, performed over the blood, destroys him.

In a west coast tradition, Hine-nui-te-pō has within her the power of the renewal of life. Māui noticed that the sun and moon always come back to life because they bathe in Tāne's waters of life

*The fantail laughed, Hine-nui-te-pō awoke, and death came into the world.*

[te wai-ora a Tāne]. He decided to do the same, and to enter the womb of Hine-nui-te-pō – for that is the underworld, where the waters of life are situated.

Hine-nui-te-pō draws all into her womb, but permits none to return. Māui determined to try, trusting to his great powers, but the fantail laughed, the woman awoke, and Māui was cut in two. If the fantail had not laughed, Māui would have drunk from the waters of life and human beings would have lived forever.

Yet while Hine-nui-te-pō is the cause of death, she is also a mother who cares for her children after their death. On the west coast her darkness was associated not only with death but with the beginning of the world; she is the most important of the gods of the night who were there in the beginning, before the gods of the light, and she is therefore the ancestor of all who followed. From this region it is recorded further (by Richard Taylor, in a manuscript) that Hine-nui-te-pō 'is the goddess of dreams, and all revelations made to men in dreams proceeded from her, prayers were regularly said to her every night as the great guardian of night and the giver of rest'.

## Hine-poupou
### The woman who swam Raukawa

Hine-poupou and her husband Te Oripāroa lived on Kapiti Island, north of Raukawa (Cook Strait), until the day they quarrelled and he abandoned her. He took his people and his waka across the wide water and settled on the southern shore, on Rangitoto (D'Urville Island). Hine-poupou's father accompanied him.

She was greatly distressed to find her people gone. For some days she stayed on Kapiti, finding what food she could, then she consulted the omens. When they became favourable, she knew she could swim this stormy strait. So she recited a ritual chant and entered the water.

For many nights and days she swam, until she came at last to a rock in the middle of the strait. She rested, then swam on for many nights and days until she reached a rock quite close to the island of Rangitoto, where her husband was living. Again she rested. On one side of the rock there were taniwha, and on the other side enormous hāpuku, more powerful even than the taniwha.

Hine-poupou swam on until she reached the village where her husband and father were living. She lay in the sun to warm herself, then that night she approached her father's house. Her father wept over her, and at dawn he performed a ceremony in recognition of their reunion.

Her husband pretended to be ashamed of having deserted her, and she lived with him once more. But when a month had passed, Te Oripāroa again treated her badly and she decided to take her revenge. She told her people about the fishing rock she had found, and all of them – her brothers, her husband and their people – put to sea in their waka to visit it.

When Hine-poupou and her brothers reached the place, they anchored at the side where the hāpuku lived. They threw out their lines and

*Hāpuku are large fish, up to sixty kilograms in weight and excellent eating, which inhabit rocky grounds at a great depth. These were very difficult to discover.*

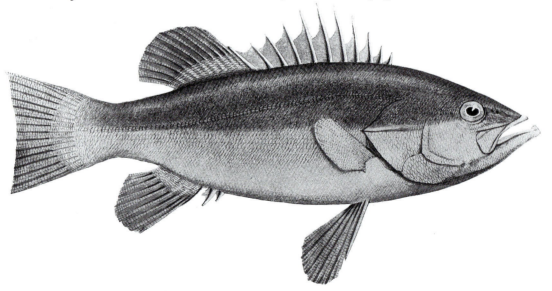

soon had many fish. Then Te Oripāroa and his people arrived. She told him to go to the other side, and at the same time she aroused the taniwha and made them an offering. The taniwha sent a great wind, and Te Oripāroa's waka were thrown about in confusion. Hine-poupou's waka returned safely to land, but Te Oripāroa's people were destroyed and the woman gained her revenge.

Sometimes the story ends here, but one storyteller goes on to say that Te Oripāroa and his younger brother, Mānini-pounamu, did not die. Instead their vessel was blown across the ocean to the island of Hawaiki, a land so tapu that the people ate only raw food. The brothers encountered an old woman who was at first revolted by their cooked food, then learned to like it.

This old women told them about an immense bird, Te Pouākai, which was preying upon the people of Hawaiki. To destroy this bird, the two men built a house with walls made from trees still rooted in the ground. Mānini-pounamu set out to lure Te Pouākai towards the house, it pursued him, and he got there just in time.

The enraged bird tried to batter the house down, but when it thrust a wing inside, the men cut it off. The other wing went in, and again their weapons came down – only the stump was left waving about. Finally Te Pouākai pushed in its head. The brothers swung their weapons and the creature fell dead.

# Hine-pūkohu-rangi
## Woman of the mist

In the Urewera Mountains, Hine-pūkohu-rangi [Sky mist woman] is the mist and her younger sister, Hine-wai [Water woman], is the light rain that falls in foggy weather. These women are fairies [tūrehu]. One night they came down from the sky so that Hine-pūkohu-rangi could visit a human man, Uenuku. At dawn Hine-wai called a warning, and the mist took them back up. When Uenuku awoke, his woman was gone.

After this, Hine-pūkohu-rangi visited Uenuku every night when the fire had gone out. She told him, 'You mustn't say anything about me until we have a child. If you deceive me, I won't stay with you.'

But Uenuku did tell, because he couldn't keep silent about his wife's beauty, which was so different from that of the women of this world. His people advised him to stop up the chinks around the door and window so that the house would stay dark.

That night Hine-pūkohu-rangi came as usual.

In the version of the story known to Paitini Wī Tapeka of Tūhoe, it was Tairi-ā-kohu [Suspended like mist] who loved Uenuku and was deceived. She later had a daughter, Heheurangi.

At dawn Hine-wai called out her warning, but Uenuku said, 'Lie down, it isn't daylight yet. See how dark the house is still.'

So the woman lay down, and Hine-wai alone went back to the sky. Meanwhile the people were gathering in front of the house. When the sun was high they slid the door across, and the woman saw she had been deceived. She stood under the hole where the smoke went up, her long hair her only garment, she sang a song of farewell, then she flew up to the sky.

Uenuku searched for her until he died. Then at last he did find her, because after his death he became the rainbow, which accompanies mist.

In another tradition, Hine-pūkohu-rangi married Te Maunga [The Mountain], who came from the skies – or some say Hawaiki. In the Ruatāhuna Valley, a tapu flax bush used to mark the place where their union occurred. Their son Pōtiki is one of the main ancestors from whom the people of Tūhoe trace their descent, and it is for this reason that Tūhoe are known as the Children of the Mist.

Others say it was Tāiri-ā-kohu [Suspended like mist] who visited Uenuku, then deserted him when he deceived her.

## Hine-rauāmoa
### Youngest of the Children of Light

In the Urewera Mountains and southern Bay of Plenty, Rangi the sky and Papa the earth were often believed to have had three children. They are Tāne, Tangotango and Wainui, who is female.

Tangotango married Wainui and they had six children, known as the Children of Light [te Whānau Mārama]. These were the origin of light in its different forms. The youngest, Hine-rauāmoa, who gave only a faint glimmering light, married her uncle Tāne and they had eight children: Rongo-mā-Tāne, Hine-te-iwaiwa, Tangaroa, Tū, Tāwhirimātea, Haumia, Ioio-whenua and Pū-tē-hue.

In this tradition, Hine-rauāmoa [Moa-plume woman] is the ancestor who initiated the art of weaving.

## Hine-rau-whārangi
### Plant and human fertility

Hine-rau-whārangi [Woman of widespread leaves] is often a daughter of Tāne and Hine-tītama. She represents and ensures the growth and development of plants, and as well she is one of the early female ancestors who assist women with their tasks and responsibilities – for this became her concern when her mother went to live in the underworld.

She is mentioned along with Hine-te-iwaiwa in a chant recited at a young woman's tattooing, and another to help women in childbirth. Sometimes she is the mother of Hine-moana [Ocean woman].

## Hine-rehia
### The discovery of weaving

According to the Hauraki peoples, the techniques of weaving and plaiting were acquired from a fairy [patupaiarehe] woman, Hine-rehia, who married a human man. This man was Karanga-roa, a rangatira of the Maruiwi people who were then living on Motuihe Island in Tikapa (the Hauraki Gulf). Hine-rehia had ventured there to gather rehia, an edible seaweed, and was drying it in the sun when Karanga-roa found her. They married and had sons and daughters.

Hine-rehia was expert in the textile arts – preparing flax fibre and dyeing it, weaving garments, plaiting baskets and mats – but she worked only at night and on foggy days. At dawn she would put away her unfinished work, hiding it from the sunlight. This, she said, was the custom of the fairy people, as the sun would otherwise undo a weaver's work and make her lose her skills.

The women of Motuihe were anxious to learn Hine-rehia's techniques but could not do so in the darkness. A tohunga agreed to confuse her senses and make her keep on working after the sun rose, and that is what happened. Hine-rehia worked on unwittingly while the women, concealed nearby, learnt her secrets.

When Hine-rehia grew tired and laid her work aside, she realised that it was long since daylight and that she had been deceived. She sang a sad farewell to the husband and children she would not see again, then a cloud came down and bore her off to her home on the Moehau Range.

Sometimes at night, or when there is a dense fog, people hear Hine-rehia's lament coming down from the roof of their house. It is an omen of death.

This is how the women of Hauraki obtained their knowledge of the textile arts. And this is why weaving, plaiting and the preparation of fibres take place only during the day, and women cover up their unfinished work before nightfall. When these skills were known only to the fairies, they belonged with the darkness. If people are

*An early engraving of the flax plant, with a hank of prepared fibre [muka]. Many varieties of flax were known and used for different purposes.*

The art of weaving, being almost entirely the concern of women, was believed to have been introduced by women. Hine-te-iwaiwa, who established women's roles, has a general responsibility in this area, though the myths also tell of specialised figures such as Hine-rehia, Hine-rauāmoa, Niwareka and Rukutia.

Many ritual usages affirm the importance of weaving, also plaiting, and give recognition to the kinship that exists between the workers and the plant materials they have harvested. The long and extremely tough leaves of the flax plant [harakeke] are the main material employed. Numerous kinds of cloaks and other garments were woven, from heavy rain capes to beautifully ornamented cloaks worn on ceremonial occasions.

For most fine garments the flax is first scraped, usually with a shell, then washed and dried. The wefts (the horizontal threads) are formed from this fibre. For the long warps (the vertical threads), the fibre is twisted into hanks and beaten well, traditionally with a stone pestle on a flat water-worn boulder, then the prepared fibre [muka] is rolled into yarn on the bare thigh. The weaver works downward on a frame consisting of two (occasionally four) short upright rods, manipulating the weft around each warp.

Right: *A Taupō weaver, sketched in 1844, beats her hank of flax fibre with a pestle.* Below: *Weaving was often a communal activity. These Urewera women in the porch of Te Whai a te Motu, probably in the 1920s, are working on tāniko that will form the border of a fine cloak.*

Plaiting was mostly done by women, though men often undertook certain tasks such as the plaiting of heavy ropes. For many everyday purposes, such as making simple kete [baskets], the green flax is split into strips. For fine kete and intricately plaited floor mats [takapau] much narrower strips are used, and to soften the material it is scraped with a shell then subjected to heat.

Above: *Women in an unknown locality early in the twentieth century.* Below: *The patterns of fine kete are endlessly varied.*

not careful now, this knowledge may return to darkness and the fairies and be lost to humans.

Trouble came to Hine-rehia when she wove by day, because the night was her proper time. But human women belong to this world and to daylight, and they would get into trouble if they wove at night. That is why a young woman who was careless about such matters might be cautioned, 'Remember how Hine-rehia came to grief' [Me mahara ki te raru o Hine-rehia].

Hine-rehia's name means 'Rehia seaweed woman', and recalls the seaweed she was drying when Karanga-roa found her by the shore. Still today there are people who trace descent from her.

## Hine-ruru
### An owl guardian

Families and larger kinship groups recognised the existence of ancestral guardians [kaitiaki] that took the form of animals of different kinds. The guardians that warn of death are often owls (moreporks). They have different names. In Northland, owl guardians are sometimes known as Hine-ruru [Owl woman].

This bird has the power to protect, warn and advise. As well as appearing at night when someone is about to die, she may announce the imminent arrival of visitors. If she is seen flying ahead or walking along the road, she is usually there as a protector at a time of danger. If she flies straight in front there is nothing to fear; if she crosses your path something is wrong. A high piercing call is bad news; an ordinary owl call is good news. Sometimes when there is a death she will appear at a window, insistently beating her wings against the glass.

Although owl guardians are not encountered as often as they once were, some people do still see them.

## Hine-te-iwaiwa
### The model wife and mother

The powers and responsibilities of women were established in the beginning by Hine-te-iwaiwa. This early ancestor is the exemplary figure of a wife and mother, the woman who provided the pattern that women now follow. All girls, therefore, were dedicated to Hine-te-iwaiwa at birth. When genealogists traced back the aristocratic female line of descent, it often ended with her.

A myth tells of Hine-te-iwaiwa's journey to find the man she has made up her mind to marry. Having heard of the handsome Tinirau, she swims

*Owls, being nocturnal predators with staring eyes, are believed in certain instances to have special powers.*

through the ocean for many days to reach his home on Motu-tapu [Sacred island]. She becomes his wife and presently has his child. When her two jealous co-wives plan to kill her, she destroys them with a potent chant that turns their bodies into greenstone – thereby introducing this treasure to the world.

In Māori society, a woman's brother had a special relationship with her sons, who sometimes inherited rank and property from him rather than their father. For this reason, Hine-te-iwaiwa's brother Rupe goes searching for her and her newborn son. Sometimes he carries her off, with the boy, because Tinirau has been neglecting her. Later, though, there is a reconciliation with Tinirau.

Women in childbirth were aided by the recitation of a ritual chant believed to have been repeated for the first time when Hine-te-iwaiwa was giving birth to her son Tūhuruhuru. This chant associates the woman with Hine-te-iwaiwa, who provided the precedent and has the power now to help her.

Another ordeal that marked an important stage in a young woman's life was the tattooing of her lips, which took place before marriage. In the chant recited while this was done, the tohunga spoke of three female ancestors: Hine-rau-whārangi, Rukutia and, as a climax, Hine-te-iwaiwa. Again they are seen as giving the girl the strength she needs to assume the role they have established for her.

Hine-te-iwaiwa is sometimes said to have been the first woman to act as a ruahine, a role performed by a high-ranking woman when she took part in a ritual to remove an excess of tapu. Māori life involved the constant interplay of elements regarded as tapu, or sacred, and those which were noa, being associated with everyday life. Since women were essentially noa, they had the power of removing tapu when this became necessary. In ritually removing much of the tapu of a new house so that people could safely live in it, Hine-te-iwaiwa established a precedent that has been followed ever since. In one of the chants recited now at the ceremony to remove tapu from a new house, the woman performing this role is identified with Hine-te-iwaiwa.

Hine-te-iwaiwa is always a very early ancestor, though her parentage is variously given. Sometimes she is Tāne's daughter and marries Tangaroa, while in other traditions her husband is Tū, Haumia or another man. Among Ngāti Awa in the southern Bay of Plenty, it is she rather than Hine-tītama who becomes Hine-nui-te-pō and brings death to the world.

It is sometimes said that Hine-te-iwaiwa's son Tūhuruhuru was killed in his young manhood and that she was sent by her husband Tinirau to ask a warrior, Whakatau, to avenge his death. This incident reflects the fact that while a woman could not herself avenge the death of a relative, it was her task to ensure that her menfolk did so.

As well, Hine-te-iwaiwa is often said to have introduced the art of weaving (though other women, more specialised figures, were also associated with this).

Occasionally it is said that Hina, not Hine-te-iwaiwa, sought out Tinirau, married him and bore his son. But the ritual chants relating to women's activities usually, if not always, speak of Hine-te-iwaiwa rather than Hina.

## Hine-tītama
### Tāne's daughter

After Tāne formed the first woman from the soil of Hawaiki, he made her his wife and they had a daughter. In many versions of the myth this girl was Hine-tītama. She was very beautiful, so much so that in later times a beautiful woman could be complimented by being told, 'You are Hine-tītama, the sight of you brings tears to our eyes'

[Ko Hine-tītama koe, matawai ana te whatu i te tirohanga].

When his daughter grew up, Tāne took her to wife as well. She bore him children, then was greatly shamed one day to discover that Tāne was her father as well as her husband. She ran down to the underworld and there her name changed, it is often said, to Hine-nui-te-pō [Great woman the night]. Tāne followed and begged her to return, but she told him that he must go back to the world and rear up their offspring, while she would remain below to receive them when they died.

This myth is known in parts of the east coast and the South Island, and perhaps other regions. Elsewhere, Hine-tītama is named at an early stage in mythic genealogies but is assigned different parents and has no association with Hine-nui-te-pō.

## Hine-tua-hōanga
### The sandstone woman

Sandstone was an important resource for shaping, polishing and sharpening stone tools and ornaments, and other tasks as well. Usually it was personified as a woman named Hine-tua-hōanga [Sandstone woman], though sometimes this name belonged to one particular kind of sandstone, while others, with differing degrees of fineness, bore such names as Hine-maheni [Smooth woman] and Hine-kiri-taratara [Woman with a rough skin].

At Rotorua, by a tapu stream known as Wai-oro-toki [Adze-grinding waters], a flat block of sandstone about a metre in diameter, lying half in the water, bears upon its surface deep grooves left by generations of workmen. Many such whetstones existed, as well as small, portable ones, but this is a revered relic believed to have been brought from Hawaiki by an early ancestor, Ihenga. Its mana is such that it is known as Hine-tua-hōanga.

When asked in earlier years how such a weighty object could have been conveyed from Hawaiki, the local people explained that Hine-tua-hōanga had once been light but that she had grown heavy through lying there so long, and from the extreme tapu she had acquired during this time.

The use of sandstone was established in the beginning by the hero Rata, when he was faced with the task of avenging his father. To do this he needed a waka, and to build his waka he needed a sharp adze. So his mother, who was Hine-tua-hōanga, offered her advice. (In one version of

# Birds

B1

B2

The forests, wetlands and shores of Aotearoa were full of birds, each kind behaving in their own way. Myths explained why some looked and acted as they did.

Pūkeko (*above*) were a nuisance to gardeners, sneaking up from the swamps to raid kūmara fields – so why did this thieving bird possess a handsome red bill and shield? The explanation was that the pūkeko was the offspring of Punga, father of objectionable creatures such as sharks, geckos and wētā, but had been adopted at birth by the noble Tāwhaki, Punga's nephew. Tāwhaki marked the bird's brow with his own blood in token of their relationship.

Saddlebacks (*above right*) used to follow flocks of tiny whiteheads through the forest, snapping up the insects they disturbed. Regarded therefore as guardians, they were sometimes believed to watch over ancient, buried treasures.

The pigeon (*right*) has beautiful plumage because Māui, when he turned himself into the first pigeon, wore his mother's skirt (see page 115).

B3

In the south especially, the enormous New Zealand eagle (*above*) preyed upon the large flightless moa (*left*). Both birds disappeared some five hundred years ago, but have survived in folklore (see pages 119–20, 200–1, 204–5).

*Right:* Huia lived only in high ranges in the southern part of the North Island, but their treasured skins and tail feathers were traded throughout the country. In the far south, greenstone was given in exchange; in the far north, a return present was teeth of the mako shark. The birds themselves were regarded as tapu, so were not eaten.

Huia plumes were worn by high-ranking men and women on ceremonial occasions, and warriors might wear them into battle. They were stored in narrow, beautifully carved boxes [waka huia] hung from the rafters of the houses of rangatira.

After Pākehā colonisation the birds became rare. Early in the twentieth century, the last of the huia disappeared from their mountain home.

While plumes of the huia, white heron and albatross were the most treasured, those of the gannet, kākāpō, long-tailed cuckoo and other birds were worn as well. Poahu, son of a leading rangatira in Tūranga (the Gisborne district), wears the wings of a hawk, fastened with flax. His companion, Koti, also wears hawk feathers.

Since people and birds were often associated in poetic metaphor, the choice of a plume must have involved a degree of association between the human and the chosen bird. It is known that a warrior who wore a plume of the New Zealand falcon was asserting that he was as fierce and reckless as that bird.

this myth, her instructions were to sharpen his adze upon her back, which consisted of sandstone. This is because the name Hine-tua-hōanga was understood by some to mean 'Woman with a sandstone back'.)

Rata did as she told him, then sailed to take his revenge.

A Ngāti Porou myth explains that sandstone deposits are present in Aotearoa because Hine-tua-hōanga (or Hine-tua-hōhanga) left Hawaiki to pursue over the ocean a fish, the pet of a man named Ngahue, which later became greenstone. (This is intelligible, since sandstone, being employed to work greenstone, is its enemy.) After a struggle between Hine-tua-hōhanga and her rival Ngahue, she took up her residence in this land. At the same time she introduced two other valuable stones, obsidian and waiapu.

## Hine-waiapu
### A supernatural boulder

The Waiapu River and its valley, near East Cape, are said to take their name from Hine-waiapu [Waiapu woman], a tipua in the form of a boulder. Hine-waiapu consists of a siliceous stone, termed waiapu, which was employed in polishing stone adzes. In that respect she is similar in her nature to sandstone, and it was Hine-tua-hōhanga [Sandstone woman] who placed her at the river mouth long ago. This was during Hine-tua-hōhanga's struggle with her enemy Ngahue, and the idea was that Hine-waiapu's presence would make it impossible for Ngahue's fish (which is greenstone) to enter the river.

At the same time, Hine-tua-hōhanga introduced other supplies of waiapu to the East Cape region. All of this stone, a much-valued resource, could be spoken of as Hine-waiapu.

Hine-waiapu herself, the boulder at the river mouth, is a guardian of the local people.

## Hingānga-roa
### Founder of a house of learning

A great woodcarver, Hingānga-roa founded at Ūawa (Tolaga Bay) a famous house of learning [whare wānanga] known as Te Rāwheoro, where both carving and history were taught. He married Iranui, sister of Kahungunu, and they had three sons, Taua, Māhaki and Hauiti.

Hauiti fought bitterly with his two elder brothers; some blame one side, some the other. Eventually Taua and Māhaki left the district. Hauiti himself remained there and became the founding ancestor of Te Aitanga-a-Hauiti.

*A Ngāti Porou ancestor, Iwirākau, forms the lower part of a pillar that supported the ridgepole of a nineteenth-century house at Tikapa, in the Waiapu Valley. Iwirākau was a master carver, having learnt this art after becoming a student in about 1700 in the house of learning [whare wānanga] established by Hingānga-roa at Ūawa. He later returned to his own region and passed on his knowledge. The stylistic tradition he founded continued until the early twentieth century.*

Taua became the father of Apanui-waipapa, founding ancestor of Te Whānau-ā-Apanui, and Māhaki became an important ancestor of some sections of Ngāti Porou.

## Horoirangi
### An Arawa ancestor

Horoirangi is an early ancestor of the Uenuku-kōpako people in the Rotorua district. These people take their name from their ancestor Uenuku-kōpako, and Horoirangi was the principal wife of Uenuku-kōpako's son Taharangi. She lived about four hundred years ago.

It was thought that important ancestors continued after their death to take an interest in their descendants' welfare and to protect them. At Te Whetengu, a pā on a hill named Te Tihi-o-Tonga, Horoirangi's image, carved some three hundred and fifty years ago in a hidden recess in a cliff, became the mauri (the source of fertility) of the lands owned by the people there.

It was Horoirangi who brought great flocks of tūī, kākā and other birds to the forests, made wild plant resources plentiful and produced abundant kūmara crops. As well, her powers ensured that her descendants possessed the strength and vitality that would enable them to fight off invaders and keep possession of their lands.

The first birds caught each season, and the

*Rangiriri (above), last of the tohunga at Te Whetengu. Early in the twentieth century, when the pā had been long deserted, he removed Horoirangi (right) from her cliff and presented her to the Auckland Museum Te Papa Whakahiku for safekeeping. She has now been lent to the Rotorua Art and History Museum Te Whare Taonga o Te Arawa.*

first fruits of the kūmara harvest, were offered to Horoirangi. On other occasions, too, tapu food was offered to her by the ruahine of the pā (a woman with a special ritual role).

Horoirangi was not, however, responsible for the conduct of warfare. This was under the control of a male deity, Maru-te-whare-aitu, whose emblem lay in a sacred enclosure nearby.

## Horo-matangi
### A taniwha in Lake Taupō

This fierce taniwha lives by Motutaiko, an island in Lake Taupō, in an underwater cave on the western side. People used to avoid the island because Horo-matangi, if he saw them, would lash the water into high waves, overturn their waka and carry them down to his cave. This happened in good weather as well as bad.

At times Horo-matangi assumes the form of a reptile, but in the lake he takes the form of a black rock. Some say he is an old man red as fire. His attendant Ātiamuri, a taniwha in the shape of a man, was not dangerous in himself but would act as a decoy, attempting to lure unsuspecting travellers in Horo-matangi's direction. At twilight he would paddle a waka towards a settlement by the lake, going just near enough to be dimly seen. When the villagers called a welcome, he would disappear into the darkness and they would realise that Ātiamuri had been trying to lure them to their death.

Many people considered Horo-matangi to be the custodian of the mana of Lake Taupō. Certain tohunga were his mediums, such as Te Ihu at Tapuaeharuru, who was said sometimes to live with him in his cave. As well, Horo-matangi is associated with two stone dogs high up on the Karangahape cliffs, on the lake's western shore. These dogs are never seen but may be heard howling on misty mornings. If paddlers on the lake were ever foolish enough to insult them by pointing their paddle or calling to them, Horo-matangi would at once send a storm.

## Horouta
### An east coast waka

Some learned men of Ngāti Porou, such as Mohi Ruatapu, said that the *Horouta* set out in the first place from the homeland of Hawaiki. Others, such as Pita Kāpiti, taught that this waka sailed first from the east coast of Aotearoa, reached Hawaiki, then made a return voyage. When the voyage begins in Aotearoa, it is to obtain the kūmara.

Pita Kāpiti tells us that the early ancestor Toi, who did not possess the kūmara, lived at Whitianga (Mercury Bay). There he was visited one day by Kahukura and Rongo-i-amo, who had arrived by magical means from Hawaiki. When these men were offered Toi's usual foods, such as fernroot, they gave him in return some dried kūmara. Toi liked this so much that he arranged for his waka, the *Horouta*, to make a voyage to Hawaiki to acquire the kūmara.

Kahukura led this expedition; Toi did not go. At Hawaiki the crew took their vessel alongside cliffs that consisted entirely of kūmara. Kahukura recited a ritual chant and thrust in his digging stick, and the cliffs of Hawaiki slid down until the waka was full of kūmara.

The leader of the return voyage was a man named Pāwa (or Pāoa); Kahukura remained behind. Before the vessel set sail, Kahukura warned the crew never to allow the kūmara to come into contact with fernroot (for these two plants must always be kept apart). But when *Horouta* made landfall at Ahuahu (Great Mercury Island), a woman named Kanawa disregarded these instructions. She stole some fernroot and hid it on board when the vessel sailed on.

*Horouta* was now coasting south, distributing kūmara to Toi at Whitianga and to other people living at Tauranga and Maketū. But the gods that had been protecting the waka were angry at Kanawa's breach of tapu, and they sent a storm. Just outside Whakatāne, near the Ōhiwa Harbour, the woman was flung into the water by the waves. She rose to the surface and seized the bow of the waka; the crew called to let go, but she clung on. So the vessel overturned and Kanawa died there.

The bowpiece of the *Horouta* was damaged and the ship was cast up on the shore; the cargo too was taken ashore. Then the crew conferred as to how the vessel could be mended. While some stayed to guard the waka, a party of men under the leadership of Pāwa made a journey into the interior. There Pāwa felled a tree and adzed a new bowpiece, while others in his party, led by Awapāka, went to snare and spear birds so they would have good food to offer the workmen who would presently be mending the ship.

But when the bowpiece was ready and the birds were potted in gourds, Pāwa and his men learnt that the vessel had been fixed without them and had sailed on around the East Coast. So they themselves ate most of the potted birds they had prepared (and the remains of their feast can still be seen, turned to stone). Then they set off along the coast, hoping to catch up. They were not able to do so because the waka was too fast,

but in the course of his journey Pāwa created many landmarks still to be seen in the territory of Ngāti Porou. And the crew of the *Horouta*, as they sailed along, continued to distribute kūmara to places that they passed.

Many incidents in this myth were regarded as having set the pattern in the beginning for people's behaviour in later times. The episode where Kahukura obtains the kūmara from the cliffs of Hawaiki relates to the annual ceremony in which, when the planting season arrived, the tohunga took the seed kūmara from the store-house (in this context, identified with Hawaiki). And since Kahukura had introduced this food, an image of Kahukura was presented with an offering of seed kūmara.

When Awapāka and his companions initiated the rituals and methods employed in hunting birds, they established patterns of behaviour for those who followed them.

The damage done to the *Horouta* was a warning of the disasters that would follow if tapu restrictions were not observed. At the same time, the fact that *Horouta* was successfully mended, and sailed on, showed that if all of Ngāti Porou worked together for a cause they would be certain of success.

## Hotumauea

### A very tall man

This ancestor of the Waikato peoples was very tall indeed and could jump prodigious distances. One day he and his wife, with their baby son,

*In winter especially, pigeons, kākā, tūī and other birds were speared and snared, then preserved in their own fat in large gourd vessels. When Awapāka and his companions went hunting birds after their arrival on the* Horouta, *their actions set precedents for their descendants in later times.*

were in a pit in some sand dunes drawing water from a spring when his treacherous brothers-in-law came with others to kill him. The men surrounded the pit and there seemed no way for Hotumauea to escape. But he gave a great leap, reached the top, struck about him with his patu and was gone.

The brothers-in-law asked their sister about her baby, for a boy would have to be killed or he would later seek revenge. She deceived them into thinking the child was a girl, so they allowed him to live. They pursued Hotumauea to the bank of the Waikato River and thought they had him cornered. But Hotumauea leapt to the top of a tawa tree, then jumped right across the great river. On the far side his feet sank into the rock, and his footprints are still there now.

Another storyteller describes a race between Hotumauea and a rival rangatira. The two men ran alongside the Marokopa River, following its winding course inland till they reached the turbulent waters above the Marokopa Falls. The river here is some thirteen metres wide. While the other man attempted to swim, Hotumauea climbed a high bank, leapt to a mudbank on the opposite side and was off.

His height was proverbial. When people saw a tall man they would say, 'Yes, that man is Hotumauea!'

# Hotupuku

## A taniwha at Kaingaroa

At Kapenga on the Kaingaroa Plains, a taniwha named Hotupuku used to prey upon travellers passing through the region. When these people kept disappearing, their relatives at Taupō feared they had encountered a war party and went to investigate. These men reached the place where Hotupuku lived, and the taniwha smelt human flesh and emerged from his den. Suddenly they saw him approaching like a hill. They fled, and some survived and some did not.

When the news reached Rotorua, a party of men from Ngāti Tama set out for Kapenga. They plaited a strong rope of cabbage tree leaves and made a large noose, then most of them positioned themselves at the ends of the rope while others went forward to entice the taniwha from his den.

Hotupuku thundered towards them, his mouth gaping wide. The decoys ran through the noose, the taniwha followed, and the rope was pulled tight around his body. Hotupuku lashed about but could do nothing. The men kept attacking with their weapons, and soon he lay dead.

It was seen then that he was like a tuatara in appearance, though like a whale in size. They cut open the great belly and found inside the bodies of men, women and children, along with weapons, greenstone and fine cloaks of every kind. Afterwards the warriors ate their enemy, then returned to their homes at Ōhinemutu.

This party was led by the sons of Tama-ihu-tōroa, whose father was the explorer Ihenga. Later these brave men fought and conquered two other taniwha, Pekehaua and Kataore.

# Houmea

## An evil woman

This woman was really an atua, a spirit, but at first her family did not realise this. When her husband Uta returned from fishing, she would go to the shore and swallow down all the fish he had caught, then pretend they had been stolen by a war party. In the end her two sons hid and discovered what she was doing.

In revenge Houmea swallowed down her sons, Tū-tawake and Nini. But when Uta came back, he recited a ritual chant and brought them up again.

Now knowing what she was, Uta tried to escape. He sent Houmea off to draw water, then sailed away with his boys. On her return she entered a shag and pursued them. She reached the waka, her throat gaping wide to swallow them, but the boys had hidden their father, and they had roasted a fish on a fire in the waka. They gave her the fish to eat, then when she demanded more they threw down her throat a hot stone from the fireplace. And so the monster died. She lives now in the form of a shag, and the name Houmea is still given to evil, thievish women in this world.

This is a Ngāti Porou myth. Since Houmea's elder son Tū-tawake is a fierce warrior, Houmea was sometimes regarded as having been responsible for the introduction of warfare.

*Wiremu Maihi Te Rangikāheke (c.1815–1896), leading rangatira of Ngāti Rangiwewehi of Te Arawa, and a brilliant writer who in the middle years of the nineteenth century produced nearly eight hundred pages of manuscript. Among his published writings is the story of Hotupuku.*

# Houses of learning

## Famous schools and teachers

Sons of high-ranking men, especially the elder sons, sometimes attended a formal course of instruction in their people's history, genealogy, religious practices and other subjects at a house of learning [whare wānanga or whare kura]. They were taught by leading tohunga, generally, it seems, in the winter months. Schools with high reputations attracted young men from far around.

A building was set aside for the purpose, and a strict tapu governed the actions of teachers and students. Much ritual surrounded the students' entrance to the school and the conditions under which they lived during their period of instruction. These rituals varied somewhat from one region to another. They seem always to have involved the use of whatu kura, small tapu stones that students either swallowed during initiation or held in their mouths during the memorisation of traditions and chants. In some districts the teaching was conducted at night-time. The subjects taught are generally said to have included esoteric traditions and ritual chants which were not communicated to other persons.

Myths provided distinguished precedents. In Hawaiki, two such houses of learning were Te

Whare Kura (in west coast tradition) and Te Kohurau (in Tākitimu tradition). And in the traditions of a number of peoples we are told that soon after the ancestors made the voyage from Hawaiki to Aotearoa, they erected a house of learning near the place where they had landed. In Tainui history, the first house of learning was Te Ahurei, near a tūāhu of the same name. In Māhuhu tradition, the first house of learning was established at Tāporapora in the Kaipara region.

Teaching in important houses often continued down through the generations. Among Ngāti Porou, the house of learning known as Te Rāwheoro was established at Ūawa by the early ancestor Hingānga-roa, who taught woodcarving as well as history. Sessions were held periodically from this time on; the last opened in 1836, when the leading tohunga were 'Rangiuia who recited the genealogies, Tokipuanga who supplemented them, and Mohi Ruatapu who elaborated upon them'.

A considerable number of leading tohunga, among them Mohi Ruatapu, were among the authorities who wrote or dictated accounts of their peoples' histories and religious practices in the second half of the nineteenth century. We have therefore some knowledge of some of the subjects taught in houses of learning.

There are also numerous written records stemming from the Ngāti Kahungunu tohunga Te Mātorohanga and his associates, who from the late 1850s developed a body of doctrine which

*Villages on the banks of the Ūawa River at Ūawa (Tolaga Bay) in the mid-1830s. The famous house of learning Te Rāwheoro was in session there at this time.*

was in many ways innovative. In 1865 in the Wairarapa, when Te Mātorohanga opened the final session of his house of learning, students were for the first time allowed to record the teachings in writing.

Young men of rank might also have esoteric knowledge communicated to them privately by their fathers or grandfathers; often the eldest son had this information passed on to him, though in some high-ranking families a younger son might be chosen to become a tohunga. In addition, all young people were taught skills such as martial arts, horticulture, the manufacture of implements, fishing, bird-hunting and weaving (some of these skills being appropriate for males and others for females). And boys and girls learnt a great deal by watching their relatives at work and assisting them.

Even the less privileged had a great many practical skills and a general knowledge of history and tradition, gained in part from listening to orators and taking part in singing.

## Humuhumu

### A taniwha guardian

This taniwha was one of those that escorted the *Māhuhu* on its voyage from Hawaiki. Later he accompanied his people, Ngāti Whātua, to the Kaipara district, and lived in a lagoon near the north head of the harbour. His sign was a tōtara log that drifted about there for many generations, revealing his mana by moving against the currents and the wind.

When Humuhumu disappeared in 1820, it was a warning of trouble to come, and sure enough an enemy army soon afterwards laid waste to the region. In about 1885 he made a brief reappearance, but his people belittled his mana by taking eels and shellfish from the sacred waters of his lagoon. They did this to provide seafood for an important meeting, but that made no difference. Humuhumu disappeared once more and did not return, and soon afterwards an epidemic brought illness to the people there.

## Īhenga

### An explorer

This man was a grandson of Tama-te-kapua, captain of *Te Arawa*, and is generally said to have arrived with him from Hawaiki. He lived for a time on the Moehau Range, and it was there that he buried his father Tūhoro-mata-kakā. Later he returned to Maketū so that his uncle Kahu-mata-momoe could free him from the tapu con-

*Hōri Haupapa (d. 1879) of Ngāti Whakaue, one of a number of Arawa historians who communicated traditional knowledge to Pākehā studying the history of their adopted country.*

sequent upon this tapu duty. When the ceremony was concluded he married Kahu's daughter Hine-te-kakara.

Īhenga is best known as an explorer. While living with his uncle he went into the interior to hunt kiwi with his dog Pōtaka-tawhiti. With the dog's help he discovered Lakes Rotoiti and Rotorua, and he rejoiced at the abundance of whitebait, freshwater crayfish and freshwater mussels.

He was not the first person to reach the region, as another Arawa immigrant, Tua-rotorua, was already living with his people among the hot springs at Ōhinemutu. But Īhenga tricked Tua-rotorua into believing he had the prior claim, so Tua-rotorua went to live on Mokoia Island while Īhenga and his people settled at Ōhinemutu.

Mount Ngongotahā, quite close to Ōhinemutu, at this time had many fairies [patupaiarehe] living on its heights. These beings are atua, but apart from their pale skins they look like people. On misty days at Rotorua the humans down below would hear them singing and playing their flutes.

Īhenga decided to climb the mountain, and on the summit he discovered the fairies' pā. He was thirsty and asked for water. A good-looking woman offered him a drink from her gourd, and because of this he later named the mountain Ngongo-tahā [Drink from gourd].

The fairies were very curious about Īhenga, and they crowded around him. He became frightened and fled down the mountain with the fairies in pursuit. Presently all were left behind except the woman who had given him the water.

Īhenga knew this woman wanted him as her husband, and that if she caught him he would never see his human wife again. He remembered the red ochre he carried in his girdle, and he painted himself as he ran. So the woman stopped chasing him then, because her people were frightened of red ochre.

Despite this encounter, Īhenga later became very friendly with the fairies. When he left on a further journey of exploration, some of the fairies went searching for him and found him on the Moehau Range. After this they lived on that mountain.

Īhenga's last journey was undertaken with Kahu-mata-momoe to visit two of his brothers in the far north and another brother at Moehau. He and Kahu, with some companions, crossed to the west coast, walked north, then later returned through Tāmaki and Moehau. On the way they bestowed names upon the places to which they came. Afterwards they returned separately to their home at Rotorua.

Īhenga's close relationship with the fairies was perpetuated through the ages by the leading tohunga at Ōhinemutu, who at certain times would climb Ngongotahā to communicate with them. This tradition continued until relatively recent times.

# Io

## A high god

New resources, technologies and contacts began changing Māori life and thought early in the nineteenth century, then in the 1830s and '40s most Māori people became Christian. In 1840 the country came under British rule, and hitherto inconceivable numbers of European settlers began arriving and demanding land. By the late 1850s it was clear that the country was being overrun and that the Government's main concern was to protect Pākehā interests.

In this highly stressful situation, Māori society and thought survived through the creative adaptation of new ideas. While some peoples remained with the missionaries and the government, in several parts of the country religious leaders founded and promulgated new faiths. These

*As a young man, H. T. Te Whatahoro (1841–1923) of Ngāti Kahungunu recorded the teachings of tohunga concerning the high god Io. Much later some of these documents were published.*

responses were shaped by the experience of Christianity, a need for religious and intellectual independence from Pākehā, and a strong desire for political power.

Two faiths in particular made much use of traditional concepts but were mainly Christian in that they were based upon interpretations of the Bible. Both were associated, initially at least, with armed resistance. They were the millenial Hauhau faith, founded in 1862 by Te Ua, and the Ringatū faith, founded in the late 1860s by Te Kooti.

Another approach was to turn back to traditional beliefs and modify and extend them so that they became a viable alternative to Christianity. This was the direction taken, from the late 1850s onward, by a group of Ngāti Kahungunu thinkers in the Wairarapa and Hawke's Bay. Initially their leaders were the tohunga Te Mātorohanga and Nēpia Pōhūhū. Te Mātorohanga had studied at two Ngāti Kahungunu houses of learning, and in about 1836 he had spent four months at Te Rāwheoro, the Ngāti Porou house of learning at Ūawa (Tolaga Bay).

At some point this group acquired a belief in a high god, Io, in the highest of the skies. This was an innovation. The only Io on record on the east coast (in a Ngāti Kahungunu document dating from 1861) appears to be a mythical figure whose activity is that of building pā. This suggests a protective role, but it is not known whether this Io played any part in the evolution of the high god.

The teachings of these tohunga were recorded by two young men, H. T. Te Whatahoro and Āporo Kumeroa. Te Whatahoro in particular recorded a great deal of material from a variety of sources, and collected other manuscripts as well. His writings, with those of others, present a convincing picture of Ngāti Kahungunu thought at a late stage in its development.

Materials derived from these records were published long afterwards, in 1913 and 1915, in a two-volume work, *The Lore of the Whare Wānanga*. Percy Smith, a Pākehā scholar obsessed with the idea that the traditions of the Māori 'recall' their Asian and Pacific origins, contributed a heavily edited translation and a commentary. Smith was one of a number of scholars delighted to discover, as they thought, a 'higher', esoteric body of Māori religious belief.

Despite his great power and status, Io is not presented in Te Whatahoro's documents as being all-powerful; it seems inappropriate for Percy Smith and others to describe him as supreme. He is not, for instance, responsible for the creation of Rangi the sky and Papa the earth; in the beginning these two simply exist. It is Rangi, furthermore, who clothes Papa in plants, and places other living things in their homes.

Rangi and Papa then have seventy sons, very many more than in other accounts; these sons are atua [gods] rather than the tāngata [people] of earlier traditions. One of them, Tāne, separates his parents and props up Rangi, whose full name is Rangi-nui [Great Rangi]. Above Rangi-nui rise eleven other skies, each with its own name and significance.

In the highest sky, Tikitiki-o-ngā-rangi or Te Toi-o-ngā-rangi [The summit of the skies], Io lives in a house, Matangi-reia, which is the original house of learning [whare wānanga], the model followed in the establishment of all others. Another house in this highest sky, Rangiātea, contains the whatu kura, sacred stones employed in the rituals of the house of learning.

These stones are in the charge of companies of spirits, male (Whatukura) and female (Mareikura), who move through the twelve skies and even down to the earth. Meanwhile, companies of other spirits, known as apa, do Io's bidding in the lower skies but venture to the highest level only when commanded to do so.

After the separation of Rangi and Papa, the sons live in different houses because Whiro, Tāne's elder brother, is jealous of him. Soon Io orders two of his attendant spirits to make their way down to Maunga-nui [Great mountain] and perform over Tāne and his younger brother Tūpai the tohi ceremony, which bestows their full names upon them and dedicates them to their future roles, and the pure ceremony, which makes permanent their mana. This is done.

Next, Io sends messengers to discover which of the gods will be able to ascend to his home in the twelfth sky. When Tāne asserts that he has this power, Whiro is furious and attempts to precede him to the skies, but the winds – Tāwhirimātea and his offspring – blow Tāne upwards, leaving Whiro behind. When Whiro sends insects and birds in pursuit of Tāne, the winds whirl them away.

Finally Tāne reaches Tawhirirangi, in the eleventh sky. In this house is located Te Pūmotomoto, the entrance to the highest of the skies. The pure ceremony is once more performed over him, then he enters Matangi-reia and stands in the presence of Io.

Tāne asks Io for the three kete [baskets] of knowledge, and is given them. These kete contain all wisdom [wānanga], with directions as to how the world should be ordered; their contents are

*Āporo Kumeroa of Ngāti Kahungunu, who in his younger years assisted in recording accounts relating to Io.*

peace and love, ritual chants [karakia] and practical knowledge. Io also gives Tāne two whatu kura, small sacred stones, both white in colour, to be used in the rituals of the house of learning.

Back on earth, Tāne proceeds to the first house of learning, which he has already built. This house, called Whare Kura, is the model for all later houses of learning (and is also sometimes identified with Hawaiki-rangi, mentioned below). At the back of the house he places his baskets and sacred stones. He then undertakes the governance of the earth. In each part of the world he places guardians, called Poutiriao, who ensure that order prevails.

There follows a war, known as Te Paerangi, with the evil Whiro and his faction. When Tāne and his companions win, Whiro goes down Tāheke-roa [Long descent] to live with Hine-nui-te-pō and Whakaruaimoko in Rarohenga, Te Muriwaihou and the different levels of Night [Te Pō]. From there he makes continual war against all beings on the earth.

Tāne, however, with assistance from Io and from his brother gods, now creates the first woman, Hine-ahu-one, from the soil at Kura-waka. He takes her to wife, and their descendants are human beings.

We are told in this account that when human beings reach the end of their life, their wairua make their way first to a house called Hawaiki-rangi (or Hawaiki-nui). This has four doors, and the wairua enter from the direction in which they have been living. Good people then depart through the eastern door and ascend to the skies, following the path taken by Tāne, while treacherous people and murderers pass through the southern door and down Tāheke-roa to Whiro. (They go in these different directions because good people love Rangi-nui and the higher skies, while bad people have an affinity with Whiro.) Others again, who have shown love for their mother the earth, proceed to the bounds of Hine-moana [Ocean woman] and there remain. And some go to the summits of the mountains.

Apart from Io himself, most of the figures and episodes in these myths (and other myths recorded with them) have their origins in the earlier traditions of a cultural region that extended, broadly speaking, from the southernmost part of the North Island up to the Whanganui River district in the west, and along the coastal districts of Heretaunga (Hawke's Bay) and Te Wairoa (Wairoa) in the east. Much has been modified and elaborated. Rangi and Papa have many more sons than before, and the companies of spirits in the skies are different in many ways; the creation of the first woman is told in more detail than usual, and the idea of different destinations for good and bad persons is a new concept. However, the extent of the similarities is surprising. Ancient songs from this region contain much that might otherwise have been assumed to be recent. The idea, for example, that wairua can enter Hawaiki-rangi, then pass either upwards to the skies or down below, is found (without any reference to moral issues) in a Whanganui song composed in the early eighteenth century.

In the years before the publication of Te Whatahoro's records, a few brief references to Io surfaced in writings from other parts of the country. It seems that these beliefs had spread from the Wairarapa, changing somewhat as they did so. In particular, a short account from the Hauraki district, published in 1907, has Io creating the world in a manner reminiscent of the creation described in Genesis.

By the time that Te Whatahoro's texts were published, in 1913–15, belief in Io had lessened considerably in the Wairarapa, although there was still a keen interest in tradition and a concern that the ancient stories should be correctly recorded. Publication led to further Māori interest in Io, and belief in him, in many parts of the country.

In the Waikato region, within the King Movement [Te Kīngitanga], beliefs concerning Io had meanwhile taken a rather different course, one much influenced by earlier Tainui tradition. A book published in 1960 by Pei Te Hurinui presents esoteric teachings taken from manuscripts dating, it seems, from the late nineteenth century. Here Io becomes fully evolved only after two entities, Hani and Puna, are merged within him. Hani and Puna embody and represent respectively the male essence and the female essence, so that Io now possesses both male and female powers. Later, Tāwhaki (rather than Tāne) ascends to the highest of the skies and returns with the three baskets of knowledge.

## Ioio-whenua
### A peacemaker

Among Tūhoe in the Urewera mountains and Ngāti Awa in the southern Bay of Plenty, Ioio-whenua is a son of Tāne and Hine-rauāmoa. When others began to stir up strife, he made peace.

He was associated in this undertaking with Rongo and, some say, Haumia and Pū-tē-hue. These last three are personifications of food plants – which is appropriate, since horticulture was traditionally a peaceful pursuit. It is not known whether Ioio-whenua was also involved with the cultivation of food.

# Irakau

### A woman of great mana

Irakau had mana over all the creatures in the ocean, including the whales and taniwha. This was not surprising, since her father was the famous Raka-taura who had ridden from Hawaiki on the back of a taniwha. Her mother belonged to the earliest peoples in the land.

Irakau was the main ancestor of the Waitaha people on the shores of the Hauraki Gulf, and she passed on her powers to them. These people possessed as a consequence a special relationship with whales.

On the coast, at a place called Rangiriri, a mauri for whales represented and contained the life force of these great creatures. This tapu place was located in an area where certain rituals were performed, such as the removal of tapu from people who been placed temporarily under its restrictions.

The mauri took the visible form of a sandbank, overgrown with coastal grasses, which resembled the back of a whale with the head pointing inland. From all over the ocean, whales were drawn to this supernatural whale.

When a death occurred, the careful observance of tapu restrictions ensured that the whales would attend the funeral, honouring the dead by providing an abundance of fine food on this sad occasion. After three or four days, if everything had been done correctly, a school of whales would be seen swimming towards the mauri at Rangiriri. Their leader would take them straight up on to the beach, but he himself would escape from the shallow waters.

The tohunga then walked slowly towards the sea, quickly and quietly reciting ritual chants, and at the water's edge he swallowed a mouthful of salt water. This was an act of homage, taking into himself the substance of the whales' home so that none of them would be able to return to that realm. So long as no selfishness or quarrelling marred the feast, all would then be well. But if anyone took more than their share, the tohunga would recite a chant that would send the disputed whale back to the sea, no matter how mutilated it might be or how distant the deep water. If the whale meat was in the oven when the people quarrelled, it would become inedible.

Nor did whales strand themselves only after a death. If a tohunga happened to suffer an injury, then washed the blood from the wound near the mauri, that very day would see one or more whales on the shore. By offering themselves as payment they righted this wrong.

Irakau's descendants were able to summon their taniwha, Ihu-moana, when in danger out at sea. If a man found himself in the water, his waka overturned, he would at once – if he knew the procedure – call loudly, 'My hosts of the land and my multitudes of the water, look, I am dying! My friends, come to my assistance and take me to the shore.'

Ihu-moana would respond at once to this appeal. He could be recognised by a hollow place at the back of his head, large enough to hold several people; he would dive below and catch them in this cavity. No matter how nasty the salt water, the men he saved could on no account insult the taniwha by spitting it out in mid-ocean.

On the shore the people he had saved would perform a ceremony of thanksgiving. They would first gather a handful of seaweed and place it, reciting a chant, a short distance inland. Then they would pull up some weeds or grass from that place and throw it into the sea as an offering to Tangaroa, whose realm is the ocean.

# Irākewa

### A precursor

In the homeland of Hawaiki, as Irākewa lay sleeping one night, his wairua went out across the water to Aotearoa. There it visited Whakatāne, and other places. Afterwards it returned to Hawaiki.

When Irākewa awoke he told his people, 'There is a land far away which is a good land for you to go to. There is a waterfall in that place, and a cave on the hillside, and the rock standing in the river there is myself.'

So his people sailed from Hawaiki on the *Mātaatua*. At Whakatāne they found the waterfall, and the cave, which became a home for the captain's sister Muriwai, and at the entrance to the river they saw the rock that is Irākewa himself. They settled at Whakatāne as he had instructed and became ancestors of Ngāti Awa.

In another account, Irākewa visited Aotearoa not in spirit but in bodily form, and at Whakatāne he was eaten by a fish, a warehou. His wairua then returned to Hawaiki and told his descendants to travel to Whakatāne. This they did. And never afterwards would they eat the warehou – for since this fish had fed upon the body of Irākewa, eating it would have been equivalent to eating their ancestor himself.

Irākewa was believed by some to take the

form of a taniwha who lived at Kawerau and protected his descendants. As well he was an atua who was appealed to in times of war.

## Irawaru
### The first dog

Irawaru began life as a man, but then his sister married the trickster Māui, the two men quarrelled, and Māui turned Irawaru into a dog.

According to a story from Ngāti Porou, this happened because Māui coveted Irawaru's white dogtail cape. So he offered to tattoo Irawaru's lips, and his offer was accepted. With Irawaru at his mercy, he pulled out his back, tail, nose and

*Māui is sometimes said to have turned Irawaru into a dog in order to acquire his dogtail cape. Dogskin cloaks were greatly treasured and owned only by high-ranking men.*

ears, then dragged out his forequarters and hindquarters. He recited a ritual chant, and Irawaru became the first dog. Because of the tattooing, his nose and lips were dark.

Māui then seized the white cape. Some say he tricked Irawaru into eating excrement, as dogs sometimes do now, and that Māui thought this a great joke. He further degraded Irawaru by telling his sister, when she came searching for her husband, to call 'Moi, moi,' – this being the expression used in calling a dog, not a person.

The sister did as she was told, and Irawaru howled in reply. When she reached him – alas, he was a dog!

While dogs were highly valued in traditional Māori society, their close association with humans led, it seems, to a feeling that they had to be sharply distinguished from humans, that a distance had to be maintained. So dogs are seen in

many proverbs as greedy, lazy and cowardly.

These attitudes find expression in the myth of Irawaru. Given the human relationship with dogs, it is not surprising that the first dog was once a human. But Irawaru was completely outwitted, tricked and demeaned by being turned into a dog.

The fact that Irawaru was Māui's brother-in-law (and the relationship between brothers-in-law was often difficult) made the story funnier still.

## Iwi-katere

### Owner of a wise bird

Tūī were often kept in cages and taught words and songs. Long ago, at Te Wairoa on the east coast, a rangatira named Iwi-katere owned a pet tūī, called Tāne-miti-rangi, which he taught ritual chants of every kind. The bird became so knowledgeable that it recited all the chants at the rituals performed at harvest time.

One year a neighbouring rangatira, Tamaterā, sent a messenger to ask if the bird could recite the

*The beautiful tūī, with its extraordinary powers of mimicry, was a popular cage bird. Some were taught recitations containing as many as forty or fifty words.*

chants for his kūmara-harvest ceremony. Iwi-katere replied that Tamaterā could borrow the tūī, but that first it would have to officiate at his own ceremony. Tamaterā regarded this as an insult, and that night he sent the messenger back to steal the bird.

As the thief approached the house, the tūī awoke and called to Iwi-katere, 'I'm being carried off, carried off by a thief, wake up!'

But Iwi-katere slept on, and the thief got away with the bird. Next morning Iwi-katere listened in vain for the accustomed sound of his tūī's voice as it spoke to the people. He wept for his bird, and knowing that Tamaterā had stolen it, he raised an army.

In the end the thief's people were defeated and migrated from Te Wairoa to Heretaunga (Hawke's Bay). Their descendants are still there, and Iwi-katere's descendants are still at Te Wairoa.

# Kahukura
## The discovery of net-making

In the far north it was believed that the knowledge of net-making was first acquired from the fairies [patupaiarehe] by a man named Kahukura. Under a strange compulsion he made a journey to Rangiaohia, in Tokerau (Doubtless Bay), and on the beach there he saw where the fairies had been fishing. So he returned that night and found them netting mackerel.

As they hauled in their great net, they shouted with joy at the thought of their catch. Kahukura joined them and pulled on the net as well; he was as fair-skinned as the fairies, so he was not noticed. As the first light of dawn appeared, the fish were brought up on the beach. The fairies started tying them together, threading strings through the gills and calling, 'Come on, hurry up, before the sun rises!'

Kahukura was tying his fish as well, but he used a slip-knot, so when his string was loaded with fish they all fell off. He started again, and a fairy came up and tied the knot for him, but afterwards Kahukura untied the knot and let the fish slip off again. He kept delaying them like this until it was quite light and people's faces could be seen.

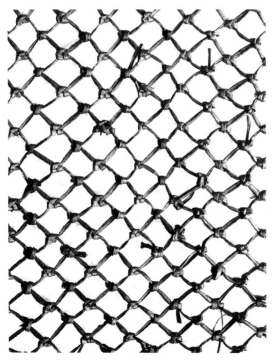

*There were many different kinds of nets, small and large. Their manufacture was a tapu task undertaken by men, although women did much of the cutting and preparation of the flax.*

The fairies discovered Kahukura and they fled, leaving behind their fish, net and waka. Kahukura took the net and used it as a pattern. He learnt how the knots were tied, and he taught net-making to his children.

# Kahukura
## A powerful god

At Waiapu on the east coast, the tohunga Pita Kāpiti taught that Kahukura was an atua, in the form of a man, who travelled with Rongo-i-amo from Hawaiki to Aotearoa. Kahukura created a double rainbow and Rongo-i-amo walked across it, then Kahukura himself leapt from one land to the other. These two then visited the early ancestor Toi at Whitianga and introduced him to the kūmara. To acquire seed kūmara for Toi, Kahukura led a voyage to Hawaiki on the *Horouta*. There he gave the crew the kūmara and told them how to handle this tapu plant. Afterwards the crew returned without him.

We also learn from Pita Kāpiti's writings that before the fields were planted in the spring, the tohunga made an offering of seed kūmara to an image of Kahukura; if the atua moved slightly, it was known that the growing crop would be undisturbed by enemies. So the god Kahukura, having given people the kūmara in the beginning, each year placed the plants under his protection.

Other peoples have other stories. Often Kahukura is a war god, and the rainbow comes as his sign. He was the main god brought on the *Tākitimu* from Hawaiki. Elsewhere, as among the Tainui peoples, he was identified with the great Uenuku, whose sign is also the rainbow.

# Kahukura
## A sorcerer

In many places Kahukura was a war god, while at Waiapu he was a god who brought the kūmara (see the previous entry).

At Ūawa (Tolaga Bay), the tohunga Mohi Ruatapu recognised the existence of more than one Kahukura, but writes only about an early ancestor of this name who is a son of Tangaroa. The rest of Tangaroa's children are fish, but Kahukura takes the form of a man, and some humans are descended from him. He is known mainly as the origin of a ritual chant that strikes people down.

In this way he provided a role model for the exercise of sorcery. The ritual performed to destroy an enemy was believed to possess its power because it had been first employed by Kahukura.

## Kahu-mata-momoe

### An early Arawa ancestor

This man came from Hawaiki on *Te Arawa*, being a son of its captain Tama-te-kapua. Soon after *Te Arawa* made landfall at Maketū (in the Bay of Plenty), some of the crew set out on journeys of exploration and settled on lands elsewhere. Kahu-mata-momoe also made expeditions into the interior, but always returned to Maketū.

It was there that a dispute arose between Kahu and Tama-te-kapua as to the ownership of a kūmara plantation. Kahu claimed it as his own, since he had worked in it, but Tama-te-kapua thought it remained his property because he was Kahu's father. Finally Tama-te-kapua left in a rage and went to live on the Moehau Range.

Later there was a fight between Kahu and his elder brother, Tūhoro-mata-kakā, and Tūhoro tore Kahu's greenstone pendant from his ear. He and his family then abandoned Maketū and went to live with Tama-te-kapua.

This was not the end of the story. When the time came for Tama-te-kapua to die, he gave his son Tūhoro strict instructions as to the tapu restrictions to be observed after his death. But Tūhoro did not perform this task properly. He broke tapu, and accordingly became ill and knew that he too would die.

Tūhoro had four sons: Taramainuku, Warenga, Huarere and Īhenga. Yet it was his youngest, Īhenga, on whom he now bestowed his mana and whom he made responsible for the procedures to be followed after his death. And he told Īhenga that afterwards he must make the journey to Maketū to find his uncle Kahu-mata-momoe and ask him to remove his tapu.

Īhenga did as he was instructed. At the proper time he journeyed to Maketū, then boldly entered Kahu's house in his absence and seated himself upon his uncle's tapu headrest. Kahu was told of the intruder and ran to kill him, but he saw the resemblance to his brother and he wept over his nephew. When he heard why Īhenga had come, he began the ceremonies to remove his tapu.

This procedure took twenty days, and it was a long time for Īhenga because by now he was in love with Kahu-mata-momoe's daughter Hine-te-kakara. Finally the rituals were over and he was free to marry her.

One thing remained to be done. Following his father's instructions, Īhenga retrieved from its hiding-place the greenstone pendant which, long before, Tūhoro had taken from Kahu-mata-momoe when the brothers had quarrelled. This pendant, named Kaukau-matua, had been brought from Hawaiki. Īhenga now placed it in Hine-te-kakara's ear and sent her to her father. Seeing his lost treasure, Kahu wept for his brother. And he told his daughter that she and Īhenga could keep Kaukau-matua.

Some time later Īhenga settled by Lake Rotorua, and Kahu joined him there. Then Kahu decided to travel to the far north to visit his nephews Taramainuku and Warenga, who were now living there. So Kahu, Īhenga and some companions set out on this long expedition. They crossed to the west coast then turned to the north, naming the places to which they came. They found Taramainuku at Kaipara and stayed with him for some time.

Īhenga went on to visit Warenga, but Kahu returned through Tāmaki. He continued to give names to the places through which he passed; in the Waitematā Harbour, one place that now bears his name is Ōkahu Bay.

Kahu visited his other nephew, Huarere, at Moehau, then afterwards lived at Rotorua with his daughter. Finally as an old man he returned to Maketū and died there.

Kahu-mata-momoe's name means 'Kahu with drowsy eyes' (or some say 'Kahu with a droopy eyelid'). His elder brother's name, Tūhoro-mata-kakā, means 'Tūhoro with fiery eyes'.

## Kahungunu

### Founder of a numerous people

Kahungunu was a man like no other. A son of the famous Tamatea, he made his way in the world not as a warrior but through his ability as a provider and through a series of marriages to attractive and important women.

He is often said to have been born in Kaitaia, in the far north. There he mastered the skills required for the production of food on the land and on the ocean, showing himself to be able and industrious. But while he was still young, his father was driven from the north and removed his household to Te Mangatawa near Tauranga.

There Kahungunu grew to manhood in the company of his elder half-brother, Whāene. Finally he quarrelled with Whāene over the distribution of fish from the nets; some say Whāene was mean and lazy, others that Kahungunu was greedy and would not wait. Whāene heard that Kahungunu had helped himself to fish, and was so angry that he seized a fish, a snapper, and hit Kahungunu on the face.

So Kahungunu left Tauranga and went south to Ōpōtiki, where his first cousin Haumanga was living with her husband Haruatai. While he was

there they had a son, and at Kahungunu's request they named him Tū-tāmure [Hit by snapper] to ensure that Whāene's insult would not be forgotten.

Presently Kahungunu set out again, making his way around the east coast. Eventually he reached Tūranga (the Gisborne district), and there he married a daughter of the great rangatira Ruapani. Usually it is said that this woman was Ruapani's eldest child, Rua-rau-hanga, and that she bore Kahungunu two sons, Rua-roa and Rongo-maire, who became leading ancestors of the peoples of Ngāti Porou and Rongo-whakaata. Some authorities, however, give her name as Rua-rere-tai and say that she had a daughter, Rua-herehere-tīeke.

After a while Kahungunu became restless and moved south to Whareongaonga. There he married Hine-pūariari and Kahukura-waiaraia, two daughters of Pānui. With each of these women he had two children.

But Kahungunu kept hearing about Rongo-mai-wahine, a high-ranking woman who lived at Tawapata on the Māhia Peninsula, and eventually he left his home and went with a party of men to visit her people. On his arrival he found that Rongomai-wahine had just married a man named Tama-taku-tai. But he was not dismayed. He saw that she was as beautiful as he had heard, and he started thinking how he could win her.

He decided he would do it with food. He took all his men to dig fernroot up on the mountains, and they came back carrying large bundles. When they got to a cliff just above the village, he put all the bundles together into one enormous bundle, then let this fall over the cliff and right down into the village. The bundle burst open and covered the marae, and the people came eagerly to get food for themselves. All the women said, 'How good this man is at getting food!'

Kahungunu went on living there, still wanting the woman, and presently he had another idea. Watching a shag diving into the sea, he found he could hold his breath for longer than the bird. So he decided that he would be able to dive down into the deep water where these people had to get their pāua. His men made a big basket, and he dived down to the pāua bed. He filled his basket, and repeated this feat until he had sufficient shellfish to feed the whole village. The last time he went down, he stuck pāua all over his body; they remained there by suction, and he came up covered with them. And once more the women were loud in their praise.

Then Kahungunu told his men, 'When you eat the pāua, keep the roes for me.'

*Kahungunu formed the base of the central pillar in a Tū-ranga house built in about 1830 by Te Aitanga-a-Māhaki, descendants of his grandson Māhaki. The name of this house was Te Poho o Māhaki [Māhaki's bosom], the concept being that Māhaki's descendants sheltered within his embrace.*

*Rua-rau-hanga, daughter of the great Ruapani and one of Kahungunu's many wives. A painting in Rongopai, a house dating from 1887 which stands at Waituhi near Gisborne.*

So he ate the pāua roes till his stomach was full. That night he went as usual to his bed in the house shared by Tama-taku-tai and Rongomai-wahine; he was on one side, and the man and his wife on the other. Then the wind in Kahungunu's stomach rose up because of the pāua. The scoundrel got up, and boldly went over to the two of them as they lay sleeping. He pulled up the cloaks that covered them, let go a fart, then put them back again.

The man and his wife slept on, covered with their cloaks. Presently the stench that Kahungunu had let loose made its way up and hit the noses of the man and his wife. They jumped up at once and started quarrelling, each blaming the other, then after a while they lay down again, while Kahungunu laughed to himself.

When they were asleep once more, he went over and did the same thing again. This time there was a serious quarrel and the man spoke ill

of his wife's parents and brothers. So the woman went off to tell her parents, who were deeply upset.

Some writers tell us that Rongomai-wahine was given to Kahungunu at this point, while others say this happened after Kahungunu managed to drown Tama-taku-tai next day while he was surfing in a small waka. Certainly Kahungunu married her, and stayed with her. Their sons were Kahukura-nui, Tamatea-kota and Māhaki-nui, their daughters Rongomai-pāpā and Tauhei-kurī.

Kahungunu was a peaceable man who avoided fighting whenever possible. When his pā was besieged in his old age, he was greatly relieved when the leader of his enemies turned out to be a relative, Tū-tāmure. To make peace, he asked his daughter Tauhei-kurī to leave the pā and marry Tū-tāmure. She went out to the besieging force and the pā was saved – though she then insisted upon marrying Tū-tāmure's better-looking younger brother, Tama-taipū-noa.

There are conflicting stories about Kahungunu; some writers name other wives and children besides those mentioned here. Many of his children became important ancestors. Through his son Kahukura-nui, Kahungunu was the founder of Ngāti Kahungunu, whose numerous divisions extend from Wairoa southwards through Heretaunga (Hawke's Bay) to the Wairarapa.

## Kaiwhare
### A taniwha near Piha

This taniwha lives near the Manukau Harbour in an underwater cave and blowhole, known as The Gap, just south of Piha. He used to visit the Manukau to receive offerings from the people there. A small piece of fish or porpoise meat would be put inside a miniature house on a little raft, and this would be set adrift on an ebb tide. If the food was gone next day, Kaiwhare had accepted his offering and would send plenty of fish.

But then Kaiwhare began killing and eating the men and women who went fishing in waka and spearing flounder on the mudflats. It became too dangerous to go out on the harbour, and the people were desperate. At last they heard of Tāmure, a man at Hauraki who possessed a mere with special powers that could kill any taniwha, if only it could be brought close enough.

Tāmure agreed to help them and he came very fast, striding from hilltop to hilltop and stepping over rivers. He instructed some men to go out spearing flounder while he himself hid close to

Kaiwhare's den. Seeing the fishermen's torches, the taniwha began to stir, and as he emerged from his den Tāmure struck him on the head with his weapon. Kaiwhare lashed about, sweeping away cliffs with his tail, and Tāmure made off inland to avoid the falling rocks.

After this, Kaiwhare contented himself with the crayfish and octopuses he could catch near his cave. Around his den the level stretch of rock he cleared in his struggles can still be seen.

This is probably the same Tāmure as the man of that name who, in a different story, overcame an evil tohunga named Kiki.

In one version of his story, Kaiwhare is killed not by Tāmure but by Hakawau. He first weakens the taniwha with a series of powerful chants, then kills him with his whalebone patu as he comes out from his cave.

## Kametara
### A man with a demon wife

Kametara married a woman who bore him a boy and a girl. Then another woman, a tipua [demon], made her appearance. Not knowing what she was, Kametara married her as well.

The demon woman wanted to kill her co-wife, so she suggested that they went out fishing. Then when it was time to return, she told the human woman that the anchor was caught fast and she would have to dive to free it. As soon as she went down, the demon cut the rope, paddled off and left her there.

But the woman did not drown. She swam to an uninhabited island nearby and she survived by eating shellfish and plant foods. She built herself a house, and wove garments. She was pregnant at the time, and presently she gave birth to twin boys, whom she reared carefully. One day as these boys were walking along the beach they saw some potatoes washed up on the sand. They took them to their mother, she planted them next summer, and after that they had plenty of potatoes.

As the woman worked, weaving garments for her sons, she was composing a song lamenting her separation from her people and her husband. She taught her sons to sing this song and play its tune on the flute.

When the twins were old enough, she told them to fell a tree and adze a waka. They did this, then set out on a voyage to find their father, elder brother, sister and other relatives. When they met them and revealed their identity, their relatives wept and greeted them. One of the boys stood up, returned their greetings, and sang their

mother's song. Afterwards they taught it to all the people.

The brothers did not see their father because he was living at the home of his demon wife. They returned and told their mother that their relatives were coming, and she prepared a welcome. During her years on the island she had worked so industriously that she was able now to appear before them clothed in fine korowai cloaks. There was much weeping, then the woman sang her song and offered her people a meal of potted birds, dried fish, shellfish and potatoes, and as well she presented them with the garments she had woven. Then they all lived permanently on the island.

This is a Taranaki version of an ancient Polynesian tale about a demon woman who marries an unsuspecting man, taking the place of his real, human wife; often she is killed when her true nature is revealed. The potatoes are a modern substitution for kūmara.

## Kapu-manawa-whiti
### Hidden intentions

Kapu belonged to Ngāti Raukawa and Ngāti Maniapoto in the southern Waikato. He was given his full name, Kapu-manawa-whiti [Kapu with hidden intentions], when he acquired a well-earned reputation as a schemer.

The Waikato people tell a story about a time when Tūhourangi, from Lake Rotorua, came with a retinue to visit Kapu. Instead of sending a messenger beforehand and coming in the autumn after the kūmara had been lifted, Tūhourangi turned up without any warning in the early summer when food was scarce.

This was highly embarrassing, and Kapu wanted revenge. When Tūhourangi invited him to return the visit in the autumn, he pretended to agree but then set out almost at once with a large party. They reached Rotorua soon after Tūhourangi, and the people there were ashamed because they had little to give them.

During this visit the two rangatira talked about food. Tūhourangi said that what he liked best were preserved birds and seafood, but Kapu maintained that water was best of all. Afterwards he surprised Tūhourangi by inviting him to visit him again, and suggesting he came in the early summer.

Kapu, of course, had something in mind. He prepared for Tūhourangi's arrival by laying in stores of preserved game and dried seafood, and by building a new pā on a hilltop far from any rivers. When all was ready his people built a

*To call a man 'a descendant of Kapu-manawa-whiti' was to imply that he was certainly planning trouble, but that no-one could guess what it would be. The saying was sometimes applied to the much-feared Te Rauparaha (1768–1849), a brilliant political and military leader.*

house, dug down inside until they came to water, then covered over the well they had made.

Tūhourangi duly arrived with a large party and was feasted upon his favourite foods. After eating a great deal he began to suffer from thirst, but when men were sent for water they found that in the summer weather all the streams had dried up. By this time Tūhourangi was crying and groaning – yet there was water in this very house. Kapu had been sitting on the cover. Now he reminded Tūhourangi that he had told him water was best, then leapt to one side and offered him water. Tūhourangi drank and recovered.

So Tūhourangi knew then that the best food really is water. He went back home very much ashamed at being twice overcome by Kapu.

When a man keeps his intentions to himself and people have reason to be suspicious, they may say, 'He's a descendant of Kapu-manawa-whiti' [Ko te uri o Kapu-manawa-whiti].

## Karitehe
### An uncanny people

These yellow-haired, white-skinned people lived in the forests of the far north, some of them in the Kauhoehoe Caves. Sometimes they would seize human girls who were out gathering the edible bracts of the kiekie flowers – for the Karitehe were often up among these climbing plants, high in the trees. The girls they caught were never seen again.

When an ancestor of Te Rārawa made one of their women his wife, the Karitehe abandoned their caves and the trouble ended.

## Kataore
### Hinemihi's pet

Some writers say this was a reptile on the Matawhāura Range above Lake Rotoiti, and that travellers passing his home made offerings of food to ensure their safety. If the reptile chattered as a war party went past, it presaged doom for the warriors.

Most authorities say, however, that Kataore was a taniwha living in a cave overlooking Lake Tikitapu (the Blue Lake) at Te Wairoa. The people there were Tūhourangi, and Kataore was owned by a high-ranking woman, Hinemihi.

*Kataore, the taniwha at Lake Tikitapu, guards the porch of the meeting house Nuku Te Apiapi, which formerly stood at Rotorua. He is portrayed twice so that he can look in both directions.*

These people thought Kataore quite harmless because he always behaved well when they went to feed him, but afterwards, when travellers approached, he would rush out and devour them. In the end he was destroyed by warriors of Ngāti Tama in revenge for their relatives he had killed and eaten. Their leader was Pitaka, who with his brothers was already famous for having killed two other taniwha, Hotupuku and Pekehaua. Some say Pitaka lured Kataore into a snare, others that his potent chants incapacitated the monster and allowed his companions to spear him to death.

This was the start of a war that involved a number of peoples in the region. Eventually Ngāti Tama were forced to leave Rotorua for the west coast and other places.

Kaukau-matua, the precious greenstone pendant believed by Ngāti Tūwharetoa to have been brought from Hawaiki, was owned until the early 1880s by Te Heuheu Tūkino (Horonuku).

## Kaukau-matua
### A treasured heirloom

In several myths this greenstone ear pendant is shaped by Ngahue in Hawaiki, brought to Aotearoa by the captain of an ancestral waka and passed down through the generations. There is disagreement as to its owners.

One tradition has Kaukau-matua brought on *Te Arawa* by Tama-te-kapua and inherited by his descendants. In the early nineteenth century a beautiful pendant owned by Te Heuheu, a leading rangatira in the Taupō region, was believed to be this very piece. When Te Heuheu died in 1846 in a mudslide that engulfed his home, Kaukau-matua was thought lost forever. Later it was dug from the wreckage. Then in the early 1880s, when one of Te Heuheu's grand-daughters was swimming in Lake Taupō, Kaukau-matua slipped from a ribbon around her neck and was gone. (This was not entirely unexpected because greenstone has an affinity with water, from which it comes in the first place.)

In another account, Kaukau-matua came on the *Tainui*. It was in the possession of leading Waikato families until 1853, when it was presented by Hōne Te Paki to George Grey, an early British governor of the country.

## Kawharu
### The Kaipara giant

This great warrior was four spans tall, about eight metres. His body was one span in circumference, and his face as long as the length from an ordinary person's fingertips to elbow. He is thought to have lived in the second half of the seventeenth century.

Kawharu won many battles in the Kaipara region for his Ngāti Whātua people, who had moved south from Hokianga. On one occasion a force under his command assaulted a pā on Moturemu Island, a stronghold of the Kawerau people on the eastern side of the Kaipara Harbour. This island is nearly fifty metres high, with precipitous cliffs, and the pā was thought impregnable. Kawharu leant against a cliff with his arms outstretched, and his men climbed up his huge body, took the pā by surprise and conquered its occupants.

Other battles followed, and Ngāti Whātua were triumphant. Kawharu, though, was eventually killed through treachery. By now his people occupied the northern part of the Kaipara, and the Kawerau people the southern section. Kawharu's sister had married a Kawerau man, and Kawharu went with some companions to visit her. According to custom this should have been quite safe, but after a display of friendship the Kawerau treacherously attacked their guests. The gateway was blocked, so Kawharu climbed the three rows of palisades. As he was jumping from the last palisade, he was caught and killed.

While it is said in the far north that Kawharu grew up there, others maintain that he was born at Kāwhia and won fame in that region before being visited by a party of Ngāti Whātua and asked for his assistance. At Kāwhia a long, red-streaked sandstone rock is Kawharu's Girdle [Te Tātua a Kawharu], a hollow in a rock is Kawharu's Footprint, and a never-failing spring is named after Kawharu's wife Koata.

## Kēhua

### Supernatural visitors

The word kēhua, meaning 'ghost', seems to have entered the language in about the 1850s. Before this, apparitions had generally been termed wairua. This word remained in use, but people sometimes now spoke of kēhua instead.

There was much debate about the nature of kēhua, and this reflected an uncertainty about the nature of supernatural beings which many people were experiencing at the time. Some were convinced they had encountered kēhua (or in some cases, wairua), while others denied that either of these could be seen. One approach, which was in accord with orthodox Christianity, was to say that wairua existed but were invisible, while kēhua were merely figments of the imagination.

Kēhua were often thought to be souls of the dead (which in the past had always been known as wairua); they were believed to be encountered especially in the far north while making their way to Te Rēinga, where they leapt to the under-world. But not all kēhua took human form. One Māori writer tells how a party of fishermen in the far north came across a herd of wild horses that were really kēhua. It was getting dark, so they drove the horses on to a headland from which they could not escape. They planned to capture some the next day, and spent the night plaiting flax ropes. But at dawn the horses had vanished and not a hoofprint was to be seen.

## Kiharoa

### A giant in the southern Waikato

This warrior was twice the height of an ordinary man. A rangatira of two related peoples, Ngāti Raukawa and Ngāti Whakatere, he lived in about 1800 at Tokanui Pā, just south of the present town of Te Awamutu.

For a long time Kiharoa was thought invincible. But then, as he led his men against invaders from Ngāti Maniapoto, he slipped and fell on some karaka fruit lying on the path. This was a bad omen, and despite his great size he was soon overcome. His body was cooked and eaten. Until recent years a depression marking the site of this enormous oven was a well-known landmark.

## Kiki and Tāmure

### A trial of strength

Kiki, who lived on the Waikato River, was a sorcerer so powerful that on sunny days he could not go outside because his shadow would have withered the plants it fell upon. When strangers came, this old man remained in his house and destroyed them simply by opening his door. Even when their waka were still on the river, if he merely opened the shutter of his window the crews would stiffen and die.

Kiki's fame spread throughout the country, and at Kāwhia a man named Tāmure decided to challenge his powers. With two men, and his young daughter as well, he crossed the ranges and paddled down to Kiki's village. As they approached, he recited chants to collect his atua around them and ward off the atua of the enemy. When he was ready they landed.

Kiki called a welcome, and they went forward on to the marae. Some of Kiki's people began to cook food for the strangers – but they did so in a tapu oven. Meanwhile Kiki remained inside his house. And Tāmure, seated just outside, quietly recited chants to destroy Kiki when he crossed the threshold.

When the food was offered to Tāmure and his party they knew it was bewitched, so Tāmure said that his daughter was very hungry and that she would eat it. All the while he was repeating chants to protect his party and kill Kiki. Meanwhile his daughter ate only a little, and each time she first passed the piece of food under her leg, destroying its power – because women can over-come tapu in this way.

Kiki emerged from his house and sat waiting for Tāmure to eat and die, then when this did not happen he went back inside. As soon as the girl had finished her meal, Tāmure told his companions to launch their waka. They did so, and paddled off quickly.

Meanwhile Kiki became ill, and presently grew worse. His people knew Tāmure was responsible and they followed his party along the river, but

Tāmure had asked some people at a village they passed to tell Kiki's men that they were long gone. The pursuers turned back, discouraged, and before long Kiki died, defeated by Tāmure.

# Kiwa

### An early Tūranga ancestor

Many east coast authorities consider that Kiwa captained a waka on its voyage from Hawaiki to Tūranga (the Gisborne district). Some say it was the *Tākitimu*, others the *Horouta* or the *Hirauta*.

Kiwa's son Kahutuanui married Hine-akua, daughter of Pāwa, who had made the voyage from Hawaiki on the *Horouta*. From this union came many high-ranking ancestors, including Ruapani, Tūhoropunga and their sister Papawharanui.

The region is sometimes known as Tūranga-nui-a-Kiwa [Great Tūranga of Kiwa] in recognition of Kiwa's role as a founding ancestor.

# Kiwa

### Guardian of the ocean

In some east coast traditions the sea is a female, Hine-moana [Ocean woman], and her husband (sometimes brother or guardian) is a man named Kiwa.

When they are husband and wife, these two are often said to have had a number of children, who were the origin of different kinds of beings that live in the sea. From their child Uru-kāhi-kahika, for instance, came conger eels, frostfish, hagfish, freshwater eels and lamprey. From Pipi-hura came many kinds of shellfish. From Kai-waha-wera came the octopus. From Whare-rimu [Seaweed house] came the different kinds of seaweed, which shelter fish.

Others, though, say that Kiwa married Para-whenua-mea, who is the waters that flow from the land to the sea.

A poetic, rhetorical name for the sea is the Great Ocean of Kiwa [Te Moana Nui a Kiwa]. In recent times this name has been given specifically to the Pacific Ocean.

# Kiwi

### Powerful ruler of Tāmaki

The Tāmaki Isthmus (where Auckland now stands) was always much coveted for its fertile soil, good climate, and excellent fishing and shellfish beds. By the sixteenth century extensive gardens helped support a large population and many of the extinct volcanic cones in the region

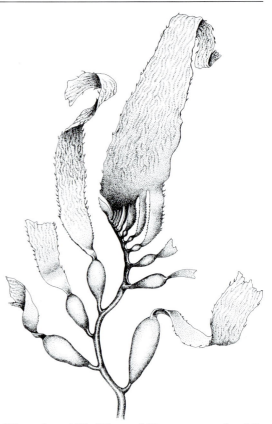

*Whare-rimu, child of Kiwa and Hine-moana, produced the different kinds of seaweed, which shelter fish.*

had become pā, with wide terraces and high scarps cut into their steep slopes. The largest of these great fortresses was on the highest hill, Maunga-kiekie (One Tree Hill). This immense stronghold is said to have been divided into seven sections, each with its own fortifications.

The inhabitants of Tāmaki traced their descent from many ancient peoples who had mingled there: first the fairies [patupaiarehe], then sections of Ngā Oho (whose ancestor was Toi), Ngāti Awa (of Mātaatua origin), Kawerau, and peoples of Tainui and Arawa origin. Eventually they became known collectively as Te Waiohua.

They were so numerous, 'like ants', that they were well able to man their formidable pā against attacks from envious neighbours. They held the isthmus for many generations and their prosperity was proverbial.

Kiwi was born into the ruling family in the early eighteenth century, when his people were at the height of their success. His father was Te Ika-mau-poho and his mother Te Tahuri. They lived mainly on Maunga-kiekie. The gardens surrounding their home may have occupied as much as a thousand hectares; his mother was so

*According to legend, the principal rangatira of Tāmaki possessed a greenstone gong that could be heard throughout his realm. In reality, a war gong took the form of a plank of resonant wood, sometimes grooved on the underside and one and a half metres or more in length. Suspended from a watchtower in the palisades of a pā and struck with a rod, it produced a booming sound heard over long distances.*

renowned for the skill with which she organised the people working in them that the Maungakiekie district became known as Ngā Māra-a-Tahuri [Tahuri's gardens].

As a young man, Kiwi became ruler of the isthmus from the Tāmaki River in the south to the Whau River in the north. At this time many of the pā in the region were occupied, and the population was perhaps as dense as it ever became in Aotearoa. This must have produced a more hierarchical society than usual. It is known that Kiwi lived in luxury, with the best of foods presented as tribute.

Legend has it that on Maunga-kiekie Kiwi possessed an enormous gong [pahū] which was made not of hard wood, in the usual way, but of greenstone. When this sounded in times of danger it was heard throughout his realm.

In fact there were few dangers that threatened them; Te Waiohua were so numerous that with good diplomacy they would have continued to occupy their lands in peace. Kiwi, however, possessed an arrogant and turbulent disposition. To the north-west, the people of Ngāti Whātua had

*This basalt figure from the south-east slopes of Maunga-kiekie (One Tree Hill) is a taumata atua, the resting place of an atua. The god it housed was probably a guardian of the enormous kūmara gardens around the pā.*

become powerful. While attending a Ngāti Whātua funeral at Waituoro (in the region now known as Helensville), Kiwi and his party, as the result of a previous quarrel, treacherously killed a number of rangatira, including a high-ranking woman, Tahataha. They then retreated to their own territory, with Kiwi confident that their safety would be ensured by his god Rehua and by his people's great numbers.

Ngāti Whātua, under the leadership of Te Waha-akiaki and Tuperiri (brother of Tahataha), retaliated by attacking villages on the shores of the Waitematā. Then came a battle at Titirangi, which Kiwi lost. Later there were further gains by Ngāti Whātua, then a second battle, in which the Ngāti Whātua army invaded the shores of the Manukau, feigned retreat, then rapidly advanced. Recognising Kiwi by the plumes he wore, Te Waha-akiaki rushed forward and succeeded in killing him. Seeing their leader fall, Kiwi's great army turned and fled. Few escaped, and all their important rangatira were killed.

This happened in about 1750. Ngāti Whātua took possession of most of Tāmaki and it was Tuperiri who now lived on Maunga-kiekie, although the newcomers did not have the numbers to hold all the pā their predecessors had occupied. Later, at the turn of the century, Ngāti Whātua suffered greatly from epidemics introduced by Pākehā visitors. Afterwards there were Ngā Puhi raiders from the north, with muskets newly acquired from the Pākehā. The old methods of warfare were now useless, and the old way of life was soon to disappear.

Kiwi, who lost Tāmaki, was known to Ngāti Whātua as Kiwi Tāmaki to distinguish him from other men called Kiwi.

## Kōhine-mataroa
### A northern ancestor

This woman was the daughter of Puna-te-ariari, sister of the early ancestor Rāhiri. She crossed from South Hokianga to the northern side of the

*Maunga-kiekie (One Tree Hill) as it is today. The terraces and scarps remain.*

harbour, explored the region and named all the places she found. She was a skilled gardener and in several suitable areas, such as Waihou and Motuti, established plantations of kūmara and taro.

Kōhine-mataroa married Kaharau, a son of Rāhiri by his second wife Whakaruru. Numerous peoples in the region trace their descent from these ancestors.

# Kōkako

### A Tainui ancestor

This sixteenth-century rangatira, a son of Manutongatea and Wawara, lived in the district south of the Manukau Heads then later in the interior. Some authorities tell us that he was responsible for the drowning of Tūheitia, a rival rangatira at Te Ākau who after his death became a taniwha.

During a visit to Kāwhia, Kōkako one night forced his attentions upon a woman, Whaea-tapoko, who had gone to draw water from a spring. Afterwards he told her that if she had a son, he was to be named Tama-inu-pō [Boy drink in the night]; if the child was a daughter, she would be Pare-inu-pō [Girl drink in the night]. He then returned to his home in the north. The child was a boy and was named accordingly.

When Tama-inu-pō grew to manhood he set out to find his father. On the way he visited the home of Māhanga, a rangatira living at Pūrākau, north of Mount Pirongia. This man's daughter Tū-kōtuku fell in love with Tama, and he married her and lived there with his father-in-law.

It happened that Māhanga was the son of Tūheitia, whom Kōkako had killed many years previously, and that he was soon to lead an army against Kōkako to avenge his father's death. Tama-inu-pō, who had not revealed his father's name, joined this expedition.

Kōkako was then living in a pā on the south side of the Waikato Heads. He had heard of Māhanga's approach and was prepared for the attack, but after fierce fighting his men retreated and Māhanga's forces entered the pā. Tama-inu-pō all this time had been searching for Kōkako. Now he found him, recognising him by his red cloak. Without revealing his identity he overcame his father, seized his cloak and patu, and allowed him to escape. Later he managed to convince Māhanga and his warriors that he had killed Kōkako, and the army returned.

Some time after these events a son was born to Tama-inu-pō and Tū-kōtuku. It was necessary for the father's father to be present at the tohi ceremony to be performed over the infant, so

*A figure of Kōhine-mataroa at the Motuti Marae in North Hokianga. Motuti is in one of the areas where this early ancestor cultivated her gardens, and her name has been given to the dining room [whare kai] which stands near the meeting house [whare hui] Tamatea. In this way Kōhine-mataroa continues to offer hospitality and sustenance to all.*

Māhanga asked Tama-inu-pō about his father. To his great surprise he learnt that Tama-inu-pō's father was Kōkako, and that he was still alive.

Tama-inu-pō determined to visit his father, in the company only of his wife and son, in an attempt to make peace. Māhanga agreed to this and indicated that he would be happy with such an outcome. So the three of them embarked on a small waka and travelled down the Waipā River and on into the Waikato. On the island near Rangiriri where Kōkako was now living, Tama-inu-pō saw a house standing apart and knew it was his father's. He went on boldly, despite angry shouts telling him the house was tapu, and confronted his father. He revealed his identity, showing the cloak and patu he had taken from Kōkako, then led forward his wife – daughter of his father's enemy – and held out their son.

Kōkako at once took his grandson to the tūāhu and performed the tohi ceremony over him, naming him Wairere. Tama-inu-pō then asked Kōkako to accompany him to his home and make peace with Māhanga. He agreed to this, and at Pūrākau the two men, with much ritual, oratory and festivity, made peace.

# Kōpū
## The morning star

The planet Venus, seen before dawn in the eastern sky, was often known as Kōpū. The brightest of the visible 'stars' [whetū], it was thought to rise as a sign that daylight was coming. Its size and beauty made it the focus of much emotion.

A beautiful woman, or one wearing fine clothes, might be said to be 'like Kōpū coming up over the horizon', and the wide shining eyes of haka performers were likened to Kōpū.

Another name for the morning star is Tāwera. The evening star (also Venus) is usually Meremere.

# Kōpūwai
## A dog-headed monster

This creature had a man's body but a dog's head, and was covered in scales. He lived in a cave in rugged country in the upper reaches of the Matau (Clutha) River, and he hunted human beings with a pack of two-headed dogs. He himself could scent the presence of humans from far away.

During the harsh winters the local people lived in a village near the river mouth, but in the warm months they went inland in small parties to gather plant foods, snare weka, and catch ducks and eels in the river and lakes. Many were then the victims of Kōpūwai and his terrible dogs.

On one occasion, having caught a woman named Kaiamio, he decided not to eat her but keep her as a slave wife. He carried her off to his cave, and his hideous pack sat guarding the entrance.

Every day Kaiamio had to leave the cave to draw water from the river and perform other tasks. So she could not escape, Kōpūwai made a long rope and plaited one end into her hair. He himself held the other end as he lay in the cave. When he jerked it, she tugged in reply.

For many years she lived like this, fretting at her servitude and longing for her home. Then she devised a plan. Every day at the river she gathered some raupō stalks, and when she had enough she lashed them into bundles and built a raft. After this she waited for a north-west wind to bring hot, enervating weather, for she knew Kōpūwai would then lie drowsing in his cave.

When the wind came she set off with the rope in her hair as usual, but at the river bank she untied it and fastened it to a raupō root so it would rebound a little when pulled. She launched the raft, and the great river carried her swiftly towards her home.

Meanwhile Kōpūwai lay drowsily in his cave, pulling on the rope from time to time. After she had been gone a long time he grew suspicious. He shouted from the mouth of the cave, there was no reply, and he knew she had escaped. In a rage he called up his dogs, and at the river bank he found the rope tied to the raupō root. He and the dogs sniffed about, then he realised she had gone by water. So he tried to drink the river dry, hoping her raft would be stranded, but the river filled up again as fast as he emptied it. His dogs drank the water too, but still the river filled up.

Kaiamio reached the river mouth safely, and after washing the monster's scales from her body she entered the village. The people were astonished and delighted to find her alive. She told her story and they planned their revenge.

When the summer was well advanced they made their way upriver, gathering raupō stalks as they went, then waited for a north-west wind. When it came, Kaiamio cautiously approached the cave and found Kōpūwai and the dogs asleep. Some of the men hid by a hole in the roof of the cave while the others piled their raupō at the entrance and set it alight.

Awakening to the flames, Kōpūwai tried to climb through the roof, but the men battered his fearful head to pieces. Most of his dogs were killed as well, though two ran off to a small cave near the Waitaki River where they are still to be seen, turned to stone.

Some say the monster lived further down the river, in high hills which were named Kōpūwai after him, and that a tall pillar of rock at the top of this range is Kōpūwai himself. Old Man Range and The Obelisk are the English names for these hills and pillar.

The name Kōpūwai [Belly of water] must relate to his attempt to drink the river dry.

# Korotangi
## A bird lost and found

In a song known to the Tainui peoples and some others, a poet mourns the loss of his pet, a beautiful bird named Korotangi. This man had given his bird the best of food, but his wife had thought this a waste and in his absence took the good food for herself and treated Korotangi badly. Finally the angry bird escaped – or perhaps the woman let it out of its cage. The man searched for his pet but found only a few of its feathers. He kept these plumes in a carved box made for the purpose, and he composed a lament that was soon widely known.

A stone bird of unknown origin, carved in a

*The mysterious Korotangi, a taonga [treasure] of the Tainui peoples.*

style that is not Māori, was found in the Waikato district in about 1879, reportedly among the roots of a mānuka tree blown down in a gale. This bird was at once recognised by leading rangatira as being Korotangi, now turned to stone. The people wept over their bird, singing the old lament, and it was explained by some that this treasure had been brought on the *Tainui* from Hawaiki.

## Kūī

### An ancient woman

In Hokianga it was believed that the first inhabitants in the region, Tuputupu-whenua and his wife Kūī, still lived there under the ground. Kūī now took the form of an insect, named kūī, which lives in holes in the ground (this is the larva of the tiger beetle). When a man built a house he would make a ritual offering of grass to Kūī, presenting her with this food in recognition of the fact that she was the real owner of the land upon which his house stood.

In myths elsewhere, the name Kūī belongs to a race of people who were very early inhabitants of Aotearoa. One story is that Māui, having fished up the land, presented it to these people (though some say Kupe gave it to them). Later the Kūī were conquered by another early race, the Tutumaiao. These in turn were dispossessed by the fairies [tūrehu], who finally intermarried with the human immigrants.

## Kūmara

### The sweet potato

This plant was subtropical in its origins and could be grown in Aotearoa only in the warmer and more fertile regions. Even there, much skill and labour were required. So kūmara were a luxury, reserved most of the time for important people and the entertainment of visitors.

Since it was eaten on festive occasions and required a state of peace for its cultivation, the kūmara was symbolically associated with peace – in opposition to fernroot, which in many situations was associated with warfare. This distinction found expression in ritual usages, and the two plants were always stored apart.

The father of the kūmara is Rongo, who was born in the beginning; he is usually one of the sons of Rangi and Papa, earth and sky, or a son of Tāne. But this myth of origin does not explain how human beings later acquired the kūmara.

*Stone figures placed beside kūmara gardens as guardians sometimes represented Rongo and sometimes local ancestors.*

*After the men had turned over the ground with digging-sticks [kō], the women broke up the clods of earth and prepared rows of hillocks for planting the kūmara. Wooden tools made this work slow and strenuous, and iron hoes were much in demand when they became available. These women in the 1820s appear to be using them.*

Each people possessed another myth which told this.

Sometimes the kūmara is acquired from Hawaiki (or in one account, the star Whānui) by a man who has a special association with the plant (and whose name is sometimes an extended form of the name Rongo). In some regions this acquisition was enacted, or referred to, in annual rituals accompanying the planting or harvesting of the kūmara crop.

In other accounts the kūmara, along with much else, is brought on an ancestral waka from the homeland of Hawaiki. Often the wife of the captain of the vessel is mainly responsible for preserving the precious seed tubers.

## Kupe

### The explorer

The first person to visit Aotearoa was Kupe. When he arrived the land had not yet assumed its present form. Kupe established landmarks and prepared the way for those who were to follow.

The waka in which he sailed from Hawaiki is variously said to have been the *Mātāhourua*, the *Mātāwhao-rua*, and *Ngā-toki-mātāwhaorua*.

According to one story, Kupe overtook the land as it was floating along on the ocean; he found that the ground was soft and trembling, and his first task was to make it firm and stationary. Some say he cut Aotearoa off from Hawaiki, to which it was then joined, and others that when Māui caught his great fish it was Kupe, not Māui's brothers, who jumped on its back and sliced it up, making it twist into hills and valleys.

Often Kupe was believed to have cut the strait that separates the North and South Islands, forming as he did so numerous landmarks – in particular, Kapiti, Māna and Arapawa Islands – which still bear witness to this exploit. In one story, he came to Aotearoa in pursuit of a giant octopus and finally killed it in this region.

He was thought to have sailed around much of the coast of Aotearoa, especially the west coast of the North Island, and to have left behind him many possessions turned to stone, such as his sail, fishing net, bailer and dogs. Two small islands in Te Whanga-nui-a-Tara (Wellington Harbour) are Kupe's daughters, Mātiu and Makaro, whom he left there.

Right above: *A large boulder, formerly at the entrance to Porirua Harbour, is believed to be the anchor stone [punga] of Kupe's waka, the* Mātāwhaorua. *Many generations have honoured this tapu stone for its association with Kupe. Fitted with a rope, it is now a treasured possession in the Museum of New Zealand Te Papa Tongarewa.*

Right: *On the coastline Kupe left many possessions, turned to stone. Two of his triangular sails [Ngā Rā o Kupe] stand near Cape Palliser; one of them is visible in this photograph.*

Kupe has an association with the rough seas and heavy surf on the west coast; sometimes he encounters these obstructing seas on his way here, and sometimes he raises them behind him while being pursued from Hawaiki by a man whose wives he has stolen. As other obstructions he introduces the prickly bush lawyer, the thorny matagouri and the stinging ongaonga, or tree nettle, which so often barred the way for travellers in the forest.

Because Kupe was a forerunner, a precursor, he returned to Hawaiki when his task was completed. Often it is said that he left from Hokianga, and that this region owes its name, literally 'Place of returning', to this event. When asked in Hawaiki if he would go back to Aotearoa, he replied, 'Will Kupe keep returning?' [E hokihoki Kupe?] This remark is quoted as a proverb by those who wish to indicate indirectly but firmly that they will never return to a place.

## *Kurahaupō*
### A waka claimed by many

In most of the traditions about waka that sailed from the homeland of Hawaiki to Aotearoa, the people who trace descent from them live in a single region. The *Kurahaupō*, however, is claimed by peoples in different parts of the country.

In the far north, the peoples of Te Aupōuri and Te Rārawa say that its captain was Pō, and that the vessel is now a reef at Kapo-wairua (Spirits Bay).

On the west coast, the Taranaki people living near that mountain believe that in Hawaiki the *Kurahoupō* (as they call it) was broken by enemy sorcery and that its owners, led by Te Mounga-roa and Turu, then accepted an invitation to sail to Aotearoa on *Mātaatua* instead. Te Mounga-roa brought with him the kura, the mystic sources of knowledge and power, which *Kurahoupō* had contained. The two men landed at Whāngārā then travelled to the west coast.

The historians of the *Aotea* acknowledge that the *Kurahaupō* was wrecked but claim that its captain was Ruatea, and that he and his crew then joined their vessel rather than the *Mātaatua*.

In the southern part of the North Island, in the coastal regions from the Whanganui River district to Hawke's Bay, a number of peoples claim descent from *Kurahaupō*. These peoples believe that the vessel was under the captaincy of Whātonga and that it landed at Te Māhia (the Māhia Peninsula). They include Te Āti Haunui-ā-Pāpārangi in the Whanganui region, Ngāti Apa

at Rangitīkei, some sections of Mūaupoko in the Horowhenua region, Rangitāne in the Manawatū, and Ngāti Kahungunu in Wairoa, Heretaunga (Hawke's Bay) and the Wairarapa.

## Lightning and thunder
### Messages from the sky

In every district there is a hill or mountain where lightning used to warn the local people of a coming event. These hills are known as rua kōhā or rua kanapu. When lightning appeared on such a hilltop, or thunder was heard among their 'rumbling mountains' [maunga haruru], the people sought to discover the meaning of the omen. Lightning that came straight down warned that they were in danger; if it pointed towards the territory of another people, they were the ones who would experience misfortune.

Lightning is spoken of as supernatural fire [ahi tipua]. Many different kinds were recognised. Among the best known in some regions were Hine-te-uira [Lightning woman], who is sheet lightning, and Tama-te-uira [Lightning man], forked lightning.

The mythical Tāwhaki is associated with lightning. When he reveals his powers in the sky, lightning flashes from his armpits.

Thunder in general is known as whaitiri, and was often associated with the mythical Whaitiri. But again there were numerous kinds of thunder, each with its own origin, name and significance.

It was believed that on an important occasion a tohunga of mana could rouse the sky [oho i te rangi] and make it speak in thunder. When an infant of high rank was being dedicated to his or her future life in the tohi ritual, the tohunga might end by striking two stones together and throwing them into the air. At once the voice of Hine-whaitiri [Thunder woman] would be heard, giving mana to the ceremony. Thunder from the east or north augured well for the child, but thunder from the west or south warned of trouble to come.

## Maero
### Wild people

These savage, hairy people had long bony fingers and speared their prey with their jagged nails. They ate their food raw, like fairies [patupaiarehe], but unlike fairies they were often solitary beings. While fairies could be dangerous, maero were especially feared. They kidnapped men and women and would fight to the death.

They inhabited the great forests in the rugged

interior of Taranaki and Whanganui, to which they had retreated when human beings arrived from Hawaiki and desecrated the tapu of their homes.

In the hills and mountains of the South Island, where they were numerous, they were known as māeroero. They speared fish, and were expert flute players. Sometimes people who were fishing or cutting flax would hear a voice warning that they had taken enough and must leave some for the māeroero.

Another name for these wild men is mohoao. In the Whanganui forests a man named Tukoio once met a mohoao with hair so long it trailed upon the ground. This mohoao was spearing birds with his fingernails. He attacked Tukoio and fought fiercely until his arms and legs had been severed. Then Tukoio cut off the shaggy head, but as he was walking back with his trophy the head began to speak: 'Children, I'm being carried off!'

Tukoio dropped the head and fled. Later he returned with others to the place where he had left the body, but it had disappeared. The pieces had joined together and gone back to the forest.

## Māhaki
### A Tūranga ancestor

The people known as Te Aitanga-a-Māhaki [The descendants of Māhaki] trace their origin to this early ancestor, who lived at Tūranga (the Gisborne district). His mother, Tauhei-kurī, was a daughter of Kahungunu and his father, Tama-taipū-noa, was from Ōpōtiki (and a half-brother of the famous Tū-tāmure).

Māhaki himself won fame as a warrior. In particular he avenged the death of his elder brother Tāwhiwhi, who had been killed by Ngāti Ira, a people living on Titirangi (Kaiti Hill). Māhaki broke the power of Ngāti Ira and expelled them from Tūranga.

It is generally agreed that two other ancestors named Māhaki must be distinguished from this man. One is the son of Hingānga-roa and Iranui. The other is Māhaki-rau, who is sometimes held responsible for the acquisition by Te Aitanga-a-Māhaki of a vast kahikatea forest.

## Māhaki-rau
### Origin of the kahikatea

When Pou, having visited Hawaiki, was flying back to Aotearoa seated upon a bird lent him by Tāne, he pulled some feathers from under the bird's wings and threw them into the ocean.

Pou's bird, carved in the early 1880s in the meeting house Te Mana o Tūranga at Manutūkē, south of Gisborne.

Under the water, on a rock known as Toka-pū-huruhuru (Ariel Reef), the feathers turned into a kahikatea tree, called Makauri. It is still down there now, bearing fruit.

Later a branch from the tree came ashore. Some say it was washed up on the beach, others that a man named Māhaki-rau had a tame shark, Ika-hoea, which used to bring him fish when he was out on the ocean. To test the story of the under-water tree, Māhaki told his shark to fetch a branch, the shark did so, and Māhaki planted it. The branch grew into a tree, then into a forest.

Kahikatea trees are tall and feathery, and because they come from the sea they grow now in swamps, surrounded by water. They were greatly valued for their fruit, although the fruit were small and the trees dangerous to climb. In Tūranga a poetic, honorific term for the kahikatea is 'Māhaki's treasure' [te kura a Māhaki].

## Māhanga
### Reckless disregard for property

Māhanga was a man who readily abandoned his assets. The stories about him differ, but are always associated with a proverb that was quoted when someone was behaving as he was thought to have done. Of such a person it would be said, 'He's a descendant of Māhanga, who abandoned food and waka' [Te uri o Māhanga whakarere kai, whakarere waka].

In the Waikato district, Ngāti Māhanga say that their founding ancestor Māhanga, son of

Tūheitia, was of a roving disposition. Several times he settled down with a people, acquired a wife and children, then abandoned them – along with his provisions – and moved on. He left the Waikato, lived in the far north, and died finally on the Moehau Range.

Waikato peoples quoted the proverb concerning Māhanga when travellers saw one of their number hurrying on ahead of the rest. The impatient person would be called 'a descendant of Māhanga, who abandoned food and waka'.

Among the people of Tūhoe, Māhanga was a son of the early ancestor Tāne-atua. After adzing a waka in a forest near Pūtauaki (Mount Edgecumbe), Māhanga assembled a large party of men to haul it to the water, but as the vessel was being lowered from a cliff the ropes broke and it shattered to pieces. Māhanga was so shamed at the disaster that he resolved to seek a new home. He would not even eat before he went. He set out at once, and never returned.

Other peoples again used the proverb without reference to any particular ancestor. Sometimes Māhanga was thought to be a very generous man who had given away provisions and waka.

## Mahina
### Discovered treasure

In the traditions of both *Tainui* and *Te Arawa* the crews of these waka, as they are about to make landfall at Whangaparāoa, see on the cliffs the scarlet flowers of pōhutukawa or rātā trees. One of the men believes them to be red plumes and thinks that in this new land such treasures are lying around everywhere. So he throws into the sea the red plumes he has brought from Hawaiki – and by the time he discovers his mistake, the real treasures have floated away.

The plumes are washed up on the beach and are found by a man named Mahina, who keeps them. When asked to give them back, he replies, 'This is Mahina's treasure that's been washed up' [Ko te kura pae a Mahina]. These words are now a saying, equivalent to 'Finders keepers.' If the previous owner wants his possession back, he will have to pay.

In the Tainui and Arawa traditions, the man who makes the mistake is usually Tai-ninihi or Tau-ninihi though in one story he is Hāpōpō.

In Te Whānau-ā-Apanui tradition the plumes are lost in different circumstances, when the Tauira-mai-tawhiti, captained by Pou, is wrecked off Tikirau (Cape Runaway). They drift ashore, are found by Māhia, and are placed in a burial cave.

## Māhu
### An ancestor in the Urewera

Māhu, a man of mysterious origins, lived in the early days in the Urewera Mountains with two wives and eight children. Their home was on the shore of Wairau-moana (now the western arm of Lake Waikaremoana).

Māhu owned a tapu spring, with a tūāhu [shrine] nearby. One day he sent six of his children for water, but they brought it from the tapu spring instead of the common one. In his rage he turned them into great round boulders, Te Whānau-a-Māhu [Māhu's Family], which lie by the shore.

He then told his daughter Haumapūhia to draw water from the common spring, but she refused to go. He attempted to drown her, but she turned into a taniwha. She struggled and tunnelled, forming hollows and channels, until she had created the broad waters of Lake Waikaremoana. Then she became a rock, a tipua still to be seen there.

Only the youngest of Māhu's children, a boy named Te Rangi-taupiri, survived in human form. His descendants belong to Ngāti Awa at Te Teko.

## Māhu and Taewa
### The acquisition of sorcery

Māhu lived long ago at Nukutaurua, on Te Māhia (Māhia Peninsula). He and his wife Te Ati-nuku had stored up a good supply of kūmara, and they were outraged to discover one day that thieves had taken them.

Māhu determined to destroy the thieves through sorcery, and to acquire the necessary knowledge he set out to visit Taewa-a-rangi, a powerful sorcerer who was married to his sister Mawake-roa. These two were living near Porangahau, far to the south.

When Māhu reached their home, Taewa taught him all the ritual chants that destroy human beings. Then Māhu did what was usual in these circumstances: he first directed his powers against a relative, his own flesh and blood. This relative was Kurapatiu, a daughter of Mawake-roa and Taewa, who at that moment was cutting flax in a lagoon. She was turned to stone and she stands there still.

When Taewa's people came to mourn her (some say to avenge her), Māhu turned them all to stone. They are still up on the Kohuipu ridge near Maungawharau. You can see the people, and the children carried on their backs.

On the way home Māhu destroyed enemies who confronted him. Then at Nukutaurua he

The largest surviving kauri tree is known because of its enormous size as
Tāne-mahuta – this being one of the names of Tāne, father of the forests.
Fifty-one metres high, it stands in the Waipoua Forest Sanctuary in Northland.

C2

*Above:* The greatly valued tōtara, son of Tāne and Mūmūwhango.

*Right:* In east coast belief, kahikatea trees first took root in the ocean (see page 141). Because of this they grow now in swampy places.

C3

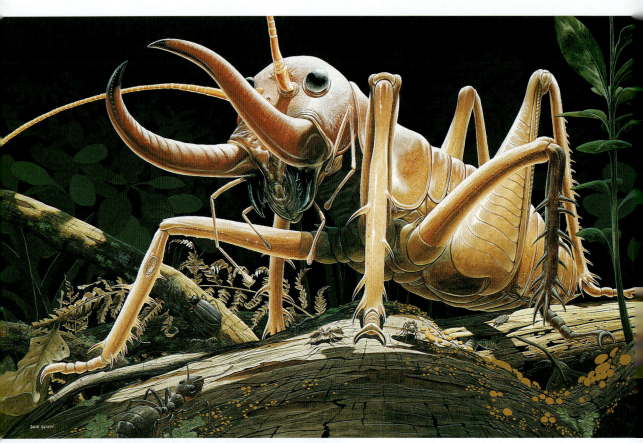

Among the inhabitants of the forests were wētā, which were proverbially ugly (*above:* the Mercury Island tusked wētā). Since Punga was the parent of ugly creatures, the giant wētā was known as Punga's wētā [te wētā a Punga].

Wētā are occasionally mentioned, along with geckos, as guardians of tapu places. These were special wētā; ordinary ones were not thought to possess such powers.

The little green or brown geckos, however, were always feared. They were especially dreaded when they assumed an open-mouthed defence posture (*left*) and made a sound thought to be laughter. This was a very bad omen (see pages 154–56).

slew the two men, Koko-uri and Koko-tea, who had stolen his kūmara.

In Ngāti Kahungunu tradition, Māhu was held responsible for the acquisition of sorcery and all that happened as a consequence. Taewa-a-rangi is sometimes known as Taewha.

## Māhuhu
### Ancestral waka of Ngāti Whātua

Descent from *Māhuhu*, which arrived from the homeland of Hawaiki, is claimed especially by the people of Ngāti Whātua in the Kaipara and Tāmaki regions, although peoples further north trace their origins to this waka as well.

When the ship landed by the Kaipara Heads, her crew settled nearby at a place called Tāporapora. There they established a house of learning [whare wānanga] where they taught ritual chants and history. Many generations later the sea carried away this stretch of land and overwhelmed their sacred house.

The captain of the *Māhuhu*, a man named Rongomai, was drowned when fishing out at sea, and his body was eaten by the trevally. For this reason the fish became tapu and was never eaten by his descendants.

## Mahuika
### Origin of fire

The trickster Māui acquired or invented many things necessary for human existence. Among them was fire, which he took from his grandmother (some say grandfather) Mahuika. Māui's family had not known how to kindle fire and had been given it as they needed it by Mahuika. But Māui tricked his grandmother into parting with all her fire, and from this time humans were in control of it.

This old woman Mahuika was all fire: her body, arms, legs, head and hair were all fire. She offered Māui her little finger, and he marvelled at the fire inside.

He went off, but when he came to a stream he put out the fire, then went back and told Mahuika he had fallen in the water. She gave him another finger, and he did the same thing again. It went on like this until all her fingers were gone, and all but one of her toes.

She realised she had been tricked and flew into a rage: 'You must be this Māui I've heard about. I'll give you fire soon enough!'

She pulled out the last of her toes and flung it on the ground, and the trees blazed up. Māui ran off, but wherever he went, fire was in front of

him. He leapt into the water, but the water was boiling. He turned into a pigeon and flew right up, but nearly died in the flames and smoke. In desperation he called to his brothers in the world above (or some say to Tāwhirimātea and Whaitiri).

The brothers sent light rain, but that was no use. Heavy rain came, and still the fire did not go out. Then torrents of rain poured down, and Mahuika's fire was overcome at last.

*Māui with the fire he took from Mahuika's fingers. A drawing by Theo Schoon.*

The old woman suffered terribly in the flood. She gathered up the remnants of her fire and placed them for protection in certain trees, especially the kaikōmako, and they are still there now. That is why fire can be kindled from fireploughs of kaikōmako wood. With such an instrument a skilled operator can produce a blazing fire in a few minutes.

Poets, orators, and others as well spoke of Mahuika's fire and Mahuika's spark. When fire was needed, someone might be told, 'Go and get Mahuika's fingers.'

## Māhunui
### The South Island

In the south they say that when Māui fished up Te Ika a Māui (the North Island), his waka the *Māhunui* became the South Island – which is consequently the older of the two. Māhunui is therefore a poetic, classical name for the South Island. Another name is Te Waka-a-Māui [Māui's waka].

While hauling up his great fish, Māui braced himself with his foot on a thwart that became the Kaikōura Ranges, and these are known accordingly as Te Taumanu-o-te-waka-a-Māui [The thwart of Māui's waka]. Rakiura (Stewart Island) is Te Puka-o-te-waka-a-Māui [The anchor of Māui's waka].

## Māhutonga
### The Southern Cross

This group of stars is always moving around the southern sky. Ice, snow and frost live upon its summit, along with Pārāwera-nui, the south wind. A tohunga wishing to make the south wind blow would 'pull out the plug of Māhutonga so that great Pārāwera could come forth'.

Its name is sometimes employed as a poetic expression for the cold south.

## Māia
### Origin of the gourd

Gourds were used as containers, and the immature fruit were a favourite vegetable. On the east coast of the North Island their origin was often attributed to Māia, who brought them from Hawaiki and initiated the rituals and practices associated with their cultivation.

At Waiapu, the tohunga Pita Kāpiti taught that Māia came to Aotearoa to escape from the great Uenuku, whom he had insulted. The trouble began when Uenuku, building a house, ordered

Māia to carry the food each day to the workmen. Perhaps annoyed at being assigned this humble task, Māia ate the best food before giving the rest to the workmen. Uenuku soon heard of this.

Uenuku was in fact Māia's brother-in-law, being married to his sister Te Rangatoro. She now warned Māia that he must leave at once or he would be killed. She advised him to travel across the ocean inside a gourd with special powers, known as Te Ika-roa-a-Rauru [Rauru's long fish], and she gave him some gourd seeds and told him how to care for them. So Māia entered Te Ika-roa-a-Rauru, the thunder resounded, and he went bobbing along on the crests of the waves. A potent chant ensured his safe passage.

He came ashore at Tūranga (the Gisborne district), planted his seeds and looked after them carefully.

In Tūranga itself, some say Māia came on a raft of gourds and others that he was the captain of an ordinary waka. According to this tradition, he was a younger brother of men who had sailed previously on the *Horouta* and the *Tākitimu*. After being delayed by a quarrel with Uenuku, he set out on a ship named *Te Ika-roa-a-Rauru* and made landfall at Tawararo (near the present Cook monument). He brought the seeds of the gourd and knowledge of its cultivation. Among his descendants were Ngā Ariki, an ancient people now partially merged into others in the region.

## Makawe
### A guardian god

The village of Ōhinemutu, on the southern shore of Lake Rotorua, belongs to Ngāti Whakaue, one of the peoples of Te Arawa. On the hill above, known as Pukeroa, there stood the tūāhu of Makawe, who for many generations was the main atua of Ngāti Whakaue. This shrine was located at the place where a high-ranking woman ancestor, Ngāhuahua, had given birth to the god in a small house.

While Makawe is best known as an atua whose guidance was sought in times of war, he was probably consulted for many reasons. An affirm-

Right: *A Tūranga (Gisborne) belief is that Māia captained the waka* Te Ika-roa-a-Rauru [Rauru's long fish] *during its voyage from Hawaiki. This voyage was recalled in 1990 when the Māori people of Tūranga built a vessel of this name as one of twenty-two waka, constructed by peoples in different parts of the country, which took part in sesquicentennial celebrations held at Waitangi. Afterwards* Te Ika-roa-a-Rauru *returned to Te Poho o Rāwiri Marae in Tūranga for the homecoming ceremony.*

ative response took the form of a rainbow that arched up, then came to earth at Ōkoumapihi, a tūāhu further along the shore of the lake.

A Catholic church built in about 1844 was located, no doubt deliberately, very close to this shrine. There is now a commemorative rock within a special enclosure.

## *Māmari*
### A northern waka

This vessel sailed from the homeland of Hawaiki to the Hokianga Harbour. Some say it was captained by Nuku-tawhiti, and that his brother-in-law Rūānui accompanied him. Others believe that Rūānui captained the *Māmari* while Nuku-tawhiti came on a different vessel.

Certain large rocks in the Hokianga region are objects and creatures that arrived on *Māmari* then turned to stone. Among them are the vessel's petrified bailer, Nuku-tawhiti's dog, and food baskets used at a feast given by Nuku-tawhiti. As well, on a rocky face north of the Hokianga Heads the crew can be seen pulling in a fishing net. The ship itself is said to lie keel upwards, turned to stone, at the entrance to the Waimā River.

People living further south, however, maintain that *Māmari* later sailed down the west coast and was wrecked near the beach at Riripo, just beyond the Maunganui Bluff. It lies there now, turned into a reef, at Ōmāmari [The place of *Māmari*].

## Mana
### Inherent power

This word mana can usually be defined, in its traditional use, as 'authority, influence, prestige, power, psychic force'. Traditionally, men and women who possessed mana had received it from their ancestors, both recent ancestors and early ones. It was not something that tūtūā [low-born people] could possess.

The mana of a rangatira could, however, increase or be lost, depending upon the possessor's actions. If the person failed to observe the rules of tapu required by their position, this would anger their atua and so endanger their mana. Incompetence as a leader would weaken it, and being

taken prisoner by enemies (even if later released) would seriously affect it. An insult or breach of etiquette, anything that could be understood as 'treading down' his mana [takahi mana], would endanger his position, so could not be countenanced. On the other hand successful leadership, a proper self-respect, appropriate hospitality, good fortune, will power, and skill in important undertakings would increase a person's mana.

The potent chants recited by tohunga possessed much mana, yet a crucial factor in their success was the mana possessed by the tohunga who employed them. Similarly a contest between two tohunga, as happened with sorcery, was essentially a contest of mana.

A people collectively possessed mana, and again this could be lost, in battle or in other ways.

Tapu mountains, those where lightning flashed as a sign to the people and where the bones of the dead lie buried, also possess mana [he maunga whai mana]. Sacred landmarks known as tipua – rocks or trees with special powers – possess mana. Any resource or important article, in fact, possessed its own mana.

An object as much as a person might lose its mana. Asked about the food offering traditionally made to Whiro after a battle, a warrior who had been involved in this explained that while Whiro, being a god, could not actually consume food, he absorbed the mana (the virtue or essence) of the food that had been presented to him.

In many circumstances, mana had to be protected by being entrusted to a guardian. A powerful rangatira might possess (and be responsible for) the mana of his people, and the mana of their land as well; his mana would ensure the safety of these other mana. (This was very much a two-way relationship, since the status, or mana, of such a leader depended upon his having been entrusted with this role.)

Individuals might be responsible in this way for a single resource. In Lake Rotorua in the 1860s, when kōaro (a species of *Galaxias*) were plentiful at certain times, a high-ranking woman of Ngāti Rangiwewehi, Makuini, held the mana of the kōaro fishing. It was she who told her people the proper time for them to be taken (this depended upon the state of the moon), and who gave her permission for this to be done.

As well as human guardians of mana, there were supernatural ones. The mana of a kūmara plantation might be ritually conveyed to Rongo (who might be present in a stone figure termed a mauri). Rongo would then assume responsibility for the crop by transferring his own mana to the field. In effect, these two mana became one.

All mauri, in fact, worked this way. The mana of a resource or some other entity, even that of an entire people, would be transferred to them, and this mana would then be protected by (because identified with) the mana of the mauri. The mana of the village of Ōhinemutu was formerly centred upon a mauri, a red pointed stone about a metre in height, which stood by the shore (near the site of the present church). This tapu stone was spoken of both as the mauri of Ōhinemutu and as its mana. It was placed there by the early ancestor Ihenga, and down through the generations it was an object of veneration to which visitors made offerings.

Guardians of mana could take many forms. The taniwha Horo-matangi was regarded by some people as the mana, or the custodian of the mana, of Lake Taupō. The adze Te Awhiorangi, an ancient heirloom brought from Hawaiki, was the mana of all the adzes in the world, their spiritual prototype. In the far north, animal guardians were often spoken of as mana.

# Manaia
## An enemy three times defeated

The powerful tohunga Ngātoro-i-rangi, who came from Hawaiki on *Te Arawa*, was residing peacefully at Maketū when he discovered that his brother-in-law Manaia was attempting to destroy him. At this time Manaia was living back in Hawaiki with Ngātoro's sister Kuiwai. One day she sent five women across the water to inform Ngatoro that Manaia was every morning asking his gods to kill him.

Ngātoro and his fellow tohunga performed rituals to avert this evil, then searched for a tōtara tree to serve as a vessel. The tree they found was dug from the ground rather than felled in the usual manner, so became known as *Tōtara-i-karia* [Tōtara that was dug up]. Ngātoro and a company of seven-score warriors put to sea on this vessel, and in seven days reached Hawaiki.

Knowing that Manaia and his tohunga would proceed at dawn to their tūāhu, Ngātoro decided that his men would pretend to have been overcome by their sorcery. Under cover of darkness they made their way to the tūāhu, where earth ovens lay ready for their bodies – such was the confidence of Manaia's tohunga that their atua would deliver Ngātoro and his men to them. Ngātoro instructed his warriors to hit themselves on the nose, smear blood over their bodies and lie stiff as corpses inside the ovens.

Next morning the tohunga shouted with delight when they saw the bloodied bodies stretched out in the ovens, apparently brought by their gods. The people in the pā heard the commotion and came running. Seeing the bodies, each claimed a shoulder or thigh for the feast that would follow.

As Manaia's tohunga came forward, Ngātoro's tohunga rushed from their place of concealment and slew their enemies beside their own tūāhu. And the warriors rose from the ovens and fought Manaia's men, and all were killed, except Manaia himself. This great victory became known as Ihu-motomotokia [Thumped noses].

Afterwards Ngātoro-i-rangi and his party returned to their vessel, not knowing that Manaia had fled to other sections of his people and was already raising an army to avenge the defeat. This army was in pursuit as they reached the ship, and before setting sail they had to fight and win another battle. This event became known as Tara-i-whenua-kura. Again Manaia survived.

Having gained revenge, Ngātoro-i-rangi and his men returned to Aotearoa. Afterwards Ngātoro and his old wife went off to Mōtītī Island, near Tauranga. They lived on their own there, growing their kūmara.

And there one evening Manaia appeared again, out on the water with a great fleet of ships. When he shouted his challenge, Ngātoro replied that it was too dark to fight and that he should anchor his vessels and they would fight next day. Manaia agreed to this.

Meanwhile Ngātoro was reciting chants at his tūāhu. Eventually he returned to their house and continued his chants while his wife, by the window, listened to the taunting songs coming across the water. Manaia and his men were amusing themselves with games and songs, anticipating a victory next day. They did not know that they would be killed. They thought that Ngātoro and his wife, being on their own, would be the ones to die.

Then Ngātoro shed his garments and called upon Tāwhirimātea to destroy Manaia's multitudes, and Tāwhirimātea sent the rain, wind, thunder and lightning against that company as they lay asleep and snoring. When Ngātoro and his wife heard the roaring and the great waves out on the ocean, they fastened their house securely and lay down. There were shrieks and groans, then silence. The wind stopped and there was only the sound of the waves on the shore.

When the old woman went out next morning she found the bodies lying on the beach. This defeat became known as Maikuku-tea [Whitened fingernails] because all that were left were bones and fingernails. None of that great company

*In one version of the myth, the five women who came from Hawaiki to warn Ngatoro-i-rangi of Manaia's enmity took an inland route. While they were crossing the Kaingaroa Plains, Haungaroa was teased by two of her companions and became so angry that she turned them into cabbage trees. These are still there. When travellers try to approach, they keep moving ahead. A drawing by Russell Clark.*

survived. Manaia, among the dead, was recognised by a tattoo on part of his hand.

These three battles, especially Ihu-moto-motokia and Maikuku-tea, set precedents for overwhelming defeats in later times. They were recalled by orators and poets when prophesying disaster for enemies or lamenting and dignifying their own peoples' defeats.

## Manaia
### A family turned to rocks

The bold peak of Mount Manaia, part of the Whāngārei Heads, is sometimes said to have been one of a group of hills that arrived one night from their home across the western ocean. Manaia, being the largest and strongest, travelled the furthest before he was transfixed by the rays of the rising sun. Smaller peaks such as Tokatoka and Maungaraho remained far behind in the west.

Another belief is that Manaia is a rangatira of this name who arrived from Hawaiki with his family in the early times, then turned to stone. He and his wife, his daughters, his slave and his dog are now jagged rocks on the skyline.

According to the traditions of Ngāti Wai, who belong to this district and other places on the eastern shore, Manaia made his journey from Hawaiki on the *Māhuhu-ki-te-rangi*. After living in the area for a number of years he began building a causeway across the harbour mouth. Because this task was tapu he warned his people not to approach, but that night his daughter climbed on to the causeway and his work was spoilt. So he killed his daughter and threw her into the water, where she can still be seen, turned to stone and with seaweed hair. The unfinished causeway is there as well.

Later, Manaia had reason to suspect his wife of adultery with his slave, Paeko. There was a contest of powers, with both these men reciting ritual chants, and the outcome was that all those people turned to stone. They are still up there on the hill.

Other descendants of Manaia became known as Ngāti Manaia. The people of Ngāti Wai trace descent from them.

## Mangamangai-atua
### Singing spirits

Some said that every utterance of these atua, their speech, laughter and shouting, took the form of ritual chants, ancient ones that cannot now be understood. Others heard the Mangamangai-atua singing songs that were perfectly intelligible. The quivering of the air on hot summer days was caused by the Mangamangai-atua as they danced in the sky, singing this song:

> Tirohia atu te rangi ka kapo mai.
> Ka kōhikohiko, ē, ka kapokapo –
> Ka kapo, ka kapo,
> Ka hiko mai i te pae ki te rangi, auē.

> Look over at the sky, it's shining there,
> It's flashing and shining,
> It shines, shines,
> Flashing on the horizon, *auē*.

## Mangapuera
### A taniwha on the Whanganui

Some twenty generations ago this taniwha arrived in the Whanganui region, no-one knows from where, and made his lair in a cave by the Ahuahu Stream, a tributary of the Whanganui. He was four metres in length and two metres tall,

*Two oystercatchers were placed on Whanga-o-keno,
and their offspring are there still.*

with a scaly skin, a head like a featherless bird's head, shark teeth, bat wings, forelegs with claws, hindquarters with webbed feet, and a row of spines from head to tail.

Unlike many taniwha Mangapuera had no association with the local people, and he preyed upon men and women he found in the forest. Soon they fled the region and their pā lay deserted. Then Tarawhiti, a man from Waitōtara, came to visit his wife, expecting to find her at Ahuahu. He knew nothing about the taniwha. As he walked along the track he felt thirsty and went down to drink at a place near Mangapuera's cave. On the way back he heard the monster crashing towards him.

He ran, but the taniwha gained on him, so he climbed a miro tree and prepared to defend himself with his adze. As the taniwha reached up, he chopped off one of his forelegs. The other foreleg came up, and he chopped that off as well. The infuriated creature lashed out with his tail, sweeping both tree and man to the ground, but he misjudged his strength and brought away the whole hillside. Caught in this landslide, the wounded taniwha moved slowly to extricate himself. Tarawhiti got out more quickly and dealt him a final blow.

Mangapuera's cave can still be seen near Parikino.

Left: *In their rugged forested lands, communities on the Whanganui River retained much of their traditional way of life until the early twentieth century. People of Parikino in the porch of Wharewhiti in 1885.*

## Mangarara
### An ancestral waka of Ngāti Porou

Sailing westward from Hawaiki, *Mangarara* came first to Whanga-o-keno (East Island), a small island by East Cape. The rangatira on board were Wheke-toro, Te Wai-o-potango, Rau-ariki-ao and Tarawhata.

The waka brought a cargo of reptiles (tuatara and different kinds of geckos), centipedes, stick insects and wētā, and two kinds of birds, pipits and oystercatchers. All these were liberated by Wheke-toro. They spread over the island, and that is why they are there now.

To protect his pets, Wheke-toro lit a ritual fire and made the island tapu. Despite the precipitous cliffs there was one place where access was possible, so he threw a stone from his fire and created a landslide that made the island safe from intruders. He threw another stone on to the rocky beach, and a spring burst up. He made a home for Tuakeke, the reptiles' rangatira, in a bundle of fern, then he left the oystercatchers and pipits in charge of the island and with his companions (among them, some reptiles) he set out for the mainland.

But on the way the ship was wrecked. One of the crew, Tarawhata, had a dog with extraordinary powers, named Mohorangi, and as the vessel neared the shore this man and his dog were thrown overboard. The dog kicked with such force that the waves rose up and the vessel was overturned. It came ashore at Pari-whero [Red cliff], where it can still be seen, turned to stone.

The humans and the reptiles tried in vain to haul up their ship, and when day came they left it there. The reptiles ran under overhanging banks, and the men settled down in the East Cape region. Their Ngāti Porou descendants are still there now.

Much later, a man named Kaiawa was living in Tūranga (the Gisborne district). He heard how abundant the kahawai were in the river mouths at Wharekāhika (Hicks Bay), and he made the journey north to see this sight. On the way he visited Ōpure, near Whanga-o-keno, where the rangatira was Tangaroa-hau.

Wanting him as a son-in-law, Tangaroa-hau told him that the fish were just as plentiful in this region. As proof he pointed to Whanga-o-keno, without, however, mentioning that the island was still tapu and could not be fished. So Kaiawa settled down there and married Tangaroa-hau's daughter Whatumori. In time they had two daughters.

After some years, Kaiawa decided to remove the tapu from the island. The local people encouraged him in this dangerous task and he set out with his elder daughter, Pōnuiahine, whose assistance would be required in kindling the ritual fire.

At Whanga-o-keno they saw Tarawhata's dog, Mohorangi, which now took the form of a cliff. And they had made a mistake, because Pōnuiahine's eyes should have been shaded with a wreath of leaves to avoid the dog's intensely tapu gaze. As it was, the dog fixed his eyes upon her.

Kaiawa made an offering of seaweed to the male pipit in charge of the island, then with his daughter he kindled a tapu 'woman's fire' [ahi ruahine]. When this was done he put his daughter to sleep while he went to destroy Wheketoro's tapu. He lighted fires at five tapu sites, and he overcame the tapu. He smothered his fire, making a great smoke, and with this he tamed the pipits, Tuhaka and Tongawhiti. The two oystercatchers,

*Tapu fire for ritual use had to be specially kindled by a man and a woman.*
*Paitini Wī Tapeka of Tūhoe and his wife demonstrate this ritual.*

however, Wehiwehi and Hine-ki-tōrea, flew out to sea and could not be tamed. Their offspring have wild and shy of human beings.

When Kaiawa returned to the place where he had left Pōnuiahine sleeping, she was nowhere to be seen. Then he looked out to sea and saw her there, turned into a rock by Mohorangi. All Kaiawa could do was to weep.

So although he had removed the tapu, Kaiawa had paid a price. As a female, Pōnuiahine possessed the powers necessary for the ritual creation of fire and the removal of tapu, but she could not withstand the gaze of Mohorangi.

Because of her fate, women never visited the island. Men did go from this time on, but if they were strangers they shaded their eyes.

## Mango-huruhuru
### Sand brought from Hawaiki

Long ago a tohunga named Mango-huruhuru, who lived on the east coast of Te Wai Pounamu (the South Island), was visited by Pōtiki-roa, who had come from Taranaki seeking greenstone. Pōtiki-roa fell in love with one of the tohunga's daughters, Puna-te-rito, and he married her and for some years lived with her people. Then he grew homesick and persuaded his father-in-law to accompany him to Taranaki. They constructed a waka and safely crossed the waters of Raukawa (Cook Strait).

At Waitaha (just south of Cape Egmont) the party were welcomed by Pōtiki-roa's relatives. Mango-huruhuru and his people built a large house on low land near the sea, while Pōtiki-roa lived with his wife on higher ground further inland.

The stony shore made it difficult to land their waka, and Mango-huruhuru decided to use his powers to solve this problem. Soon after sunset the old tohunga climbed to the ridgepole of his house, faced out to sea, and recited a long chant asking Papa the earth and Tangaroa in the ocean to send sand from the homeland of Hawaiki.

A dark cloud appeared on the horizon and rapidly advanced; it was a great storm bringing sand. By the end of the chant it had reached the people assembled on the shore. Soon they were buried, then the house as well, with Mango-huruhuru on the roof, and all the countryside round about. Mango-huruhuru's young daughter Heihana was turned to stone, and stands there now as proof of this story.

Pōtiki-roa and Puna-te-rito, in their house further inland, were the only survivors. The stone foundations of their house can be seen to this day.

## Maniapoto
### Founder of Ngāti Maniapoto

A rangatira generally had a principal wife and several secondary wives. Usually he married his principal wife first, so that her children, as well as being high-born, would have the further advantage of primogeniture. This simplified questions of succession.

But Rereahu, eldest son of Raukawa, first took a wife, Rangianewa, who was not of high rank. Only many years later, when her children had grown up, did he marry another woman, the high-born Hine-au-pounamu. With her he had Maniapoto, then seven other children.

When Rereahu was on his death-bed he had to decide which son would inherit his mana. The choice lay between Te Ihingārangi, eldest son of his first wife, and Maniapoto. Although Te Ihingārangi was much older, Rereahu chose Maniapoto because of his high rank and ability. Te Ihingārangi, who was standing waiting, was sent off on an errand, and Rereahu summoned Maniapoto and bestowed his mana upon him. This was done ritually; Rereahu's tapu head, anointed with red ochre, was bitten by Maniapoto, who thereby absorbed his father's mana.

When Te Ihingārangi returned and saw the red ochre on Maniapoto's face, he knew he had come too late. Afterwards there was trouble between the brothers. In the end Maniapoto fought the jealous Te Ihingārangi, conquered him and spared his life.

Maniapoto's descendants include the people of Ngāti Maniapoto, who belong to the Waipā Valley and the region south to the Mokau River.

## Marakihau
### Carved figures of taniwha

In some parts of the country, especially in the southern Bay of Plenty and the Urewera, taniwha are depicted in meeting-houses as marakihau, creatures with fishlike bodies below the waist and heads rather like those of humans but with long hollow tongues. They are said to use these tongues to suck down fish, and sometimes people and waka.

Yet taniwha in the ocean were usually said to take the form of whales, or sometimes sharks. There are few, if any, recorded stories concerning taniwha with hollow tongues. It seems that the word marakihau generally refers to carvings depicting taniwha rather than to the creatures themselves.

The concept must be ancient in its origins,

*A marakihau, with fish, alongside the early ancestor Toi in the porch of the meeting house Te Tokanga-nui-a-Noho, opened at Te Kūiti in 1873.*

because the word exists elsewhere in Polynesia. In the Tuamotuan atolls a marakihau is 'a mythological sea creature with a human form above the navel, but a tail like a fish below it'.

## Mārere-o-tonga
### A source of knowledge

In some traditions this man and his companion, Takataka-pūtea, are a source of religious knowledge. They are, for instance, the two tohunga on the *Nukutere* during its voyage from Hawaiki.

Tūhoe people associate Mārere-o-tonga and Takataka-pūtea with knowledge of a different kind, regarding them as the originators of games and amusements such as dancing, playing musical instruments, string games and storytelling.

In some Arawa traditions they are twin sons of Rangi the sky and Papa the earth.

As a source of religious teachings, Mārere-o-tonga is sometimes associated not with Takataka-pūtea but with Timu-whakairia. Sometimes he is a star that 'leads,' or precedes, the star Atutahi (Canopus).

## Maru
### A fierce god

In the Rotorua region, Maru was a powerful atua whose protection was sought in times of war. His full name was Maru-te-whare-aitu [Maru the house of disaster]. There were tūāhu dedicated to him in different settlements, each with an intensely tapu symbol inhabited by the god.

At Te Whetengu, for instance, a recess cut in the side of a cliff was known as the storehouse [pātaka] of Maru. His sacred symbol, a lock of human hair, lay in this shrine in a lidded box [waka] of tōtara wood which was wrapped in rimu bark and fastened with vines. Here the tohunga came to ask Maru's assistance when war was imminent, and again when warriors were about to set out. After a victory, Maru was rewarded with enemy flesh. Often the heart of the first man slain in battle became his food.

On the west coast from Whanganui to northern Taranaki, Maru had other roles as well. At Whanganui he was described as the greatest of the gods. If a person had broken tapu and was about to die as a consequence, Maru might relent and save him if the appropriate chant was recited. Almost certainly he would be merciful if this ritual was followed by the sacrifice of a dog and the presentation of its cooked head.

Maru was sometimes kind, sometimes evil. He was a hungry god, always crying for food. If he was given the heads of all the fish people caught, and plenty of other food and property, and if he was put in charge of the kūmara plantations and house-building, he would see that things went well. If he was neglected, there would be serious trouble.

A west coast myth tells of a large sacred building called Te Whare Kura [The crimson house] which stood at Hawaiki. Many persons occupied the interior of this house. Some say there were two opposed groups, one led by the great Uenuku and the other by Maru (whose associates, in this account, include the evil Whiro and a group of reptile gods). Others deny there were factions, saying that Te Whare Kura was built so that those inside could make offerings to Maru.

# Maruiwi

## A disastrous journey

When the Maruiwi people were forced to leave their homes at Waimana, inland from Ōhiwa in the southern Bay of Plenty, they decided to migrate to Heretaunga (Hawke's Bay), making their way through the Taupō region. While on this journey, travelling secretly by night through the rugged country north of Heretaunga, their party came to a great chasm. They did not see it in the darkness and they fell in one by one, first the leaders then those behind. Only seven survivors reached Heretaunga.

Orators and poets recall this occurrence when speaking of any people who have been destroyed, or may be in the future. Proverbial expressions are quoted, such as 'Maruiwi's descent to the underworld' [Te heke o Maruiwi ki te pō]. One poet identifies her people's deaths with this event:

E tama ē, kāore he uri tāngata i te ao nei,
Tēnā ka riro atu i te waro i heke ai a Maruiwi.

My child, there are no sons of men left in this world,
They are taken by the chasm where Maruiwi went down.

On such occasions the disaster that befell Maruiwi provided a precedent which, being so well known, gave added force to the speaker's message. The fate of Maruiwi became the fate of all who could be likened to them.

It is not clear whether there really were a people named Maruiwi who met disaster, or whether their story began as myth and became localised in the southern Bay of Plenty. Some consider Maruiwi to be the leader of the party of travellers rather than their collective name.

# Maru-tūahu

## Founder of Ngāti Maru

Maru-tūahu's father was Hotunui, an early ancestor sometimes believed to have come on the *Tainui* but often said to be a son of Uenuku-tuwhatu. While living at Kāwhia, Hotunui was accused of the theft of some kūmara. He felt so insulted at this that he abandoned his home and his wife Mihi-rāwhiti, who was pregnant at the time. He crossed the ranges to the Hauraki Gulf and finally settled at Whakatīwai among the people of Ngāti Pou. He married Waitapu, sister of a rangatira named Te Whatu, and they presently had a son, Pāka.

Meanwhile Mihi-rāwhiti, back at Kāwhia, also had a son. Following Hotunui's instructions, she called the boy Maru-tūahu. When Maru grew up, he questioned his mother about his father, then set out with a servant to find him. The two men passed through the mountains, taking a long bird-spear to catch themselves food. After travelling for a month they reached the forests near Hotunui's home.

Now while Maru was up in a tree spearing tūī, and his servant was sitting on the ground below, it happened that the two daughters of Te Whatu approached them. The younger sister was beautiful and the elder sister was ugly. These women saw the servant and each claimed him as their slave, but the younger sister ran faster and she got him. Then a screeching tūī fell from the tree and the younger sister looked up, saw Maru and claimed him as her husband. So then the two girls argued about him, because he was a fine-looking man.

The girls went on ahead to the village; Maru adorned himself with plumes and fine garments, then followed. At the village he was greeted by his father Hotunui. And late that night Te Whatu's younger daughter went to Maru and they slept together. When the elder sister found out, it was too late.

So Maru-tūahu married Te Whatu's younger daughter and they became the founding ancestors of Ngāti Maru. They had three famous sons: Tamatepō, whose descendants became the people

*Originally the property of Hotunui, and named Maru-tūahu, this mauri guards the mana of the descendants of Maru-tūahu.*

of Ngāti Rongou; Tamaterā, whose descendants became Ngāti Tamaterā, and Whanaunga, who founded Ngāti Whanaunga.

Maru and Hotunui went on living among Ngāti Pou, but there was trouble and it led to fighting. Hotunui was insulted by these people, and told Maru what had happened. When his servant had gone to get him a fish from the catch of some newly returned fishermen, their leader refused to give him one. Instead he cursed Hotunui.

Maru planned his revenge. He displayed no anger, but announced the construction of a large

*An early photograph of figures in the porch of Hotunui, a large meeting house built and carved in 1878 under the supervision of Wepiha Apanui, a rangatira of Ngāti Awa, and presented by Wepiha to his sister Mereana and her husband Hoterini Taipari of Ngāti Maru on the occasion of their marriage. The house stood for many years at Pārāwai near Thames. It is now in the Auckland Museum Te Papa Whakahiku.*

seine net; each section of the people would make the part assigned to them, then all would meet to join up the parts. After months of work the time came for their meeting.

The visitors saw heaps of food on display, and rejoiced at the thought of the feast that would follow; they did not know that these heaps had rubbish inside. Then when the parts of the net had been joined together and it was ready for its first, ceremonial use, Maru's seven-score men stood alongside with hidden weapons. They lifted the net, threw it over the visitors, then killed them all.

So Maru-tūahu took possession of that place. His descendants continued to live there.

## Mataaho
### The overturning of the earth

A giant, Mataaho, is often held responsible, along with Rūaumoko, for earthquakes and volcanic

*Te Puhi-o-Mātaatua [The plume of Mātaatua], a small house that stood on Te Pipi Marae near Ruatāhuna, celebrated the Mātaatua ancestry of the people of Tūhoe. A photograph taken in 1898.*

activity. Some authorities trace the origin of these disturbances to a time long ago when Mataaho turned his mother Papa, the earth, face downwards so that she would no longer be made unhappy by the sight of Rangi the sky, from whom she was separated. Others claim that Mataaho did this at the command of the high god Io, to protect Papa from the sight of the strife between her sons Whiro and Tāne. Either way, the expression 'Mataaho's overturning' [te hurihanga a Mataaho] is taken as referring to this early event.

Elsewhere the expression is rather different. In the saying 'the overwhelming of Mataaho' [te hurihanga i Mataaho], Mataaho is not the person who performs the action but a country that long ago was destroyed by a flood. This happened when the hero Tāwhaki, to revenge himself on brothers-in-law who had tried to kill him, caused a great deluge that overwhelmed the land.

In a related tradition, a giant named Mataao is held responsible for the mountainous nature of the country. He became very angry and jumped all over the land, making valleys and hills, because another man, Rua, had introduced volcanoes to the Tāmaki (Auckland) district. What happened was that Rua had arrived from Hawaiki in pursuit of his wife, and while searching in the interior he had become very cold. So he called upon his god to bring fire from Hawaiki, and the god brought the fire in the form of burning mountains.

Similar stories are told about an ancestor named Mataoho.

## Mātaatua
### Landfall at Whakatāne

Among the leading men who sailed from Hawaiki on the *Mātaatua* were the captain Tōroa, his father Hikaroa, and his brothers Puhi and Tāneatua. The women included Tōroa's sister Muriwai and his daughter Wairaka. Tōroa's mother Wairakewa came by magical means of her own.

When the waka landed at Whakatāne, only its stern was brought up on the shore. Next morning the waves were washing over the vessel, and Wairaka called a warning. But the men were intent upon exploring their new land and they took no notice. Wairaka had to secure the waka herself, having first remarked, 'Oh, I must make myself a man!' [Ē, kia whakatāne ake au i ahau!] This, it is said, is how Whakatāne gained its name.

Still preoccupied with exploration, Tōroa forgot to perform the ritual to mark their safe arrival. Muriwai had to do this herself, though it was the wrong thing for a woman to do. Back in Hawaiki, their mother Wairakewa sensed that something was amiss and set out for Whakatāne. She made the voyage seated on the trunk of a mānuka tree, and on her arrival she planted the tree on a mound on the foreshore. It became a mauri of the Mātaatua peoples, a potent force

109

referred to in songs and healing rituals.

Tōroa and many of his family remained at Whakatāne, but one of his brothers, Puhi, sailed north with others and became an important ancestor in the far north. Meanwhile another brother, Tāne-atua, set out to explore the hinterland with his wife Hine-mataroa. Only the youngest of their children were human. The others are rivers, rocks, ponds and other features in the landscape.

The peoples who trace descent to *Mātaatua* include Ngāti Awa, Te Whakatōhea and Tūhoe in the southern Bay of Plenty and the interior, Ngāi Te Rangi in Tauranga, and Ngā Puhi and Te Rārawa in the far north. Some say it was Muriwai, not Wairaka, who saved the vessel and spoke the words that gave Whakatāne its name.

## Matakauri
### A giant-killer

Lake Wakatipu in the South Island had its origin in the death of a giant, Matau. When this monster carried off a girl named Manata, the daughter of a rangatira, the broken-hearted father promised her in marriage to any man who could rescue her.

A brave warrior named Matakauri determined to do so. He waited for a hot north-west wind, knowing that Matau would be asleep at this time, then he armed himself and set out. Towards evening he found Manata. She told him, sobbing bitterly, that her captor had tied her to him with a long cord which could not be cut, because it was plaited from the hide of one of his ferocious two-headed dogs.

Nevertheless, Matakauri went to a nearby river and built a raft to carry the girl away. When all was ready and they still could not cut the cord, she wept all the more; and when her tears fell upon the cord it parted at once. Matakauri's raft took them to safety and soon they were married.

The next time there was a north-west wind, Matakauri returned to kill Matau. He climbed the hill where the giant lay sleeping with his knees drawn up, and he piled bracken around him and set it on fire. The monster was burnt to death, and the fire left a deep hole in the ground in the shape of his body. The rivers from the mountains filled this hole with water, forming Lake Wakatipu.

## Matamata
### A taniwha near Kaikōura

In the later years of the seventeenth century the people of Ngāi Tahu were invading the South Island. Just north of Kaikōura there was a place where the only track along the coast passed high limestone bluffs. To prevent Ngāi Tahu from entering the region, the local people, Ngāti Mamoe, stationed their taniwha, Matamata, at the mouth of a stream there (its English name is Lyell Creek).

Matamata, a vicious-looking creature with a long neck and scaly body, for some time killed and devoured all the Ngāi Tahu warriors who came along the track. His method, we are told, was first to eject 'a noxious fluid' that stupefied them. This fluid must have been scalding hot urine, which was also employed by another taniwha in this region.

Eventually Matamata was overcome by a Ngāi Tahu rangatira named Maru. A strong noose was prepared, Maru hid nearby with some companions, then fast runners lured Matamata from his den. The taniwha thrust his head into the noose, it was pulled tight, and Maru dispatched him with his adze, which possessed special powers. Inside the creature's great body the warriors found the clothes, ornaments and weapons of the victims he had devoured.

## Mataoho
### Cause of Tāmaki's volcanoes

In Tāmaki (Auckland) the ancestor responsible for volcanic activity is usually said to be Mataoho, though sometimes his name is given as Mataaho. This giant felt cold one day, and asked his gods to send subterranean fires to warm him. The gods made a vigorous response, forming the sixty or so volcanic hills and basins that now exist in the region.

Several place names refer to Mataoho. The large crater of Maunga-whau (Mount Eden) is known as Te Ipu-a-Mataoho [Mataoho's bowl], and was sacred to him.

## Mataora and Niwareka
### Originators of tattooing and weaving

Niwareka was beaten by her husband Mataora and ran down to her father Uetonga in the underworld. Mataora followed; Kūwatawata, guardian of the path, showed him its entrance at the back of her house.

In the underworld he came to a place where there was a ritual fire and Uetonga was tattooing a man. When Uetonga saw the designs painted on Mataora's face he wiped them off, saying, 'The people up there cannot tattoo properly.'

Then Mataora was thrown down and Uetonga

began to tattoo him. When he felt the pain, Mataora sang a song to Niwareka. She heard of this in the house where she sat weaving garments, and she left her work and came to him. Again he sang, and though his face was covered with blood she knew him from his words. She took him to her house and cared for him until his wounds had healed.

He told her then that they must go back to the world. They reached Kūwatawata's house and passed through safely, but when Mataora failed to give one of Niwareka's garments in payment, Kūwatawata called, 'Farewell, Mataora! The path to Night and the path to Day are now shut off, and living men will no longer pass over them.'

After this Mataora lived with his wife in the world, and taught people the art of tattooing.

Often we are told that Niwareka brought up from the underworld a finely woven cloak, called Te Rangi-haupapa, which became the model for all such cloaks in the world above. Some say she was prevented from taking her cloak up with her, but that she was nevertheless able to teach weaving in the world.

This myth seems to belong mainly to Ngāti Kahungunu, on the east coast between Wairoa and the Wairarapa. However, Mataora is mentioned elsewhere, usually as the man who introduced the art of tattooing to the world. The Tūhoe people say that when the trickster Māui

Above: *A small, finely carved container for pigment to be used in tattooing. Such possessions were tapu.*

Below: *In the early years of contact with Pākehā, Māori men often signed legal documents or important letters with drawings of their facial tattoo [moko]. This self-portrait was drawn in 1844 by Tūhawaiki, principal rangatira in the far south.*

had himself tattooed in the beginning, Mataora was the expert who did this.

In songs and chants the expression 'Mataora's chisel' [te uhi a Mataora] refers usually to the tattooer's tools and is used in praise of a fine tattoo [moko]. But occasionally this expression acquires a new significance. When a poet speaks of someone who has died as having been 'pierced by Mataora's chisel', Mataora has become a demonic personification of fate.

There is a parallel between this myth and that of Tama-nui-a-raki, who in the South Island is tattooed in the underworld. His wife Rukutia is similarly associated with weaving, although this is recorded only in old songs.

## Matariki

### Stars bringing the new year

The English name for this small cluster of stars is the Pleiades; the Māori name, Matariki, means literally 'Little eyes' or 'Little points'. For peoples in many parts of Aotearoa, their appearance at dawn (or sometimes the first new moon after their appearance) marked the end of the old year and the beginning of the new. Generally seven stars were discerned.

Matariki is usually a woman. The seven stars were often regarded as Matariki and her six daughters, though others considered the entire group to be a single female. Near the end of the Māori year, in mid-April, she was lost to sight in the west in the evening, then near the end of May she became visible in the east shortly before dawn.

So the end of the year was identified with Matariki's disappearance in the west as darkness came on – and these were the direction and the time of day traditionally associated with death and sorrow. The start of the new year was marked by her reappearance in the north-east before dawn – this direction and time being associated with light, life and wellbeing. The new year began, furthermore, close to the time of the shortest day, when the light was about to return.

When Matariki first reappeared, she and her daughters were greeted with songs lamenting

*King Tāwhiao's coat of arms, devised at his request late in the nineteenth century, includes the seven stars of Matariki and is known as Te Paki o Matariki [The fine weather of Matariki]. This expression, which is also the name given to a periodical published by the King, referred on one level to his senior men, whose support sustained the King Movement [Te Kīngitanga].*

Ko te Mana Motuhake.

# TE PAKI O MATARIKI

the loss of those who had died in the previous year. But the singers' tears were joyful too, because the new year had begun:

Tirohia atu nei, ka whetūrangitia Matariki,
Te whitu o te tau e whakamoe mai rā.
He hōmai ana rongo kia kōmai atu au –
Ka mate nei au i te matapōuri, i te
    matapōrehu o roto i a au!

See where Matariki are risen over the horizon,
The seven of the year winking up there.
They come with their message so I can rejoice.
Here I am full of sorrow, full of sadness within!

Parties of women sang and danced to the stars, and there was much festivity.

Appearing as she did in winter, Matariki was closely examined for signs as to the seasons that would follow. If the seven stars seemed indistinct and quivering, it would be a poor season. If each star stood out clearly and distinctly, a warm prolific season would ensue.

It was believed that Matariki brought food supplies to human beings, and offerings were made to them during the kūmara harvest. They were closely associated with the taking of game, because their reappearance came at the time of year when birds and rats, grown fat on berries and other foods, were caught and preserved.

It is recorded that in parts of Taranaki the old people would watch in midwinter for Matariki to appear at dawn. They might watch for several nights before this happened, and while waiting they would make a small hāngi [earth oven]. When Matariki rose up, they would weep and tell the stars the names of those who had died since the stars had set. Then they would uncover the oven so that the scent of the food would rise and strengthen Matariki, who were weak and cold.

This was still being done in the 1890s. Near New Plymouth, one old lady carried on the custom until her death in about 1940.

The Pleiades occupy a place very close to the ecliptic, the path that the sun annually follows. With this placement in the sky and their conspicuous appearance, this star cluster has been associated in many traditional societies with the yearly cycle of the seasons.

## Mataterā and Waerotā
### Distant lands of origin

According to an early tradition in the far north, people migrated to Aotea (the North Island) from the islands of Mataterā, Waerotā, and Hawaiki.

These were lands of plenty where the kūmara grew wild and abundant food was available without toil. But the people became numerous, there was fighting, and the ancestors set out across the ocean to find a new home for themselves.

Of these three mythic islands, Hawaiki is most often spoken of in tradition. But on the east coast an ancient harvest chant identifies the kūmara plantation, with its abundant crop, with Mataterā, and a lament from the far north speaks of Mataterā and Waerotā as lands to which the wairua of the dead make their way:

Tama i torohakina, e koe, ki Mataterā,
Ki Waerotā, tē tau mai hoki koe nā!

O my son who sped off to Mataterā
And Waerotā, oh you did not stay!

Because they are lands of origin, islands from which the ancestors came in the beginning, the wairua return to them after death.

Some poets speak of two lands named Waerotī and Waerotā. This is a consequence of the Māori fondness, in rhetorical speech, for pairs of words that are identical in meaning and form except that the first has the letter i and the second the letter a. Thus the land of Waerotī evolved as a variant of Waerotā.

Waerotā was known in Polynesian tradition outside Aotearoa. In the Tuamotu atolls there is a legendary land known as Vaerotā (a name equivalent to Waerotā).

## Matuatonga
### A fertility god

On Mokoia Island in Lake Rotorua, an ancient stone figure known as Matuatonga was the dwelling place of an atua of this name who was believed to possess the power to ensure the fertility and abundance of the kūmara crop.

Before the fields were planted each year, the peoples in the region sent some of their seed kūmara across to the island. There they were taken to the tūāhu and ceremonially brought into contact with Matuatonga, while the tohunga recited ritual chants to ensure a bountiful harvest. Most of the kūmara then returned to their owners, conveying with them the mana of Matuatonga.

A few of the kūmara were ritually presented to Matuatonga to ensure his protection. This offering was placed in a small basket of raupō leaves, plaited in the shape of a waka, then after the singing of a sacred chant the vessel with its cargo was set adrift upon the lake. It was believed to find its way to Hawaiki, from which Matua-tonga had come.

It was Matuatonga's continuing association with the land of Hawaiki, the source of fertility, which gave him his power. While his image [taumata atua] had been brought from Hawaiki on *Te Arawa* and he himself alighted and dwelt in Aotearoa, at the same time he continued to live in Hawaiki. He was therefore a point of contact between Hawaiki and Mokoia, bringing fertility to the crops.

Kūmara grew very well on Mokoia Island, since its soil is fertile and the lake creates a relatively mild microclimate. The ancient figure of Matuatonga, which at one time was buried there to ensure its safety, is now in the Auckland Museum. But another figure of Matuatonga, apparently carved in the nineteenth century as a replacement, still stands upon the slopes of Mokoia.

The name occurs as well in the traditions of the Tūranga (Gisborne) district. Some regard Matuatonga as an early ancestor associated with the kūmara who arrived from Hawaiki on the *Tākitimu*, while others in the region assert that Matuatonga is the name of the carry-belt in which the kūmara was brought to Aotearoa.

## Matuku-tangotango
### Rata's enemy

This demonic being kills and devours Wahieroa, the father of Rata, and Rata accordingly sets out on a voyage to avenge his father's death. He succeeds in this undertaking, usually by catching Matuku-tangotango in a great noose. In some versions of the myth, this happens on a path near the monster's home; in other accounts Matuku-tangotango lives underground and emerges only when there is a new moon, so Rata snares him at this time. Afterwards Rata tears out his heart, reciting a chant of triumph, and eats it.

Rata's noose is proverbially secure, and sure in its result. In many important undertakings a saying might be quoted: 'Bind it with Matuku-tangotango's bonds, which cannot be loosened' [Me here ki te here o Matuku-tangotango, e kore nei e taea te wewete].

On the west coast of the North Island it is said that when Matuku-tangotango died he turned into the bittern, which still goes by his name [matuku]. Although Matuku-tangotango in one account appears to takes the form of a man (he washes his hair in a pool), his name and Rata's use of a noose must generally have been sufficient to give him something of the character of a bittern.

This bird was regarded as unattractive, un-sociable and melancholy, so a giant bittern could perhaps be readily envisaged as an enemy.

## Māui
### The trickster hero

This man comes early in the genealogies, at a point where the world and its inhabitants have been formed but human beings still lack many of the things they need. Māui shapes the environment further, providing important resources for humans and demonstrating useful skills.

He himself is very much a human being, despite his extraordinary powers. He achieves his ends through trickery, very often, and by breaking the rules. In this he forms a contrast with another early hero, Tāwhaki, a glorious figure who avenges his father's death and mounts to the skies. Māui, on the other hand, performs no feats of arms, concerns himself often with practical, domestic matters, and tends to do things the 'wrong', non-prestigious way. Much of his power, it seems, comes from breaking tapu.

There is first the remarkable manner of his birth; he is a miscarried foetus that survives and grows in the sea (or some other unpromising environment). In mythologies it is quite common for heroes to be born in unlikely ways; this is a demonstration of their powers, for one thing. In this case, though, a further consideration must be that in Maori belief an aborted foetus or stillborn child might turn into a spirit of an especially dangerous kind (atua kahukahu). Be-cause these beings had not been accepted into the kinship group, they owed no loyalty towards it and were ill-disposed towards the living.

Māui himself is not such a spirit. Having miraculously survived, cared for by the people of the sea (or other guardians), he is finally accepted into his kinship group. Nevertheless the resemblance is there, and makes for ambiguity. No wonder there is a recognition scene where Māui persuades his mother Taranga, with dif-ficulty, that he is her son.

Māui in fact is the youngest of five brothers – or some say four. (His full name is Māui-tikitiki-o-Taranga, and the others are variously known as Māui-mua, Māui-taha, Māui-roto, Māui-waho and Māui-pae.) Like many heroes in mythology, he acts vigorously to overcome the low status accorded him as the youngest son.

There is also his name. Many figures in Māori tradition have names that suggest their nature (such as Tāne, Rangi, Papa), so it must be sig-nificant in this case that the word māui is the term for the left, and the left hand. This was the noa [profane, ordinary] side of the body, as opposed to the tapu [sacred] right side. Māui is not a personification as such, but this area of meaning is relevant to the way he behaves, with his notorious lack of respect for tapu and convention generally.

Māui's close relationship with his mother rather than his father is unusual in a hero, and again seems in accord with his nature (in that women, intrinsically and in general, were noa, whereas men in the same general sense were tapu). Wanting to know what Taranga does all day, he spies on her, then turns himself into a pigeon (to do this, he sometimes wears her garment). He follows her down to a place under the ground, and there is a second recognition scene between mother and son. Occasionally his father is present and performs over him the tohi ceremony, which dedicates the boy to his future life. (The father is Irawhaki, or sometimes Makeatūtara.)

This underground region is not Night [Te Pō], home of the dead, but simply another land where people are living. It seems that Māui is exploring a place down below, just as Tāwhaki, Tāne and Rupe explore places in the skies where people are to be found. They are the ones who can reach those other realms, which fantasy so readily populates.

Certainly Māui, being a 'low' figure rather than a 'high' one, belongs in the earth rather than the sky. Also he has an association with horticulture, and may be in the earth partly because kūmara crops belong there. Probably, though, it is the other way round, and the association with crops follows from the fact that he goes under the ground.

His mother's association with the earth is natural enough, in that it can be viewed as a female realm.

Most of Māui's major exploits involve tricks of one kind and another. This is in accord with the Māori assumption (as expressed in myth) that valuable assets are not given freely, for no reason, but must be bought, or taken through force or trickery.

Clever tricks and deceptions are highly entertaining, furthermore, and the stories evolved accordingly. In the story telling how Māui stole fire from Mahuika, going back for more and more until all is gone, Māui's dramatic victory over Mahuika and her fire is a victory for all human beings.

The funniest trick may have been Māui's persuading his brother-in-law to let him tattoo him and then – with Irawaru at his mercy, and with the aid of a potent chant – pulling him out into the shape of a dog. It must have been most satisfying to think of such a solution to a brother-in-law problem. At the same time the episode convincingly explains the origin of dogs.

Māui often used ritual chants, along with other methods. Because the days were too short, he conquered the sun, sometimes with the help of his brothers; he noosed it as it came up, and recited a chant that forced it to go more slowly. So now the days are long enough for the things people have to do. As well, a traveller with a long way to go before sunset can, if he has the mana, act as Māui did. By reciting a chant that refers to this feat of Māui's, he can slow the sun and lengthen the day.

The most spectacular of Māui's exploits, the one most often spoken of in oratory, songs and proverbs, was his fishing up the land. The North Island is Māui's Fish [Te Ika-a-Māui] and the South Island, according to its inhabitants, is the waka from which Māui caught his fish. While the earth itself is Papa, the first mother, it was Māui who created these islands.

For a long time Māui was too lazy to go out fishing, and lay in his house while his brothers were toiling out there. When his wives kept complaining, he was finally shamed into acquiring a fish hook. He did this his own way, by visiting the tapu cave that contained the bones of his grandparent, Murirangawhenua; he took the jawbone, and it became his hook.

Normally only an enemy would use a human bone for this purpose, and then only if he intended the worst insult possible. Yet Māui was able to break tapu in this horrendous way without any ill effects. Indeed he gained great power by doing so.

His elder brothers did not want him in their waka, fearing his tricks, but he hid, then sprang up when out on the ocean. They anchored above the fishing rock and the elder brothers set to work, but they would not give Māui any bait. So he punched himself on the nose and used his own blood as bait, and a fish took his hook at once.

The waka was lifted up then down, it spun round, and his brothers cried out in fear. But Māui would not let go his fish. He recited a powerful chant, and the fish came up. Soon it stretched out upon the surface, the vessel high and dry on its back.

Māui left for their home to make offerings to the gods, telling his brothers to leave the fish alone until his return. But the greedy brothers

began at once to chop it up. It was not yet dead, and it thrashed and writhed into mountains, cliffs and gorges. That is why the lie of the land is now so bad.

And the fish's shape can still be seen. The head is in the south, the mouth being Te Whanga-nui-a-Tara (Wellington Harbour) and one of the eyes Lake Wairarapa. The heart is Lake Taupō – or some say the Urewera Mountains. The fish hook is Cape Kidnappers. The fins are Taranaki and the East Coast, and the tail is Northland.

There are other stories about Māui, some told only in certain parts of the country. He was clever with his hands as well, and he invented string games, juggling, crayfish pots and other things, though usually the storytellers do not go into detail about this.

Much is said about his encounter with Hine-nui-te-pō [Great woman the night], who gathers to herself the wairua of the dead. This was the most ambitious of his tricks, and like several others it involved meddling with the body of an opponent. This time he was not successful.

He wanted to pass through Hine's body to kill her, and do away with death. He was warned, but he would not listen. He approached the great woman as she lay sleeping, he entered her body, she brought her legs together, and that was the end of Māui. He had tried once too often to reverse the normal order of things.

It is because of this defeat that people die now.

# Mauri
## Repositories of vitality

It was believed that a person, a people, a pā or house or waka, a river or forest, a food resource of any kind – any entity of value – possessed a life force, a vitality, which was termed a hau. In the case of a person, this hau was identified with the breath, and a number of bodily states involving the breath – such as being startled or sneezing – were said to be the act of the person's mauri. With a person, then, the hau and the mauri were both located within the body.

With other entities they were closely related, but in a different way. In every other case, the hau (the vitality of the entity, understood as being equivalent to a person's breath) was strengthened and protected from enemies by being ritually

*Two interpretations of the myth of Māui's fishing up the land.* Left: *A drawing published in 1907 by Wilhelm Dittmer, a German artist who had visited the country to study its mythology, and* (right) *a wall pillar carved at about the same time by an Arawa artist.*

located within a material counterpart, usually a stone, which was termed a mauri. At the same time an atua, sometimes more than one, was located in the stone as well.

In this way the mauri brought together the vitality of the entity and a guardian spirit. If the mauri was kept safe, all would be well with the people, the land, the structure or the resource with which it was identified. For this reason it was often hidden, as when a mauri for birds was buried in a forest where no enemy could find it. The main protection, though, came from the atua that had been located in the stone or other object used. The mana of these spirits protected the mana of the entity the mauri represented.

The mauri that represented and protected the mana of an entire people were sometimes believed to have been brought from the homeland of Hawaiki. At Whakatāne, a mauri of the Mātaatua peoples was the mānuka tree upon which their female ancestor Wairakewa rode from Hawaiki. At Kāwhia, where two limestone rocks mark the resting place of the *Tainui*, one of these rocks (a female named Puna) is responsible in a general way for the people's wellbeing and must have been regarded as a mauri. When *Te Arawa* entered Tikapa (the Hauraki Gulf) after her voyage, the tohunga Ngātoro-i-rangi placed a tapu stone upon a small island near the Moehau Range so that in later times this would be the mauri of the Arawa peoples.

Some of these mauri established by immigrants from Hawaiki had more specialised roles, representing and attracting birds or fish. At Te Māhia (Māhia Peninsula), the tohunga on the *Tākitimu* poured out a small quantity of sand that had been brought from Hawaiki; this became a mauri of the whales, and the very next day a whale was lying on the beach. Another mauri at Te Māhia took the form of a hillock by the shore which was shaped like a whale, its spout a māpou tree. Such was the power of these two mauri that whales in the region regularly stranded themselves on the shore.

Sometimes the protective deity was an early ancestor of the people concerned. At Tihi-o-Tonga, in Arawa territory, the image of a female ancestor, Horoirangi, was carved into a cliff-face in a highly tapu area below a hilltop pā. She was the mauri who preserved the fertility of her people's lands and gave them the strength to hold that land, and offerings of tapu food were laid at her feet.

Similarly, the Taranaki people possess a stone sculpture of their female ancestor Hine-o-tanga, whose powers protected her people.

Mauri for kūmara sometimes took the form of

*A mauri that formerly belonged to Ngāti Whātua and was used in sea fishing. Like many mauri it is quite small, some sixteen centimetres in diameter at the widest point.*

stone images representing Rongo, the mythic originator of horticulture. These images stood beside the fields, or sometimes at the tūāhu associated with horticulture.

Mauri for fish and birds seem usually to have been non-figurative, as indeed were most mauri; generally the stones were left unworked or were simply shaped, hollowed out perhaps, or formed into a phallus or vulva. A fishing mauri might be hidden together with the gills of a fish of the kind most important in the region. The mauri of the forest birds was often placed beside the right wing of a kākā, since this parrot was regarded as the rangatira of all the birds in the forest.

The mauri of an ocean-going waka was usually a small stone over which rituals had been performed to make it a medium between the vessel and the atua; after the first, ceremonial voyage it was hidden somewhere on land, perhaps in the roots of a tree. The mauri of a pā was a stone that might be placed under the first palisade post to be erected, or buried near the tūāhu, or hidden at the foot of a tree in a nearby forest. The god located within this mauri would be the war god under whose protection the fortress had been ritually placed; an east coast authority tells us it might be Rongomai, Kahukura, Tū-nui-a-te-ika or Tama-i-waho.

The mauri of a large house was buried under or beside a central pillar [pou-toko-manawa], or that supporting the ridgepole in the rear wall. Occasionally the mana of a house was so great that a human being was required as a mauri. Usually a slave was sacrificed for this role.

If a mauri were stolen by an enemy who then performed sorcery over it, the consequences would be serious unless he was at once opposed by more powerful rituals. Even if no enemy were involved, a lost mauri had to be replaced immediately, as the people could not be left without the protection of their gods.

## Miru
### Ruler of Night

In a tradition of the Taranaki people, Miru lives in a house down below that is known as Te Tatau o Te Pō [The Door to Night]. His companions are atua that afflict human beings with illness and misfortune, and are involved in sorcery. Miru himself possesses much knowledge of history, ritual chants, and sorcery.

Two men in Hawaiki, Ihenga and Rongomai, lead an expedition to visit him. They climb down a rope, are invited into Miru's house, and remain there for many days and nights, acquiring knowledge. But Miru's manner changes and the men become suspicious. When they rush from the house, Miru seizes two laggards, Ngo and Kewa, and keeps them as payment for the knowledge he has imparted.

*Te Kāhui Kararehe (1846–1904) of Taranaki preserved many of the traditions of his people, among them the myth of Miru, who lives down below.*

The travellers soon find that their rope has been cut. Then they see that Ngo and Kewa are missing. They return, but Miru will not give up his captives and presently he kills them. Ihenga and his companions then plan their revenge. While Miru and his attendant spirits are asleep in their house they set it on fire, and its occupants are burnt to ashes.

Only with great difficulty, after a dangerous voyage, do the survivors of the expedition return to their home in Hawaiki.

Other versions of the myth explain that as a result of these or similar events, much knowledge was gained by human beings. The story belongs mainly to the west coast, though poets elsewhere speak of Miru as living in the underworld of Te Rēinga. Miru's house is sometimes Rua-ki-pōuri or Mirimiri-te-pō. Occasionally Miru is a woman, and sometimes the name is Meru. In a tradition apparently from the far north, a woman of this name kills timid spirits in the lowest levels of the underworld.

Related myths exist elsewhere in Polynesia.

## Moa
### Extraordinary birds

Eleven species of moa once browsed on trees and shrubs in Aotearoa, being especially common in the eastern part of the South Island. The tallest of these wingless birds were two and a half metres in height, and the heaviest weighed more than two hundred kilograms. When the first settlers arrived about a thousand years ago, they called these new birds by the same name as the domestic fowls [moa] they had left behind in their previous home.

The presence of these huge birds, along with smaller species of flightless birds and numerous colonies of seals – none of them used to humans – must have led to a rapid increase in the population. As a result, the moa did not last very long. Moa-hunting reached its peak in about 1300, great numbers were killed in the century that followed, by 1500 they had become rare, and soon afterwards they disappeared completely.

A common expression, 'lost like the moa' [mate-ā-moa], means 'lost utterly and hopelessly'. As well, moa appear in tradition as remote creatures with extraordinary attributes which live on the summits of certain mountains. A solitary moa that stood on one leg was believed to guard Hikurangi on the east coast, another was on the heights of Whakapunake (inland between Gisborne and Wairoa), and another lived with giant reptiles on the icy peak of Taranaki.

These moa were sometimes said to be similar in appearance to human beings but to feed only on the wind. So a person who did not eat very much, or a girl in love who had lost her appetite, might be called 'a moa that feeds on air' [he moa kai hau].

## Moeahu
### A dog-headed man

This fierce creature was like a man except that he had a dog's head and feet. He barked, but had human intelligence. He could run very fast and no man could escape him. His weapons were a taiaha and a whalebone patu, and as well he used his muzzle and feet. He lived with his brothers and sisters in a forest in the Tūranga (Gisborne) region.

A man named Te Kowha once stole some fish that Moeahu's people had left drying on a stage, and in retaliation Moeahu ate some preserved birds belonging to Te Kowha. The man seized his spear, but the monster broke it; he fled but was clubbed to the ground.

Te Kowha's three brothers armed themselves and ran to his assistance, but found him dead. They fought Moeahu so bravely that the monster fled and there was a long chase. Then Moeahu saw that one of the brothers was ahead of the others, so he turned back and killed him. A second brother ran ahead and was killed in the same way, then the last of the brothers was killed.

## Moko-hiku-waru
### A powerful reptile

In the Taranaki and Whanganui regions, Moko-hiku-waru (sometimes Moko-hiku-aru or Moko-huku-waru) is a fierce reptile god, often linked with a similar god named Tū-tangata-kino. These two reptiles guarded the house of Miru, ruler of the underworld. They were very dangerous and might attack human beings, especially when employed in sorcery by knowledgeable persons. In some circumstances, though, humans could employ them as guardians.

Treasures hidden in remote places were often believed to be watched over by guardians, which frequently took the form of geckos. These were sometimes regarded as the descendants of Tū-tangata-kino and Moko-hiku-waru.

*Geckos were generally thought to be agents of evil, yet were also believed to guard hidden treasures and tapu places such as caves that held the bones of the dead. When acting as guardians they were regarded by some as descendants of Moko-hiku-waru and Tū-tangata-kino.*

## Moko-ika-hiku-waru
### An eight-tailed taniwha

In Tainui tradition, Moko-ika-hiku-waru is a taniwha in the form of an eight-tailed reptile (his name means something like 'Eight-tailed fish reptile').

One of the taniwha that guided the *Tainui* on its voyage from Hawaiki, he left the ship at Tāmaki (the Auckland district), along with those of the crew who had decided to settle there. He made his home in a deep pool at the entrance to a lagoon that became known as Te Wai-roto-o-Moko-ika [The lake waters of Moko-ika], he drank from a famous spring nearby and fed upon the eels, flounder and yellow-eyed mullet that abounded in the lagoon – so that these fish were tapu, never eaten by human beings. (The English name of this lagoon is the Panmure Basin.)

The region's fertile soil and abundant seafood attracted a large population. Moko-ika-hiku-waru remained there with his people, a branch of Ngāti Pāoa, until in 1820 they foolishly killed a rangatira of the Ngā Puhi peoples who was visiting them. Moko-ika-hiku-waru was furious, knowing that Ngā Puhi would take a terrible revenge. He swam up and down the Tāmaki River lashing the water with his tails, then swam out to sea and was never seen again.

Yet the restriction against taking fish from the lagoon was still in force in the early years of the twentieth century.

## Moko's Great Dog
### A ferocious beast

The forested Ngāmoko Range borders the eastern shore of Lake Waikaremoana. Men who climbed its precipitous slopes to hunt kākā, pigeons and other birds sometimes failed to return, and it was discovered at last that they had been devoured by a savage creature known as Moko's Great Dog [Te Kurī-nui-a-Moko].

The warriors of Waikaremoana resolved to trap and kill this monster. They constructed a strong cage from saplings and supplejack vines, baited it with meat, cautiously placed it near the animal's den, then hid nearby. The dog scented the meat and entered the cage, the door was quickly shut, and the men speared the howling beast through the lattice-work sides of the cage. Soon it lay dead.

The dog had no mate, so after this the bird-hunters were undisturbed. Sometimes they camped in the large, comfortable cave where the monster had lived.

## Monoa
### Whiro's son, who escaped

Some authorities on the west coast of the North Island say that a great house named Te Whare Kura [The crimson house] was erected at Hawaiki as a place in which to impart sacred knowledge. The rangatira in this house belonged to two great factions, and there was feuding between them. When the house was completed, one of these factions sent a treacherous message inviting their enemy, the evil Whiro, to attend as a leading orator.

Whiro told the messenger that two of his sons, Marama-nui-o-hotu and Tai-nui-o-aitu-rourou-ātea, would go instead. So these young men entered Te Whare Kura, and were attacked and killed at once.

Other messengers were sent to bring Whiro and his remaining son, Monoa. Whiro again declined, and said that Monoa would go in his place. But he warned Monoa that his brothers might have been killed, and told him before leaving to perform the niu ceremony, throwing sticks to determine his fate. Monoa did so, and the omen was unfavourable.

Whiro instructed him then to make his way cautiously to the house, climb the roof and look down through the smoke-hole. When Monoa did this, he saw the hearts and lungs of his brothers being offered to the gods by the tohunga. He fled, and the men in the house pursued him.

As he went, Monoa recited a chant to make himself run faster. He ran into a flock of shags, but they could not hide him. He ran into a flock of ducks, but they could do nothing. He went among godwits, then oystercatchers, then black-backed gulls, but in vain. Then he ran into a flock of terns – small birds that fly in large flocks – and there he was completely hidden. His pursuers could not find him, and he escaped.

## Moon
### A return to life

All living beings beneath the moon will die, while those above will live forever. The fate of Te Marama [The Moon] is different, because every month he dies, then lives once more. He bathes in Tāne's waters of life [Te Waiora-a-Tane], and three nights later he is restored to life.

Sayings and songs contrast this renewal with the fate of human beings. Poets mourned,

> Me i pēnei te mate ki a koe
> Me te mate i te marama, ka ea mai, e au!

If your death were like that of the moon
You would rise up again, *e au!*

When heroes in mythology come back to life (as Tāwhaki sometimes does), they generally do so after three days and nights.

Since people counted by nights of the moon rather than by days, the changing shape of this bright being served to measure time. For longer periods there were the months of the year, again regulated by the moon.

Like the sun, the moon was male. Since his cycles correlate with women's menstrual cycles, he was believed to control their cycles and to be their real husband. When he came back to life the call went up, 'The husband of all the women in the world has appeared!'

There is a woman in the moon, called Rona. He seized her and took her up when she rashly cursed him one dark night.

Sometimes the moon is considered to be one of the sons of Tāne's brother, Tangotango. Tāne obtained him from his brother and placed him in the sky in the same way as he did the sun (and sometimes the stars).

## Motu-tapu
### A sacred island

In a myth known throughout Polynesia, Hina (or Hine) hears about the handsome Tinirau and wants him as her husband. She swims through the ocean for many days to reach his island (which is often called Motu-tapu), she finds him there, marries him and has his son.

In Aotearoa, this woman is occasionally Hina but usually Hine-te-iwaiwa, and the story often takes place in the homeland of Hawaiki or in an unnamed land. However, there is an island in the middle of Lake Rotorua which was known originally as Te Motu-tapu-a-Tinirau [Tinirau's sacred island]. It was, we are told, given this name by the explorer Īhenga. Later its name was changed to Mokoia.

The interesting thing is that while there is no story associating the mythical Hina or Hine with this island, a well-known legend tells how an ancestor, Hinemoa, evaded her relatives and swam across Rotorua in the darkness to reach the island and marry Tūtānekai, whom she loved; again, all ends happily. According to the genealogies, this event occurred after the island had been given its new name of Mokoia, but the old name was remembered. Perhaps the legend of Hinemoa has been shaped by the ancient story of Hine, who swam bravely across the water to find the man she had made up her mind to marry.

In the Hauraki Gulf, an island named Motu-tapu is said to have been named by Taikehu of the *Tainui* 'in commemoration of an island in Hawaiki'. This is probably a reference to Tinirau's island.

## Mountains
### The high places

Every people had a special association with a hill or mountain of mana [he maunga whai mana]. Its tapu summit stood apart, a source and expression of the people's mana and their point of contact with the sky. Lightning and thunder brought messages concerning the future, and the bones of high-ranking people were often laid to rest in caves upon their mountains' heights.

Some high mountains, such as Taranaki (Mount Egmont), were so frightening, their high snows guarded by atua, that they were spoken of as supernatural mountains [maunga tipua]. But all tapu mountains and hills were treated by their people with the respect their status required.

The people of Ngāti Mahuta in the lower Waikato claimed for their mountain, Taupiri, priority over all others – because when Māui pulled up the fish that became Aotea (the North Island), it was the first land to rise above the waves. The same thing was said by Ngāti Porou of their mountain, Hikurangi; this is why the light shines upon it every morning while all else is still in darkness.

Unfortunately, Māui's brothers ignored his instructions and hacked up his fish while it was still alive, so that it writhed into hills and ridges. Volcanoes were sometimes thought to have been caused by a giant named Mataaho, though others thought Rūaumoko responsible, and it was Ngātoro-i-rangi who had summoned from Hawaiki the volcanic fires and hot springs now to be seen in the territories of his descendants.

In the south, the men who came on the *Āraiteuru* arrived by night and spread out over the countryside, then turned into mountains when the sun rose. In other places, the mountains themselves had moved around under cover of darkness, then been transfixed by the light.

Traditionally, the name Tongariro belonged to the peaks known now as Tongariro, Ruapehu and Ngāuruhoe, since these three were regarded

Right: *Wairehu Te Huri of Ngāti Hikairo, on the paepae of his people's house Ōkahukura near Lake Rotoaira and Tongariro. Wairehu's account of the events that led the mountains around his home to move to their present locations was recorded and published.*

as a single mountain. Tongariro lives now where he has always done, but others separated from him and went their own ways. Two rounded hills, Pihanga and Hauhungatahi, are his wives, but they now stand at some distance. Another male, Taranaki, once lived with Tongariro, but they fought, some say over Pihanga, and Taranaki went rushing off in the darkness, dropping rocks on the way and digging with his great bulk the gorge of the Whanganui River. When the sun rose he was far in the west, and he has been there ever since.

Some say that others, among them Tauhara and Pūtauaki (Mount Edgecumbe), were involved in the quarrel as well and moved to their positions at this time.

## Mumuhau and Takeretou
### Two wise birds

The saddleback is a dark bird with a chestnut 'saddle' and orange wattles. Its cries were often taken to be good or bad omens, and it was believed to act as a guardian. Ancient, buried treasures were sometimes thought to be protected by these birds.

It was believed that the *Mātaatua*, while sailing from Hawaiki, was guarded and guided by two saddlebacks with extraordinary powers, Mumuhau and Takeretou. At the entrance to the Hauraki Gulf the crew placed these tipua on Repanga (Cuvier Island), and they are living there still. They are wise birds that foretell the weather by their cries and their manner of flying.

Mumuhau is also present as an atua among Tūhoe and Ngāti Awa, two Mātaatua peoples living further to the south.

According to Arawa tradition, the birds Mumuhau and Takeretō were pets of the tohunga Ngātoro-i-rangi. After the voyage of *Te Arawa* he left them on Ahuahu (Great Mercury Island).

## Muturangi's Octopus
### The monster killed by Kupe

In Hawaiki, or some say Rarotonga, a giant octopus, the pet of an ill-disposed tohunga named Muturangi, kept stealing the bait from Kupe's fishing lines. This creature is generally known as Muturangi's Octopus [Te Wheke a Muturangi].

When Kupe angrily pursued the octopus, it sped across the ocean to Aotearoa. Kupe followed and caught up with it in Raukawa (Cook Strait). He fought the great creature, hacking at its arms, then threw overboard a bundle of gourds. The octopus attacked these, thinking them a person, and this gave Kupe the opportunity he needed.

After killing the octopus, Kupe placed its eyes upon a group of small rocky islands that henceforth became known as Ngā Whatu [The eyes]. (Their English name is The Brothers.)

Because Ngā Whatu were very tapu, Kupe created a strong current in the ocean nearby to ensure that voyagers would respect their sacredness and stay well away. And travellers did indeed observe great care in passing this dangerous place. In particular they avoided meeting the gaze of Ngā Whatu; often they wore eye-shades of leaves to prevent their looking at them. This was especially important when people were making their first crossing.

In another story, a giant octopus kills many voyagers in Raukawa, pulling their waka under

*Fighting Muturangi's Octopus, Kupe deceives it with a gourd. A drawing by Russell Clark.*

water, but is conquered by warriors led by two Whanganui men, Popea and Tama-ngākau. Muturangi and Kupe are not mentioned, and Ngā Whatu occurs only as the place where the octopus has his home.

The Māori word wheke is used both of the octopus and the squid, and it may here refer to either; there would have been no difficulty in imagining a gigantic octopus or squid. Giant squid do in fact exist, though they would have been seen only rarely, when a dead one was washed ashore.

## Ngahue
### Owner of the greenstone fish

In the homeland of Hawaiki, two people each had a pet fish consisting of stone. Ngahue's fish, named Poutini, was greenstone. Hine-tua-hōanga's fish, Waiapu, had a back of obsidian and a belly of flint.

These people used to allow their pets to swim in the ocean. But Hine-tua-hōanga grew jealous and wanted her fish to be the only one in the sea.

So she drove Ngahue and his fish away from Hawaiki, pursuing them across the ocean and finding them at last on Tūhua (Mayor Island). She threw part of her own fish, Waiapu, on to this island – and that is why it now contains large deposits of obsidian.

The greenstone fish, Poutini, took fright at this and went swimming away across the ocean, pursued by its owner, Ngahue. Hine-tua-hōanga swam after them for a while, throwing obsidian ashore in certain places as she went, then she herself settled down on the land.

The greenstone fish swam all the way to Arahura on the west coast of the South Island, and has ever since lived in the rivers where it is now found. Ngahue, however, returned home, taking part of his fish with him.

Back in Hawaiki, Ngahue spoke about the land he had discovered – and that, it is said, is why the ancestors later migrated to Aotearoa. From the greenstone he had brought back with him, he made adzes, tiki and ear pendants. The adzes, some say, were used subsequently in making the waka that brought the ancestors to Aotearoa.

This myth explains how precious resources of stone – greenstone, obsidian, flint and sandstone – had their origin, like other treasures, in Hawaiki, and how they then came to be located in different parts of Aotearoa. As for the greenstone adzes and pendants that Ngahue made in Hawaiki after his return, they provided the models, the spiritual prototypes, for all the similar objects that people made later.

Hine-tua-hōanga [Sandstone woman] was a natural enemy of greenstone because sandstone was used by craftsmen in working this stone. Obsidian and flint were also used for this purpose, to a rather lesser extent.

## Ngāi-te-heke-o-te-rangi
### Taniwha at Kāwhia

This group of fifteen taniwha live near Te Māhoe, by the Wai-harakeke inlet of the Kāwhia Harbour. One of them, Ngā-tara-tū, is a man-eater. The others are kindly disposed, and save people who call upon them when in danger of drowning.

A man named Ue-kaha was spearing flounder on the mud-flats one night, going further and further out, when suddenly the ground gave way under his feet and he found himself in a spacious, waterless cavern where many taniwha were lying around.

The taniwha treated him well, and after a few days they took him back to the world. Close to his home a spring gushed up, and out came Ue-kaha. His hair was matted with water-weed, but he was well in mind and body.

## Ngake
### Kupe's companion

The early explorer Kupe is sometimes regarded as having been accompanied by a companion, Ngake. It is said that when Kupe pursued Mutu-rangi's Octopus from Rarotonga to Raukawa (Cook Strait), he and his men sailed on *Mātāhorua* while Ngake and his men travelled on *Tawhiri-rangi*. At Raukawa they together fought and killed the octopus.

The two leaders then explored Te Wai Pou-namu (the South Island), discovering greenstone at Arahura on the west coast. When they reached the far south, Kupe told Ngake's wife Hine-waihua that since there were no people to be seen it would be a good place for her to leave her pet seals and penguins. She did so, and they are still there now.

One writer, Hōri Ropiha of Ngāti Kahungunu, tells us that Kupe and Ngake left their children at intervals along the coast; they are now rocks and islands, and their food is the wind. Afterwards Kupe and Ngake returned to Rarotonga.

Ngake is sometimes identified with Ngahue, owner of the greenstone fish.

*Fiordland crested penguins are among the pets which Ngake's wife Hine-waihua left in the far south during their exploratory voyage.*

## Ngake and Whātaitai
### Taniwha that formed a harbour

In the early times two taniwha, Ngake and Whātaitai, were confined within a great lake. Both tried to escape to the ocean by forcing a passage through the surrounding land. Whātaitai failed to do so, but Ngake succeeded in opened up a channel to the sea, thereby forming Te Whanga-nui-a-Tara (Wellington Harbour).

Whātaitai's struggles did, however, create the indentation now known as Evans Bay. The Miramar Peninsula was called after him, and as Hātaitai his name is still in use as the name of a nearby suburb.

As for Whātaitai himself, after this he assumed the form of a bird and flew to the top of a hill close by (Mount Victoria). On windy days the bird's harsh cries can still be heard on this peak, which for this reason is known traditionally as Tangi-te-keo [The screeching sound].

## Ngātokowaru
### A rangatira of Ngāti Raukawa

This renowned warrior lived in the Wharepū-hunga Range south of Mount Maungatautari in the first half of the eighteenth century. He fought and defeated Te Arawa at Te Tumu in the Bay of Plenty, then later attacked the Waikato peoples in the region of Maungatautari. He was at first successful, but in the end his army was defeated near Taupiri by Ngāti Mahuta. In that battle Ngātokowaru himself was taken prisoner by Tāwhia-ki-te-rangi, son of the great rangatira Te Putu.

Knowing he would be killed, Ngātokowaru asked if he could first meet Te Putu. This wish was granted. And as Te Putu – who was then an old man – bent forward courteously to hongi with him, Ngātokowaru pulled from his cloak a hidden dagger and stabbed him in the throat. He then quickly smeared himself with Te Putu's blood.

At once he was killed. But because of this contact with Te Putu's blood, he escaped the victors' ovens, as he had known he would, and his bold act won him lasting fame.

## Ngātoro-i-rangi
### A great tohunga

This ancestor of the Arawa peoples was a tohunga with extraordinary powers. During the voyage of Te Arawa from the homeland of Hawaiki, he flew into a rage when the captain, Tama-te-kapua,

stole his wife Kearoa, and he sent the vessel down towards the abyss at the edge of the ocean. Only at the last moment did he relent and bring it back up.

On reaching Aotearoa, Ngātoro-i-rangi placed two guardian saddlebacks on Ahuahu (Great Mercury Island) and established his people's mauri near Moehau (Cape Colville). Then after the ship made landfall at Maketū he set out into the interior on a journey of discovery.

On the way he created springs in waterless places by stamping on the ground, he placed fairies [patupaiarehe] in the hills as a sign of his ownership, and the shreds that fell from his cape grew into tall trees. Finding that Lake Taupō was lacking in fish, he created inanga and kōkopu, which live there now.

At Taupō he encountered Tia, a relative who had come on Te Arawa and was now seeking land for himself and his descendants. Ngatoro tricked Tia into believing that he had a prior claim, so Tia left that region to Ngātoro and made his way to Tokaanu, on the southern shore.

Ngātoro also met Hape, a man belonging to one of the early peoples already established in the country. Realising that Hape was also looking for land, Ngātoro set out to establish his own claim by climbing the snowy peak of Tongariro (which is now known as Ngāuruhoe). Hape attempted the climb as well, but Ngatoro called upon his gods and they sent a snowstorm that destroyed his rival.

When Ngātoro and his slave stood upon the summit they were benumbed with cold, so Ngātoro called to his sisters back in Hawaiki and asked them for fire. Te Pupū and Te Hoata heard him and came at once. Their fire warmed Ngātoro, though it came too late for his slave; it burns still in the crater of Ngāuruhoe, and in the many other places in Arawa territory where thermal and volcanic activity is to be found.

On his way back to the coast, Ngātoro was challenged near Mount Tarawera by an early demonic inhabitant named Tama-o-hoi. He overcame this adversary and thrust him down into the mountain.

After his return to Maketū, Ngātoro still had before him a series of encounters with a brother-in-law, Manaia, who was trying to destroy him. In this contest of powers Ngātoro won three great victories.

The name Ngātoro-i-rangi [Resound in the sky] must relate to Ngātoro's powers. Tohunga were believed to make the thunder resound, and Ngātoro-i-rangi was after all the greatest of the tohunga.

*Ngāuruhoe's volcanic fire was brought from Hawaiki by Ngātoro-i-rangi's sisters.*
*It burns there still as a sign of his mana.*

Evidence from Tahiti suggests that his name was brought to Aotearoa from there (or from an island with similar traditions) by the first settlers, and that the accompanying story was then adapted to suit the new circumstances, in particular the presence of thermal and volcanic activity. A Tahitian god named 'Atoro-i-ra'i is described in an early dictionary as 'an active god', while the Tahitian word 'atoro-i-ra'i is given as meaning 'strong and active' and 'to ascend towards the sky'. This name 'Atoro-i-ra'i is equivalent to Ngātoro-i-rangi (the only difference being that in Tahitian the sound *ng* has been replaced by a glottal stop).

# Night

## The darkness

In the beginning there was darkness. Some say the world began with the embraced sky and earth, others that generations of beings, or entities, first evolved and coupled. These had names, some of them, such as Te Pō Uriuri [Dark Night] and Te Pō Tangotango [Black Night]. Later came the sky and earth, then the light.

The eternal lights, the sun by day and the moon and stars by night, belong with Rangi the sky father. Darkness belongs with Papa the earth mother, who lies below, for within her, or beneath, there is the underworld to which the wairua of the dead leap down. In this underworld, furthermore, there lives Hine-nui-te-pō [Great woman the night], the woman who brought death into the world.

Night and the underworld were inseparably associated, both being known by the one expression, Te Pō [Night]. Like many peoples the Māori feared the darkness and the spirits that moved about in the dark, and would not venture out at night without good reason. But in sleep their wairua might move through the darkness. If someone dreamt of a meeting with another person, whether alive or dead, the explanation was that their wairua had met in the underworld.

Since night belonged with Papa and Hine-nui-te-pō, females generally were associated with darkness – which in ritual, oratory and poetry had negative associations with defeat and death. Males, predictably, were associated with the light – which was associated with life and success.

Also the east, being the source of light, was in many contexts regarded as a male domain, while the west was associated with women.

Yet the darkness had great power, as women in fact did. The world after all had come from darkness, just as new life came from women, and it was darkness (and the woman Hine-nui-te-pō) that received people at the end of their lives. The powers of darkness and of light were in reality more evenly balanced in Māori thought and experience than a simplistic interpretation might suggest.

## Nukumaitore's Descendants
### An island of women

Tales about an island inhabited only by women, and a man who is shipwrecked there, were told in many parts of Polynesia. On Manihiki in the Cook Islands, this place is Nukumautere.

In two Māori stories, the name Nukumaitore belongs not to the island but the women's ancestor, and the women are known accordingly as Nukumaitore's Descendants [Te Aitanga-a-Nukumaitore]. Sometimes there are men as well, but the emphasis is on the women's presence.

When a man named Tura visits the island, he finds that the women make no use of fire. He teaches them how to kindle fire and cook in an oven, then having taken a wife, he discovers that he must teach the proper methods of childbirth. In introducing the knowledge of these things, he establishes the procedures that human beings have followed ever since.

In the other tale, from the far south, two castaways, Pungarehu and Kōkōmuka, teach the islanders, who include men, how to kindle fire and cook. Then they show them how to kill a giant bird, Te Pouākai, which has been preying upon them. Afterwards they feel homesick, and they sail back to their own land and are united with their wives once more.

## Nuku-tawhiti and Rūānui
### Ancestors of Ngā Puhi

Two ancestors, Nuku-tawhiti and Rūānui, are held mainly responsible for the settlement of the Hokianga region in the far north. The story begins with the explorer Kupe, who was there first. Some say Nuku-tawhiti met him in Hokianga on his arrival, others that the meeting occurred back in Hawaiki and that Kupe, who had just returned from his stay in Hokianga, gave Nuku sailing directions and also his own ship, *Ngā-toki-mātā-whao-rua*. Rūānui meanwhile decided to

*Mohi Tāwhai (1827–1894) of Hokianga was one of a number of Ngā Puhi authorities who gave information about their traditional history to writers who recorded it.*

accompany Nuku and made ready his vessel, the *Māmari*. Kupe gave much good advice and provided taniwha guardians for both waka.

Safely arrived in Hokianga with their followers, the two rangatira set about building themselves carved houses. This made them rivals, because Rūānui finished his house first and would not agree to wait so that both houses could be ceremonially opened at the same time. Then in a further demonstration of his mana, Rūānui summoned a whale to strand itself on the beach to provide meat for the feast that would accompany his opening ceremony.

Enraged at this, Nuku-tawhiti created a huge sandbank and shut out the whale, but Rūānui called upon Tangaroa, ruler of the sea, and a great wave swept the whale over the sandbank and towards his house. In this way he defeated Nuku-tawhiti, despite his powers, and he never afterwards submitted to him.

The quarrel between the two men continued between their successors and followers for some six generations. After this, though, they began to intermarry.

The traditions vary somewhat. There are those who say it was Nuku-tawhiti who captained *Māmari* on its voyage from Hawaiki, and that

# Landscape

Myths explained that certain prominent mountains had moved of their own accord to their present positions – or sometimes, that these peaks were people who had turned to stone. Both stories were told of Mount Manaia, highest peak in the Whāngārei Heads (*above*), and his companion Mount Tokatoka, a volcanic peak near the Kaipara Harbour (*below*).

Two ancient landmarks, both tapu for many generations, have been preserved at Whakatāne.

*Right:* Muriwai, sister of Tōroa, captain of *Mātaatua*, and a woman of great mana, occupied this cave after their waka arrived from Hawaiki (see pages 75, 109–10).

*Below:* Pōhaturoa [Long rock], a religious centre of great importance to Ngāti Awa and allied peoples. Just beyond, in a tapu pool [wai tapu] in a nearby stream, the tohi ritual was performed over newborn babies. In a tapu cave (now a tunnel) at its base, young men were tattooed. Meetings of rangatira were held under its shadow. And the bones of high-ranking people were laid to rest on its ledges.

Now in the centre of the town of Whakatāne, Pōhaturoa has also become the region's official War Memorial.

On the summit of Old Man Range in Central Otago, in a harsh alpine environment,
a tall rock pillar was believed to be the dog-headed monster Kōpūwai, turned to
stone (see page 90). The English name of this pillar is The Obelisk.

The homeland of Hawaiki was believed to lie in the east, this being the direction of the rising sun by day and the rising stars by night (see pages 51–52). For this reason, certain of the islands on the east coast of the North Island have a special association with Hawaiki.

The supernatural fires [ahi tipua] of Whakaari (White Island, *above*) were thought to have been brought from Hawaiki, and a myth explained that this happened when Whakaari became a resting-place for two women who were bringing fire from Hawaiki to warm their brother Ngātoro-i-rangi (see pages 205–6).

It was also apparent that the valuable deposits of obsidian on Tūhua (Mayor Island, *right*) had been brought across the water from Hawaiki (see pages 124–25).

By Ōtiki (East Cape), Whanga-o-keno (East Island, *above right*) was the place where the *Mangarara*, on its voyage from Hawaiki, first landed before continuing on to the mainland (see pages 103–5). When the wairua of the recently dead set out from Ōtiki on their eastward journey to Hawaiki (see page 208), they also passed by Whanga-o-keno.

A long headland to the south of the present city of Gisborne is Pāwa's Dog
[Te Kurī a Pāwa], turned to stone (see page 136). Its English name is
Young Nicks Head.

When Māui pulled up his fish, his fish hook became part of the land and can be seen now in the sweeping curve of Hawke Bay (see page 117). The sharp point is Te Matau a Māui [Māui's fish hook]; its English name is Cape Kidnappers.

In every region people have their own tapu mountain.
*Above:* Mount Taupiri, the revered mountain of Ngāti Mahuta in the lower
Waikato, viewed from Kaitotehe Pā in 1844.

*Below:* The many volcanoes in the Tāmaki region were believed to have
been brought into existence by a giant named Mataoho (see page 100). The
deep round crater of Maunga-whau (Mount Eden) was tapu to Mataoho,
being known as Te Ipu-a-Mataoho [Mataoho's bowl].

Rūānui accompanied him on the vessel. Some say Rūānui was Nuku's junior relative, others that he was a brother-in-law. Nuku-tawhiti is also known as Nuku-mai-tawhiti [Nuku from the distance].

Nuku-tawhiti and Rūānui are among the founding ancestors of Ngā Puhi. Rūānui is also one of the early ancestors of the peoples of Te Rārawa and Te Aupōuri.

## Ocean
### The surrounding waters

The ocean, like the earth, is female. In some regions, such as Whanganui and Heretaunga (Hawke's Bay), she is Hine-moana [Ocean woman]. Since the ocean is formed from the rivers, Hine-moana is often the daughter of Parawhenua-mea (the rivers, lakes and swamps).

Hine-moana unceasingly assails her forebear Papa the earth, but Papa is guarded by Hine-one [Sand woman], Hine-tuakirikiri [Gravel woman] and Rakahore (who is the rocks). Sometimes Hine-moana is said to be watched over by her husband Kiwa, and certain kinds of fish, shellfish and seaweed are regarded as their progeny. Each of these living things was placed in its proper position by her.

In the southern Bay of Plenty the ocean is Wainui [Great waters], one of the three children of Rangi the sky and Papa the earth. Since she is the mother and origin of water, the rivers make their way towards her.

Moana-nui [Great ocean] is her name in Tūranga (the Gisborne district). There she is the daughter of Rangi and his second wife Wainui-ātea [Vast expanse of waters].

## Owheao
### A taniwha at Taupō

In the sixteenth and early seventeenth centuries an ancient people known as Ngāti Hotu, occupants of the Taupō district, came under pressure from certain sections of Ngāti Tūwharetoa who had taken up arms against them. The fighting continued for several generations, with Ngāti Tūwharetoa gradually establishing themselves in the region. Victory was finally assured when Tūrangi-tukua and other rangatira of Ngāti Tūwharetoa managed to destroy Owheao, the taniwha guardian of Ngāti Hotu.

This took place at Te Hemo, near the present town of Tūrangi (which is called after Tūrangi-tukua). After many unsuccessful attempts had been made, strong ropes were plaited and a snare

was set at the entrance to Owheao's cave. When Waikari's daughter Hine-rauāmoa approached the cave as a decoy, Owheao emerged at once and was caught in the snare. The ropes were pulled tight and the taniwha was killed.

Ngāti Tūwharetoa were now able to build a pā nearby, and from this stronghold mount attacks upon the local people. With their guardian gone, Ngāti Hotu were soon conquered.

## Pahiko
### A voyage to Hawaiki

At Reporua on the east coast the people of Te Wahine-iti (or Ngāti Pakura), a section of Ngāti Porou, lost a series of battles with the peoples around them. When the survivors were enslaved, their leader Pahiko determined to seek another home.

He instructed his people to steal their masters' seed kūmara from the storehouses and cook and preserve them so they could be eaten on the voyage. This was done, and when the slaves were ordered to plant the kūmara, they planted instead the young shoots of the tutu shrub which appear in the spring.

They sent out their atua to find the way, and he returned bearing a kūmara. This sign represented Hawaiki, source of the kūmara, so the people knew that they would be able to reach it safely.

When all was ready they sailed one night in a vessel belonging to their masters. Next morning those people found that their slaves had disappeared with their precious seed kūmara and their waka.

Pahiko and his people set their course towards the rising sun and sailed back to the homeland of Hawaiki. They found their relatives who had stayed behind and they greeted them, weeping, in the porches of the houses.

## Paia
### Tāne's assistant

In the beginning Tāne separated his father Rangi the sky from his mother Papa the earth so that their children would have room to move, and light could be seen. Mostly he is said to perform this feat on his own, but sometimes he is helped by a brother, or sister, named Paia.

When Paia is a man, he often possesses ritual powers. A Ngāti Kahungunu story from Heretaunga (Hawke's Bay) has Paia as a tapu man who at Tāne's urging, and with the aid of a potent chant, lifts Rangi upon his back. In a South Island story, Paia is a younger brother who recites a chant and helps prop their parents apart. In the far south, a younger brother named Paiao attempts unsuccessfully to separate their parents before Tāne finally succeeds.

Another Ngāti Kahungunu myth has Paia as a younger sister, and this time her role is to encourage Tāne to perform the deed. In a story told at Moeraki, Tāne and his sister Paia marry and produce the first human beings.

Some Tūhoe people say that Paia-te-rangi supported the sky after it had been forced upwards by Tāne, while others assert that Tāne and Paia-te-rangi are one and the same person.

## Paikea

### A journey on a whale

In Hawaiki, Paikea was one of seven-score sons of the great rangatira Uenuku. Another of these young men, Ruatapu, felt himself insulted by his father and determined to gain revenge by murdering his brothers. A new ship had been built, and the sons set out on its first voyage in ignorance of the fact that Ruatapu had bored a hole in the bilge and was covering it with his foot. Far out on the ocean he let the water rush in, and the vessel capsized. Then Ruatapu drowned his brothers one by one. The only brother to escape was Paikea, who was borne up by ritual chants.

So Ruatapu called a farewell and Paikea went on his way. To make himself swim, he recited a long and famous chant, and a taniwha in the form of a whale came and carried him on his back.

Paikea thought the whale was taking him back to Hawaiki, but instead his journey ended at Ahuahu (Great Mercury Island) in Aotearoa. Thinking he was in Hawaiki, he walked south. At Whakatāne he married a woman, Manawatina. But still he wanted to find the home he had left, so after a while he abandoned his wife and children and continued on.

At Te Kautuku, near East Cape, he met Huturangi, daughter of Whiro-nui and Ārai-awa. He married Huturangi and lived there for some time, then went on again, accompanied by his wife and her parents. Still he was looking for his home in Hawaiki.

At last the travellers reached a place on the coast which was very similar to Whāngārā-i-tawhiti [Whāngārā in the distance], Paikea's lost home. Paikea liked this place very much. He named it Whāngārā after his home, and he named the hills and rivers after those he had known. It was here that he and his wife spent the rest of their days.

His descendants regard Paikea as one of the most important ancestors of Ngāti Porou. Some say he was the eldest of Uenuku's sons, and that until his journey his name was Kahutia-te-rangi.

*Paikea rides his whale on Whitireia, a meeting house at Whāngārā on the east coast. A carving by Pine Taiapa in 1939.*

# Pane-iraira

## A taniwha guardian

Some say this was one of the taniwha that guided the *Tainui* during its voyage from Hawaiki, and that when the ship was close to Tāmaki a strong wind blew from the east and Pane-iraira swam back towards Hawaiki. Seeing their guardian abandon them, the people knew there was trouble to come. Soon they found that Marama, the secondary wife of their captain Hoturoa, had broken tapu by taking a lover.

Others claim that the tohunga Raka-taura, instead of coming on the *Tainui*, made his own way across the ocean seated upon the back of Pane-iraira.

Pane-iraira continued his association with the people of Tainui. When a vessel capsized at sea he sometimes carried the crew to safety. From time to time he would communicate with a tohunga possessed of special powers, and on the death of one of these men he would send a whale to strand itself on the shore so that the best food would be available for the funeral.

Pane-iraira's name means 'Spotted head', and describes his appearance. He was last seen in 1863, just before the war with the Pākehā, when he came to warn his people of impending disaster.

# Pani

## Mother of the kūmara

The main idea in this myth is that a woman, Pani, gave birth to the kūmara, or sweet potato. The details vary. According to a Ngāti Awa authority, Hāmiora Pio, a man named Rongo-māui climbed to the sky to acquire the kūmara from his elder brother Whānui (the star Vega). Whānui would not part with the kūmara, but Rongo-māui stole it anyway and placed it in his penis. He then went back down to his wife Pani-tinaku [Seed-kūmara Pani].

When Pani became pregnant, she told her husband to take her to the waters of Mona-ariki. There she recited a ritual chant and gave birth to her 'kūmara children' [tamariki kūmara], the many different varieties of kūmara. Rongo-māui then performed the rituals appropriate to the kūmara harvest, in this way setting the pattern for the future.

Pani, in this version of the story, is the step-mother of the trickster Māui and his brothers. These young men were delighted with their new food but could not get Pani to tell them where it came from. So Māui hid, discovered the truth,

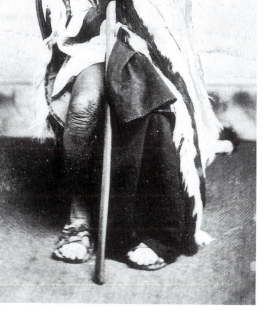

*Etara Te Muru, the last widely acknowledged tohunga in Canterbury, must have taken part in the rituals that ensured Pani's support. In 1873, when more than a hundred years old, he accepted Christianity and was baptised at Kaiapoi.*

and expressed his disgust. Greatly shamed, Pani fled to the underworld, where she cultivates her kūmara. Māui later joined her there.

Unfortunately, Whānui is still angry with Rongo-māui. Since Rongo-māui acquired the kūmara from him, Whānui sends it down each year to the earth, but in revenge for its theft he also sends the caterpillars that attack it.

In Ngāti Porou tradition there is no journey to Whānui, and Pani's husband is Māui-whare-kino. Again there is a preliminary episode; this time a man named Rongo-marae-roa (son of Tāne and parent of the kūmara) takes refuge in Pani's belly after losing a battle with the warrior Tū. When Pani's oven is lit and she needs some kūmara, she goes to the waters of Moana-ariki [Lordly ocean], produces the kūmara and rinses them in the water. She is shamed when a man surprises her there one day.

The mythologies of many peoples recognise an association between women's power of fertility and the fertility of the natural world. In this case, the Māori were assigning a human birth to their most valued food plant (just as the dog, their close companion, was the animal they regarded as having once been human).

But naturally men are involved as well, in one case Rongo-māui and in the other Rongo-marae-roa and Māui-whare-kino. And there is a male ambivalence about Pani's role. Hence the shame she is said to show when a man spies on her; although she apparently retains her power.

Among Ngāti Porou, episodes in the story of Pani were enacted during the elaborate ceremonies that accompanied the planting and harvesting of the kūmara. Rituals elsewhere are not so well recorded, but it is known that chants were addressed to Pani during planting ceremonies at Mokoia in Lake Rotorua. At Kaiapoi in the south, Pani was one of two beings responsible for the welfare of the kūmara gardens. Small shrines nearby took the form of tapu gardens, one dedicated to Pani and the other to her fellow deity Marihaka.

# Pānia

## A woman from the sea

Pānia's home was in the sea, but every evening she swam ashore. She would spend the night by a spring at Hukarere, near the entrance to the harbour at Ahuriri (Napier), then at dawn she would go back to her people in the sea.

One night a young rangatira, Karitoki, went to draw water and discovered her there; he took her to his house and they slept together. After this she visited her husband every evening, but always at dawn she returned to the sea. In time she gave birth to a son; he was quite bald, so they called him Moremore [Baldy].

Karitoki became anxious, thinking the boy might be taken away by the people of the sea, and he asked a tohunga how he could keep his son and wife. The tohunga told Karitoki to wait until they were asleep, then remove their tapu by placing cooked food upon them. When this was done they would no longer be able to return to the sea.

The husband did as he was told, but perhaps the food was not properly cooked, because Pānia went back to her people and never returned. Her son Moremore became a taniwha, the guardian [kaitiaki] of the rich resources of the great harbour of Te Whanga-nui-a-Ōrotu. He appears in different forms – a shark, octopus, log – warning his

people of impending danger while they are gathering sea-food.

Pānia now takes the form of a reef (out from Napier). She can be seen, when the sea is calm, lying face downwards with her arms stretched towards the shore. The fish in her left armpit are rock cod, those in her right armpit are snapper, and those between her thighs are hāpuku. She was once a tapu fishing ground, but now the tapu has been broken and there are not as many fish as before. And most of the harbour of Te Whanga-nui-a-Ōrotu was destroyed in an earthquake in 1931.

Moremore may have been bald as a baby because the human part of him had come into contact with the tapu of the sea people. There are other stories in which contact with too much tapu makes people lose their hair.

# Pāoa

## A Hauraki ancestor

This early ancestor of Ngāti Pāoa came to Hauraki from the Waikato region. At Kaitotehe, by Taupiri Mountain, he had married a high-ranking woman and had two sons, Toa-whena and Toa-poto, then had fell in love with a beautiful slave woman and deserted his family. So then there were two households. His high-ranking wife lived alone with her sons, assisted by a loyal slave, while Pāoa lived some distance away with his new wife.

Both households worked hard cultivating their crops, but Pāoa's supplies of kūmara were always being depleted by visitors. One day some visitors came and he had no kūmara to give them, so in desperation he sent his new wife to beg for kūmara from his first wife. When she refused to help, Pāoa was overwhelmed with shame and abandoned his home that very night.

He went straight up the Mangawara Stream, and from its headwaters he looked back at the Waikato and saw Hauraki before him. He wept for the people he was leaving, then resumed his journey. He came to the Mirimiri-rau Pā on the bank of the Piako River, and he lived with the people there and became their rangatira.

His fame spread throughout Hauraki and finally reached Ruawhea, where the rangatira was Taharua. This man's daughter Tukutuku was well known for her industry and good management, and she was not yet married, having so far rejected all suitors. It happened that a party from Pāoa's pā visited Ruawhea, and the young woman questioned them eagerly about him. She entertained her visitors lavishly, as was her custom, and they told Pāoa about her.

So that autumn, when the crops had been harvested and stored, Pāoa set out to visit Tukutuku. His party paddled down the Piako River and up the Waihou, and came at last to Ruawhea. There they were entertained for several days. At first Tukutuku was too shy to approach Paoa, but her parents encouraged her and they soon married.

A month later, Pāoa and Tukutuku set out for his home. On the way they visited many of her people and Pāoa saw their high regard for her. At Mirimiri-rau her skills, industry and generosity were quickly seen. People began working hard for her, and more of them collected around her.

Tukutuku bore Pāoa ten children, the youngest being the great warrior Horo-whenua. In Pāoa's old age he persuaded his Hauraki sons to take him to the Waikato to visit his sons there, whom he had not seen since his departure. They did this, but the encounter led to a fight in which the Waikato men were killed.

Some writers identify this man with the Pāwa (or Pāoa) who captained the *Horouta*. Their accounts begin with Pāoa travelling from the east coast to the Waikato in search of a wife who has run away.

## Papa
### The first woman, the earth

Papa's name means 'Foundation' or 'Flat surface'. She is the earth that stretches out beneath her husband Rangi, the sky, and at the same time she is the first woman. The world came into being when Tāne separated Rangi and Papa, pushing Rangi upwards and allowing light to come between them.

The sky and earth did not resist when this occurred, for it was their fate to be parted. They do, though, mourn their separation. The mist rising at dawn conveys Papa's love to her husband, and the rain is Rangi's tears.

Papa has a number of extended names, such as Papa-tūā-nuku [Widespread Papa] and Papamatua [Papa the parent]. She supports and sustains her human children, providing food and the other conditions necessary for life, yet inevitably she is inferior to her husband Rangi because she lies below that sacred realm, and Night [Te Pō] is within her. The earth is the house of Aituā [Misfortune], and her children enter her body when they die. The sky, on the other hand, is the house of life, because the persons who light it live forever.

As the primal parents, Rangi and Papa set the pattern for their descendants. Women were thought to take their nature from the first female; like her, they were fertile and productive, greatly loved and valued, though beyond question less important than men. While men were sacred and set apart [tapu], women's nature was everyday, ordinary, profane [noa]. All this and much more was established in the beginning.

The genealogies that trace the history of the world usually begin with Rangi and Papa, then come down through the generations to the present day. A polite and indirect way of asking a person's name was to chant, 'From whom are the two of us descended?'

The other person would sing in reply, 'We are from Great Rangi, and from Papa who lies stretched out here.'

Having established a relationship, the people would then identify themselves.

The separation of Rangi and Papa was re-enacted in a ritual that took place after a divorce when one of the pair still loved the other and wished to be rid of their longing. A chant identified the husband with Rangi and the wife with Papa, making it clear that the first divorce had created a precedent. This later separation was as inevitable as the first one.

## Papa-kauri
### A tipua of Hauraki

This was a tipua, a supernatural being, who belonged to the Hauraki peoples and was their mauri, a source and symbol of their vitality and mana. He took the form of a stump of a kauri tree [papa-kauri], easily recognisable by the flax bush growing upon it.

When someone of Ngāti Maru was about to die, Papa-kauri left his resting place at Hauhau-pounamu, near the mouth of the Waihou River, and moved out over the water. The direction of the tide made no difference; he kept moving outward.

In the beginning, Papa-kauri had been a tree in the vicinity of Ōkauia, near the headwaters of the Waihou (just east of the present town of Matamata). This tree finally fell, and lay there for several generations. It possessed special powers and was associated with an atua, Hina-repe, who took the form of a reptile (probably a gecko). Papa-kauri and Hina-repe had a close relationship with the local people, whose rangatira was a man named Tāmure.

Then a great flood swept Papa-kauri downstream, with Hina-repe riding upon him. On the way they stopped at Te Konehu, a sacred place belonging to the people with whom they were associated; it was here that lightning foretold important events in these people's lives. Hina-repe bit the stone that was the shrine of this lightning, in this way taking its mana. Afterwards the two of them continued their journey down the Waihou, around the many bends of that long slow river.

Eventually they came to Te Kairere, in the territory of Ngāti Maru. Hina-repe went ashore there and established a sacred place with the lightning brought from Te Konehu, then the two went on out into the waters of Tikapa (Hauraki Gulf). Hina-repe landed at Hauturu (Little Barrier Island) and remained there.

Papa-kauri returned to the Waihou and was quietly returning to his home at Ōkauia when Maiotaki, a rangatira and tohunga of Ngāti Maru, saw him moving against the current and recognised him as a tipua of great mana. To keep this valuable tipua in his own people's territory, he recited a potent chant that prevented Papa-kauri from moving.

Meanwhile, back at Ōkauia, Tāmure, the tohunga with whom Papa-kauri had previously been associated, discovered he was gone and asked his atua to locate him. Soon he learnt that Papa-kauri was in the lower reaches of the Waihou, and he set off in his waka to recover him. On the way he recited a chant so powerful that Maiotaki, near the river mouth, realised what was happening.

So began a contest between these two tohunga. Papa-kauri struggled to free himself but was held fast by Maiotaki's atua. Tāmure, when he arrived, had to admit himself beaten. He yielded gracefully, saying, 'You have our ancestor. Behave generously towards him.'

Maiotaki acted as a high-born man should. He received Tāmure hospitably, and next morning allowed him to obtain for himself a share of the lightning that Hinarepe had located at the shrine at Te Kairere. He made propitiatory offerings of fine garments to Papa-kauri, then when the ritual was completed he presented these garments to Tāmure.

Afterwards Tāmure returned to his home, and at Te Konehu he replaced the lightning in the stone where it belonged.

From this time on, Papa-kauri remained with Ngāti Maru near the mouth of the Waihou. He was last seen just before the great pā at Te Tōtara (on a hill near the present town of Thames) was taken by Ngā Puhi forces under the command of Hongi in 1821. He drifted moaning into the waters of the Hauraki Gulf and never returned.

## Para-whenua-mea
### Rivers and streams

Para-whenua-mea is generally the origin of the waters of the earth. She is the streams flowing from the mountains, and she is floodwaters, so it is not surprising that she is often regarded as a daughter of Tāne and Hine-tūpari-maunga [Mountain cliff woman]. Sometimes her husband is Kiwa, guardian of the ocean.

The glow-worm, which lives near water, is under the care of Para-whenua-mea. It was given the power of emitting light so that she would not lose it in the darkness.

Para-whenua-mea's name is related to that of Pele, the volcano goddess in Hawai'i, who is sometimes known as Pele-honua-mea [Pele of the sacred earth]. In Aotearoa, Para-whenua-mea came to be associated with flood waters, apparently because her name changed somewhat and was then differently interpreted. While the Māori word whenua means 'land', like the Hawaiian honua, the word para means 'sediment, silt'.

Another tradition makes Para-whenua-mea the parent of Te Pupū and Te Hoata, who in some regions are the origin of volcanic fire. Here the old significance of the name remains.

## Pare and Hutu
### The woman who was brought back

Pare was a great lady who remained unmarried, cherished and guarded by her people, because they could not find a man worthy to be her husband. She lived in a finely carved house scented with kawakawa leaves, with beautiful cloaks inside and three fences around it.

One day when her people were playing games, whipping tops and throwing darts, they were joined by an unknown rangatira. This man, Hutu, showed great skill, and the people applauded so loudly that Pare came to the door of her house. Hutu's dart landed by the door, and Pare caught it up. When he went to fetch it, she asked him into her house and said she loved him.

Hutu told her he already had a wife and children, but Pare said this did not matter. She kept insisting, and in the end he ran off. So then Pare, suffering from love and shame, ordered her attendants to adorn her house. When everything was ready she killed herself.

Pare's people said that Hutu must die for this. Hutu told them he was willing to die, but that first he must go to the underworld, and they were not to bury her body until his return. He set off, and at Te Rēinga he met Hine-nui-te-pō [Great woman the night]. In return for a present of greenstone she showed him the path and told him how to jump down.

In the underworld he found that Pare was inside a house and would not come out. He showed the people how to throw darts and whip tops, but still she would not come out. So he taught them to make a swing from a tall tree. They plaited ropes, fastened them to the treetop, bent the tree to the ground, and Hutu sat upon it with someone on his shoulders. Then they let go the ropes and the tree sprang upright.

The people were delighted and made such a commotion that Pare's wairua came to watch. Soon she asked to sit on his shoulders. Overjoyed, he told her, 'Hold on tight to my neck.'

They pulled the tree right down, then it sprang back with such force that the ropes flew up to the land above. Hutu kept climbing upwards with Pare on his shoulders, and at last they reached the upper world. When Pare's wairua returned to her body she was alive again, and her grateful people gave her to Hutu as his second wife.

Rangatira often had more than one wife, but a woman of rank was not usually allowed by her people to accept the lesser status of a second wife.

## Pare-ārau

### A woman with loose morals

Pare-ārau is usually identified with the planet Jupiter, though sometimes with Saturn. It was recognised that this bright 'star' [whetū] moves in a different way from most others, and the explanation was that Pare-ārau is a promiscuous woman who goes wandering around at night, up to no good.

She is sometimes said to be the wife of Kōpū (Venus as the morning star). Kōpū told her, 'Stay here till daylight, then we'll go.' But Pare-ārau paid no attention. She went off in the darkness, and at midnight she was found clinging to another man. That is how she got the name Hine-i-tiweka [Woman who sleeps around].

Pare-ārau was sometimes regarded as the leader of the Milky Way, the star that precedes it. Seafarers consulted her when a storm was threatening, believing that if she looked light and misty the storm would pass them by.

## Parikoritawa

### A god in a tree

North of Parinui on the upper Whanganui River

*A swing [mōrere]. In reality people would swing out over a stream, then let go the rope. In the story of Pare and Hutu, the top of the swing is pulled to the ground by its ropes, the two of them sit upon it, then the ropes are let go and they are flung up to the world above.*

there is a high hill, Whirinaki. On this hill there stood a tawa tree named Parikoritawa. Long ago a woman named Matakaha married and had three children, then her husband died. Having to provide for her family, she went to get berries from Parikoritawa. But no sooner had she set to work than a man appeared from the tree. He was not an ordinary man, but half man and half atua. His name was Mata-o-te-rangi.

He made love to her, then gave her his instructions. If she had his daughter, the girl was to be named Parikoritawa after the tree. If she had a boy, he would be named Takaiteiwa, but in this case the child would emerge from her back between the shoulders and she would die.

The child was a boy. He was born in the same way that the cicada emerges from its nymphal husk, and the mother died. An uncle cared for the boy, and he grew up to be the greatest tohunga in the upper Whanganui region.

Because of these events Parikoritawa became

very tapu, and many people died from violating the tapu. Sometimes its leaves were used in healing, but only by those with a knowledge of the proper ritual chants.

## Patito
### A dead man who came back

This man died and set out for Te Rēinga, where the wairua leap down. His grand-daughter followed, begging him to return, but Patito looked back and his gaze turned her to stone.

Patito left behind a son, Toa-kai, who was a brave and skilful warrior. Down below, Patito heard much about his son's valour from newly arrived wairua, and he decided upon a trial of strength – for in his time he had been an expert spearsman. So he sought out his son in the world and challenged him to a duel with koikoi (spears about the length of a man, pointed at both ends). Although Toa-kai was the champion warrior of his Ngā Puhi people at this time, he was unable to ward off his father's thrusts.

Satisfied with his victory, the old man went back down. If his son had proved the better spearsman, Patito would have continued to live upon the earth and human beings would not have been subject to death.

Patito is an ancestor of many of the leading families of Ngā Puhi and Te Rārawa. He lived about fourteen generations ago.

## Pāwa
### Captain of the *Horouta*

According to east coast tradition, the *Horouta* sailed from Hawaiki with a precious cargo of kūmara and other treasures under the command of Pāwa (or Pāoa). Off Whakatāne the vessel was damaged and required a new bowpiece.

So Pāwa took a party of men into the interior to fell a tree and adze a bowpiece. Then, needing a river to float this to the coast, he recited a chant and urinated, in this way bringing into existence four rivers the country required, the Waioeka, Mōtū, Waipāoa and Waiapu.

But Pāwa and his companions soon learnt that their work was in vain, because the *Horouta* was already rebuilt and had sailed on without them. They abandoned the bowpiece, which became the mountain known as Maungahaumi [Bowpiece mountain], and they went on by land. On the way Pāwa created many landmarks, and many places received their names from events that occurred.

At Wharekāhika (Hicks Bay) Pāwa left his child Maroheia, who is still to be seen there in the form of a rock; his stingray [te whai a Pāwa] is a grey rock visible under the water at Matakaoa Point. Then he stirred up the waters, creating strong currents in the ocean that are still there now; the name given them is Te Koringa-o-Pāwa [The place where Pāwa stirred it up]. An echoing cliff at Awatere is Pāwa's house, and his voice can still be heard there.

Then Pāwa heard about an enormous kiwi which could not be killed by human beings. Between Waipiro Bay and Tokomaru Bay he set a trap for this bird, a very large version of a rat trap. Some say this kiwi was a pet of Rongokako, a giant who was Pāwa's enemy; certainly Rongokako came across the trap and dealt it a blow. The rod flew up and is now Mount Arowhana, far inland. The place where the trap stood has become the mountain known as Tāwhiti [Rat trap].

Pāwa continued on and created more landmarks in Tūranga. Among them is the long white headland that is his dog, turned to a cliff. This is Te Kurī-a-Pāwa [Pāwa's dog]; its English name is Young Nicks Head.

*The giant Rongokako, Pāwa's rival, had a pet kiwi, a huge bird that could not be killed by human beings. Pāwa was unable to snare it, but his trap turned into Mount Tāwhiti.*

Pāwa's daughter Hine-akua married Kahu-tuanui, son of Kiwa. Their descendants became important ancestors in the Tūranga region.

## Pekehaua
### A taniwha at Rotorua

Te Awahou Stream, flowing down to Lake Rotorua's north-western shore, has as its source a large spring that wells up from a great depth. This is Te Waro-uri [The dark pit]; its English name is Taniwha Springs.

It was formerly the home of a taniwha, Pekehaua, who devoured human beings. After many parties of travellers had been lost, it was discovered that Pekehaua was to blame, and some warriors of Ngāti Tama, led by Pitaka, made ready to fight him. These men had won fame by defeating another taniwha, Hotupuku, on the Kaingaroa Plains. But this time their enemy was a taniwha that lived under the water.

From supplejack and bush lawyer they constructed a strong basket, decorated with pigeon feathers and large enough to hold several men. Stout ropes were plaited as well, then they made their way upstream, reciting ritual chants.

On the bank above the spring, Pitaka and some companions entered the basket. It was weighted with stones then lowered into the dark depths, with the men on the bank reciting chants to weaken the taniwha, send it to sleep and destroy its powers.

At first the spines on the taniwha's back were angrily erect, then they grew soft as the chants took effect. When the men reached the bottom they found the taniwha stretched out there in its fine home. Pitaka quietly placed a noose around its body, then he and his companions tugged on a rope.

The people above recognised the signal and pulled on the ropes, slowly hauling up the men in the basket and Pekehaua as well. They were dragged ashore, and the now helpless creature was clubbed to death. Then people came from far around to look at their victim. Stretched out on the shore, it was as large as a right whale – not a fully grown right whale, but a calf. The men cut it up for food and found inside the bodies of women, children and men, and garments and weapons of every kind. Afterwards they returned to their homes.

## Peketahi
### A taniwha in the Waikato

In the Waikato region, Peketahi is a rangatira of the taniwha people. One of the stories about him concerns a tohunga, Poraka, who was a medium for Peketahi; he made him offerings, and the taniwha communicated with him.

One day Poraka instructed his daughter Parekawa to cut his hair. Since his head was tapu, Parekawa's hands had to remain tapu for some days afterwards. But while she was still in this condition, visitors arrived at her home. No-one else was there to cook for them, so Parekawa, deeply shamed, cooked the food despite her tapu hands.

So then the taniwha punished her for breaking the tapu. She went crazy, and ran away. No-one could catch her, and in the end she jumped into a stream and disappeared from sight. It was thought that she was dead.

Parekawa made her way through the water then the earth, and came at last to a place where Peketahi and the other taniwha were living; there were houses, plantations and places where they gathered food. She was offered a meal, but Peketahi would not let her eat. He told her that if she ate the food down below, she would have to stay there always.

Because her father was Peketahi's medium, he allowed her to return to the world. After three days she came back up. By now she looked like a taniwha, and she was instructed to keep out of sight until she had jumped on to the tūāhu.

The first time she was discovered, but the second time she reached the tūāhu and her father found her there. Rituals were performed, and she once more assumed her human appearance. After a while she told what she had seen.

There are many taniwha in the water and under the earth, but Peketahi is the one with the mana. And it is Peketahi that people know about, because they listen to the tohunga when he tells them, 'Don't go on to the tapu places or you'll be carried off by Peketahi and dragged into the water.'

## Peketua
### Origin of the tuatara

Reptiles are generally held to be offspring of Punga, but in some east coast traditions the tuatara was created by Peketua. This man made an egg from clay, then on the advice of his brother Tāne he endowed the egg with life. It cracked open and out came the tuatara.

Sometimes Peketua has a wife, Mihamiha, and these two are the parents of all reptiles and insects. Reptiles and insects might therefore be spoken of as Peketua's Family [Te Whānau a Peketua].

## Pikiao
### Ancestor of Ngāti Pikiao

This high-ranking rangatira lived at Ōwhata on the eastern shore of Lake Rotorua. He was sixth in descent from Tama-te-kapua, captain of *Te Arawa* on its voyage from Hawaiki.

When Pikiao's first wife Rakeiti gave him only daughters, his father Kawatapuārangi urged him to take another wife so that he would have a son to carry the family name abroad. In response to this, Pikiao travelled across the island to a Ngāti Maniapoto community on the slopes of Mount Pirongia and there married a woman named Rereiao. Her first child proved to be a boy and was named Hekemaru.

Later Pikiao returned to his first wife and she at last bore him a son, Tamakari. In due course the descendants of Tamakari became Ngāti Pikiao, who belong to Lake Rotoiti in the Rotorua region.

Meanwhile Hekemaru, Pikiao's other son who had remained in the Waikato, became an important ancestor in that region. The descendants of Pōtatau, the first Māori king, are among those who trace descent from Tama-te-kapua through Hekemaru. This link between the Arawa peoples in the Rotorua district and the Tainui peoples in the Waikato is still of much significance.

## Pikopiko-i-whiti
### A harbour at Hawaiki

In accounts of ancestral voyages from Hawaiki to Aotearoa, the waka often sets sail from a harbour, or river mouth or long channel, named Pikopiko-i-whiti. In a sense this waterway makes possible the voyages of the vessels that are launched there.

There were other beliefs. A South Island authority, Tāre Tikao, considered the earth to be circular (like a plate) and 'the sands at Pikopiko-i-whiti' [te one i Pikopiko-i-whiti] to be a sandbank that stretched around the world as a rim, restraining the oceans. This encircling sandbank was itself held in place by Hine-ahu-one [Woman formed from sand].

Certain places in Aotearoa were known as Pikopiko-i-whiti, the belief being that this name had been brought from Hawaiki. Two such localities exist in the Rotorua district. On the lake, Pikopiko-i-whiti is a deep channel between Ōhinemutu and Mokoia Island. At Whakarewarewa, in an intensely tapu area that is now a cemetery, a large pool of this name was a tūāhu where the bones of the dead were prepared after exhumation for their final resting place.

*At Pikopiko-i-whiti, a tapu pool at Whakarewarewa, the bones of the dead were prepared. Patara Te Ngungukai was the last tohunga to perform this duty.*

Such places had a close association with the Pikopiko-i-whiti in Hawaiki. Since people's wairua were frequently believed to return to Hawaiki after death, the ceremonial cleansing of bones at Whakarewarewa must have been understood as having involved in some way a return to Hawaiki.

## Pokopoko
### A taniwha at Kaipara

According to one account, Pokopoko was the great taniwha of the Kaipara Harbour. On a cliff on the south-western shore of the harbour, near a place known now as Shelly Beach, there stood a large pā called Ōkāka. Pokopoko lived in the water nearby, and it was there that he would assemble his army of taniwha. He would watch them gambolling, then place his red-ochre mark upon their backs.

Nine generations ago a tohunga named Mawe at Taiāmai (inland from the Bay of Islands) harboured a grudge against the people of Ngāti Whātua, so he came in secret and recited powerful chants calling upon Pokopoko to rise and destroy the Ōkāka pā. In response, Pokopoko raised his voice like thunder, summoned the wind and waves, burrowed under the cliff and brought the hill and pā crumbling and crashing into the surf.

Other authorities say that Pokopoko was a

man, not a taniwha, and that his full name was Pokopoko-herehere-taniwha [Pokopoko who binds taniwha]. He gained this name when he fought and conquered an army of taniwha near Shelly Beach. The only ones to escape were Ārai-teuru and Te Niniwa (or Niua), who now live at the Hokianga Heads.

Some say that as well as killing taniwha, Pokopoko was a celebrated peacemaker. In honour of this, another of his names was Pokopoko-whiti-te-rā [Pokopoko who makes the sun shine].

When Pokopoko died he was given sea-burial, as he had wished, at the entrance to the Kaipara Harbour. After this, when the harbour was rough the people would say, 'Pokopoko's wrath is kindled.' When the waters were calm they remarked, 'Pokopoko is happy.'

It seems that this man Pokopoko-herehere-taniwha was thought to have become a taniwha after his death.

## Ponaturi
### Uncanny beings in the ocean

These supernatural beings resemble people. They live in the sea and sometimes come ashore, especially at night; their footprints would sometimes be seen on the beach in the morning.

They are generally hostile to humans. The hero Tāwhaki, in one version of his story, avenges his father's death and his mother's enslavement at the hands of the Ponaturi. In this instance they live in a country beneath the waves, but come ashore in the evening to sleep in a large house called Manawa-tāne.

In one version of the myth of Rata, who also has to avenge his father's death, it is the Ponaturi who are the enemy. Rata sets sail with his warriors and at nightfall they reach the pā of the Ponaturi on the shore. After fierce fighting and the recital of potent chants, the multitude of the Ponaturi are slain.

## Porourangi
### Founding ancestor of Ngāti Porou

This high-ranking man was a descendant of Paikea, who rode a whale from Hawaiki. He also traced his descent from Ruatapu, who back in Hawaiki had attempted to kill Paikea.

Porourangi became an important ancestor of Ngāti Porou, a people who take their name from him. As well he is an ancestor of peoples right down the east coast from Tūranga (the Gisborne district) to the Wairarapa.

*The meeting house Porourangi at Waiomatatini, in the Waiapu Valley, during the tangi in 1897 for Rōpata Wahawaha, the leading rangatira who had been largely responsible for its erection in 1888.*

He was a very tapu man, having inherited the extreme tapu of his ancestor Pouheni (a son of Paikea). According to one tradition, his death occurred when under great stress he deliberately chose to break his tapu.

Porourangi's younger brothers knew that he was too tapu to go fishing or birding, or cultivate crops, and they willingly supplied him with food. But Porourangi's wife Hamo kept telling him how lazy he was not to get food for his household, until in the end Porourangi could put up with it no longer. He made himself a fish hook from the curved part of a pāua shell, and he boarded the waka his younger brothers used for fishing.

His younger brothers and his people angrily remonstrated, but he would not listen because he was overcome with shame at his wife's scornful words. At the same time he knew – and so did his people – that disaster would befall him because he had been set apart on account of his ancestor.

So he boarded the waka and, with his brothers, paddled out from Whāngārā. They let out their lines, and Porourangi caught a fish on his hook; he hauled it in and found it was a nohu, a sea perch. (This reddish fish has spines that give painful jabs. It was considered very dangerous by the people in the region.) As soon as the fish entered the vessel, Porourangi became ill and died.

His younger brothers were busy fishing so they did not see him there in the stern. Then they listened, and they could not hear him moving about. They looked into the bilge of the waka, and it was full of blood. Then they looked back and saw he was dead. Blood was pouring from his mouth and nose, and that fish was on his hook.

Porourangi had three sons, Hau, Ueroa and Awapururu, and a daughter, Rongomai-āniwaniwa; important lines of descent are traced through all of them. After his death his widow

Hamo married one of his younger brothers, Tahu (or Tahu-pōtiki). Tahu's descendants moved south, and some of them became Ngāi Tahu in the South Island.

## Pōtaka-tawhiti
### A chief's pet

In the traditions of the Arawa peoples, a dog was the cause of their ancestors' migration from Hawaiki. This dog, Pōtaka-tawhiti, belonged to the great rangatira Hou (or Hou-mai-tawhiti).

Another leading man, Uenuku, was suffering from a boil, and Pōtaka-tawhiti was seen eating the discarded dressings. In effect the dog was eating Uenuku's own body, a terrible insult, so Uenuku and his son Toi at once killed and ate the animal.

Hou's sons Tama-te-kapua and Whakatūria went searching for Pōtaka-tawhiti, calling as they went. When they reached Toi's village, the dog howled his reply from inside Toi's stomach. Toi kept his mouth shut tight, but Pōtaka-tawhiti kept on howling and was heard.

'If only,' Tama-te-kapua told Toi, 'you had killed the dog and returned his body to me, so that we could still have been friends!'

As it was, a great war took place between Hou's people and those of Uenuku. This struggle ended with the migration to Aotearoa of Tama-te-kapua and his followers.

Some years after their arrival one of their number, Īhenga, went hunting kiwi in the interior. He took with him his dog, which was also called Pōtaka-tawhiti. In the Rotorua district the dog ran on ahead chasing a kiwi, and came upon a

*Among Arawa peoples in the Bay of Plenty, visiting rangatira would occasionally be honoured by being presented with food in a bowl carved in the shape of a dog. These bowls were named Pōtaka-tawhiti.*

lake that was alive with little fish. Pōtaka-tawhiti gulped some down, ran back to his master and promptly brought them up again. Īhenga, seeing the whitebait wriggling on the grass, knew that his dog had discovered a lake that would be a treasure for his people.

In yet another Arawa tradition a dog named Pōtaka-tawhiti, the pet of a man named Uenuku-kōpako, was killed by the people of Mokoia Island. In retaliation his master fought them and defeated them, winning the island for himself.

The name Pōtaka-tawhiti occurs as well in the west coast tradition of the *Aotea*. When this ship was given to Turi in Hawaiki by his brother-in-law Toto, Turi in return presented Toto with a magnificent dogskin cloak. Pōtaka-tawhiti was among the eight dogs whose skins were used for this cloak.

## Pou

### Treasures from Hawaiki

The best known myth about Pou, or Pou-rangahua, is that one day this man left his home at Tūranga (Gisborne) and travelled to Hawaiki; some say he was carried off by the taniwha Ruamano, others that his waka was blown there in a storm. At Hawaiki he lived at Pari-nui-te-rā (cliffs that are the origin of the kūmara).

After a while he became homesick, and the leading rangatira at Hawaiki, who was Tāne, allowed him to fly home on the back of a giant bird named Te Manu-nui-a-Ruakapanga [Rua-kapanga's great bird]. As a farewell present Tāne gave him two baskets of kūmara from the summit of Pari-nui-te-rā, and two wooden spades to employ in the cultivation of this valuable plant. Lastly he warned him to treat the bird well.

But Pou disregarded his instructions. As they approached Tūranga he pulled a feather from under the bird's wing (it fell into the ocean and grew into the first kahikatea tree). And he made the bird take him all the way home, delaying the creature so much that on the return flight he was caught and killed by the demonic Tama-i-waho.

Pou's kūmara were planted by Hākirirangi at Manawarū in Tūranga, and they flourished. But in retaliation for the bird's death three kinds of caterpillars are sent each year from Hawaiki to attack the young plants, and it is a laborious task to defeat them.

At Whangaparāoa in the southern Bay of Plenty, the myth takes a different form. Pou brings two plumes from Ruakapanga's great bird, but he travels by waka and is responsible for the arrival of an important fish, the moki.

*Having gained the kūmara, Pou flies back to Aotearoa on Tāne's great bird. A drawing by Theo Schoon.*

This story begins with the arrival from Hawaiki of the *Tainui*. After making landfall at Whanga-parāoa the vessel sailed north, leaving behind one of the crew, Rua-moe-ngārara. Later this man decided to return to Hawaiki to fetch his relative Pou, so he rode there on the backs of his three taniwha. He found that Pou had just finished work on a waka named *Tauira-mai-tawhiti* [Tauira from afar].

Pou agreed to sail to Aotearoa and made his preparations. In particular he acquired certain possessions. First he visited Rehua and asked for one of his sons. Rehua promised him the fish called moki, saying that every winter this son of his would arrive from Hawaiki.

Pou then visited Ruakapanga and asked for two red plumes [kura] from his great bird. Rua-kapanga gave him a plume named Tau-ninihi from under the bird's right wing, and another named Moko-nui-ā-rangi (some say Ko-nui-ā-rangi) from the left wing. These tapu treasures

141

were stored in a gourd on *Tauira-mai-tawhiti*, and Pou and his companions set sail.

Just off Tikirau (Cape Runaway) their waka struck a rock, because the rituals had been performed incorrectly. The ship was wrecked, and now takes the form of a rock known as Tauira.

The gourd with the red plumes drifted ashore and a man named Māhia claimed them for himself. Because of this, the saying 'Māhia's stranded plume' [te kura pae a Māhia] indicates that something that has been lost will be kept by the person who has found it. Since the plumes were wet, Māhia spread them to dry on rocks at Rātānui; some of their colour ran into the rocks, which are still red now. Afterwards the plumes were placed in burial caves.

As for the moki, Rehua kept his promise. Every winter these tapu fish migrate from Hawaiki to Whangaparāoa and are caught by the people there.

Another tradition, also belonging to Te Whānau-ā-Apanui, has nothing about plumes or the moki but tells how Pou arranged for great schools of kahawai to migrate each summer to the mouth of the Mōtū River. This happened after Pou's son Hekopara was drowned at the river mouth.

Suspecting that his son had been abducted by Tangaroa, whose home is in the ocean, Pou visited him in Hawaiki. (Tangaroa, it seems, was a relative.) At Hawaiki he found Tangaroa living in a house full of different kinds of fish. Tangaroa denied taking the boy, though he had apparently done so. When asked to attend the mourning ceremony, he promised to arrive in the early summer.

So Pou returned home and made careful preparations to catch and kill Tangaroa. The nets and lines, firewood and oven stones were made ready. The experts watched from the lookout place, and when the time was right they saw Tangaroa, in the form of large schools of kahawai, approaching from Hawaiki in the east. Then for three months the people caught great quantities of kahawai, cooking them in enormous ovens and drying them for the winter.

Every year this happened. And every year, until the early 1900s, the first kahawai caught was hung as an offering to Pou in a rātā tree at the mouth of the Mōtū River. This rātā was the mauri of the local people, the source and representation of their life force and mana.

Several tipua play their part with Pou in ensuring that the kahawai visit the Mōtū. Kōhine-Mōtū [Mōtū woman], who takes the form of a rock at the river mouth, is still revered. Heko-

para, Pou's drowned son, is a rock quite a long way up the river. He is a mauri of the kahawai, attracting them to the waters around him.

## Poutini
### The origin of greenstone

The usual explanation for the origin of greenstone is that Ngahue and his pet fish Poutini were chased from Hawaiki to Aotearoa by their enemy Hine-tua-hōanga, and that in this country the fish turned into greenstone.

In other traditions Poutini, while still greenstone, is a star (which has not been identified). It is explained that 'One of the chiefs living in the sky is the star Poutini . . . Poutini's people are greenstone. Those people migrated here from Hawaiki, having been attacked by enemies. They came down from the sky, but their principal rangatira, Poutini, remained there.'

In Mātaatua tradition Poutini is a son of Tangotango, whose children include the stars, sun and moon. Among Poutini's descendants are famous greenstone weapons and ornaments.

While the expression 'Poutini's stone' [te whatu o Poutini] usually referred to greenstone, in some districts it was used instead of the berries of the hīnau tree, which when steamed were a favourite food.

## Poutū-te-rangi
### A harvest star

Poutū-te-rangi is usually identified with the star Altair. His reappearance in the east before sunrise during the ninth month of the Māori year (February–March) marked the approach of autumn, and the tenth month (March–April) was often known by his name.

Arriving at this time, Poutū-te-rangi was one of the main food-bringing stars. In some parts of the country he presides over the kūmara harvest itself. Elsewhere he tells the people to prepare for the harvest, and Whānui then brings it.

## Puanga
### The start of the new year

Puanga is the star Rigel in the constellation of Orion. While the rising of Matariki (the Pleiades) marked the start of the new year in many parts of the country, in the far north and the South Island the new year began after Puanga had come up brilliantly at dawn in the east. This took place in mid-June (a month after the rising of the Pleiades). Often the start of the year was calculated from the first new moon following the rising of Puanga.

Puanga was often believed to be female and was regarded as one of the most beautiful of stars. When she first appeared the marae was swept in her honour, offerings of tapu food were made and she was greeted with tears and ritual chants. In the South Island the appearance of Puanga (or Puaka, as she was known there) marked the ceremonial opening of the tapu house of learning that was attended each year by young men of rank.

At this time the women studied Puanga's aspect intently. If they considered that her rays were directed towards the south, they predicted a poor season for crops, forest foods and fish; if her rays shone northward, all foods would be plentiful.

The word puanga can mean 'blossom,' and her name was understood in this way. The constellation of Orion was often seen as a bird snare with a shaft, and a perch to which a flower was fastened to attract birds. In the sky this flower was Puanga.

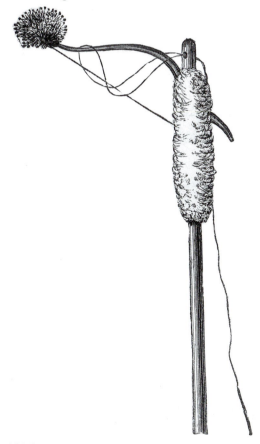

*A bird snare with a nectar-bearing flower on the perch. The constellation of Orion was often viewed as a bird snare, its flower being Puanga (the star Rigel).*

## Pūhaorangi
### A lover from the sky

The stories differ, but all agree that Pūhaorangi was a man in the sky who in ancient times came down to earth to visit a human woman, Kura-i-monoa (or Te Kura-nui-a-monoa), whose earthly husband was Toi. Some say he came as a pigeon, which Te Kura fondled, others that she thought in the dark house that Pūhaorangi was her husband. She bore his son Oho-mai-rangi [Oho from the sky].

In the traditions of the Arawa peoples, Pūhaorangi's visit occurred in Hawaiki. His son Oho-mai-rangi had descendants who took his name, becoming known as Ngā Oho, and it was these people who afterwards came to Aotearoa on *Te Arawa*. As their numbers increased they acquired other names, then in the nineteenth century most of these peoples came together under the general name of Te Arawa. But the orators of Te Arawa still speak of their people as Te Heketanga-ā-rangi [Those come down from the sky] in proud remembrance of the origin of their ancestor Oho-mai-rangi.

Other peoples, such as Tūhoe and Ngāti Awa, trace descent from Oho-mai-rangi. In their traditions Te Kura-i-monoa and Toi live not in Hawaiki but in Aotearoa, at Whakatāne, and the celestial visitor is not Pūhaorangi but Tama-i-waho.

## Puha-o-te-rangi
### A high-ranking Whanganui man

This ancestor is said to have been so tapu that most people did not greet him by pressing their nose to his nose [hongi] in the usual way, but instead pressed their nose to his knee – for his head was too sacred to be in contact with common people.

Among his descendants are people belonging to the Whanganui region and the coastal strip extending northwards to Taranaki, also some Ngāti Tūwharetoa in the Taupō region. In southern Taupō, for instance, the nineteenth-century rangatira Te Here-kiekie was a descendant of Puha-o-te-rangi through his mother, Te Kahu-rangi.

## Puhi
### A journey northwards

This man was a younger brother of Tōroa, who captained the *Mātaatua* on its voyage from the homeland of Hawaiki. At first Puhi lived with his relatives at Whakatāne, but after a quarrel with Tōroa he left to find a new home.

He and his people sailed north in *Mātaatua*. Some say they went right up the east coast, others that at Tāmaki they portaged the vessel across to the Manukau Harbour, continued north to Hokianga, lived there for a while, then dragged their ship across to Kerikeri on the east coast. All agree that Puhi and his people made their home at Takou Bay (just north of the Bay of Islands) and that *Mātaatua*, turned to stone, lies at the mouth of a little river there, the Kopua-kawai.

During this long journey many places received their names as the result of incidents concerning Puhi which occurred on the way.

Puhi is an important ancestor of Ngā Puhi, a people who are sometimes said to take their name from him. Some say his full name was Puhi-kai-ariki, and that his grandson was the great rangatira Rāhiri. Others consider Rāhiri to be the grandson of a brother of Puhi, a man who bore the similar name Puhi-moana-ariki.

## Punga
### Parent of ugly creatures

There had to be a reason for the presence of ugly, nasty creatures, and that reason was Punga.

*Eagle rays and other rays have dangerous spines; in shallow water it is possible to step on one and receive a painful wound. No wonder these unpleasant creatures were believed to be children of Punga.*

Sometimes he is the father of reptiles, sharks, and fish such as stingrays. In one region he is the father of marine mammals. Elsewhere he is the parent of insects.

According to the Arawa peoples, Punga was a son of Tangaroa, the father of fish, and he in his turn had two sons, Ika-tere [Swimming fish] and Tū-te-wehiwehi [Fear and awe]. When Tāwhirimātea, the wind, attacked his brothers, Ika-tere fled to the sea and Tū-te-wehiwehi made for the land. Ika-tere's children are fish and Tū-te-wehiwehi's children are reptiles.

This myth explains the similarity between fish and reptiles in terms of their common parentage. It also explains why fish and reptiles now inhabit different realms.

On the west coast of the North Island, Punga and Karihi are the ugly elder brothers (or uncles or brothers-in-law) of the handsome rangatira Tāwhaki. These brothers have unpleasant offspring, sharks and reptiles. Jealous of Tāwhaki, they attack and kill him, but he comes back to life and mounts to the sky.

In the South Island, where marine mammals were common, Punga's children are the sea lions, fur seals, leopard seals and whales. These creatures once lived in the sky, but Tāwhaki climbed up to avenge their murder of his father and threw them down into the ocean. That is why they live there now.

While Punga is generally male, in one story the creator Tāne takes to wife a woman named Punga who becomes the mother of insects. It seems to have been thought that the ugliest of all insects was the giant wētā, because this was known as Punga's wētā.

In proverbial expressions and songs an ugly person might be spoken of disparagingly as Punga's offspring, and someone who had been rejected might speak of themselves ironically as Punga's child.

In Ngāti Porou tradition, Hunga is a son of Rangi and Papa and the father of lice. This is probably a related belief.

## Pururau
### An extraordinary fish

This huge fish was a tipua, an uncanny being. He was a kahawai, and was first sighted near Whangaparāoa in the Bay of Plenty, where these fish are plentiful. Apart from his enormous size, he could be recognised by the fact that his head was always partly above the water and had a small tree growing upon it.

A man and woman, Tāne-patua and Mamoe,

made up their minds to capture Pururau. For months they followed the fish in their waka, taking with them a kahawai net of great mana and tapu. After Pururau had swum right around the east coast and across to the west coast, they caught him at last at Waingongoro in southern Taranaki.

This happened about seventeen generations ago.

## Pū-tē-hue
### Origin of the gourd

Gourds were carefully cultivated. In summer the young fruit were enjoyed as a vegetable, but the plant was grown mainly for the ripened fruit. Dried and hollowed out, sliced open or with a hole bored at the top, they became containers used for many purposes.

Among Ngāti Awa in the Bay of Plenty, the origin of the gourd plant was Pū-tē-hue, a female who was the last-born of the children of Tāne and Hine-rauāmoa. During quarrels between the offspring of Rangi and Papa, Pū-tē-hue joined Rongo (who is the kūmara) and Haumia (fernroot) in striving to maintain the peace – for these three plants are peaceable people who live very quietly.

It is sometimes said that Pū-tē-hue's husband is Tangaroa and that one of their daughters is Rona. Other accounts name her husband as Tāwhirimātea.

## Rāhiri
### A northern ancestor

Nearly all of Ngā Puhi in the far north trace their descent from Rāhiri, whose grandfather Puhi came from Hawaiki on the *Mātaatua*. Puhi travelled north from Whakatāne to Hokianga, married there and had a daughter; this girl's name is usually given as Ihenga-parāoa, though the traditions vary. She married Tauramoko, a descendant of Nuku-tawhiti. Rāhiri was their son.

Rāhiri was born about sixteen generations ago at the foot of Whiria Hill at Pakanae, on the southern shore of the Hokianga Harbour. When he became a man he captured the strongly fortified pā that stood upon this hill and drove its occupants, Ngāti Awa, away from the north. For much of his life he lived with his people in this pā. The remains of its fortifications are still to be seen, and a handsome monument to his memory now stands upon the summit.

Rāhiri had three wives. His first, Āhua-iti of Ngāi Tāhuhu, belonged to Pakaraka near Kaikohe, and Rāhiri lived with her there for a

*Kamariera Te Hautakiri Wharepapa, who lived in the Mangakāhia Valley inland from Whāngārei, was an authority on his Ngā Puhi people's traditions and a well-known storyteller. He died at a great age in 1919.*

while, but they quarrelled when she offered her brothers a meal of fernroot that had been set aside for Rāhiri. So they separated, but afterwards she bore his son, Uenuku-kūare. This man had many famous descendants, among them Ue-oneone, who married Rei-tū from the Waikato.

Rāhiri's second wife, Whakaruru, had a son named Kaharau; many peoples trace their descent to him. His third wife was Moetonga.

## Rakahore
### Father of rocks

Rakahore is the origin of rocks of all kinds. Along with Hine-one [Sand woman] and Hine-tua-kirikiri [Gravel woman], he protects the sides of Papa, the earth, from the attacks of Hine-moana [Ocean woman].

On the east coast he is sometimes a son of Kiwa, guardian of the ocean, and Para-whenua-mea, the waters of the earth. He has two wives. With Hine-māukuuku he produces rocks and stones on the land, while with Hine-wai-pipī [Woman of soaking waters] he is the source of rocks and reefs in the ocean.

Other genealogies give Rakahore different parents, wives and children. Sometimes he fathers sand and gravel. Sometimes, with Hine-ukurangi [Clay woman], he is the origin of valuable rocks such as Whatu-aho [Shining stone], who is obsidian, and Hine-tua-hōanga [Sandstone woman], who is the different kinds of sandstone used for shaping stone tools and ornaments.

His name and sex can change. Rangihore, in an account probably from the far north, personifies rocks and stones; a son of Māui and Rohe, he is the father of Maru, a sinister figure associated with warfare. Rangahore, in Arawa myth, is a woman whom Tāne takes to wife then abandons when he finds she gives birth only to stones.

## Raka-maomao
### Father of the south wind

Raka-maomao is associated especially with the cold south wind, which is often his youngest child. Other winds as well are sometimes his progeny. And some say he is the father of all tapu birds, such as Te Hōkioi, the white heron, the long-tailed cuckoo and the huia.

Tāwhirimātea is also regarded as the parent of winds, and the existence of these two figures is variously explained. Sometimes strong winds are the offspring of Tāwhirimātea, and ordinary winds the children of Raka-maomao.

## Raka-taura
### Tohunga of the *Tainui*

In traditions about voyages from the homeland of Hawaiki to Aotearoa, each waka has a leading tohunga. In the story of the *Tainui* there is a struggle between the ship's captain, Hoturoa, and its main tohunga, Raka-taura.

Some say Raka-taura was a lazy man, others that he was a thief. Certainly Hoturoa did not want him. He took another tohunga, Riu-ki-uta, and thought he had left Raka behind.

But Raka was not so easily evaded. Some say he turned into a rat and hid on board, then revealed himself when the ship arrived. Others believe he and his wife rode across the water on the back of their people's taniwha, Pane-iraira, or that they walked or swam across the ocean, keeping close to the *Tainui* so that Raka could hear what was going on.

Some claim the two of them were left behind in the Bay of Plenty but that they dived into the sea, made their way underground and came up in the Waikato River, in a place that still bears their names. From there they walked underground to the west coast, arriving before the *Tainui*. When the crew tried to land, Raka at first prevented them by imitating the sound of a confused hubbub of voices on the shore, so that they were frightened, thinking people were already there. Finally he relented and allowed the ship to land. He and Hoturoa were reconciled, and near Maketū at Kāwhia they established sacred landmarks.

Raka now undertook the task of preparing the land for his descendants. With his wife Kahu-keke (or Kahu-rere) he travelled through the territory of the Tainui peoples inspecting the land and establishing mauri, brought from Hawaiki, to keep the birds in the forested ranges. Then Kahu died on a hill in the Waipā Valley, which Raka named Puke-o-Kahu [Kahu's hill] in her memory.

He made his way eastwards, and at the far boundary of Tainui territory he climbed the mountain now known as Te Aroha. Gazing back the way he had come, he called one peak Te Aroha-ā-uta [Longing for the inland places] and another Te Aroha-ā-tai [Longing for the sea coast] as he mourned his wife who lay in the interior, and wept for the children he had left by the coast. And it was in this region that Raka-taura died.

## Rākeiao
### A warrior with special powers

Hordes of dragonflies under the command of Rākeiao drove from the Rotorua region the early Maruiwi people whom the ancestors of Te Arawa had found there on their arrival and who were still living among them.

A son of the great Rangitihi and his wife Manawa-kotokoto, Rākeiao spent his later years at Lake Ōkataina. His descendants continued to live there.

## Rangi
### The sky father

Rangi's name means 'sky'. The world came into being when Rangi and Papa, the first parents, were separated by their son Tāne. Rangi was thrust high above his wife Papa, the earth, so that there would be room for people to move around and light could enter the world. He was accompanied only by his son Tāwhirimātea, the wind.

Rangi is the first male and Papa the first female, and at the same time Rangi is the sky and Papa the earth. This means that human society and the physical world came into existence at the same time. Each is inseparable from the other.

Being the first male, Rangi in important respects set the pattern for his male descendants. Coming as he does at the very beginning, he is an unspecialised figure; later, male ancestors establish patterns of behaviour in more specific ways. But men's general nature is due to Rangi. Like him, men (in general) are high, associated with light, and tapu. Women on the other hand are like their mother Papa. While their fertility and their skills are essential to the continuance of human life and they are greatly loved and valued, they are in general of lower status than men.

Rangi and Papa are so huge, always so close to humans, that they are generalised figures and often rather passive. Their main role is to be themselves, and so provide the conditions for human existence.

*Rangi and Papa are separated by Tāne (who here, head down, takes the form of a cabbage tree). A drawing by Wilhelm Dittmer.*

# Rangiātea
## A sacred place

Rangiātea [Clear sky] is generally regarded as a sacred place of origin in the homeland of Hawaiki. It is best known from proverbial sayings, such as 'I cannot be lost, I am the seed scattered from Rangiātea' [E kore au e ngaro, te kākano i ruia mai i Rangiātea]. A people whose ancestors came from Rangiātea and successfully crossed the wide seas to Aotearoa cannot be defeated. They will forever survive and flourish.

Originally such sayings referred to the speaker's own people, though they are often applied now to Māori people in general. There are variations in their wording and interpretation. One commentator takes them to mean that high-ranking families 'must originate from the true and proper seeds'.

It seems that in earlier times these sayings were especially important on the west coast of the North Island. In that region Rangiātea was usually believed to be a shrine, sacred house or mountain in Hawaiki.

As well as having this location in Hawaiki, Rangiātea was sometimes the name of a place of strong spiritual significance in Aotearoa. When Tāwhao and his son Tūrongo built a pā on a hill in the Waipā Valley and established an important house of learning there, both the hill and the cultural centre were named Rangiātea. Two centuries later, soon after the acceptance of Christianity, a beautiful church built by the people of Ōtaki was also called Rangiātea.

Another ancient tradition locates Rangiātea in the highest of the skies, the heavenly summit. There, on the Rauroha marae, this sacred building is the source of life and ritual power. For some persons of mana it is also the final destination of the wairua after death.

When beliefs about a high god, Io, evolved in the nineteenth century, Rangiātea was regarded as second only to the abode of Io.

Māori settlers may well have come to Aotearoa from the Society Islands, where the culture is broadly similar. One of the islands in this group, Ra'iatea, has a name which, allowing for a sound shift, is identical with that of Rangiātea. Ra'iatea is now often regarded as the place referred to in the saying about 'the seed scattered from Rangiātea'.

# Rangiriri
## The source of fish

In the sea near Hawaiki there is a spring that is the origin and home of the fish and other creatures in the ocean. Often this is known as the spring at Rangiriri [te puna i Rangiriri]. The name occurs in fishermen's chants that ask Tangaroa, father of the fish, to send his children from the spring at Rangiriri.

Sometimes instead people spoke of Tinirau's spring [te puna a Tinirau], in recognition of Tinirau's position as lord of all the fishes in the sea. But Tinirau is not asked to send fish, for that is not his role.

# Rangitāne
## A founding ancestor

The Rangitāne people trace their descent from this grandson of Whātonga, whom they believe to have been one of three rangatira who arrived from Hawaiki on *Kurahaupō*. The vessel landed at Nukutaurua on Māhia Peninsula, then turned to stone.

Whātonga's second wife, Reretua, bore him a son, Tautoki. He married Waipuna, a great-granddaughter of Kupe, and their son was Rangitāne.

Not a great deal is known about Rangitāne, despite his importance as an ancestor. He lived in Heretaunga (Hawke's Bay), and with his uncle Tara he took part in fighting in the region. With his first wife, Mahue, he had a son, Kōpu-para-para, and with his second wife, Mahiti, a child named Whetuki.

Rangitāne was also known as Tāne-nui-a-rangi and Rangitāne-nui-a-rangi.

At one time the descendants of Rangitāne were (in alliance with the closely related Ngāi Tara) the dominant people in a vast area that included the region now known as Hawke's Bay, the Wellington district up to Dannevirke, the Marlborough Sounds, and part of Nelson. They are now based in the Manawatū region.

# Rangitihi
## An important Arawa ancestor

Rangitihi was a great-great-grandson of Tama-te-kapua, who had captained *Te Arawa* on its voyage from Hawaiki. He married three sisters, then later took a fourth wife. His eight children became the ancestors of most of the peoples in the Rotorua lakes district. They were Kawata-puārangi, Rakeiao, Apumoana, Rātōrua, Rangi-

*The meeting house Rangitihi, opened at Te Tāheke, Rotoiti, in 1951. Around the base of the central pillar in the porch are Rangitihi's four wives. Above are his seven sons and one daughter.*

whakaekeau, Rangiaowhia, Tauruao (a daughter) and Tūhourangi.

It is proverbial that rangatira possess eight talents, or capacities [pūmanawa]. Reinterpreted, this saying was applied to Rangitihi's children, who became known as 'The eight talents of Te Arawa' [Ngā pūmanawa e waru o Te Arawa]. Another saying applies to Rangitihi himself:

Rangitihi ūpoko whakahirahira!
Nō Rangitihi te ūpoko i takaia ki te akatea.

Rangitihi with the great head!
It was Rangitihi whose head was bound with white rātā vine.

This is generally believed to refer to an occasion during a battle when Rangitihi's head was split open by an enemy. Undeterred, Rangitihi called for a length of white rātā vine, and his head was bound with this (some say by Apumoana). He then rallied his men and led them to victory.

So this proud saying celebrates Rangitihi's mana, and the mana of those descended from him – all the more so because the head of an important rangatira was highly tapu. And it can imply to his descendants, 'Never despair!'

In another interpretation, the saying's origin is attributed to circumstances that arose at Rangitihi's funeral. His mana was so great that none of his elder sons felt able to perform the funerary rites – for if they made a mistake, they would die. Finally a younger son, Apumoana, successfully performed the ceremonies, binding the body into the traditional sitting position with a white rātā vine.

## Rarotonga
### Plants firmly rooted

Rarotonga is mentioned in tradition as a place associated with the homeland of Hawaiki. In proverbs it is a place where things are established firmly and cannot be shaken. One saying asserts that 'We cannot be overcome, we are a firmly-rooted cabbage tree from Rarotonga' [E kore e riro, he tī tāmore nō Rarotonga].

This is an affirmation of strength. The persons to whom the saying is applied are as difficult to move as a cabbage tree, with its long taproot. And the cabbage tree, being so strongly rooted, belongs to Rarotonga.

Another saying praises fernroot as 'the firmly rooted plant from Rarotonga' [te tāmore i Rarotonga]. Fernroot was an important food because it was readily available. In this saying its value is associated with its strong roots – and because of

these strong roots, the plant is given an origin in Rarotonga.

## Rata
### Revenge for a father's death

Wahieroa, son of Tāwhaki, was killed by Matuku-tangotango, a demonic being. His own son Rata grew up knowing it was his sacred duty to avenge his father's death.

For this he needed a waka, so he felled a tall tōtara. At dawn next day he returned to adze his tree, but to his astonishment he found it standing upright once more. Again he cut it down with his stone adze, but again next day the tree was standing there. Realising a trick was being played on him, he felled the tree then hid nearby.

Before long he heard the sound of chanting as the Multitude of the Hākuturi approached his tree. Their chant was so powerful that the tree returned to its stump, all the chips flew back, and soon it was growing there as it had done before.

The Multitude of the Hākuturi discovered Rata and they upbraided him: 'It was your doing, for cutting down Tāne's tapu forest without authority. Didn't you think to go to your ancestors, so they could give their assent?'

Rata was shamed by their words, and ever since this time people have performed the proper rituals before they cut down a tōtara or any other important tree.

The Hākuturi themselves adzed Rata's waka, completing it with extraordinary speed. They then, it is sometimes said, formed his crew as he set out to accomplish his task. At dawn they launched their waka, Rata recited a ritual chant and it sped across the sea to Matuku-tangotango's home. Then Rata killed the monster and avenged his father's death.

There are many variations. Rata's waka is named *Riwaru*, *Niwaru* or *Aniuwaru*. In a Ngāti Toa tradition he first kills Matuku-tangotango, then builds his vessel and makes his voyage in order to recover his father's bones. Sometimes Matuku-tangotango has a companion, Poua-hao-kai or Whiti, who is killed as well. In one account Rata is not the avenger of Wahie-roa but the builder of the *Tainui*.

Sometimes Rata succeeds only with the advice of his mother Hine-tua-hōanga [Sandstone woman]. When he builds the *Tainui*, Hine-tua-hōanga is his sister rather than his mother; she tells him to rub his adze upon her back, and he does so. (Sandstone was used in sharpening adzes, and the name Hine-tua-hōanga can be taken as meaning 'Woman with the sandstone back'.)

*The Ngāti Toa version of the myth of Rata is one of a number of traditions communicated by Te Rangihaeata (c.1785–1855) (above) to his sister's son Mātene Te Whiwhi (d. 1881). Mātene (below) wrote them down, and some were later published.*

# Rats
## Weak, greedy, cunning

Having an abundance of fish but very little meat, Polynesians valued their mainly herbivorous rats and carefully transported them from one island to another. Probably the Māori, having discovered the big flightless birds of Aotearoa, did not bother much at first with the rats they had liberated in the forests, but in time these birds grew scarce and meanwhile the rats had flourished.

These rats [kiore] run considerable distances at night from one feeding ground to another, scampering in single file along narrow paths which for economy of effort keep to the highest ground. Traps were laid along their paths and the tiny creatures were singed or plucked. They were then barbecued, or cooked in vessels and potted in their own fat ready to be presented to guests.

On the west coast of the North Island the father of rats was Hinamoki, while on the east coast their mother was Hine-mataiti. The names of these parents were often used in formal speech when speaking of rats.

It was thought that rats could cross water, still in single file, each holding in its mouth the tail of the rat in front; in this formation they safely crossed rivers and even Raukawa (Cook Strait). Some said that in the beginning, rats had swum the wide ocean between Hawaiki and Aotearoa. Others believed they had arrived on ancestral waka such as *Horouta*.

Rats were proverbially weak, but it was a constant struggle keeping them away from store-houses, especially kūmara stores, so there were many complaints about the greed and cunning of 'long-toothed rats' and 'rats that eat through baskets'. Such expressions were also used of greedy people.

# Raukata-ura
## A powerful ancestor in the north

In the far north, Raukata-ura [Crimson Raukata] introduced music to the world. Her flute was once the tough leathery cocoon of the case moth, but later she went to live in this cocoon. Since she has lost her flute, her music now takes the form of sudden, unintelligible noises heard in the forest.

When enemy sorcery had to be countered by the tohunga, Raukata-ura's powers were invoked. Some distance from the village the tohunga cleared a space of weeds and grass, then dug a small pit and thrust into it pebbles that represented the hearts of the enemy (and therefore their bodies). This grave was covered over, then next day the tohunga returned to entrap the wairua of the enemy.

The wairua were imprisoned in a small basket the tohunga made for the purpose. Since plaiting was really women's work, the tohunga enlisted the assistance of the ancestors of the female line by addressing a chant to Raukata-ura as he plaited the basket. Whiro, whose domain is death, was then invoked.

But if the enemy sorcery had been very potent, it was necessary as well to plait a little mat and place upon it an effigy of Raukata-ura formed from a stick, with leaves tied around for head, arms and clothing. The tohunga then asked Raukata-ura to go down to the underworld and take with her the wairua of the persons against whom his sorcery was directed. To ensure she did so, he turned her face downwards.

*On an eighteenth-century carving from the Te Kaha region an ancestor plays a pūtōrino. Large pūtōrino are trumpets; small ones can also be blown as bugle-flutes.*

When war was imminent, Raukata-ura and Whiro were again consulted. Sometimes the tohunga led his people into battle with an effigy of Rakata-ura in one hand and his spear in the other.

## Raukata-uri and Raukata-mea
### Originators of the arts of pleasure

Games, music and dancing were introduced to the world by Raukata-uri [Dark Raukata] and her sister Raukata-mea [Red Raukata]. Sometimes Raukata-uri occurs on her own in these stories. When the two are spoken of together, Raukata-uri is always mentioned first.

In the forest Raukata-uri is an elusive presence. The case moth is thought to be her flute, or the woman herself, the cicada with its insistent song is sometimes said to be her, the mountain foxglove found on Taranaki (Mount Egmont) is her gourd plant, and some say her daughter is Whēke, 'a voice heard in the forest, a female who sings to the world'.

The hanging spleenwort, a fern with pendulous narrow fronds which grows high on forest trees, is known as 'Raukata-uri's ringlets' – or sometimes 'the ringlets of Raukata-uri and Raukata-mea'.

Because Raukata-uri is skilled in women's tasks, an intricate square plait formed from eight strands is 'Raukata-uri's plait'. And she is sometimes the owner of a tapu storehouse where property can be safely stored.

In the story of Tinirau and Kae, Kae visits Tinirau on his island and is kindly treated, then returns home on the back of Tinirau's pet whale. But Kae kills and eats the whale, and Tinirau plans revenge. To this end he summons his sisters Raukata-uri and Raukata-mea, with others, and sends them in search of Kae.

At each village they teach the people the arts of Raukata-uri, such as dancing and singing, dart-throwing, top-spinning and string games. Finally, when all else fails, an erotic dance makes Kae laugh, revealing crooked teeth that betray his identity. By magical means the women carry Kae back to Tinirau's island, and there he is killed.

Stories about these women are over a thousand years old. In the Society Islands, which form part of the cultural region from which the ancestors of the Māori migrated to Aotearoa, Rau'ata-ura and Rau'ata-mea were 'goddesses of the forest' – and these names are equivalent to the Māori names Raukata-ura and Raukata-mea.

What happened, apparently, was that these two figures were brought from the Society Islands

Raukawa's son Rereahu had many children, who became famous. Among them were Maniapoto and Matakore, each the founding ancestor of a people, and a daughter, Te Rongorito, who was very influential.

Raukawa himself became the founding ancestor of Ngāti Raukawa, in the region around Mount Maungatautari (between the present towns of Te Awamutu and Putaruru). In the early 1820s, sections of these people migrated to Te Whanga-nui-a-Tara (the Wellington region).

A huge conical stone in a valley near the village of Te Whetū (between Rotorua and Tokoroa) was traditionally believed to be Raukawa himself.

## Rauru
### The first carver

Many different peoples claim Rauru as their early ancestor, and the traditions about him vary accordingly. On the east coast he is frequently the son of Toi, the first person to live in this land; on the west coast (where Toi is often said to have lived not in Aotearoa but in Hawaiki), he is generally Toi's grandson.

He is an important ancestor of the Tauranga

*Te Kiwi Amohau of Ōhinemutu with the kōauau. These flutes can play the melodies of waiata, the most complex of Maori songs, and they were apparently used mainly to accompany group singing.*

(or somewhere else in that cultural region) to Aotearoa, along with their accompanying stories, and Raukata-ura then became established on her own in the mythology of the far north. Elsewhere her name changed to Raukata-uri, and in this form she was still often associated with Raukata-mea.

In Aotearoa there is a close correspondence between the roles of Raukata-ura and those of the sisters Raukata-uri and Raukata-mea. Apart from their association with music, the case moth and plaiting, both the northern woman and the two sisters have it in common that – in different stories – they carry off the enemy.

## Raukawa
### Founder of Ngāti Raukawa

Raukawa was the son of Tūrongo and Māhina-ā-rangi, whose marriage joined the descent lines of the Waikato and east coast peoples. When he in his turn married Tūrongo-ihi, a descendant of Tia, he allied his Waikato peoples with the peoples of Te Arawa.

*A carving pattern named after Rauru, in many regions the originator of carving.*

peoples, to whom he is known as Rauru-kī-tahi. This name means literally 'Rauru who spoke only once'. The implication is that Rauru always kept his word, also that he commanded such unquestioning obedience that he never had to repeat an order.

In southern Taranaki the people of Ngā Rauru have taken his name and regard him as an ancestor who lived in Hawaiki before the departure of the *Aotea*.

Rauru is regarded in many regions as the originator of the art of wood-carving. The expression 'Rauru's skills' [ngā mahi a Rauru] is applied to the work of an expert carver.

## Rehua
### A great rangatira in the sky

Rehua is a very tapu man who lives in the highest of the skies, often the tenth sky. In a Tūhoe myth, Māui-mua, searching for his sister Hina-uri, transforms himself into a pigeon, takes the name Rupe and flies right up to Rehua. He asks if Rehua, from his high vantage point, has seen his sister, and Rehua tells him where to find her.

Elsewhere it is not Rupe but Tāne who makes the journey to the sky and encounters Rehua. According to Ngāi Tahu in the south, Rehua was the eldest son of Rangi the sky and Papa the earth; he first appeared as lightning but assumed human form when he ascended to the skies. His younger brother Tāne later went up to visit him.

In both of these stories the visitor is shocked when Rehua prepares a meal for him by untying his long hair and shaking into a vessel the birds that have been feeding on the lice on his head. When these birds – they are tūī – are cooked by his attendants and placed before them, neither Rupe nor Tāne will touch them, because they have fed on the lice that have fed on Rehua's tapu head. Tāne, however, receives permission from Rehua to take the birds down to the earth below, and he is told how to snare them. As well he takes the trees with the fruits on which the birds feed; and so we now have birds and forests.

Rehua is also a bright, powerful star. Among some peoples, such as Tūhoe, he was identified with Antares. To others he was Betelgeuse, or sometimes Sirius.

In Tūhoe belief, Rehua has two wives, Rūhī (or Peke-hāwani) and Whakaonge-kai, who are the visible stars closest to him on either side. He lives with his wife Rūhī in the early summer, when she rises near dawn on the eastern horizon; at this time her feet rest upon the earth and she brings food to human beings (because fruits and crops then begin their growth). But in midsummer Rehua returns to his other wife, Whakaonge-kai [Make food scarce]. Food is in short supply and the summer heat is exhausting.

Because of this, and because of the warfare that might take place once crops were planted, Rehua was sometimes called 'Rehua who devours humankind' [Rehua-kai-tangata].

Yet Rehua, living as he does in the highest of the skies, inhabits the realm where there is eternal life. He can therefore 'cure the blind, resuscitate the dead, and cure all diseases'. For this reason and for others, offerings were made to him and he was approached in ritual.

In the south, some people associated him with the sun.

## Rei-tū and Rei-pae
### Northern ancestors

The stories vary, but these girls are usually considered to be daughters of Tuihu, a rangatira in the southern Waikato who was a great-grandson of Whatihua and Apakura. A young rangatira from the north, Ue-oneone, visited their home and fell in love with Rei-tū. After returning to Whangapē, he called his great bird and told it to fetch her.

The bird flew off and landed by the house where Rei-tū and Rei-pae were living. When it conveyed its message, Rei-tū agreed to go. Then Rei-pae begged to be taken as well, so both of them climbed on the huge back. When they reached the district now known as Whāngārei, Rei-pae asked to be let down to relieve herself. The bird landed near a village and she decided to stay there, while the bird flew on with Rei-tū.

Rei-pae married a rangatira named Tāhuhu-pōtiki in the village where she had been left, while Rei-tū married Ue-oneone. Both women became important ancestors. The links they established between the northern peoples and those of the Waikato are still of much significance.

## Reptiles
### Enemies of human beings

Geckos and tuatara were believed to have extraordinary powers and were regarded with fear and awe. They were, it seems, thought to be anomalous creatures, closely related to fish yet living on the land and even, in some cases, climbing trees. Green geckos were especially dreaded when they lifted their heads and emitted chattering sounds thought to be laughter. This was a terrible omen.

Most illness was thought to be caused by a gecko's having invaded the person's body. Such a gecko might have been sent by an atua as a punishment for having broken a tapu restriction, perhaps unknowingly, or it might have come from a sorcerer. If all went well, a tohunga could expel the gecko and heal the patient.

Atua might manifest themselves as geckos, birds or spiders, and those that took the form of geckos were especially feared. Yet the powers of such spirits were sometimes employed for the benefit of human beings, as when a captured gecko was ceremonially released to watch over a burial cave or the mauri of a food resource. It was thought to stay there forever, down through the generations, and would occasionally be glimpsed gliding from its home.

Tuatara are ancient reptiles much larger than geckos, up to sixty centimetres in length, and the male has a row of spines on his head and back which he erects, when excited, in an alarming manner. Yet while they were feared, they were not dreaded as geckos were. They were even eaten.

Reptiles [ngārara] were generally regarded as the offspring of Punga, whose children are all ugly. At first they lived in the sea, then they became dissatisfied and moved to their present home.

In traditional stories, human beings encounter

Below: *A chest in the form of a reptile, ritually endowed with the power to guard a burial cave at Waimamaku, near Hokianga. This reptile could bite in both directions, having a head at its tail end as well (the tail forms the nose). Its powers made it highly dangerous, even to persons with a legitimate reason for entering the cave.*

*It is recorded that one man went to the cave to deposit the bones of a relative, and on entering it stepped over the lizard.*

*'He must have been confused; he did not go round as was the custom. He stepped back again over the lizard, and was bitten by the spirit of the lizard. He felt sick when he got out; went home, and died.'*

Above: *Much illness was thought to be due to the person's body being invaded and devoured by a gecko. It was different, though, when a gecko was swallowed deliberately; on these rare occasions the human generally overcame the reptile.*

*A Rotorua warrior, it is said, persuaded a Waikato woman to elope with him. Later, when she sought her elders' forgiveness, they challenged him to prove his mana by submitting to the ordeal of swallowing a reptile, did so successfully and won lasting fame, also a new name, Ngārara Nui [Great reptile]. Because of this victory over the powers of evil, he is sometimes placed as a guardian on the front of a house.*

giant reptiles that are as much as ten spans in length (nearly twenty metres). Sometimes the monster devours all the human beings it encounters, but is eventually killed by the humans. In a popular tale, a giant reptile kidnaps a human woman and keeps her as his wife, then visits his brothers-in-law and tries to get accepted into human society. The humans invite him into an enormous house built for the purpose, then set fire to the building.

One story tells of a giant reptile that was at first helpful to humans, being the guardian of a pā, but became angry when he did not receive his usual food offering.

While taniwha are beings of a different kind, some of them possess certain of the characteristics of geckos or tuatara.

## Rona
### The woman in the moon

In the far north, Rona is a woman who set out one night to draw water, carrying her gourd. When the moon passed behind a cloud, she stumbled among the bushes and cursed the moon for not giving light. So then the enraged moon came down and seized her. Rona clung to a tree, but it was pulled from the ground, roots and all. She was carried right up to the moon, along with the tree and her gourd.

When the moon is full, Rona can be seen there with her tree and her gourd. The insults she shouted at the moon were sometimes regarded as the origin of curses and vilification in this world, and a saying warned, 'Remember Rona's mistake' [Kia mahara ki te hē o Rona].

She was thought to regulate the tides (along with Te Parata), so another of her names was Rona-whakamau-tai [Rona the controller of the tides]. And she was sometimes held responsible for regulating the months of the year.

On the west coast of the North Island the story is much the same except that Rona is a man, a rangatira who to his annoyance has to draw water for himself in his wife's absence.

In the southern Bay of Plenty and the Urewera, Rona went for water with her sister Tangaroa-a-roto; when she cursed the moon, both women were carried up to become the moon's wives.

In Heretaunga (Hawke's Bay) and some parts of the South Island, the phases of the moon, along with eclipses, were thought to be due to the struggles that periodically occur between the moon and Rona. After they exhaust themselves, the two are revived in Tāne's living waters [Te Wai-ora a Tāne].

In the far south a different tale is told about a man named Rona who kills his wife's lover, then ends up mysteriously in the moon with his gourd.

Elsewhere in Polynesia there is a myth about a woman in the moon, but her name is Hina and she beats barkcloth with her mallet. Sometimes, as in Sāmoa, she is carried up by the moon after she insults it.

Very little barkcloth was made in Aotearoa, so the Māori story changed. Storytellers kept the idea of a woman in the moon, but now associated her with different things. And the name of the woman was transferred, it seems, from one mythical figure to another. In Tahiti and the Tuamotus, Rona was Hina's mother. In Aotearoa other stories came to be told about Hina and the woman in the moon became Rona.

## Rongo
### Origin of the kūmara

The kūmara, or sweet potato, was the most highly valued of plants. In some regions its father Rongo is a son of Rangi and Papa; elsewhere he is a son of Tāne and a grandson of these first parents.

There are the many extended versions of his name. Some belong to Rongo himself, who brings the kūmara into existence, while others refer to secondary figures who later convey the kūmara to human beings.

In Ngāti Porou tradition, Rongo-marae-roa [Rongo of the long marae] is the primary figure, being a son of Tāne and father of the kūmara, while the secondary figure is a man named Rongo-i-amo who later sails to Aotearoa, where he introduces the kūmara to human beings. Rongo-i-amo (whose name seems to mean something like 'Rongo ceremonially presented') represents the kūmara and at the same time is the person who makes it available.

In a related South Island tradition, Rongo-i-tua brings the kūmara from Hawaiki.

In Ngāti Awa tradition, there are again two men with related names and roles. Rongo is a son of Tāne and father of the kūmara, while Rongo-māui is the man who later acquires the kūmara from the star Whānui and brings it down to the earth.

The kūmara was associated with peace and was seen as being opposed to the fernroot, which was often associated with warfare. Naturally then, Rongo is a peacemaker. In fact the word rongo means 'peace'.

Tūhoe account tells us that when the offspring of Rangi and Papa quarrelled among themselves, Rongo was the leader of those who tried to keep the peace. 'Had Rongo acquired the management of this world and its affairs, then . . . agriculture and arts of peace alone would have been followed by all peoples, war and quarrels would have been unknown.'

In Ngāti Kahungunu tradition, Rongo-marae-roa occupies himself with the cultivation of food and other peaceful activities such as assembling travelling parties, dancing, and building houses. There was once a quarrel between Rongo-marae-roa and Tū, his warrior brother, but in the end peace was made between them.

## Rongokako
### Giant strides

Some say this man arrived from Hawaiki on the *Tākitimu* and was the father of the famous Tamatea, some say he came on the *Horouta*, and others again believe he came by mysterious methods of his own. He was a giant and could stride enormous distances.

There was a struggle between Rongokako and Pāwa, who had come (most people say) on the *Horouta*. The two of them raced down the east coast; Rongokako took tremendous steps, and Pāwa was unable to catch him. In some places Rongokako's feet sank into flat rocks, and his footprints have been pointed out by later generations. One such footprint is at Wharekāhika (Hicks Bay), another is a few kilometres south of Whāngārā, another at Tūranga, and another at Nukutaurua on the Māhia Peninsula. From there Rongokako stepped across to Te Matau-a-Māui (Cape Kidnappers), then right down to the shore of Raukawa (Cook Strait). In one stride he crossed Raukawa and was gone.

Pāwa set a trap, hoping to catch Rongokako, but his adversary sprang the trap, and it is now a mountain. This trap is sometimes thought to have been intended not for Rongokako but for his pet bird, a giant kiwi that accompanied him.

## Rongomai
### A powerful god

In many parts of the country Rongomai was an atua who provided guidance and protection in times of war.

In the Taupō region, Rongomai was the main god. Te Heuheu Tūkino, the leading rangatira of Ngāti Tūwharetoa, explained in about 1905 that Rongomai still appeared to him: 'I am a Christian, but nevertheless my own god has not vanished. [Rongomai] is our guardian atua, and our god of war. His ariā [form] is a star; in the olden days it

was a shooting star. Rongomai still appears on certain occasions. He has accompanied me on my travels at night. I was once riding along the shore of Lake Taupō, when the tohu [sign] of Rongomai appeared to follow me in the sky as I went on my way. He is my protector.'

*For generations after the acceptance of Christianity, people continued to experience the presence of protective atua. In Taupō, Te Heuheu Tūkino (Tūreiti) still encountered his own god Rongomai.*

## Rongo-tākāwhiu
### A fierce adversary

This was a man with dreadful powers. The Tūhoe people regarded him as a tohunga, a sorcerer who, when he anticipated the approach of an enemy, would score a line with his staff across the path the enemy warriors would take and recite a chant ensuring that if they crossed that line they would weaken and die. This precedent empowered Tūhoe's own tohunga to perform the same ritual and gain the same result.

On the west coast, Rongo-tākāwhiu was much feared. A poet complaining of illness blames it upon Rongo-tākāwhiu's 'destroying adzes' which have attacked his body.

In one myth, Rongo-tākāwhiu is a creator rather than a destroyer. According to Ngāti Raukawa and some others, the hero Whakatau was not born in the usual way but came from his mother's girdle, which she had thrown into the sea while walking along the shore. At the bottom of the ocean Rongo-tākāwhiu gave life to the girdle, then nurtured and taught the boy he had produced.

But Rongo-tākāwhiu was still acting in character. The boy he reared had one sacred task in life, to avenge a murdered relative. The ritual chants he learnt from Rongo-tākāwhiu helped him to achieve his purpose.

## Rongo-whakaata
### An ancestor in Tūranga

The Rongo-whakaata people trace their descent from this rangatira, who was a great warrior. In Tūranga (the Gisborne district) he ruled large pā at Manutūkē and Waerenga-a-hika.

Rongo-whakaata was a son of Tū-mauri-rere and a great-great-grandson of Porourangi. He married three sisters, Tūrahiri, Uetupue and Moetai.

## Ruaeo
### The giant who introduced lice

Ruaeo had intended to sail on *Te Arawa* on its voyage from Hawaiki to Aotearoa. But the captain, Tama-te-kapua, tricked him into going ashore to collect an adze he claimed to have forgotten, and the ship sailed without him. Tama-te-kapua did this because he wanted Ruaeo's wife Whakaotirangi for himself.

Ruaeo, however, mounted his own expedition, caught up with Tama-te-kapua when *Te Arawa* reached Maketū, and challenged him to single combat. Both these men were giants; Tama-te-kapua was three metres tall, Ruaeo even taller. There are no men like them now.

After a fearful struggle, Ruaeo pulled a handful of lice from a bag he wore around his neck and rubbed them into Tama-te-kapua's hair. He then said, 'I've defeated you! You can keep our woman as your compensation, because you've been defeated.'

But that brave warrior Tama-te-kapua didn't hear a word, because he was itching and stinging and scratching frantically. That is how lice came to Aotearoa.

## Rua-ki-pōuri
### A house in the ocean

In the Whanganui region it was believed that after the separation of Rangi the sky and Papa the earth, their sons Tāne and Tangaroa lived in a house in the ocean called Rua-ki-pōuri [Pit in darkness]. This house was the place from which the fish, little and big, were distributed throughout the ocean. In recalling this, poets speak as well of other houses such as Whare-papa [Reef house] and Whare-rimu [Seaweed house].

Rua-ki-pōuri may be associated with darkness because it was present in the earliest times. But in some sense this house is still there now. When a young man drowned in the Whanganui River in the early eighteenth century, his father sang a lament that spoke of his son as making his way out to the ocean and into Rua-ki-pōuri. It may have been thought that this young man, as he moved through the water, was going back to the beginning.

In other regions this house, while still associated with origins, was envisaged differently. In some parts of Taranaki, Rua-ki-pōuri was one of the names of Miru's house in the underworld, from which much knowledge was brought up to this world.

## Ruamano
### An ocean taniwha

There are many stories about a famous taniwha of this name. In the far north, Ruamano took the form of a mako shark. Further south, one belief was that he was the offspring of Tūtara-kauika, another that he sprang from Te Pupū, a personified form of volcanic fire. On the east coast, Ruamano is one of a pair of taniwha that guided *Tākitimu* on its voyage to Aotearoa.

When a waka was overturned in a storm and the crew flung into the ocean, they might call upon Ruamano and sometimes he would take them to land. And in times of illness his assistance might be requested. A chant was recited, and the affected part of the patient was sprinkled with salt water (which being associated with Ruamano, possessed his powers).

## Ruapūtahanga
### A famous Taranaki ancestor

This beautiful woman lived at Pātea in southern Taranaki; her people were Ngāti Ruanui. When a Waikato rangatira, Tūrongo, visited her home, she loved him and agreed to marry him.

So Tūrongo returned to Kāwhia to prepare for her arrival. He began enlarging his house, but his jealous half-brother Whatihua persuaded him that a smaller house would be better. And he made Tūrongo believe that Ruapūtahanga liked small kūmara, so it was these that Tūrongo put in his storehouse.

Meanwhile Whatihua was secretly constructing a fine big house at Aotea and laying in large supplies of food. His plan was successful. When Ruapūtahanga arrived with a train of attendants, as befitted her rank, Tūrongo could not accommodate or feed so large a company. Whatihua invited the party to stay in his new house, where he fed them well, and presently Ruapūtahanga changed her mind and married Whatihua instead.

But later, after she had borne two sons, she left him. What happened was this. Ruapūtahanga wanted an eel, and Whatihua went fishing. The eels were slow to take the bait, so he charmed them with a chant: 'Die because of Ruapūtahanga's great hunger!'

An eel came out of its hole and took the bait, and afterwards Whatihua went home and told how the eel had responded to his use of Ruapūtahanga's name. Then although he had caught the eel by speaking of Ruapūtahanga, he gave it not to her but to his other wife, Apakura. (Most narrators say Apakura was his principal wife, though some consider Ruapūtahanga to have been the principal wife.)

*The rugged Taranaki coastline along which Ruapūtahanga travelled on her journey south. At centre left is Kaitangata Point, where she escaped from her pursuing husband.*

Deeply shamed at this insult, Ruapūtahanga set off on the long journey back to her home in southern Taranaki. She took the route along the shore, past precipitous cliffs, and at first she carried her baby son. But near Kāwhia she left him on the beach, knowing Whatihua would find him. And soon Whatihua came running up. He found the boy and put him on his back, then he saw Ruapūtahanga and called, 'Wife, stay where you are, think of our son!'

He kept imploring her to return. But the woman kept on going, and crossed the Marokopa River. At Kaitangata Point she came to high cliffs passable only at low tide, and dangerous even then. Travellers had to climb through a cavern in the cliff, while in a cave nearby a taniwha named Rākei-mata-taniwha-rau [Rākei of a myriad taniwha eyes] lay waiting in the water. Once the tide started to rise he would occupy the cavern and seize any unwary travellers.

Ruapūtahanga climbed through just in time, then called back, in words that became famous, 'Husband, go back! The waves of Rākei-mata-taniwha-rau are rising up' [E pā, hoki atu i konā! Ka tū ngā tai o Rākei-mata-taniwha-rau].

It was too late for Whatihua to enter the cavern. He returned home with his baby son, and it was Apakura who brought the boy up.

Ruapūtahanga did not return to Pātea. Instead

she married a rangatira of Te Āti Awa whom she met in northern Taranaki. She had more sons, and when she eventually died and the news reached Kāwhia, her two sons there visited their half-brothers in Taranaki to mourn her death.

## Ruarangi and Tawhaitū
### The wife stolen by a fairy

Ruarangi and his wife Tawhaitū lived on their own together. They had two sons, then one of the sons died. They went on living there; Ruarangi spent his time hunting birds.

One day when Ruarangi was away, a fairy [patupaiarehe] man visited their home, seized Tawhaitū and carried her off. On Ruarangi's return his son told him what had happened and the two of them wept together.

That night the wairua of the dead son visited their house and told Ruarangi what he must do: 'Don't cry any more. You must set out, and keep going until you reach a river, then a second one and a third. You must stop and light a fire, catch a pig, and throw it on the fire.'

Ruarangi did this, and presently the smoke bearing the good smell of pork drifted through the forest. It reached Tawhaitū and she wept, saying to herself, 'Perhaps this smoke is from Ruarangi.'

She followed it and came to Ruarangi. They returned home and she told him to guard her closely because the fairy would soon return. But when the fairy came, he once more carried her off.

Again Ruarangi and his son wept together in the night, and again the dead son came to them: 'Don't cry any more. You must go again, and take with you a cooking pot and a gourd. When you have reached the first river, the second and the third, light another fire. Kill another pig, singe it on the fire and cook it in the pot, then go to the river and dig for red ochre. Cook the pig's fat with the red ochre, fill the gourd with the mixture and bring it back home with you.'

Ruarangi returned to the forest, and the smoke from his fire once more reached Tawhaitū. She followed as she had done before, she found him, and they worked together digging the red ochre. Then they carried it home and painted their house and marae, leaving the ridgepole of the house unpainted as an escape route for the fairy.

When he came he stayed a short distance away, afraid of the red ochre. He felled a tree, leant it against the house and climbed to the ridgepole, but still he could find no way of entering the house. He sang a lament acknowl-edging that the fairy people cannot live with human beings but must stay apart, then he rose up to his home on the mountain heights.

This story was widely known in the Waikato district, and the far north as well. The fairy's name is sometimes Te Rangi-pōuri. In some versions Ruarangi is told by the tohunga that his wife can be kept from the fairies by means of ritual chants, red ochre and the steam from opened ovens – 'so great is their dread of cooked food'.

Being atua, fairies were very tapu and could not approach fire or cooked food; Tawhaitū would have been given only raw food to eat. Probably the fairies feared red ochre because of the mana of which it was a sign. Important timbers in houses and other structures were painted with red ochre, and men and women sometimes painted their faces with it.

Pigs, which come into this version of the story, were introduced in the late eighteenth century. Iron pots were a nineteenth-century acquisition.

## Ruatāne and Tarapikau
### Rival fairy rangatira

Ruatāne was the rangatira of the fairies [patu-paiarehe] in the region extending from Te Aroha through to the Moehau Range. Far to the south, on Mount Maungatautari and the Rangitoto Range north of Lake Taupō, the fairy rangatira was Tarapikau.

One day a human woman was gathering tawa berries in forests near the Rangitoto Range, in the territory of Tarapikau, when she was kidnapped by Ruatāne and carried off to Te Aroha. The wairua of her relatives found her there, and sent a messenger to ask Tarapikau to rescue her.

Tarapikau promised to help. He told the messenger to go that night and encourage the Te Aroha fairies to dance haka; the messenger did so, and just before dawn the exhausted fairies fell fast asleep. Then Tarapikau and his men made a hole in the thatch of the house, found the woman and carried her off. They kept her for a while on Rangitoto, then returned her to her people.

When Ruatāne found the woman gone, he knew Tarapikau had taken her and he set out with an army. But when he caught sight of Tarapikau's warriors at Pae-whenua, in the Rangitoto foothills, he saw they were too numerous for his forces to engage and he returned home to Te Aroha.

As for Tarapikau's warriors, they are still at Pae-whenua. They take the form of regularly formed limestone rocks that cover a hillside there.

# Ruatapu
## An insult avenged

In the homeland of Hawaiki, the great rangatira Uenuku conquered the forces of Wheta, then took one of his enemy's relatives, a woman named Pai-māhutanga, as a secondary wife. As a consequence their son Ruatapu was of unequal parentage. On his father's side he was of high rank, but his mother was little better than a slave.

After Ruatapu had become a man, he and his brothers adzed a waka. When all was done and the young men were adorning themselves for the first, ceremonial voyage, Uenuku anointed and combed the heads of his seven-score sons – all except Ruatapu. Uenuku told Ruatapu that he could not anoint his head because he was only a bastard, of no importance.

Ruatapu wept with shame and planned his revenge. He secretly bored a hole in the bilge of the vessel, then put out to sea with his brothers. All the while his foot covered the hole he had made. When the land was lost to sight, only then did he take away his foot, and the water came in. His brothers looked for the bailer, but he had hidden it. The waka overturned and they were swimming in the sea. Then Ruatapu swam after those men and drowned them one by one.

But his brother Paikea could not be drowned, for he was borne up by ritual chants. So Ruatapu accepted that Paikea would survive, and he offered advice. He foretold that after Paikea had reached the land, he, Ruatapu, would arrive in the early summer in the form of immense waves, and he cautioned that the people must gather on the hills to survive the flood.

Paikea rode a whale to land, not back to Hawaiki but all the way to Aotearoa, and Ruatapu arrived in the early summer as he had said he would.

This is the myth as it is known to the people of Ngāti Porou, on the east coast north of Gisborne. The story explains the origin of the high waves that do in this part of the country break on the shore in early summer, and at the same time it intensifies the reality, turning the waves into a flood. The numerous jellyfish that appear at this time are also identified with Ruatapu.

Peoples related to Ngāti Porou took the story further south, where it changed somewhat. In Heretaunga (Hawke's Bay), where these large waves of early summer do not occur, the waves in the myth break in winter instead, no doubt because of the rough weather experienced then. In the far south of the South Island, unusually large waves were known as Ruatapu.

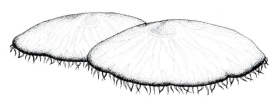

*In the traditions of Ngāti Porou, the high waves that arrive on their shores every spring are sent by Ruatapu. The many jellyfish washed up on the beaches at this time are Ruatapu himself.*

# Rua-taranaki
## The first person to climb Taranaki

Mount Taranaki (Mount Egmont) is said by some to have received its present name after being climbed by Rua-taranaki, the first person to reach those snowy heights. This man Rua-taranaki belonged to a very early people called Te Kāhui Maunga [The Assembly of Mountains].

Others say it was Tahurangi who first climbed the mountain, and so laid claim to it.

# Rua-te-pupuke
## The origin of carving

In Ngāti Porou tradition, Rua-te-pupuke was the first person to gain a knowledge of carving. He acquired it from Tangaroa, who had kidnapped his son Te Manu-hau-turuki.

Te Manu had been sailing toy boats with other boys on the beach when he went too far out, beyond the breakers, and was carried off by Tangaroa. He was taken down to Tangaroa's home in the sea and placed on top of his carved house as a gable figure, a tekoteko. Rua-te-pupuke searched for him and finally found him there.

An old woman advised Rua-te-pupuke that to overcome Tangaroa and his children he must block up the cracks in the house so that daylight could not enter. When he went to do this, he found that the carved figures in the porch were silent but that those inside were conversing together.

In the evening Tangaroa appeared with his children (who were fish), and after entertaining themselves with singing and dancing they went to sleep. Next day these creatures of darkness did not know the sun had risen, and when Rua-te-pupuke pulled open the door they were caught in the light. Rua-te-pupuke fought and killed them, avenging his son.

He burnt the house, there under the ocean, and he brought back up the carved posts from the porch of Tangaroa's house. These became the models for carvers in this world. And because

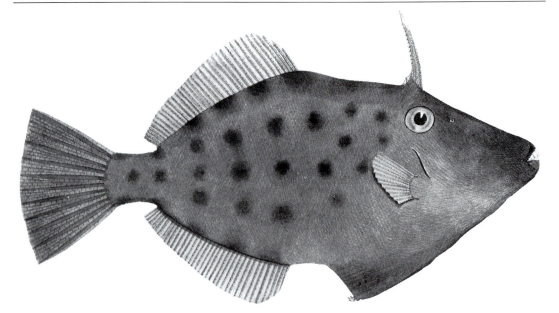

the posts came from the porch rather than the interior, carvings now cannot speak.

It is at first surprising that Mohi Ruatapu, the tohunga who wrote down this version of the story, tells us elsewhere that Tangaroa is Rua-te-pupuke's father. Yet this is quite logical. Rua-te-pupuke acquires the mana, the powers, of a carver in two ways, through descent from the original possessor of these skills and by virtue of his triumph over that person.

The victory over Tangaroa and his children was the occasion on which many of the different kinds of fish assumed their present forms and dispersed to the places where they are now to be found. It was then, for instance, that porpoises and dolphins migrated to the most distant parts of the ocean.

Related traditions are known in other areas. Instead of Rua-te-pupuke, some authorities speak of Rua-pupuke, Rua-i-te-pūkenga or simply Rua. The word puke in these names conveys the idea of thoughts rising or welling up, also (with pūkenga) the idea of a repository of knowledge. The word rua usually refers to a pit or underground storehouse, and there must be an associated meaning here.

Rua-te-pupuke is the best known of many personifications that represent forms of knowledge, the desire for knowledge, and its acquisition. Among these persons, sometimes male and sometimes female, are Rua-i-te-hiringa [Energetic Rua], Rua-i-te-mahara [Thoughtful Rua], Rua-i-te-wānanga [Rua possessed of wisdom], and Rua-i-te-wetewete [Rua who studies all aspects]. A man named Rua-i-te-hotahota [Persistent Rua]

*Leatherjackets are small coastal fish with thick skins and prominent spines. When Rua-te-pupuke attacked Tangaroa's children, most of them died. But, Mohi Ruatapu tells us, 'Leatherjacket rushed out with his throwing spear and his heavy cloak; he got right away, and lived.' Here the leatherjacket is a fierce warrior, his spine a short spear [tīmata] and his thick protective skin equivalent to the heavy cloak [kākahu pukupuku] employed as a shield in battle.*

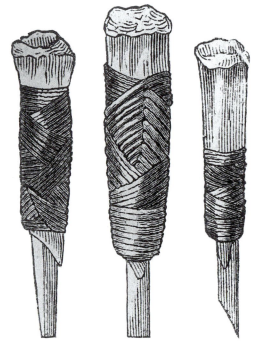

*Hafted greenstone chisels employed by wood carvers. A great variety of chisels were used, large and small, as well as adzes. The rare greenstone was greatly valued for chisels because it took a keen edge, but basalt was also used.*

is often associated with Rua-te-pupuke in his work as a carver. Sometimes all these people are Tangaroa's children.

Rua may be associated with other arts as well, such as weaving.

## Rūaumoko
### Origin of earthquakes

A son of Rangi and Papa, sky and earth, Rūaumoko was still in the womb when his parents were separated, so he remains there now. When he moves around inside his mother, there are earthquakes. By shaking her and turning her over, he divides the warmth of summer from the cold of winter.

Sometimes Rūaumoko is held responsible for volcanic activity. And living as he does in the earth, he is often associated with death. In some accounts he is married to Hine-nui-te-pō, who presides over the underworld.

Among his other names are Rūaimoko, Whakarūaimoko, Rūwaimoko and Rūaimoko-roa. In the Whanganui region, Rū (or Rūauoko) is the creator and father of lakes and rivers. It is he who dug out the great gorge of the Whanganui River.

## Rukutia
### An originator of weaving

In a South Island myth, Rukutia leaves her ugly husband Tama-nui-a-Raki for the good-looking Tū-te-koropaka (or Tū-te-koropanga). Having discovered he is ugly, Tama visits his ancestors in the underworld and they tattoo him, making him handsome. Then he returns to the world and sets out in pursuit of his wife. He gets her back, kills her, then mourns her death. When the spring comes, she returns to life.

Elsewhere in Māori tradition, though not in this story, Rukutia is an originator of weaving and plaiting. Her name must have helped to sustain this idea, since it can be understood as meaning 'Bound together' or 'Bind together'. The process of twisting flax fibre into thread was sometimes known as 'Rukutia's thread-making' [te miri o Rukutia], and her name was given to one of the finest varieties of flax.

Names related to those of Rukutia and Tū-te-koropanga (or Tū-te-koropaka) occur on other Polynesian islands, and their association must be very old. In a Hawaiian story, Lu'ukia is married to a rangatira named Olopana, but a rival suitor intrudes. Again there is an association with garment-making and plaiting: Lu'ukia invents the barkcloth skirt now worn by women and the lashing patterns used on waka and elsewhere.

## Ruru-teina
### A youngest son

In this tale from the far south, Ruru-teina [Ruru-junior] is the youngest son and is treated badly by his brothers. One day the brothers hear about a beautiful woman, Te Roronga-rahia, who lives in a village some distance away. They set out to visit her home, and Ruru accompanies them as their servant.

On their arrival, Ruru stays behind to look after the waka while the elder brothers are entertained in the village. Each brother keeps company with a woman there, and each of the women pretends to be Te Roronga-rahia.

Meanwhile Ruru, going to draw water, comes across the real Te Roronga-rahia sitting quietly in her house with her servant. Every evening he visits her, and she falls in love with him.

Some days later the elder brothers prepare to return home. That night, Ruru hides Te Roronga-rahia and her servant inside the deck-house. Each of the brothers arrives with his woman, and they sail off.

But the wind is against them, and they land in a strange country. They try to light a fire but cannot do so, and Ruru is told to go and ask for fire at a settlement in the distance. There he finds a giant reptile, an evil female named Te Ngārara-huarau (or Te Kārara-huarau) who tries to detain him.

Ruru escapes, and he and his brothers build a trap, a house with a carved figure of Ruru inside it. Presently Te Ngārara-huarau comes looking for Ruru; she enters the house and wraps her disgusting tail around the figure, thinking it Ruru himself. The brothers set fire to the house, and the monster is burnt to death.

A fair wind sends them home to their mother and father. Then each of the elder brothers claims that his wife is Te Roronga-rahia, but the parents cannot see any beauty in these women. When Ruru-teina sends his mother to look in the deck-house, it is revealed that he himself is married to Te Roronga-rahia.

## Sky
### The eternal heights

The sky is an immortal realm because of its height and inaccessibility, and because the lights that move around it live forever. The sun, moon and stars do not die like people on the earth.

163

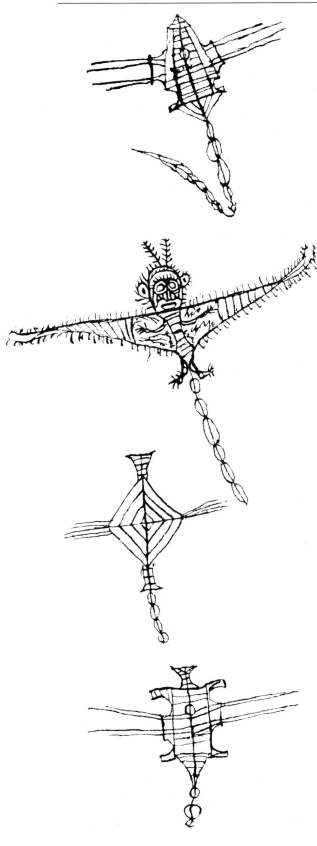

In making human existence possible, these lights give life to human beings. Days and nights are created by the sun, the year is created by the sun's annual movements and the moon's cycles, and the most important of the stars bring with them the seasons and their associated food resources.

In many places it was believed that a number of skies lie one above the other and that the highest is the most tapu and powerful of all. On the east coast, Mohi Ruatapu of Ngāti Porou tells us there are two skies, while Ngāti Kahungunu writers speak of ten, or sometimes twelve. Authorities on the west coast of the North Island say there are ten or eleven; they are solid bodies that spread out over the flat earth, each with its own nature. In one account the lowest is the abode of rain, the next has atua, the third the winds, and the fourth the light. The highest, being the most glorious, is the chief abode of persons such as Rehua.

In some traditions, especially those of Ngāti Kahungunu, Tikitiki-o-rangi is the uppermost of the twelve heavens. Within this highest realm, in a tapu region known as Te Rauroha, there is a most sacred house known as Rangiātea. This is the dwelling place of the high god Io, who is attended by females known as mareikura.

In several myths a man goes up to the skies to obtain a possession, or knowledge, from a person up there. The most important of these journeys are those made by Tāne and by Tāwhaki.

## Stars

### People in the sky

The unreachable skies with their eternal lights were a highly tapu realm, and the people up there did not know death:

Tātai whetū ki te rangi, mau tonu, mau tonu,
Tātai tāngata ki te whenua, ngaro noa, ngaro noa.

Companies of stars in the sky last forever,
   forever,
Companies of men on the earth are lost, lost.

Tohunga with a special knowledge of the stars spent much time studying them. These shining persons follow in their movements and conjunctions a yearly cycle, as does the earth below,

*Kites were popular with adults as well as children and took many forms. Large ones, often in the form of hawks, were flown ceremonially on festive occasions, bringing the earth into contact with the otherwise unreachable sky. Titore, a young rangatira from the far north, did these drawings in 1819 during a visit to England.*

so their rising and setting inevitably marked the progression of the seasons. As well, certain stars were believed actually to bring the seasons into existence, and to send down to the earth the foods that became available at the times of year associated with them.

Since the general movement of the stars is from east to west, a star or constellation that has been absent from the sky for some time will first become visible again in the east just before dawn. The stars therefore, like the sun, were seen as coming from the direction of Hawaiki. Since this mythical land was the main source of life and fertility, the association with Hawaiki supported the idea that some stars bring seasonal foods.

With some important stars, the manner of their rising predicted the nature of the season that was to follow: 'Our old men said that the stars were the cause of good and bad seasons, which are influenced by the mana of their rays.' When the stars looked bright and clear, and were perceived as shining towards the north rather than the south, it was believed that the season would be a good one and the crops would be planted early.

The new year (in early winter, May–June) generally began with the first new moon after the appearance before dawn of Matariki (The Pleiades) or, in other regions, after the rising before dawn of Puanga (Rigel). These stars brought food supplies to human beings. In early August, Whakaahu (Castor) brought the new spring growth of plants and foods of all kinds. Other food-bearing stars include Rehua, Atutahi, Poutū-te-rangi and Whānui. Rehua brought the summer as well, while Takurua was responsible for the cold months. All of these, with others, were the rangatira of the stars [whetū rangatira].

The stars were placed in the sky by Tāne. After he had pushed up his father Rangi the sky, people could move about on the earth but were still in darkness. So to create light and to make his father beautiful, Tāne flung up the stars, then the moon and the sun. Some peoples, such as Ngāti Porou, say the stars are Tāne's sweat from having laboured so hard in raising the sky. Others say he acquired them from Tangotango, others again from Wehi-nui-a-mamao.

Some stars are early ancestors, among them Rehua, Tama-i-waho, Poutini and Marere-o-tonga. Rehua and Tama-i-waho both live in the highest of the skies and are encountered by men who possess the power to climb to those sacred heights. Rehua is usually a beneficient figure, but Tama-i-waho is very dangerous.

The common stars, shining in their multitudes, are atua. The cloud formation known as a mackerel sky, with clouds in long thin parallel masses, shows that the atua are planting their kūmara, while a meteor is an atua visiting the earth – or sometimes, being expelled for misconduct.

It was thought in some regions that when a person of consequence died, the left eye became a star. Still today at a funeral, when the burial has taken place and speakers are addressing their last farewells to the dead, they may say, 'You have risen over the horizon' [Kua whetūrangitia koe].

In life, too, valorous rangatira could be spoken of admiringly as stars. Beautiful girls were compared to the morning star, Kōpū, and eyes flashing with rage or misted with tears might be likened by poets to stars.

Planets were regarded as 'stars' [whetū], although it was recognised that they moved differently from the fixed stars.

# Sun

## The light of day

Daylight was associated with life and wellbeing, and darkness with weakness and sometimes death. As an extension of this idea, the rising sun and the east were associated with life, and the setting sun and the west with death. The rising sun was often greeted with a joyful song, while the evening was a time when people sang laments.

Because of this, the east was a propitious direction. At divination ceremonies it was a good omen if rods fell towards the east, a bad one if they fell towards the west. Males were associated with the rising sun, females with the setting sun. The homeland of Hawaiki, the source of life, was generally believed to lie in the direction of the rising sun.

The Sun [Te Rā] was placed in the sky by Tāne after he had separated Rangi the sky and Papa the earth. Some east coast peoples believed that Tāne obtained Te Rā, along with Te Marama [The Moon], from his younger brother, Tangotango.

In Tūhoe tradition, Te Rā is married to Tangaroa's two daughters Hine-raumati [Summer woman] and Hine-takurua [Winter woman]. In the hot weather he lives in the south with Hine-raumati, whose tasks are those of the summer, then in the cold weather he moves north to Hine-takurua.

Hine-raumati bore Te Rā a son, Tāne-rore, who invented the first haka. He did this to celebrate the fine weather, and the quivering movements of his dance are still to be seen in the shimmering heat of summer days.

Tūhoe authorities also say that Te Rā has a

*Tāne-rore, son of Te Rā [The Sun] and Hine-raumati [Summer-woman], invented the first haka to celebrate the fine weather, and its quivering movements can still be seen in the shimmering heat of summer days.*

*A haka performed on the deck of a French ship that visited the country in the mid-1820s.*

second son, Auahi-tū-roa [Long smoke], who is the origin of comets. Te Rā decided to bestow the gift of fire upon his human descendants, so he sent Auahi-tū-roa down to the earth to marry Mahuika. The trickster Māui later took fire from Mahuika and gave it to human beings.

Some claim there is a bird in the sun, but others say that Te Manu-i-te-Rā [The bird in the sun] is the sun itself.

## Taha-rākau

### A prudent, quick-witted man

Taha-rākau, a rangatira living at Tūranga (the Gisborne district), once set off with a companion to visit Tapuae, a rangatira whose home was at Te Rēinga in the Wairoa district.

Taha-rākau's friend Te Angiangi wore his best clothes for the journey, though they had far to go. Taha-rākau, on the other hand, wrapped up his good clothes and took two rain capes with him.

When Te Angiangi scoffed at this because the sun was shining, Taha-rākau replied cryptically, 'What's above is close.'

This was a way of saying that it's always likely to rain. And in the end it did. Te Angiangi's fine garments were soaked through and the plumes in his hair were broken, but Taha-rākau put on his rain capes and was quite comfortable.

When they reached Te Rēinga, Tapuae and his people were secretly scornful because Taha-rākau had only a single companion and was wearing the rain capes. But Taha-rākau now put on his good clothes. While they were being welcomed, he noticed that Tapuae's large carved house was not inside a pā in the usual way but stood in the fields where enemies could reach it.

Later, when the visitors were being feasted, Tapuae asked Taha-rākau three questions, hoping each time to outwit him and diminish his mana. The first question was: 'Taha, wouldn't it have been better if a large party had escorted you?'

Taha-rākau calmly replied, 'When I've got my rain capes to protect me, that's a large enough party.'

The next question was: 'What do people live on in Tūranga?'

Taha-rākau told him, 'We eat from cabbage-

*Taha-rākau, portrayed in 1887 in the meeting house Rongopai at Waituhi near Gisborne.*

tree ovens by day, and make love to our women at night.'

Again Tapuae felt that Taha-rākau had got the better of him. So he asked his last question. Shaking the toggles of greenstone and marine ivory that fastened his cloaks, he said, 'Taha-rākau, what is the mark of an aristocrat?'

And Taha-rākau, remembering how Tapuae's house was positioned, replied, 'A carved house standing inside a pā is the mark of an aristocrat. A carved house standing in the open, amongst cultivations, is food for fire.'

Once more Taha-rākau had outwitted his opponent. His sayings are still repeated today.

## Tahu
### Source of good things

Tahu represents food and plenty, feasts, and tranquillity. He appears to be a personification of the word tahu, 'husband, lover', though his name may have been associated as well with another word tahu that means 'to cook'. On the west coast of the North Island he is sometimes a son of Rangi the sky and Papa the earth.

One writer tells us Tahu is 'the source of good things, life and well-being, and joyful hearts. It is because of him that husbands love and care for their wives and children, and wives love and care for their children and husbands.'

Tahu is often contrasted with Tū, who personifies warfare. Some authorities associate Tahu with the masculine attributes appropriate in times of peace, and Tū with those necessary in times of war. Others say that all females belong to Tahu and all males to Tū.

Since Tahu can personify food and hospitality, a person who had declined the offer of a meal could be told, 'Don't tread down Tahu.'

## Tahu-pōtiki
### Founder of Ngāi Tahu

This early ancestor lived on the east coast of the North Island and was a younger brother of Porourangi, from whom the people of Ngāti Porou take their name. After Porourangi's death, Tahu-pōtiki married his widow Hamo – it being customary for a surviving brother to do so. Hamo, who had borne Porourangi four children, had three more in this marriage.

Tahu's descendants lived for a while in Tūranga (the Gisborne district), then made their way further south. Some of them lived for a time at Te Whanga-nui-a-Tara (the Wellington district). Eventually, perhaps late in the seventeenth century, some migrated to the South Island. There they fought with Ngāti Mamoe and Waitaha, the main peoples in possession of the island, and formed alliances with them through marriage. In time they won a leading position and were able to call the island Tahu's House [Te Whare o Tahu].

## Tahurangi
### The man who claimed Taranaki

Tahurangi is often said to have been the first man to climb Taranaki (Mount Egmont). He belonged to the Taranaki people who live near the mountain, and he climbed it to claim it for them. At the top he lit a fire so that all could see what he had done.

When misty clouds like smoke cling to the summit of Taranaki, these are from Tahurangi's fire.

## Taiāmai
### A bird from Hawaiki

A district often takes its name from one particular place, frequently a rock, where a significant event occurred. This place is the tino, the essence, of the entire region. Formerly such places were tapu and treated with great respect.

The district inland from the Bay of Islands, with its rich volcanic soil, is traditionally known

*The great rock that gives its name to the Taiāmai district.*

as Taiāmai. Near the present town of Ōhaeawai, some six hundred metres behind the post office, there stands a rock more than three metres high, a great block of lava conspicuous on the level ground. This is the tino of Taiāmai.

The surface of the rock is pitted and furrowed, with hollows that hold pools of water. In the early days a white pigeon was seen flying towards the rock; it circled, then landed and drank from a pool. The people wondered where this strange beautiful bird had come from, and their rangatira, Kaitara, told them, 'This bird is from Hawaiki, a guest sent inland to us [taia mai] by the winds of Tangaroa. Therefore we will call him Taiāmai. He is tapu; do not approach him. He will bring us great mana.'

Every afternoon Taiāmai came to drink from the rock, and he did indeed bring the people mana. Then one evening a neighbouring rangatira, jealous of this mana, tried to capture the bird. Taiāmai vanished into the rock, and the terrified man fled. The rock now became known as Taiāmai.

Later there came a dying rangatira who wished to gaze for a last time upon Taiāmai. He sat before it for many hours, then after his death his wairua also entered the rock. Taiāmai now was highly tapu. Down through the generations, people passing the rock would observe the ceremony of uruuru-whenua; they would pluck a twig, recite a ritual chant and lay the twig as an offering beside it, in this way acknowledging the mana of Taiāmai and ensuring themselves a safe journey.

Taiāmai is still honoured. It is believed by some to be a resting-place for the wairua on their way to Te Rēinga.

## Taiau
### A fishing rock

The early ancestor Māia is best known for having brought the seeds of the gourd from Hawaiki to the Tūranga (Gisborne) district. As well, he created a valuable fishing rock.

Standing one day beside the Tūranganui River, Māia called to a girl, Taiau, on the opposite bank and told her to bring his waka to him. She did so, and he drowned her. But this was not the arbitrary act of violence that it might appear, because Taiau was transformed into a treasured fishing rock, Te Toka a Taiau [Taiau's rock].

This huge rock used to mark the boundary between the territory of Ngāti Porou to the north and the lands belonging to the peoples of Tūranga. Now that the rock has been dynamited, a bridge serves this purpose.

# Taikehu

## An ancestor's fishing resources

Harbours, with their sandbanks and mudflats, provided rich supplies of seafood. In both Arawa and Tainui traditions, these coastal fishing grounds are associated with an ancestor named Taikehu.

The Arawa peoples say that Taikehu arrived from Hawaiki on *Te Arawa* and soon began collecting seafood from a large sandbank in the Tauranga Harbour near Katikati. Ever since, this sandbank has been known as Te Ranga-a-Taikehu [Taikehu's sandbank].

The Tainui peoples believe that Taikehu came on their waka and settled at Tāmaki. In the Waitematā Harbour the *Tainui* was stranded for a while on a sandbank that became known as Te Ranga-a-Taikehu [Taikehu's sandbank], and places nearby were given names such as Taikehu's swimming-place and Taikehu's sand dunes.

Afterwards Taikehu led an exploratory expedition. At Manuka (the Manukau Harbour) his party found great flocks of seabirds and an abundance of seafood; the mullet were leaping from the water in such numbers that they could wade in and catch them in both hands. To take possession of these fishing grounds, Taikehu named the mullet 'the fearless children of Taikehu' [ngā tamariki toa o Taikehu]. Ever since, this saying has been quoted by peoples tracing descent from Taikehu as proof of their fishing rights in the harbour.

In the traditions of southern Taranaki, the early explorer Kupe left a man named Taikehu in a fertile region between two rivers that he named Te Awa-nui-a-Taikehu [Taikehu's great river] and the Wai-kākahi. Later, when Turi arrived on the *Aotea* and found him there, these rivers were renamed the Pātea and the Whenuakura.

# *Tainui*

## Waka of the Tainui peoples

The story of the *Tainui* begins in Hawaiki with Tinirau and his wife Hine-kura (whom some call Hina-uri). This woman gave birth to a stillborn son, named Tainui, who was incomplete; he was perfect from head to chest, but had no waist or legs. He was buried, and not long afterwards a tree grew up from his burial place. Many generations later, when the tree was fully grown, it became the hull of the *Tainui*.

In some accounts the tree is felled by the tohunga Raka-taura, in others this task is performed by Rata. In both cases the proper

ceremonies are at first neglected and the tree rises up once more. It remains fallen only when the appropriate rituals are performed.

When the waka was ready the captain, Hoturoa, arranged for kūmara, gourds, taro, karaka and other plants to be stowed on board. Seats were assigned to members of the crew: Hoturoa's place was at the stern, the other high-ranking men were immediately in front, and the tohunga sat at the bow beside the tūāhu.

Ngātoro-i-rangi had been chosen as tohunga, but he was kidnapped by Tama-te-kapua, captain of *Te Arawa*. Some say that Raka-taura took his place, and that during the voyage he fell in love with Hoturoa's daughter Kahu-keke, much to Hoturoa's anger. Others say that Raka was deliberately left behind in Hawaiki (because he was lazy or a thief, or because his son had been killed and the people feared his retaliation). Raka, however, crossed the ocean by methods of his own.

Riu-ki-uta is generally thought to have replaced him as tohunga. When the ship set sail he recited his ritual chants, some say nine of them. One of these chants called to the taniwha in the ocean and the birds of the air to bear the vessel forward. They heard him, and they came and did this.

*Tainui* made land on the east coast, most say at Whangaparāoa; others claim there was first a visit to Te Māhia (Māhia Peninsula) or to Whāngārā. Certainly it was at Whangaparāoa (the name means 'Bay of sperm whales') that the crew had their famous encounter with the crew of *Te Arawa*, who had arrived just before them. The men of *Te Arawa* had erected their tūāhu, they had tied a rope to a whale stranded on the beach and were now exploring the hinterland. The crew of the *Tainui* deceived them by constructing their own tūāhu from materials they had dried before a fire, and by tying a dried rope of their own to the whale. Afterwards they argued successfully that their materials were older than those of the Arawa men, and that this showed they had arrived first and had a prior claim to the land.

It was here too that Hāpōpō, as they approached the shore, saw the glowing flowers of the rātā and thought he had no more need of his precious red plumes. He threw them into the water, they drifted away, and too late he discovered his mistake.

Afterwards *Tainui* coasted north, leaving names and landmarks in the places the crew visited; at Whitianga, for instance, one of the sails was left hanging on a cliff, which became known as Te Rā o Tainui [The sail of the *Tainui*]. At certain places some of the crew settled down to live among the people who were already there.

Accounts differ as to the direction taken by the ship after it entered Tikapa-moana (the Hauraki Gulf). Some say *Tainui* went north to Muri-whenua (the far north), then returned to Tāmaki. Others say that Tāmaki was visited first, and that afterwards the vessel sailed right round Te Tai Tokerau (Northland) and down the west coast. It is generally believed, though, that *Tainui* reached the west coast by being portaged across the Tāmaki Isthmus.

At first this could not be done. When the ship had been taken up the Tāmaki River and was to be dragged over to Manuka (the Manukau Harbour), it would not move forward on the skids. The reason, we are often told, was detected by Raka-taura (this was the tohunga who had been left behind in Hawaiki, but nevertheless arrived at Tāmaki before the *Tainui* and waited there for the crew). Raka now discovered that Hoturoa's secondary wife, Marama, had broken tapu by having an affair with a slave. Marama sang a song admitting her guilt, the slave was sacrificed

*After the Waikato war of the mid-1860s many of the peoples tracing descent from the* Tainui *had their lands seized by the Government, but they continued to maintain their own political, social and religious organisation, the King Movement [Te Kīngitanga]. The flag of Mahuta, who in 1894 became the third king, has his name and those of his predecessors; the* Tainui, *with a fugleman calling the time to the paddlers; the rainbow, sign of the god Uenuku; the seven stars of Matariki (the Pleiades); and the Christian cross, the sun and the moon.*

to the gods, other necessary rituals were performed, the men again pulled on the ropes and the ship glided forward. Soon it drank the waters of Manuka.

Some of the crew remained at Tāmaki, among them the tohunga Riu-ki-uta. One of the ship's taniwha, Moko-ika-hiku-waru, also settled there. And kūmara were left at Tāmaki, which is why the land is so fertile now and kūmara grow so well.

The rest of the crew continued on, coasting south from Manuka. The explorer Kupe had left high waves on the west coast to obstruct the passage of later expeditions, but Hoturoa calmed the waves with a ritual chant. *Tainui* was sailing now towards its final resting place at Kāwhia. On the way further landmarks were established and names were given to the places they passed.

Some say the reconciliation between Hoturoa and Raka-taura occurred at Tāmaki, others that it took place at Kāwhia. In the harbour there, beside the water at Maketū, two tapu stone pillars, Hani and Puna, mark the positions of the prow and sternpost of *Tainui*; the prow belongs to Raka-taura and the sternpost to Hoturoa. The ship itself lies buried, turned to stone, between them. The skids employed in pulling it ashore took root and turned into a tree, the tainui, which formerly grew only in a small area between Kāwhia Harbour and the Mōkau River.

Nearby on a low hill a tūāhu and a house of learning [whare wānanga] were established. Hoturoa gave his daughter Kahu-keke to Raka as his wife, and Raka, with Kahu and other companions, set out on a long journey to place in the hills the mauri he had brought from Hawaiki.

Then Whakaotirangi, Hoturoa's principal wife, planted her kūmara. During the voyage the rest of the crew had eaten the seed kūmara they carried, but Whakaotirangi had prudently kept hers tied up in a corner of her basket. Now they were planted in soil brought from Hawaiki and they cropped abundantly, along with Whakaotirangi's gourds and her paper mulberry [aute] tree.

As for the disgraced Marama, Hoturoa's secondary wife, all her crops grew up the wrong way. Her kūmara became convolvulus, her gourds grew into a weed called mawhai, and her paper mulberry tree turned into the whau tree, which has rather similar leaves but bark that is useless for cloth.

## Taipō
### Supernatural intruders

The word taipō refers to many kinds of unwanted supernatural visitors. It entered the language, it seems, in the middle of the nineteenth century and is of unknown origin.

Some people thought it derived from an English word, though there is no evidence for this. Others assumed it was an expression composed of two Māori words, tai-pō, and assigned it a meaning on this basis. On the northern shores of the South Island, these words tai-pō (literally, 'sea-night') were taken to mean 'out from the sea at night.' In that region there was a belief that a dangerous people, the Poniaturi (also known as Ponaturi), lived in the ocean and came out at night to attack humans living near the coast. It was now decided that Taipō must be another name for these people.

Others again took the word to be taepō, interpreted it as tae-pō [arrive-at-night], and believed it referred to supernatural beings who intruded upon humans in the darkness.

## Takarangi and Rau-mahora
### A marriage that brought peace

Takarangi was a great warrior of Ngāti Awa (who are known now as Te Āti Awa). In about 1750 he led an army against the Whakarewa Pā, in the territory of the Taranaki people. For a long time he and his men besieged the pā, and the people inside suffered from hunger and thirst.

Finally the rangatira of the pā, an old man named Rangi-rā-runga, mounted the palisades and asked his enemies for water. Some wanted to help, but others would not agree. Then Rangi-rā-runga caught sight of Takarangi and knew from

his emblems of rank, a whalebone patu and a white-heron plume, that he was their leader. He asked his name, and Takarangi told him.

So Rangi-rā-runga, in the proud, formal language of warriors on the battlefield, asked for Takarangi's assistance. And Takarangi consented, for though he had been eager for battle he had heard of the beauty of Rangi-rā-runga's daughter, Rau-mahora, and he felt pity for her and her people. He filled a gourd at a spring and carried it to the old man, and none of his people dared intervene.

Rangi-rā-runga and his daughter drank while the young man and the girl gazed at each other. And Takarangi's warriors, seeing this, told one other, 'Friends, Takarangi wants Rau-mahora more than he wants war!'

Then Rangi-rā-runga expressed his heart's desire. He asked his daughter if she would marry Takarangi, and she agreed. She married him, and there was peace from that time on. Many people now in Taranaki trace descent from these two ancestors.

## Takere-piripiri
### A guardian insulted

In appearance this great reptile was like a tuatara, with spines down his back and a spiky tail. He was the guardian of the Ōtautahanga Pā, at this time one of the main strongholds of Ngāti Raukawa. The pā was full of people and its surrounding slopes were covered in gardens.

It was Takere-piripiri who ensured this prosperity; no enemy could conquer the people while he was protecting them. He was the pet of the leading rangatira, and his home was a cave below the walls of the pā. On sunny days he would lie basking at the entrance.

Every day Takere-piripiri was brought a basket of the best food, usually eels. One day when people were busy, the rangatira's two grandchildren, a boy and a girl, were told to take Takere-piripiri his eels. But the smell of the steamed eels was too much for them, and they ate a little bit, then more, until only the heads were left. So they put fern in the bottom of the basket, arranged the heads on top, and offered the basket to Takere-piripiri.

Out came the hungry reptile. He found the heads, pursued the children and killed them both. Soon their heads lay alongside those of the eels, and inside the cave Takere-piripiri ate his meal.

But his anger was not assuaged. That night he abandoned his home and made his way north to the Maungakawa Range. There he found another home, in a cave near a track used by travellers crossing the mountains.

Meanwhile the people in the pā were searching for the children. By the cave they saw what had happened, and mourned the childrens' deaths. But they knew it was very wrong to have robbed their guardian of his meal, and they were greatly disturbed at his loss. And indeed, soon afterwards the pā was attacked and taken by enemies.

Takere-piripiri also came to grief. Since there was no-one to bring him offerings, he ate passing travellers. Most of them belonged to Ngāti Hauā, and in the end the warriors of these people constructed an enormous wickerwork cage like an eel-pot and set it up near the reptile's cave. One of the men sat on top as bait, Takere-piripiri was lured inside, then the others rushed from their ambush and speared him to death.

## Tākitimu
### An ancestral waka

Peoples in certain parts of the east coast, the South Island and the far north trace their descent to ancestors who came from Hawaiki on the Tākitimu. Differing versions of the story are told in different parts of the country, and some accounts have been elaborated to include visits to all of these regions.

In the east coast story there is often a preliminary episode in which two men, Ruawhāro and Tūpai, insult the great rangatira Uenuku and are treated roughly by him, then go to their grandfather, Timu-whakairia, for the ritual chants that will enable them to take their revenge. Afterwards they come across Uenuku's people hauling their waka, the Tākitimu. As the humans pull on their ropes they are assisted by flocks of birds, each kind of bird with a rope of their own. These birds are the Hākituri.

Ruawhāro and Tūpai cut the ropes and then, reciting the appropriate chants, place before the ship four skids that stop it from moving forward. When the vessel's owners cannot move it, the two men offer to do so; Ruawhāro mounts the ship to call the time for the hauling song, while Tūpai puts in place another skid with special powers. The waka slides easily forward, and now belongs to Ruawhāro and Tūpai. In this way they revenge themselves for their injury.

They then prepare the Tākitimu for its voyage. As crew they take the previous owners, seven score men of high rank. As atua they put on board Kahukura, Tama-i-waho and others; these gods obey them because of their ritual chants. They take as well their five skids, their tapu

knowledge, and the mauri of the whales they have brought from Timu-whakairia's house.

Some say the leading men on the Tākitimu, apart from Ruawhāro and Tūpai, were Rongo-kako, Tamatea and his son Kahungunu. Others name Kiwa as the captain. Some believe that the famous Tamatea was born in Aotearoa, and most agree that Kahungunu was born here. Some claim that the giant Rongokako came by means of his own.

Because the gods, the knowledge and the rangatira that came on the Tākitimu were highly tapu, the vessel itself was so tapu that food supplies could not be taken on board. In the middle of the ocean the crew became very hungry, so a man named Ngu-toro-ariki called down to the pāua, and multitudes of these shellfish rose up through the water to feed the people. Later they were hungry again, and another man, Te Au-noanoa-i-ariki, called down to the mussels. They climbed up and clung to the gunwale, and again the crew ate their fill.

This happened several times, with shellfish of different kinds. Since the vessel was too tapu to contain cooked food, the people ate the shellfish raw. That is why shellfish are often eaten raw today.

When the waka reached Whanga-o-keno (East Island), sand from Hawaiki was thrown ashore – and that is why whales come ashore at Takapautahi. They paddled on and made landfall at Nukutaurua, at Te Māhia (the Māhia Peninsula). Some say the Tākitimu is still there now, along with its skids. Because the mauri of the whales was left there, and sand that Ruawhāro had brought from Hawaiki, whales now beach themselves at Te Māhia.

Later, Ruawhāro travelled south along the coast of Heretaunga (Hawke's Bay), leaving in places there his sons Matiu, Makaro and Moko-tuararo. They turned to stone and became powerful mauri that attracted whales and other fish to those regions.

When the people of Ngāi Tahu migrated to the South Island, they brought the story of the Tākitimu with them. They now believed that Tākitimu, having sailed down the east coast of

*Tākitimu, a large meeting house that took several years to carve and was opened in 1887 at Kehemane, near Martinborough. In giving their house a name identifying it with the Tākitimu, which brought the ancestors of Ngāti Kahungunu and others from Hawaiki, the owners let it be known that they regarded the house as a meeting place for all of the peoples that trace descent to this waka. The house stood until 1911, when it burned down.*

the North Island, continued on to the east coast of the South Island, then was swamped by three waves. The vessel overturned and became the Tākitimu Mountains, the waves became high hills, and the captain, Tamatea, walked back along the coast creating landmarks as he went.

People in the far north say that *Tākitimu* made its way up there, and that the hull now lies by Tokerau (Doubtless Bay), turned to stone. Some people in the region trace descent from Tamatea.

## Takurua
### The winter star

Takurua is a name often given to Sirius, the brightest star in the sky. The Tūhoe people, probably others as well, say she is a woman who brings the winter. On cold nights she shines brightly to warn that there will be a hard frost.

Winter itself is often known as takurua. It is referred to poetically as Hine-takurua [Winter woman].

There are those, however, who identify Sirius with Rehua.

## Tama
### The greenstone wives

Greenstone, or jade, was obtainable only in a few wild remote valleys in the South Island. The most famous was the Arahura Valley in Westland, and its presence there was explained by a myth telling how Tama arrived from Hawaiki on the *Tairea* in search of his three runaway wives. At Arahura he found his wives, but his slave broke a tapu restriction and the atua punished Tama by turning the women into the different kinds of greenstone now to be found there.

Further south, in the fiords of Piopio-tahi (Milford Sound), a translucent, softer kind of greenstone known as tangiwai is another of Tama's wives. This name means 'weeping tears', and the marks like drops of water which are often seen in this stone are the tears shed by Tama on discovering the petrified body of his wife.

As Tama ran frantically along the west coast looking for his wives, his cloaks were torn to ribbons. The cloaks were made of tussock, flax and other plants, and the pieces he left behind

took root. This was how these plants were introduced to the country.

## Tama-āhua

### A flying man

In the early days at Waitōtara, in the Whanganui region, Tama-āhua was able to project himself through the air without the use of wings. Some say he could do this because of his great mana; when he resolved to fly to a place, he had only to recite a ritual chant and he would be there at once. These people say that Tama-āhua lost his powers because of a woman. He married, and found next morning that he had become an ordinary man of the earth.

Others maintain that Tama-āhua owed his power of flight to the possession of a feather called Te Rauāmoa [The moa feather], which had been plucked from under the wing of Te Manu-nui-a-Ruakapanga [Ruakapanga's great bird]. They speak of Tama-āhua's mana but do not say that he lost his powers.

His feather, they say, came originally from Hawaiki. A taniwha known as Ikaroa [Long fish] became stranded on a beach in the Pātea district and was found there by Pou. Thinking him an ordinary fish, Pou began to cut him up, but the cuts closed as fast as he made them. He then began to recite ritual chants, and this alarmed Ikaroa so much that he suddenly carried Pou off to Muriwai-o-Hawaiki.

But the people of Hawaiki condemned this act because Ika-roa had been out of his element at the time, and they lent Pou a flying taniwha on which to return. When this creature, Te Manu-nui-a-Ruakapanga, neared Pou's home at Pātea, he told Pou to pull a feather from under his wing. Pou did so, and this treasure, a potent source of mana, came eventually into the possession of Tama-āhua.

Tama-āhua's full name was Tama-āhua-rere-rangi [Tama whose nature was to fly through the sky]. He often flew between the Whanganui River and Waitōtara. On one occasion he made this flight to ask Aokehu for his help in dealing with the taniwha Tūtae-poroporo.

## Tama-i-rēia

### Fairy battles

The fairy [tūrehu] people live on the hilltops and move around in the mist and darkness. Two fairy peoples lived in the Tāmaki (Auckland) region, one in the Waitakere Ranges and the other in the Hūnua Ranges to the south. Dissension arose when Hine-mai-rangi, a high-born girl of the Hūnua people, eloped with Tama-i-rēia, leader of the Waitakere people.

The rangatira of the Hūnua fairies, Kōiwi-riki, led an army against Tama-i-rēia's people, and the two forces met one night at Pakuranga. In the ensuing battle neither side at first could gain the advantage. Then the Hūnua tohunga made the sun rise before the proper time, and many of the Waitakere warriors died in the light.

The following night the Hūnua people again advanced upon their enemy, but this time the Waitakere tohunga were ready for them. They made volcanoes erupt from the earth, and the Hūnua warriors, covered in burning ashes and overwhelmed by molten lava, were driven back to their own territory. When a change of wind brought the volcanic fires back towards the Waitakere forests, the tohunga sent rain to quench the flames.

The remains of the volcanoes are still at Tāmaki, and in the Waitakere Ranges there is still a much heavier rainfall than elsewhere in the region.

## Tama-i-waho

### A god in the sky

This powerful atua in the sky was a war god of a number of Bay of Plenty and east coast peoples. His visible form was a star, which has not been identified. Before a battle he would be asked to foretell the outcome, and would reply by taking possession of a tohunga and speaking through him. He also warned of approaching enemies.

According to Ngāti Kahungunu, this god was brought from Hawaiki on their ancestral ship *Tākitimu*. Others say he flew from Hawaiki and landed on the peak of Mount Hikurangi, near the Waiapu Valley. There he remained, a dangerous ogre known sometimes as Tama-ki-Hikurangi [Tama on Hikurangi].

In the early days when Toi, the first man in Aotearoa, was living at Whakatāne, Tama-i-waho came down from the sky and made love to Toi's wife, Te Kura-i-monoa. This went on for many nights, with Te Kura sleepily thinking him her husband. By the time she learnt differently, she was pregnant. She bore a son, Oho-mai-rangi, whose name was taken by his descendants, Ngā Oho (this is the old name of the Arawa peoples). Some say that during his visits to the earth Tama-i-waho was known as Pūhaorangi, while others claim Pūhaorangi was someone different.

Tama-i-waho's position in the highest of the skies is associated with great power, including a knowledge of ritual chants. When visited by a

*Hikurangi, tapu mountain of Ngāti Porou, is in one tradition
the home of the ogre Tama-i-waho.*

stranger he may be helpful, but is more likely to destroy the intruder. A number of stories tell how the hero Tāwhaki climbed to the sky to visit Tama-i-waho; some say Tāwhaki was killed, others that he obtained a knowledge of powerful chants.

In Tūhoe tradition, Tāwhaki wanted Tama-i-waho's pack of ferocious dogs so that he could avenge his father's death. Some believe he was given them, others that he fell and died.

## Tama-nui-a-Raki

### The man who was tattooed

Tama-nui-a-Raki lost his wife to Tū-te-koropaka, who had been visiting him. When Tama asked his children why the woman had run off with Tū-te-koropaka, they explained it was because he was good-looking. As for Tama, he had an ugly face.

Realising this for the first time, Tama determined to be made beautiful. He turned into a white heron, flew down below, and there met two of his ancestors who were tattooed and beautiful. When he asked them to tattoo him, they painted curved lines on his face and body. But the lines washed off when he went to bathe, so he asked for permanent adornment. They told

him he would have to go to two other ancestors, Toka and Hā.

Tama made his way on and found these men. They were at first reluctant to tattoo him, saying the pain was as bad as death. But Tama insisted and they agreed. The instruments were sharpened and the pigment made ready, he was laid down and the operation commenced. It was long and terribly painful, and he often fainted. After many days it was done; he was carried to a house and began to recover. When his wounds healed he found that he was handsome.

Tama returned to his children, then soon afterwards set out to find his wife Rukutia. He overcame the obstructing plants and other obstacles that her new husband, Tū-te-koropaka, had left in his path, and eventually he approached the place where the two were living.

Disguised as a slave, he was accepted into their house; Rukutia was there but did not recognise him. Later he quietly left the house, washed and adorned himself, and recited a ritual chant to bring Rukutia outside. She now knew who he was, saw he was handsome, and begged to be taken back. He refused, but said he would soon return by sea.

Presently he did so, overcoming with chants and strategems the monsters and dangers of the deep which Tū-te-koropaka had put in his way. As his waka approached the place where they were living, Rukutia swam out towards it. But Tama had not forgiven his wife. He killed her, returned home with her body, buried her in a box, then sat mourning until the spring.

When the spring came and there were new shoots on the tutu bushes, a humming blowfly told Tama that Rukutia had come back to life. He opened the box in which her body lay and saw that she was alive once more and smiling at him.

This is a South Island story. Tama-nui-a-Raki was apparently regarded there as the first man to be tattooed, although it is not said that he later tattooed others. In one version, the person who tattoos him in the underworld is Mataora (also the initiator of tattooing in some parts of the North Island).

Sometimes Tama-nui-a-Raki [Great son of Raki] is identified with the Tama who came from Hawaiki seeking his runaway wives and ended up on the west coast of the South Island with them turned to greenstone. Tū-te-koropaka is a South Island form of the name Tū-te-koropanga.

## Tama-o-hoi
### A powerful atua

Tama-o-hoi is so old that some trace his descent to Māui, who fished up the land. His descendants include both humans and fairies. Some believe he lives under the ground at Rotoiti, others that his home is in Ruawāhia, the enormous crater in Mount Tarawera.

Some say that Mount Tarawera once lived in the centre of the island and was moving to his present home when he was challenged by Tama-o-hoi. The demon and the mountain fought, and Tama-o-hoi hit Tarawera so hard that he opened up Ruawāhia [Pit broken open].

Others say that when the great tohunga Ngātoro-i-rangi had arrived from Hawaiki and was exploring the countryside, he was confronted by Tama-o-hoi, who resented this intrusion. Ngātoro-i-rangi stamped upon Mount Tarawera, forming the chasm of Ruawāhia, and thrust Tama-o-hoi down inside. There he remained until 1886, when he burst free and caused a terrible volcanic eruption.

## Tama-rereti
### The waka in the sky

Tama-rereti possesses a ship, with sternpost, rope and anchor, which can be seen in the sky at night. Sometimes he has a fish hook rather than an anchor, and spends the night fishing. At dawn the vessel reaches land.

Usually his waka is identified with the tail of the Scorpion in the constellation of Scorpius. One authority, though, says that it stretches far across the sky and that the bow is Matariki (the Pleiades), the sternpost Tautoru (Orion's Belt), and the anchor Māhutonga (the Southern Cross).

Some say it is the *Uruao*; though others assign this name to a waka that brought the ancestors of the Waitaha people to Te Wai Pounamu (the South Island).

## Tamatea
### A great explorer

Tamatea is usually said to have captained the *Tākitimu* on its voyage from Hawaiki, though some say he was born in Aotearoa. All agree that he undertook ambitious journeys of exploration.

A number of extended names, such as Tamatea-ariki-nui [Tamatea the great lord], Tamatea-mai-tawhiti [Tamatea from afar] and Tamatea-pokai-whenua [Tamatea who travelled over the land], are considered by many authorities to belong to this ancestor: they believe, that is, that the one man possessed all of these names. Others assert that the extended names are employed in order to distinguish between several men who all bore the name Tamatea.

In a number of stories Tamatea is associated in one way and another with fire, which in some special sense is his possession. In the Tāmaki region his fire is located underground; Tamatea-o-te-rā [Tamatea of the sun] lives in the volcanic cones there and occasionally visits other districts, where his presence is disclosed by earthquakes and other underground activities. On parts of the east coast and the South Island the belief is that Tamatea burnt the undergrowth he found on his arrival so as to prepare the land for his descendants.

In the South Island story, after the *Tākitimu* had been wrecked in the far south and turned into a mountain range, Tamatea walked along the eastern coastline creating as he went. Many of these landmarks are marked by his fire, such as an island in Foveaux Strait (its English name is Green Island) which is called Tamatea's Firestick [Te Kauati a Tamatea].

But Tamatea lost his fire at Ōamaru, because it sank into the ground (and still smoulders there). So he and his party were very cold by the time they reached Banks Peninsula. He climbed a peak, recited a chant, and called to the great tohunga Ngātoro-i-rangi, who just at that moment had

# Recent interpretations

Works by present-day carvers. *Left:* Mauriora Kingi, of Tūhourangi (Te Arawa) and Ngāti Raukawa, portrays Tama-te-kapua, captain of *Te Arawa*, above his younger brother Whakatūria. The two men hold the stilts they used in stealing Uenuku's fruit, and the fruit itself are in Whakatūria's kete (see pages 196–97). *Right:* In a work by Roi Toia of Ngā Puhi, Tangaroa stands above Kiwa (see pages 86 and 182–83). These men together brought into existence the different kinds of fish.

*Above:* In a mural, a polychrome relief carved by Cliff Whiting of Te Whānau-ā-Apanui for the Meteorological Service of New Zealand, Tāwhirimātea, father of the winds, wrestles to control his children (who are portrayed as blue spiral forms). Te Rā, the sun, is top left; Te Marama, the moon, is in the opposite corner. At top right is a reference to the separation of Rangi and Papa, sky and earth. Blue waves and green fronds above Tāwhirimātea suggest his brothers Tangaroa and Tāne.

*Right:* Two paintings by June Northcroft Grant, of Te Arawa and Ngāti Tūwharetoa.

Whakaotirangi holds the kete of seed kūmara that she brought from Hawaiki; on her left is her first husband, Ruaeo, and on her right her second husband, Tama-te-kapua (see pages 158 and 244).

Kearoa, wife of the great tohunga Ngātoro-i-rangi (see pages 126–27). Her hair, tied to the bargeboards of the house, recalls the occasion during the voyage of *Te Arawa* when her husband, becoming suspicious of Tama-te-kapua's intentions, fastened a rope to Kearoa's hair. The blue area is the mouth of Te Parata [te waha o Te Parata]; Ngātoro-i-rangi in his anger was about to send the ship down to destruction in Te Parata when the terrified crew reminded him that in this case Kearoa would die also. The bones refer to the fact that Ngātoro-i-rangi as a great tohunga would have performed the intensely tapu duty of preparing the bones of the dead for their interment [mahi hahunga], and that Kearoa as his wife would also have led a tapu existence.

WHAKAOTIRANGI

KEA ROA

### Tāne separates Rangi and Papa

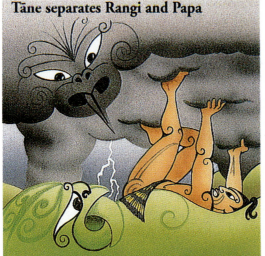

AOTEAROA NEW ZEALAND $1·20

E6

### Māui pulls up Te Ika

AOTEAROA NEW ZEALAND 45c

E7

### Māui attacks Tuna

AOTEAROA NEW ZEALAND $1·00

E8

### Rona is snatched up by Marama

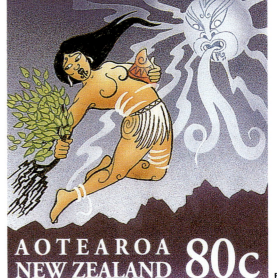

AOTEAROA NEW ZEALAND 80c

E9

### Matakauri slays the Giant of Wakatipu

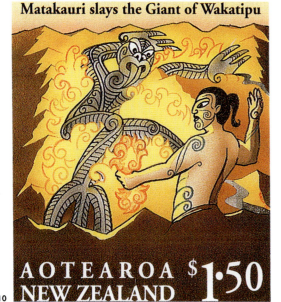

AOTEAROA NEW ZEALAND $1·50

E10

Stamps designed by Brian Gunson (of Ngāti Toa, Ngāti Raukawa and Te Āti Awa) for New Zealand Post. Tāne separates his parents Rangi and Papa; Māui pulls up the fish that becomes Aotearoa; Tuna [Eel], killed by Māui, becomes the origin of all the eels; Rona is carried up by Te Marama [The Moon]; and the giant Matua is overcome by Matakauri and forms Lake Wakatipu.

established his fires on the summit of Tongariro.

Ngātoro at once sent some of his fire through the air to Tamatea (creating more landmarks in so doing). The fire warmed and guided Tamatea's party. They continued north, walked across the ocean, and went on to a meeting with Ngātoro at Taupō.

*Tama-o-hoi, who had been imprisoned by Ngātoro-i-rangi in Tarawera, split the mountain open on 10 June 1886 and caused a dreadful volcanic eruption. Tarawera was a tapu mountain and the bones of the dead were deposited on its heights. For this reason there was a belief that whenever deaths were about to occur, a supernatural [tipua] waka would be seen travelling towards the mountain. A few days before the eruption this warning was given, it was believed, when the occupants of two boats led by Te Pāea (Guide Sophia) (left) saw a phantom waka with thirteen paddlers moving rapidly in that direction.*

*The eruption came at night. First there were earth tremors, a fierce gale and extraordinary lightning. A tremendous roaring came from the mountain, and its great summit was seen to be a mound of fire. Then volcanic mud and red-hot stones came down, the forest fell and the countryside was buried. Some villages disappeared entirely. At the village of Te Wairoa, six kilometres from Tarawera, many buildings collapsed but a few survived the night. Two that remained standing, and saved many people, were Te Pāea's house and the meeting house Hinemihi (below).*

In the Society Islands, part of the cultural region from which the ancestors of the Māori came in reality about a thousand years ago, a figure named Tamatea is one of the gods; fire is his agent of power, and it obeys him in the bowels of the earth and in the sky. This tradition, or a related one, must have been brought to Aotearoa by the first migrants, then localised and modified here. It is not surprising, then, that stories about Tamatea are widespread.

## Tama-te-kapua
### Captain of *Te Arawa*

In the homeland of Hawaiki, Tama-te-kapua and his younger brother Whakatūria became involved in a struggle between their father Hou-mai-tawhiti and the great rangatira Uenuku. Eventually this led to Tama-te-kapua's migration to Aotearoa as captain of *Te Arawa*.

The trouble began when Uenuku was suffering from a boil, and Hou-mai-tawhiti's dog Pōtaka-tawhiti was seen eating the discarded dressings – a dreadful insult, equivalent to eating Uenuku himself. Naturally Uenuku and his son Toi-te-huatahi killed the dog and ate it. Then Hou's sons, Tama-te-kapua and Whakatūria, went searching for the dog, calling as they went, and in Toi's village the dog howled back from inside Toi's stomach.

Hou had now been insulted as well, through his dog's being eaten. So Tama-te-kapua and Whakatūria retaliated by going that night to steal fruit from a tree owned by Uenuku. That led to further trouble, with Tama-te-kapua having to rescue Whakatūria from Uenuku and his men. A battle followed, and although Uenuku was defeated, Tama-te-kapua decided it was time to seek a new home. A waka was built, its crew were chosen, and they made their preparations.

It was known already that Tama-te-kapua was a bold resourceful man who did not hesitate to take what he wanted. On the voyage his character was further revealed. First, when *Te Arawa* was ready to sail, Tama persuaded the powerful tohunga Ngātoro-i-rangi to board the vessel with his wife Kearoa so that the two of them could perform the ceremony to remove the ship's tapu. As soon as they came on board the anchor was raised, the sails were spread, the ship put out to sea – and Ngātoro realised too late that they had been kidnapped.

*Tama-te-kapua, a resourceful thief, made use of stilts when he went by night with his brother Whakatūria to steal fruit from Uenuku's tree.*

At the same time Tama-te-kapua committed another theft. He wanted the wife and property of a man named Ruaeo, so at the last moment he sent Ruaeo back on shore on a pretended errand. He then set sail without him, carrying off his wife and possessions. (He did not know that Ruaeo would find his own way across the water and be waiting for him in Aotearoa, seeking revenge.)

On the voyage itself there was a further theft, which nearly proved fatal. Not content with having stolen Ngātoro-i-rangi, Tama-te-kapua now decided to steal his wife Kearoa. While Ngātoro was elsewhere on the vessel, Tama-te-kapua took her by force. But Kearoa told her husband what had happened, and the angry tohunga determined to destroy their ship. Only at the last moment was he persuaded to relent.

When *Te Arawa* arrived at Maketū, Tama-te-kapua found Ruaeo already there. Challenged to a dual, he suffered a humiliating defeat.

Afterwards the crew of *Te Arawa* spread out through the land. Tama-te-kapua lived at Maketū, then later went to live near the Moehau Range. When he died he was laid to rest on the summit of that mountain.

His habit of helping himself is recalled in proverbs, and sometimes attributed to his descendants. One such saying is: 'Tama's descendants are always stealing something or other' [Ngā uri o Tama whānako roa ki te aha, ki te aha].

## Tāminamina
### An East Cape story

Once some girls went swimming in a freshwater pool. Everyone knew about Tāminamina, the taniwha there. The elders used to warn the children that if they went near his den, or drank nectar from the flowers on the pōhutukawa trees above, Tāminamina would swallow them or drag them down into the water.

But one of these girls, Mere, was not frightened. She did drink nectar from the pōhutukawa trees, and she was dragged down by Tāminamina. The water in the stream became very dark, though before it had been clear, and it was now deep everywhere, though there had been shallow places before.

Her companions swam to the bank, terrified of the swirling water, and they ran off shouting, 'Mere is dead, the taniwha killed her!'

The girls were asked, 'How do you know it was the taniwha?'

They said, 'The water was lashed about, and it's very dark there now.'

When the people reached the stream they found the water was quite black, and kelp from far out to sea was floating there, though salt water does not reach that place. Then they knew it was the taniwha that had done this.

## Tāne
### Creator of the world

The world is made up of Rangi the sky and Papa the earth, but it was their son Tāne who pushed them apart and gave the world its proper form. Unlike most of his brothers, Tāne was in the shape of a human man. Some say he rested his shoulders upon the earth and pushed Rangi up with his legs, others that he raised Rangi through the power of a ritual chant; either way, he then placed props beneath him. On the west coast of the North Island it is said that these props can still be seen; they are the tall trees.

Next, Tāne searched for lights to adorn his father. In different myths he acquires the heavenly bodies from different people; Ngāti Awa say he got them from Tangotango, Tūhoe people speak of Tane-te-waiora, and Ngāti Kahungunu say the stars came from Wehi-nui-a-mamao. When Tāne had thrown up the stars, the moon and the sun, his father was beautiful at last.

According to some traditions Tāne then made a human male, named Tiki. More often we are told that he went looking for a human female, and that at first he found only females who were not human, and fathered plants and birds. In this way he brought into existence the tōtara with Mūmūwhango, the rātā and other climbing plants with Rere-noa [Go out everywhere], shags with Noho-tumutumu [Perch on stump], and many others. He also met Punga, the mother of ugly creatures, and with her he had the insects.

There are different stories as to how Tāne finally acquired a human woman. In the best-known tradition, he made one for himself by shaping a woman from the soil (some say the sand) of Hawaiki. He covered the figure with his garments and breathed into her mouth, she came to life, and he called her Hine-ahu-one [Woman shaped from soil].

Their first child was a daughter. Her name is Hine-tītama in some traditions, Hine-i-tauira or Hine-manuhiri in others. Sometimes it is said that when Hine-tītama (or Hine-i-tauira) grew up, Tāne took her to wife as well, and that in Tāne's absence she began asking about her father. When she discovered that her husband was also her father, she was overcome with shame and fled to the underworld. She stayed down there in the darkness; often it is said that her name now became Hine-nui-te-pō [Great woman the night].

Tāne followed his wife and begged her to return, but she told him, 'Return to the world, Tāne, to rear up our progeny, and let me go to the underworld to drag down our progeny.'

That is how death came into the world. It is the task of Hine-nui-te-pō to receive the wairua of human beings when they die, but new generations keep growing up because Tāne meanwhile creates new life. According to one tradition, he gained this power by climbing up and taking possession, in the highest of the skies, of Tāne's living waters [te wai-ora a Tāne]. From these precious waters come the wairua of newborn infants.

In some traditions, Tāne is believed to have brought down from the skies three baskets [kete] containing sacred knowledge. Sometimes too he receives a whatu kura, a sacred stone that enables

*Humans are Tāne, being his children, and waka are Tāne, since they are formed from the trees which are also children of Tāne. When people in waka venture out on to the water, Tāne is confronting his opponent Tangaroa.*

*A race on the Whanganui River in the early twentieth century.*

him to maintain order on the land below.

Being the ancestor of the trees and birds, Tāne is present now in his descendants, so must be propitiated before a tree of importance is felled. On such an occasion it may be said that 'Tāne has fallen' [Kua hinga a Tāne]. Since houses and waka are made from trees, they too are Tāne. And birds singing loudly at dawn are Tāne's mouth.

Because Tāne made the first human, his powers could be employed in healing. To heal a patient's broken bones, a tohunga might recite a ritual chant recalling, and so re-enacting, Tāne's act of creation. (The bones would, naturally, be expertly set, but a ritual such as this was considered essential as well.)

Since the word tāne ordinarily means 'male, husband, lover', Tāne's name is a personification, Male. In the myths relating to him, male energy is presented as having shaped the world and created the life forms that belong to the land. Every human man – every tāne – who fathered a child was re-enacting the occasion on which Tāne, having obtained a wife, fathered the first of his children.

Tāne has many extended names, which refer

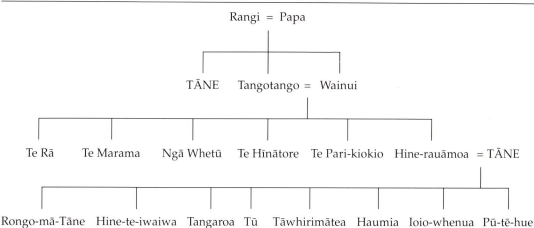

Rangi = Papa

TĀNE     Tangotango = Wainui

Te Rā    Te Marama    Ngā Whetū    Te Hīnātore    Te Pari-kiokio    Hine-rauāmoa = TĀNE

Rongo-mā-Tāne   Hine-te-iwaiwa   Tangaroa   Tū   Tāwhirimātea   Haumia   Ioio-whenua   Pū-tē-hue

*Tāne is always one of the sons of Rangi and Papa, although in other ways the names of their children differ considerably from one region to another. In the genealogies of Ngāti Awa in the southern Bay of Plenty, Rangi and Papa have two sons, Tāne and Tangotango, then a daughter, Wainui. Because there is (unusually) a woman at this stage, she must have children; but Wainui's husband cannot be Tāne, who has always to assert himself in the process of finding a wife. So Tangotango, who is the origin of the alternation of light and dark, marries Wainui, who is the origin of water and the ocean; they produce the different forms of light, then a daughter, Hine-rauāmoa. Tāne takes away his niece, then his five nephews; he locates the males in the places they now occupy, then marries the woman. With her he has eight children (some of whom, in other traditions, are children rather than great-grandchildren of Rangi and Papa).*

to his different activities. Among them, in some regions, is a series of names that recall how he slowly stretched his legs while raising his father; these include among others Tāne-tūturi [Tāne with bent up knees] and Tāne-ua-tika [Tāne with a straight backbone].

In the traditions of other peoples, such as Ngāti Porou, Tāne is said to have used a ritual chant rather than his legs, and this series of names does not belong to the one person but instead is assigned to a number of brothers, sons of Rangi and Papa, who were born one after the other. The last of these brothers, Tāne-nui-a-Rangi [Great Tāne son of Rangi], had the strength to create the world.

## Tāne-atua
### Creator of landmarks

This ancestor of the peoples of Ngāti Awa and Tūhoe was a brother of Tōroa, who captained the *Mātaatua* on its voyage from Hawaiki. Some say that Tāne-atua accompanied Tōroa and was guardian and medium of the god Rongomai.

Others claim he preceded Tōroa, travelling by mysterious means of his own.

In Aotearoa, Tāne-atua and his wife Hine-mataroa had many children. While the four youngest were apparently human, the elder children are not human but are features of special significance in the landscape.

Soon after his arrival at Whakatāne, Tāne-atua set out to explore the country. He walked up the Whakatāne Valley, then right on to the Huiarau Range, and as he went he placed some of his children in the mountains there. They are now tipua, uncanny beings that take the form of rivers, streams and unusually shaped rocks.

The ancient name of the Whakatāne River itself is Te Tamāhine a Hine-mataroa [Hine-mataroa's daughter]. At a place known as Ngā Māhanga [The twins], Kanihi and Ōhora became tributaries of this river; other children are now rocks in another tributary, the Ōwhakatoro, and at the mouth of the Manga-o-Hou Stream. Far inland, on the summit of the tapu mountain Maunga-pōhatu, Tāne-atua's child Rongo-te-māuriuri is a taniwha living in the red waters of a pond of the same name. If anyone in the old days dared approach this pond, its waters became violently disturbed and rose and pursued him.

Other tipua associated with Tāne-atua include several dogs with extraordinary powers. At the site of the present township of Tāneatua (which is called after him), one of his dogs, Ōtara-hioi, takes the form of a grassy mound. Another dog, his child Mariko, lives in a pond on a range at Te Purenga. This creature in turn had a son, Ōkiwa, who inhabits a pond nearby and can be heard howling at night by those brave enough to camp there. The ōkiwa, a local wind which blows down the gorge of the Whakatāne River at Rūātoki, is this dog's breath. It comes only at night, often with a mist that is steam from the animal's breath.

Tāne-atua is sometimes said to have been a taniwha. Two peoples in the region of the Rangitāiki River, Ngāti Hamua and Warahoe, trace descent from him.

## Tangaroa
### Father of the fish

Tangaroa is one of the sons of Rangi the sky and Papa the earth (or sometimes their grandson, and a son of Tāne). Sometimes he lives at first on the land, then escapes to the ocean when he and his brothers quarrel and go their different ways. His role as the father of the fish and other sea creatures is referred to in many sayings, as when mullet are termed 'the leaping sons of Tangaroa'. And a single fish, if especially significant for some reason, might be spoken of as Tangaroa.

Land and sea were experienced by the Māori as opposed realms, and in many situations they saw conflict between them. Their main sympathies were naturally with the land, so in myths the land generally wins over the sea (as in a tale of a great battle between land birds and seabirds). Victims and losers, such as enemies killed in battle, were often spoken of as fish.

So Tangaroa, whose realm is the ocean, is in many contexts the enemy of Tāne, who as the father of trees, birds and humans represents the land. Some authorities taught that their mutual antagonism was established in the beginning, after the separation of their parents. It was in any case apparent whenever men in waka (representatives of Tāne) ventured out on the dangerous ocean to catch Tangaroa's children. Before and after their expedition, they were careful to make offerings to Tangaroa.

In other ways as well, Tangaroa could represent

*Whenever people go fishing, Tāne is attacking the children of Tangaroa. Fishermen and their families pose with their catch at Whangaroa in 1902. The women have cleaned some of their snapper and hung them up to dry in the sun and wind before packing them into kete.*

an opponent. For instance, the saying 'Tangaroa has a multitude of paths' [Tangaroa-ara-rau] referred to fish but was often applied to enemies or cunning people.

Yet sometimes in ritual a person might be associated with Tangaroa in order to gain his powers. A man cutting down a tree (which was Tāne) might in a chant identify himself with Tangaroa in order to use Tangaroa's strength against the tree.

In some Ngāti Porou traditions Tangaroa is not only the father of the fish, he has human sons too. One of these, Kahukura, initiates the practice of sorcery, perhaps not surprisingly with such a father. Another human son, Rua-te-pupuke, ends up fighting Tangaroa and defeating him. At the bottom of the ocean he conquers the fish and burns his father's house, then brings up the carved posts from which he acquires a knowledge of carving.

Tangaroa's house occurs in other traditions as well. In Whanganui belief, in the dark beginnings of time he shared a house in the ocean with his brother Tāne.

Sometimes Tangaroa, like Tāne, is the owner of a whatu kura, a sacred red stone of great mana which enables him to control the ocean.

## Tangaroa-piri-whare

### A hidden spy

A house, being made from trees, was in a sense Tāne (since Tāne had fathered the trees and was identified with them), and a spy inside a house could therefore be associated with Tāne's opponent Tangaroa. In the Waikato district, the name Tangaroa-piri-whare [Tangaroa who clings to houses] was given to an unfriendly person who, overhearing things said in a house at night, would make mischief by repeating them later.

So the saying 'There's Tangaroa who clings to houses' [Ko Tangaroa-piri-whare] was a warning to watch what you said or did. The unrecognised enemy might be a person whose allegiance lay elsewhere. Or a tohunga might send a blowfly with special powers to spy upon some people; they would think themselves safe, but all the while this blowfly, Tangaroa-piri-whare, would be hiding in a wall, and presently it would go back and tell what it had heard.

## Tangaroa's whatu kura

### A stone of great power

In the traditions of the Whanganui region and some other areas, Tangaroa is the owner of a whatu kura, a small, highly tapu stone of great mana (often said to be red) which was given to him in the beginning by the gods. Through its power he is able to keep the sea in its proper place so that it does not overwhelm the land.

For other peoples again, 'Tangaroa's whatu kura' [te whatu kura a Tangaroa] is simply an expression expressing admiration for something of great value. In the South Island it might be used when speaking of the daughters of a rangatira.

In the southern Bay of Plenty, the people of Te Whānau-ā-Apanui have a tradition concerning a red tapu stone of this name which was discovered by ancestors in Hawaiki. In the beginning, a woman named Hine sent her two daughters, Hine-tītama and Hine-ahu-one, fishing by the shore. The girls cast their net into the sea, but all they caught was a red stone. After this happened several times they were frightened and ran to tell their mother.

When Hine heard they had thrown the stone away, she expressed her strong disapproval: 'That stone was your ancestor. Go back and try to catch it.'

The girls soon found the stone. Their mother examined it carefully and said, 'This is a great treasure. If it is properly carved, we will catch enormous quantities of fish with its assistance.'

She told them that the stone must be carved in the shape of a phallus. This was done, then she sent them off fishing once more. On the beach the girls recited chants to Tangaroa, then cast their net. Immediately they caught three thousand fish.

When the powers of the whatu kura became known, a man named Kaurepa managed to steal it. Hine sent the girls to the beach to ask the fish what had happened, and finally the kahawai told them that Kaurepa was to blame. This man at first denied his guilt, but the kahawai explained where the whatu kura was hidden and Kaurepa had to hand it back to its rightful owners.

Later, Tangaroa's whatu kura was brought from Hawaiki, some say by Motatau-mai-tawhiti when he came with Pou on the *Tauira*. It became a mauri employed by Te Whānau-ā-Apanui in sea fishing.

This heirloom was seen in public in 1895, when it was taken from its hiding-place and displayed at the funeral of a man of rank, being suspended from a bargeboard of the meeting house. It was explained at this time that while its custodian was the only person who knew the hiding-place, there was no need to fear that it might be lost through his sudden death. There was as well a supernatural guardian in the shape of a bird, a saddleback, who would if necessary disclose its location to the proper person.

This tradition brings together two different elements. One is the old belief that Tangaroa is the possessor of a whatu kura. The other is an ancient story concerning the theft of a magic fish hook (rather than a fishing mauri) which was known in Western Polynesia some two thousand years ago, and was brought to Aotearoa about a thousand years ago.

## Tangotango
### Father of the Children of Light

In the traditions of Ngāti Awa and related peoples, it is often said that the first parents, Rangi and Papa, had two sons, Tāne and Tangotango, and a daughter, Wainui [Great waters]. Tāne is the father of trees, birds and humans, Tangotango is the origin of the alternation of day and night, and Wainui is the mother of water.

Tangotango made Wainui his wife and they had six children. These were Te Rā [The Sun], Te Marama [The Moon], Ngā Whetū [The Stars], Te Hīnātore [Phosphorescence], Te Pari-kiokio [Kiokio-fern cliffs], and Hine-rauāmoa [Moa-plume woman]. Together they are known as Te Whānau Mārama [The Children of Light].

When Tāne saw how brightly the children shone, he asked Tangotango to give him a child to light the world – because all was dark. Tangotango presented Tāne with his youngest child Hine-rauāmoa, but her light was very faint. So Tāne went back and obtained Te Pari-kiokio, but his light was too dim. (Te Pari-kiokio's light comes from the glow-worms that live in kiokio ferns on cliffs.) Next, Tāne acquired Te Hīnātore, a faint light sometimes seen at night. But he was still not satisfied, and he asked for Ngā Whetū, then Te Marama. He put these two up in the sky and there was now bright light in the world. But he insisted on having Te Rā as well.

Tangotango was very angry when he realised his elder brother wanted all his children, and he sent Te Rā to destroy him. Tāne warded off the sun's fierce rays and thrust Rangi, the sky, further up so that the heat would not destroy the people on the earth. And Tangotango's three eldest children, the stars, the moon and the sun, now live in the sky. They are not subject to death like those who live below.

This quarrel between Tangotango and Tāne is the origin of human strife and warfare; that is how evil came into the world. Afterwards Tāne married Hine-rauāmoa and they had eight children.

Ngāti Porou on the east coast also list Tāne and Tangotango among the children of Rangi and Papa, and consider the sun and the moon to be Tangotango's children. But in their traditions the stars are Tāne's sweat, which ran down as he struggled to separate sky and earth.

In related traditions, the name Tangotango is replaced by Tongatonga or Tūrangi. Occasionally Tangotango is female. Some authorities identify her with the Milky Way, perhaps because its position changes before the dawn. She is sometimes believed to be the origin of all stones, including greenstone.

## Taniwha
### Spirits in the water

These beings live in the ocean and the inland waters, and some can move through the earth. Most are associated with humans, because every people have a taniwha of their own. Many famous taniwha arrived from Hawaiki, generally as guardians of ancestral waka, then settled down in Aotearoa with the descendants of the crew of the vessel they had escorted. Other taniwha are of unknown origin.

In the beginning, some taniwha created harbours by opening up channels to the sea; this happened with Ngake, and the eleven sons of the female taniwha Āraiteuru. Others have caused landslides, especially by lakes and rivers.

There are many stories of heroic battles with taniwha, on the land and in the water. Often these struggles occurred soon after the settlement of Aotearoa, usually after a taniwha had attacked and devoured persons with whom he had no connection; the creature might have been avenging an injury to one of his own people, or he might just have been feeling malicious and hungry. Always the humans win. Sometimes the taniwha's bones, turned to rock, can still be seen.

But when taniwha were respected, they usually behaved well to their own people. Their dens were in deep pools in rivers, or dark sinister-looking caves, or places where there were strong currents or dangerous breakers, and travellers avoided these places when possible. If they had to pass the taniwha's den or wanted to go fishing nearby, they were careful to make a propitiatory offering, often of a green twig, and to recite the appropriate chant. And tohunga would make them offerings, perhaps of the first kūmara and taro to be harvested and the first birds and fish to be caught in season. We are told that in the Manukau Harbour it was customary, if there was trouble of any kind (such as illness or impending

E mau ana nga Pākehā, Heturakona,
te i ngoa o te Taniwa, nana a
te Heuheu, nana ko Haperahuma

*Taniwha were often blamed for landslides. When a huge landslide, the result of thermal activity, led to the deaths of the great rangatira Te Heuheu Tūkino and many of his people at Te Rapa on Lake Taupō in 1846, a taniwha was thought responsible. This drawing of that taniwha is by the writer Te Rangikāheke. His comment below includes the remark that Pākehā would call this taniwha a dragon.*

war), to anchor overnight a very small raft with a miniature house containing mullet flesh or some other delicacy; if the food was gone next morning it was a good omen, as the taniwha's assistance was assured.

When all went well, taniwha were guardians of their people. They warned of the approach of enemies, communicating their messages to the tohunga who was their medium. On the death of an leading rangatira, they might leave their den and be seen on the water – a sign of mourning that marked the importance of the occasion. Because of their role as guardians they watched vigilantly to ensure that their people respected the tapu restrictions imposed upon them, and any violation of tapu was sure to be punished. They were usually held responsible for deaths by drowning; the person must have insulted the taniwha by breaking tapu in some way.

On the ocean, taniwha often appear in the form of a whale or large shark. In rivers and lakes they may be as big as a whale, but look more or less like a gecko or tuatara; some have a row of spines down their backs, like male tuatara. They may possess bat wings and shark teeth, and some can assume different forms. Horo-matangi in Lake Taupō sometimes takes the form of a reptile, but in the lake itself he appears as a black rock.

Many taniwha can assume the form of a floating log, which may behave in an unusual way. The guardian of Lake Rotoiti, a taniwha named Mataura, would mourn the death of a high-ranking person by appearing on the water in the form of a huge tree with many branches and a covering of water weed.

While taniwha might punish people by drowning them, they saved some persons from drowning. Some say that when a tohunga was caught in a storm at sea or on a lake, he would ask for a taniwha's protection and throw into the water as an offering a hair from the top of his head; others speak of such a ritual as being performed to protect the occupants of a waka from the taniwha that had itself caused the bad weather. It was also believed that taniwha might if necessary assist a high-ranking man by bearing his waka on their backs to the shore. And a man flung from his vessel might find himself riding to shore on the taniwha's back.

Taniwha might be spoken of as atua, or sometimes tipua (especially when they took the form of a floating log). Occasionally they were said to be the mauri of the human community with which they were associated.

A man who had been associated with taniwha might become a taniwha after his death; this happened to Pokopoko, who during his life had conquered taniwha, and to Te Tahi-o-te-rangi, who had been a medium of the taniwha and had been rescued by them. However, another early ancestor, Tūheitia, became a taniwha without any prior association. In the far north, an English missionary wrote in 1822 that people drowned by taniwha were believed to become taniwha themselves.

There are as well Hine-kōrako, a female

taniwha who was married for a while to a human man, and Pānia, a woman from the sea whose short-lived marriage to a human produced a son who later became a taniwha. There were relationships of many kinds.

In metaphor, a powerful rangatira might be spoken of as a taniwha.

## Tapu and noa
### Sacred and profane

Traditionally, Māori life was organised in all its aspects through the intricate interplay of two states of being, tapu and noa, which were complementary and of equal importance. In numerous contexts a person, place or thing would be said to be either tapu or noa.

The word tapu indicated that the person, place or object could not be freely approached, that restrictions had been placed upon access, and in this way the term referred not only to the tapu entity but also to the restricted relationship others might have with it. In many contexts it can be translated as 'restricted, forbidden' or 'sacred'. The word noa indicated unrestricted access and can generally be understood as 'ordinary, everyday, common, profane'.

Since nothing in Māori life and experience was secular – beyond the reach of religious thought and practice – noa cannot be translated as 'secular'. The noa, or profane, was a powerful counterbalance to the tapu, or sacred, and as

*People who were temporarily in a tapu condition after taking part in a ritual, or while engaged in a major undertaking such as house-building, were under more restrictions than usual as regards food, especially cooked food. This man cannot touch food with his hands, so he uses a bracken stalk as a fork; with a more severe tapu he might have to be fed by an attendant for a period of time.*

such it was an essential element in daily life, ritual and thought.

Tapu restrictions were imposed for religious, social and political reasons, so they varied greatly. Basically such a restriction marked the importance of a person or other entity by setting them apart from indiscriminate contact with others; it might also serve to protect a resource or property, or focus attention on important undertakings. Atua were extremely tapu, along with places and objects associated with them, and so were tipua and other supernatural beings. Tohunga, because of their relationship with atua and their tapu knowledge, were highly tapu. Rangatira were tapu as a consequence of their rank, with tapu restrictions being observed to a greater or lesser degree in accordance with their precise status.

The head of a tohunga or high-ranking person was extremely tapu. All of the property of such persons – houses, storehouses, garments and other possessions – was tapu (and therefore protected from thieves). This tapu extended to everything that was closely associated with them, such as the remains of their food, even the fires in their houses; a tohunga's fire could on no account be lit from a common cooking fire but had to be specially kindled.

Several early Pākehā writers describe occasions on which a slave or servant mistakenly ate the leftover food of a great rangatira. When informed of this by an appalled bystander, the unfortunate man became ill at once and might die; although sometimes a tohunga would save him. Yet a rangatira could also be seriously at risk when his tapu was infringed, however accidentally, for his atua could be expected to punish him with illness or some other disaster for allowing this to happen.

A tohunga or high-ranking person might impose a temporary tapu. This was often done to protect a seasonal food resource – birds or fish, or certain plant foods – until the time came to lift the ban [rāhui]. Kūmara gardens were protected by tapu during the growing season. After a death by drowning it was (and sometimes still is) customary to declare a stretch of coastline tapu for a certain time, so that no-one can fish those waters. Anything to do with the death of a person of rank involved severe tapu restrictions, as did such crucial events as birth and tattooing. Men building a house, carving, or adzing a waka ob-

*In a house occupied by a rangatira and his family, figures carved on the tapu lintel [pare] over the door, and sometimes another over the window, represented important ancestors. These ancestors were relatively recent ones, whose presence spoke of the ancestry and mana of the occupants. Their position guarding the doorway was crucial, as the forces of sorcery [mākutu] might otherwise enter the house and attack the inhabitants. Female ancestors were often placed in this position, because the female organ (in which female powers were concentrated) was thought to be especially powerful in overcoming enemy sorcery.*

*This great sculpture from the Hauraki region is almost two and a half metres in width, much larger than usual.*

served tapu restrictions, and warriors preparing for battle were highly tapu.

If a rangatira asserted himself by imposing a tapu upon a certain stretch of river, temporarily forbidding others to sail along it, this was a test of his power and status; people of lesser status would probably observe the restriction (or ignore it at their peril), while those of equal or greater status might pay no attention.

Intrinsically and in general, men were tapu and women were noa. In specific circumstances the situation was different; a woman might possess the tapu of high rank, a puhi (a high-ranking girl specially brought up for an important marriage) was tapu in that unlike other girls she was not allowed lovers, a low-ranking woman who had prepared a body for a funeral would be temporarily tapu. In such cases the context of the tapu, therefore its meaning, was clear to all.

But just as men belonged with the sky and women with the earth, so men in themselves were essentially tapu and women noa. Woman's main responsibilities were seen as involving the continuance of life and the patterns of day-by-day existence, that which is noa, rather than the more specialised and isolated tasks of men. In the nature of things, everyday life tends to be taken for granted; yet the entire system of Māori life and thought depended upon the subtle interplay of these two states of being.

Tapu and noa are abstract organising principles, yet at the same time they had physical counterparts in men and women; ultimately, that is, these concepts were sustained by body imagery. As well, both tapu and noa were embodied in each person, in that every individual possessed a tapu (male, right) side and a noa (female, left) side. This had many advantages, some of them practical. Warriors, for instance, while under the tapu of war could carry nothing upon their tapu backs, and although they could

carry their weapon in their male, tapu hand, they could not hold their noa provisions in this hand. Fortunately, however, they were able to carry the food in their female, noa hand.

Frequently it was necessary to remove a state of tapu, or diminish it. Generally the complex rituals performed for this purpose required the presence of women – since they were noa – and also the presence of food, especially cooked food, because this too was destructive of tapu. After a new house had been completed, its tapu had to be partially removed so that it would be safe for people to sit and sleep inside; although the mana of the house required that some tapu remain, as the atua would otherwise desert it.

One such event, in Rotorua in 1900, took place in the early morning before a large assembly. The tohunga Te Rangi-tahau instructed the chief carver Tene Waitere to make a small fire in the porch in front of the window and roast a kūmara upon it. Meanwhile he climbed to the roof, sat upon the ridgepole and recited an ancient chant to ensure the wellbeing of the house and those who would enter it, a second chant to remove the tapu from the carvers' tools, and a third chant to free the house of tapu.

He then slowly descended, took the kūmara, which by now was cooked, and entered the house with Ruihi Rongo-he-kumi, wife of Tene Waitere, and the three carvers. Ruihi's role was that of a ruahine, a woman employing female powers in ritual.

As the tohunga and the woman stepped over the tapu doorsill (the tohunga putting his left, female foot forward first), they diminished the power of the tapu. Inside there were more rituals, then at a certain point each member of the party took a piece of the kūmara and slowly ate it. The house was now safe for all to enter. Its occupants would, however, respect the house's remaining tapu by observing the usual restrictions, in particular the rule that there must be no eating inside it.

These restrictions are still respected, and a woman's presence is still required at the ceremonial opening of a meeting house.

*Precious ornaments of a rangatira and his family, such as plumes worn in the hair and greenstone pendants, were stored in treasure boxes [waka huia], often about fifty centimetres in length. The importance and the tapu of these boxes and their contents was signified by their fine carving. They were hung from rafters in the interior of the house, suspended by cords passed around lugs at the two ends. The rafters and battens in the roof, especially those near the ridgepole, were more tapu than the areas below, and it was necessary for tapu possessions to be stored in a tapu place.*

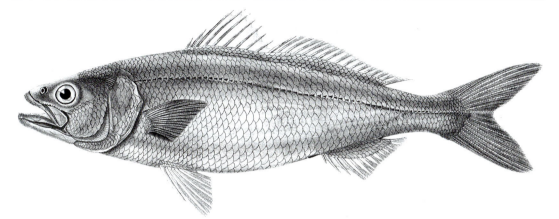

*Kahawai were believed to be attracted to the Mōtū River by Hekopara,*
*a mauri in the form of a rock some distance up the river.*

## Tāpui-kākahu
### Owner of an heirloom

This ancestor of the people of Te Whakatōhea
lived at Waiaua in the Ōpōtiki district. He was
the owner of a treasured heirloom, a greenstone
kahawai lure inlaid with pāua, and one day when
he was using this lure it was carried off by a big
kahawai. So he went ashore, very unhappy at its
loss, he put on his precious dogtail cloak, then he
started following the school of kahawai as they
moved across the surface of the sea. He ran along
the coast, knowing they would be heading for
the mouth of the Mōtū River, because that is the
source of all the kahawai in the land.

At last he came to Maraenui, on the Mōtū.
There he found the people of Te Whānau-ā-
Apanui netting the kahawai, as he had expected.
The women were gutting the fish, and soon one
of them found the greenstone lure. It was still in
the mouth of that kahawai.

She cried out and held it up, and Tāpui-kākahu
told the woman why he had come. She gave him
the lure, and in return he presented her with his
dogtail cloak.

Having regained his treasure, he then set out
on the journey back to Waiaua. He had not eaten
since morning and it was now near sunset, so the
people told him, 'Stay for a meal and go back
after you've eaten.'

His answer was: 'But there's also food at
Waiaua.' [Ā, he kai rā hoki i Waiaua rā].

This is a saying quoted by his descendants
when they are anxious to return home, so turn
down an invitation to a meal.

Some people give this ancestor's name as Tapa-
kākahu. The distance he is said to have run is
more than twenty-five kilometres.

## Tara
### Founder of Ngāi Tara

Ngāi Tara, an early people in the far south of the
North Island, traced their descent to Tara, who
was born at Te Matau a Māui (the Cape Kidnappers region). Tara's father, Whātonga, had
arrived from Hawaiki on the *Kurahaupō*.

Tara lived first at Te Aute, where he owned a
productive lake that became known as Te Roto-
a-Tara [Tara's lake]. When a wandering taniwha
named Te Awarua-o-Porirua left his home at
Porirua, arrived at this lake and began devouring
its fish and birds, Tara angrily attacked him.
During the fight the enormous creature lashed
his tail around so much that he formed an island
in the lake. Finally he was defeated and returned
to his home.

Tara later moved south and settled by the wide
stretch of water that his wife Te Umu-roimata
named in his honour Te Whanga-nui-a-Tara
[Tara's great harbour]; its English name is now
Wellington Harbour.

His people's main pā there was Te Whetū-kai-
rangi, on the high ridge now known as Seatoun
Heights.

By the nineteenth century if not before, Tara's
descendants had intermarried with other peoples
to such an extent that they no longer used the
name Ngāi Tara. In Te Whanga-nui-a-Tara and
Porirua they merged with Ngāti Ira. In the Wairarapa they became a branch of Rangitāne.

## Tara-ao and Karewa
### Rival rangatira

In the southern Waikato, Tara-ao lived in the
interior near Mount Kakepuku, and Karewa lived

189

on the western shore. Each man was married to the other one's sister.

One day they quarrelled and parted in anger. So then Tara-ao went to steal Karewa's patu, carrying his own one with him; his patu had a plaited thong and Karewa's had a thong of dogskin. He approached under cover of darkness and found Karewa and his wife snoring in their house; the thong of Karewa's patu was looped right up by his armpit, with the blade pillowing their heads. Tara-ao boldly lifted their heads and took the patu, then to show what he had done he put his own one in its place.

Next morning as Karewa went to eat, his wife looked at the patu he was holding and saw it belonged to Tara-ao. She cried out in dismay, and Karewa was greatly shamed to see that Tara-ao had had him at his mercy and spared his life. Because of this insult he summoned an army and set out to fight him.

Meanwhile Tara-ao and his people had been building a pā, with a long tunnel that could take them to safety if necessary. When Karewa besieged the pā, the armies fought through the night and Tara-ao and his warriors were hard-pressed. Just before dawn they entered their tunnel, leaving Tara-ao's wife, Karewa's sister, sitting on the cover.

Karewa came rushing into the pā but couldn't find his enemies. Then, while he was still searching, Tara-ao's trumpet sounded in the distance. The woman called to Karewa, 'That's your brother-in-law who's escaped, sounding that trumpet there!'

When Karewa found the tunnel he was furious, but he could do nothing. Tara-ao made a new home in the north, and afterwards his wife went and lived with him once more.

## Tara-i-whenua-kura
### A happy outcome

Often this is the name of a great victory won by the people with whom the listeners are identifying. In one such myth, set in the Tauranga region, the tohunga Ngātoro-i-rangi and his men overwhelm warriors led by Manaia.

On the west coast of the North Island there is a different story. A young man, Monoa, is pursued by enemies and attempts to conceal himself in flocks of birds; finally he manages to hide among a flock of terns. This occasion becomes known as Te Tara-i-whenua-kura, or (as the expression must have been understood in this context) 'The terns of the crimson land'.

Ngāti Porou on the east coast have yet another interpretation. In a chant believed to ensure possession of a treasured object, this property is personified as Tara-i-whenua-kura.

As the expression moved from one region to another it changed its meaning, but always referred to a much-desired outcome.

## Tara-ki-uta and Tara-ki-tai
### Murdered twins

In Tūranga (the Gisborne region), a rangatira named Rākai-hiku-roa [Rākai with many followers] received much tribute from the local people. His eldest son, Tūpurupuru, was also the recipient of gifts of food and valuable possessions. But then the flow of gifts lessened, and Rākai-hiku-roa became aware that they were being presented instead to the twin sons of his cousin Kahutapere. These boys, Tara-ki-uta and Tara-ki-tai, had become very popular and the people were now regarding them rather than Tūpurupuru as their future leaders.

Rākai-hiku-roa viewed this as an insult and sought revenge. On a visit to Kahutapere's pā he saw the twins whipping their tops, and as the tops spun past he knocked them into a kūmara pit. When the boys went down to retrieve their tops he killed them and hid their bodies inside the pit.

Finding his sons missing, Kahutapere summoned his tohunga. To discover the murderer the tohunga sent up a kite, reciting chants to empower it, and the kite flew straight across a valley to the hill where Rākai-hiku-roa had his pā. When it hung motionless above Rākai-hiku-roa's house, it was known that he had killed the boys.

Some say two kites were sent up, and one storyteller speaks of an army of kites, all bearing weapons. Another belief is that Rākai-hiku-roa sent up his own kite to pull down Kahutapere's one, but failed to do so.

Afterwards Kahutapere and his allies attacked Rākai-hiku-roa's pā, killed his son Tūpurupuru and forced Rākai-hiku-roa and his followers to migrate southwards from Tūranga. After much fighting these people finally settled at Te Wairoa (Wairoa) and Heretaunga (Hawke's Bay).

A rather similar story is told by the people of Te Whakatōhea in the Ōpōtiki region. Tara-ki-uta and Tara-ki-tai were sons of Tuamutu, a rangatira of Ōhiwa who lived long ago. The cord of the kite they were flying became entangled in the palisades of the Te Mawhai Pā, and when they went to retrieve it they were killed by the people there.

# Taramainuku

## The owner of a net

Some say this man came from Hawaiki on *Te Arawa*, others that he was a grandson of Tama-te-kapua and born in Aotearoa. He was a great fisherman, and his enormous seine net can be seen in a number of places.

In the Tāmaki region, dangerous rocks at the entrance to the Manukau Harbour are Taramainuku's Seine Net [Te Kupenga-o-Taramainuku] and the islands of the Waitematā Harbour are its floats. In Heretaunga (Hawke's Bay), the posts to which the net was fastened are

*Tara-ki-uta and Tara-ki-tai hold their tops on the façade of Mātaatua. This meeting house, carved by Wepiha Apanui and his team, was opened at Whakatāne in 1875 and is now in the Otago Museum. In Te Whakatōhea tradition the story of these twins differs from that known in Tūranga.*

two high rocky pinnacles. To the Tūhoe people, the entire Milky Way was his net.

# Taranga

## Māui's mother

The trickster hero Māui began life as a foetus that his mother Taranga threw into the sea after a miscarriage – or, in other versions of the myth, that she put in a prickly bush-lawyer vine or placed in the cave that held the bones of his ancestors. But Māui miraculously survived, grew up and returned to his family. At first his mother did not recognise him, but then she welcomed him.

Every day Taranga disappeared at dawn. Māui wanted to know where she went, so to slow her departure he hid her clothes one night. Next morning Taranga searched in vain for her skirt, and eventually fled without it.

Looking around the door, Māui saw his mother pull a clump of sedge from the ground and enter a hidden passage that went down under the ground. So he turned himself into a pigeon and flew down after her. (It is sometimes said that the pigeon's beautiful plumage is Taranga's skirt, which Māui wore in order to achieve this transformation.)

Down below, the disguised Māui made himself known to his mother, who greeted him with affection.

Some say it was Taranga who taught Māui how to fasten a barb to his bird-spear, so that people learnt for the first time how to spear birds.

Māui's full name is Māui-tikitiki-o-Taranga [Māui the girdle of Taranga]; this is said by one narrator to recall Māui's origin in blood from Taranga's tikitiki, or girdle. The place under the ground to which the mother and son go is not Night [Te Pō], home of the dead; it appears to be simply another region that is normally unreachable.

# Tarawhata

## Owner of a supernatural dog

This man came from Hawaiki with a dog that possessed special powers. Some say he arrived on the *Mangarara*, which brought ancestors of Ngāti Porou to East Cape. Near the shore the dog jumped overboard and kicked so hard it raised waves that wrecked the waka. Afterwards the creature turned into a cliff on the nearby island of Whanga-o-keno. In this form it remained dangerous; on one occasion its piercing gaze turned a woman to stone.

191

Others say that Tarawhata and his dog came on *Mātaatua*, and that the dog is now a rock with uncanny powers, a tipua, in the Whakatāne River near Pūkareao. It is also claimed that the two of them arrived on *Te Arawa*, and that at Tauranga the dog leapt from the waka, Tarawhata followed, and they swam ashore.

Another story is that Tarawhata came with two dogs on the back of a taniwha that took the form of a log of firewood. At Paepae Aotea he left his magic taniwha-belt, and he swam to Mauao (Mount Maunganui) in Tauranga. When he saw that his dogs were about to reach the shore before him, he was angry at their presumption and turned them to stone. They can still be seen there now.

## Taro
### A favourite food

Several varieties of taro were grown for their starchy corms and the thick succulent stems of the leaves. The plants were not irrigated, as often in tropical Polynesia, but were grown in warm parts of the country in rich damp soil, often by streams, with an upper layer of sand or gravel to warm the ground.

They were not very productive in terms of time and effort, so were a luxury reserved mostly for distinguished visitors. In certain ceremonies, such as the naming of a newborn child of rank, they formed a ritual meal. Sometimes at a funeral a seed taro would be placed in each hand so that

*Taro were a luxury food kept mostly for visitors.*

the person would have food in the underworld.

In southern Taranaki the people of Ngā Rauru and Ngāti Ruanui believed that taro was first obtained by the inhabitants of Hawaiki from an island, Te Wairua Ngangana, and that it was later brought to Aotearoa by Ruauri, captain of the *Mātaatua*. This tradition differs from those concerning *Mātaatua* which are possessed by the peoples of the southern Bay of Plenty and the Urewera.

## Tautini-awhitia
### A voyage to find a father

There was a woman who was pregnant and had a craving for birds, so her husband went off bird-spearing. He came back with a huia and a white heron, but the woman did not eat these birds. She kept them as pets.

Then the husband left the woman and returned to his own home. She stayed there, and gave birth to her son, Tautini-awhitia. When this boy grew big, the other children called him a bastard, so he asked his mother about his father and she told him where he was living.

He took the seedpod of a rewarewa tree, tried it out on the water, and found it would serve as a waka. He said farewell to his mother, and she to him. He went out over the ocean, while the mother recited a chant to speed his voyage.

At his father's village he was treated like a slave and sent to the cookhouse, because no-one knew who he was. So he went into the forest and caught two birds, a huia and a white heron. He taught those birds to speak, there in the cook-house, then that night he went to the house and found the people asleep and snoring. He thrust in his birds, putting their supplejack cage in the ashes of the fire.

The huia called, 'The fire is not burning, it is dark, dark, dark!'

The white heron called, 'The fire is not burning, light shines!'

The people cried out in amazement at these wise birds. Then the boy's father stood up and said, 'This boy is my son, because these are the birds for which his mother longed.'

He wept over his son, and at daybreak he performed the tohi ceremony that acknowledged the boy's paternity and dedicated him to his future life.

The white heron and the huia were rare, treasured, tapu birds. Since the white heron sometimes symbolised the male and the huia the female, the woman's pets together represented the child of unknown sex whom she was to have.

# Tautoru
## Three bright stars

The English name for this row of three stars is Orion's Belt. Along with another row of three stars nearby (Orion's Sword), it was often known to the Māori as Māui's Handle [Te Kakau a Māui] – the idea being that these six stars are the bent handle of an adze belonging to the trickster Māui.

Sometimes the two rows of stars were thought instead to be a bird-snare, of the kind that was baited with a rātā flower. This flower was the beautiful star Puanga (Rigel).

Tautoru was associated with the third month in the year (August–September), and indicated the time when the kūmara should be planted; according to the manner in which it rose, the crop would be planted early or late. As well it marked the approach of dawn.

# Tāwera
## The morning star

Before dawn the rising of Tāwera (Venus) in the eastern sky told restless sleepers that daylight would soon come. His bright presence was greeted with songs and sayings:

Tērā anō Tāwera kei waho kei te moana.
Ko te aho kua tae mai ki aku kamo
I te matatūtanga o te awatea nei, ha!

There is Tāwera far out over the ocean.
His shining light comes to my eyes
As the daylight wakes, *ha!*

Poets might welcome Tāwera and wish he were an absent lover or relative. Another name for him is Kōpū.

# Tāwhaki
## A journey to the skies

In the genealogies, Tāwhaki's place comes quite soon after the creation of the world. His main exploit is to climb to the skies. Being very handsome, he is loved by many women. Often he avenges his father's death.

On the east coast, the Ngāti Porou story is that Tāwhaki and his younger brother Karihi set out to visit their grandmother Whaitiri in the sky. After overcoming enemies they began their climb. Karihi fell and died, but Tāwhaki was successful.

In the sky he found Whaitiri. She was blind, and she was sitting counting a pile of twelve taro. Tāwhaki tricked her by taking away her taro, one by one, then restored her sight by giving her the eyes of Karihi, his younger brother who had died. Whaitiri gave him one of her grand-daughters, Maikuku-mākaka, as his wife, and for a time Tāwhaki lived with them there.

But then he broke a prohibition: despite a warning he slept with his wife in the open, outside their house. This was too casual a way to treat a married woman and the wife's relatives punished him by taking her up to a higher sky. Tāwhaki lamented her loss then attempted, with Whaitiri's help, to fly up on a kite. But Tama-i-waho, a demonic being in the highest sky, sent a great bird that struck the kite and made it fall.

Still longing for his wife, Tāwhaki turned himself into a harrier hawk and flew up once more. Tama-i-waho cut off one of his wings with his adze, and Tāwhaki fell and died.

On the west coast of the North Island, Tāwhaki has two uncles, Punga and Karihi, whose children are sharks, dogfish and reptiles. These ugly off-spring are jealous of their handsome cousin Tāwhaki, and they kill him. Tāwhaki, though, comes to life once more.

He then sets out to climb to the sky, seeking his grandmother Whaitiri. His uncle Karihi tries to accompany him, but fails; Tāwhaki does not help, because Karihi is one of those who had tried to kill him.

Tāwhaki climbs right up to the tenth of the skies, and there finds Whaitiri. This blind old woman is sitting counting a pile of ten taro (or sometimes seed kūmara). Tāwhaki puts them aside one by one until all are gone, and Whaitiri realises she is being tricked. He reveals himself, and later restores her sight by moistening clay with his saliva, anointing her eyes and reciting a ritual chant.

He then avenges himself upon his murderous uncles by casting into the sea their children, the sharks and dogfish. That is why they live there now.

In the South Island, the first part of Tāwhaki's journey is not to the sky but across the ocean. Accompanied by his elder brother Karihi, he walks across the water, reciting a ritual chant and being careful to tread on the crests of the waves rather than the troughs. On the way he encounters women, takes them as wives, and fathers a number of creatures, among them the seagull, the oystercatcher, the crayfish, the takahē and the weka.

In this southern story, he mounts to the skies to avenge the murder of his father Hemā at the hands of Te Whānau-a-Punga [Punga's Family]. These include not only dogfish and sharks but the different kinds of seals encountered in the south, and whales as well. These large and sometimes dangerous marine mammals are the enemies that are thrust down from the skies and assume their proper place in the ocean.

In other versions, Tāwhaki destroys his enemies while they are inside their house. In an account dictated by Te Rangihaeata of Ngāti Toa, Tāwhaki and his brother Karihi revenge themselves upon a race of water spirits, the Ponaturi, who have killed their father Hemā and enslaved their mother Urutonga. The two brothers block up the chinks in the door and window, and next day kill these creatures of darkness by exposing them to the sun.

Afterwards Tāwhaki, in some versions, marries Tangotango, a woman who has come down from the sky because she has heard of his great beauty. When their child is about to be born, this woman reverses the normal order of things. In reality, baby boys were often looked after much of the time by their fathers, and cleaned up by them when necessary, but it was the mothers who looked after the girls. Yet Tangotango now tells Tāwhaki that she will wash their baby if it is a boy, and he must perform this chore if they have a girl.

The baby is a girl, and the great Tāwhaki has to wash her. (The very thought of this must have been very funny and rather scary.) But Tāwhaki complains, 'Ooh, how bad the little thing smells!'

Deeply offended, Tangotango catches up her daughter and returns to the sky. Tāwhaki weeps for the loss of his wife and child, and climbs in search of them. Eventually, after an encounter with an old blind woman, he is successful.

In some parts of the country at least, Tāwhaki in certain respects prepares the way for human tohunga. Some South Island accounts have him receiving a knowledge of ritual chants [karakia] from Tama-i-waho in the highest sky; in another South Island text, he teaches ritual chants to tohunga; in yet another, he gains the first whatu (or whatu kura) from the sky.

Tohunga of importance were thought to be able to make the thunder sound, and they had this power, it was believed, because the thunder had obeyed Tāwhaki when he had called upon it to resound. Lightning, too, had flashed from Tāwhaki's armpits in token of his powers.

Tāwhaki's action in healing Whaitiri's eyes made him an appropriate role model for tohunga, and as well he was directly approached. On the west coast of the North Island, where he was regarded as 'a deified man', offerings were made to him in a reenactment of the scene in which Tāwhaki took Whaitiri's taro. An early writer,

*Climbing to the skies, the hero Tāwhaki reveals his powers. A drawing by Russell Clark.*

Richard Taylor, tells us that 'when baskets of food were offered to [Tāwhaki] to heal the sick, they counted out the tenth basket, and lifted it up to the god, and then they counted out the ninth and lifted that up, and so on until the entire ten were thus counted out to him', From another source we learn that the tohunga performing this ritual called Tāwhaki's name aloud as the offering was made. In this situation the invalid must have been identified with Whaitiri.

On other occasions the invalid was ritually identified with Tāwhaki, whose successful journey to the skies became the transition this person was to make from sickness to health. And when someone had died, they might in a lament or a ritual chant be identified with Tāwhaki as he mounted to the skies. This association honoured the person, and at the same time sent their wairua on its pathway to the stars.

Tāwhaki has a special association with red, the colour associated with high status. Among other things, his blood, when he died, coloured the flowers of the rātā and the pōhutukawa.

His myth is known in differing versions in many parts of Polynesia and must have existed for two thousand years or more.

## Tāwhirimātea
### Father of the winds

This man is usually regarded as a son of Rangi the sky and Papa the earth. In an Arawa account, he quarrelled with his brothers when they resolved to separate their parents, and when Rangi was pushed upwards he followed him to the realms above. From there he attacks his brothers, sending down winds and storms.

It is usually believed that all the winds are his offspring, though some say that gales are his children, and ordinary winds the children of Raka-maomao. The larger stars are also thought sometimes to be children of Tāwhirimātea.

Sometimes he is a son of Tāne, and grandson of Rangi and Papa.

*Fishermen and voyagers, anxious to placate and honour Tāwhirimātea, sometimes put him on board their waka as the inward-facing figure at the base of the sternpost. This was a place of honour, as is shown by the fact that the seat next to the sternpost (apart from the one for the steersmen) was occupied by the most high-ranking person on board.*

## Te Akē
### A story of revenge

Te Akē and his people, a small group of Ngāi Tahu, lived on the shores of the Akaroa Harbour some two hundred years ago. One day his beautiful daughter Hineao went with others to visit a related people whose village was by the Ōpāwaho River (the Heathcote).

The rangatira there was Turaki-pō. When he saw Hineao he wanted to marry her, but she rejected his advances. So Turaki-pō decided that if he could not have her, no-one else should do so. After she returned home, he went by night to his tūāhu and performed rituals to kill her through sorcery. His chants did their work and Hineao soon died.

Te Akē knew very well who had killed his daughter. He wept for her, then to revenge her he travelled north to visit Tautini, the great tohunga of Ngāi Tahu. It was Tautini who had taught Turaki-pō his sorcery; but now, in response to the presents Te Akē laid before him, the tohunga communicated chants more powerful than those he had given Te Akē's enemy. And from another tohunga, Iri-rangi, Te Akē learnt chants that allowed him to call to his aid the gods of the earth, sky and sea.

It was summer when Te Akē returned home, the time when the inland peoples visited the shore to fish and gather shellfish. Turaki-pō's people had taken their waka down to the coast and were camped in a cavern in the great rock known as Tuawera (Cave Rock, at Sumner). Seated on cliffs near his home and looking across the water at his enemies in the far distance, Te Akē recited his long chant to raise Tangaroa and Tuhirangi and all the other powers of the deep.

In the morning the people in the fishing camps woke to find a sperm whale stranded on a sand-bank near the shore. Greatly excited, they feasted upon the meat. Only Turaki-pō did not join in the celebrations. The previous night he had had an ominous dream, a warning of disaster. Saying nothing, he took the smallest of the waka and set out for his home. There he recited chants to avert sorcery.

Next morning Turaki-pō's people lay dead around their camp fires, destroyed by the terrible tapu of the whale's body. Te Akē had gained his revenge; for while it was a pity that Turaki-pō himself had not died, it was appropriate that his people should suffer for his misdeeds. From this time on, Tuawera Rock was shunned by all. It was a tapu place where spirits whistled in the night.

## Te Aoputaputa
### A lover's magic

Some twenty generations ago a young rangatira, Tahito-kura, lived on Titirangi Hill in Tūranga (the Gisborne district). On a visit to Ōpōtiki, far to the north, he fell in love with Te Aoputaputa, but she rejected him.

Back home, he decided to win her through magic. He made a neck pendant and cord, steeped them in scented oil and placed them inside a ngāruru shell [Cook's turban shell]. He recited a chant to make Te Aoputaputa love him and seek him out, then he told the shell to go to Ōpape Beach and threw it into the ocean.

The shell moved along the coast until it came to Ōpape, near Ōpōtiki. Te Aoputaputa was there, as Tahito had known she would be. She was diving for pāua with a group of women.

But she couldn't find a single pāua. The other women's baskets were full, but all she could see was this ngāruru shell. She threw it away and went somewhere else, but still the shell followed. In the end she took it ashore. Then she noticed the pendant inside, and put it around her neck. At once she thought of Tahito and she loved him.

So Te Aoputaputa walked alone through the forests and mountains from Ōpōtiki to Tūranga, and there she found Tahito and married him. Many peoples in the region are descended from these two.

## Te Ara Tāwhao
### A voyage to gain the kūmara

In the early times Toi lived with his people at Whakatāne, in a pā named Te Kapu-o-te-rangi on a high hill above the sea. Their only vegetable foods were wild plants. They lived on fernroot, inner leaves of the cabbage tree, berries, raupō roots, pith of the mamaku tree-fern, and other forest products.

One morning Toi's daughter Te Kura Whaka-ata discovered on the shore two strangers who had come from the homeland of Hawaiki. These men, Hoake (or Hoaki) and his younger brother Taukata, had floated all the way to Aotearoa on a piece of pumice stone.

Te Kura Whakaata led the visitors up to the pā, where her people offered them a meal of fernroot and other wild plant foods. The men accepted this but did not like it, and ate with difficulty. Then Taukata untied his carry-belt and produced some dried kūmara he had brought with him. He mixed it with water and offered it to his hosts, who were delighted with this new food.

When Toi asked Hoake and Taukata how he could obtain the kūmara, they told him he must construct a ship and sail to Hawaiki. Toi did not know how to do this, but was advised by the two brothers. They told him that a tōtara log, washed up on the shore, would be their waka.

Because of its origin, Toi's vessel was named *Te Ara Tāwhao* [The driftwood path]. It reached Hawaiki under the captaincy, it is sometimes said, of Toi's son Tama-ki-Hikurangi, and the crew obtained the kūmara there. They left their vessel in Hawaiki and later sailed back to Aotearoa in the *Mātaatua*.

Hoake returned to Hawaiki, but Taukata stayed at Whakatāne. To ensure that the mauri [life-force] of the kūmara would remain in Aotearoa and not go back to Hawaiki, he was killed as a sacrifice. His skull, with a seed kūmara in each eye-socket, was placed beside the plantations at planting time and rituals were performed to ensure a plentiful crop.

## Te Ara-tukutuku
### A son's revenge

Te Ara-tukutuku was a human woman whose son Te Ihi became a taniwha. Some time after this, Te Ara-tukutuku was insulted by some women while she was visiting the pā at Ōhinemutu, by Lake Rotorua. When she retaliated by calling upon her son to revenge her, the taniwha caused half of the pā to sink down into the lake.

Later, back among her people at Taupō, Te Ara-tukutuku was murdered by men who had accused her of sorcery. Again her son acted on her behalf, destroying two pā beside Lake Taupō by sending them down into the water.

## Te Arawa
### Waka of the Arawa peoples

A war in Hawaiki led to the voyage of *Te Arawa* to Aotearoa. This struggle began when the powerful rangatira Uenuku suffered from a boil, and the dog belonging to another rangatira, Hou (or Hou-mai-tawhiti), came across the discarded dressings and ate them. To avenge this terrible insult, Uenuku and his son Toi at once killed the animal and ate it.

Hou's sons Tama-te-kapua and Whakatūria went searching for the dog and discovered its fate. To revenge themselves, these two men went by night on stilts to steal fruit from a tree owned by Uenuku. Eventually they were caught; Tama-te-kapua escaped, but Whakatūria was captured

*At Ōhinemutu, where thermal activity can lead to land subsidence, Te Ara-tukutuku was blamed for the disappearance of half of the pā. Some of the palisade posts remained in the lake for long afterwards.*

and hung up inside the roof of their enemies' house. He was up there nearly choked by the smoke of the fire, while below him the warriors were dancing haka.

Learning what had happened, Tama-te-kapua climbed the roof, made a hole in the thatch and spoke to his younger brother. He had a plan, and he told Whakatūria what to do.

So Whakatūria called down to his enemies and told them how badly they were dancing and how much better he could do. They gave him a chance to prove it, and when he asked for a fine garment and a taiaha, they gave him these as well. Then he danced his haka, leaping from one side of the house to the other, his eyes shining like the evening star rising over the horizon.

Presently he asked for the door to be opened so he could cool down. Then he danced again – and straight out through the doorway! Tama-te-kapua, sitting ready in the porch, fastened the door and window so the enemy could not follow. But this led to fighting, and many were killed. In the end Tama-te-kapua decided it was time to go.

When *Te Arawa* had been constructed and lay ready, there was no tohunga to guide and protect the waka. So Tama-te-kapua decided to take with him the great tohunga Ngātoro-i-rangi, who was about to travel on the *Tainui*. Some say Tama persuaded Ngātoro to join *Te Arawa*, others that he kidnapped him.

It is certain that Tama stole Whakaotirangi, the wife of Ruaeo. He did this by tricking Ruaeo into going back at the last moment to fetch an adze Tama claimed to have forgotten – then off they went without him, and Tama had the woman to himself.

During the voyage Tama, not satisfied with this, stole Ngātoro-i-rangi's wife Kea (or Kearoa) as well. And Ngātoro, enraged, called up the winds and began to send *Te Arawa* down to destruction in the throat of Te Parata, the monster at the edge of the ocean. The crew wept and cried as the vessel began to slide into the abyss, and finally Ngātoro had pity on them. With a powerful chant he brought the ship back up – and this chant is still sung now when an Arawa orator wishes to remind his people of a danger from which they must be saved.

They sailed on, and at last approached Rātānui, near Tikirau (Cape Runaway, on the east coast). The rātā trees were in bloom, and when the

voyagers saw the crimson flowers they threw their own red treasures [kura] into the water, thinking such things were freely available in the new land. By the time they discovered their mistake, the real treasures had floated away.

The vessel then sailed straight across to Moehau (on Cape Colville), near which, on a small island, Ngātoro-i-rangi placed a stone brought from Hawaiki as a mauri for their descendants. Coasting south, they left on Reponga (Cuvier Island) the two saddlebacks that had guided their ship. (These birds have remained on the island; their task is to foretell the weather.) By now some of the leading men were claiming for themselves and their sons mountains and headlands on the shore, in this way gaining territory for their descendants. By the time they landed at Maketū (in the Bay of Plenty), all the land from Katikati in the north to Maketū in the south had been claimed.

Afterwards a number of men set out to explore the country and lay claim to territory. Tama-te-kapua returned to Moehau, Tia went inland to the Taupō region, Hei lived by Mount Hikurangi (inland from Katikati), and Tua (or Tua-rotorua) settled by Lake Rotorua, where he was later joined by Īhenga. Kahu-mate-momoe remained at first at Maketū, then went to live at Rotorua.

Ngātoro-i-rangi in his explorations revealed his great powers. He walked far inland to Tongariro, climbed that mountain and, with the help of his two sisters from Hawaiki, lit the fires that burn there now. The three of them then returned to Maketū, the sisters creating hot springs and mudpools on the way. At Tarawera, Ngātoro overcame the demon Tama-o-hoi. Later Ngātoro quarrelled with his brother-in-law Manaia and won mighty victories against him.

At about this time *Te Arawa* was burnt by an enemy rangatira, Raumati, as it lay at Maketū. This terrible crime was avenged by Hatupatu, a warrior with extraordinary powers.

Left: *A figure at Whakarewarewa, carved in the early twentieth century, relates to the famous episode in which Uenuku and Toi kill Hou-mai-tawhiti's dog Pōtaka-tawhiti. The main figure must be Uenuku; he holds his son Toi and is eating Pōtaka-tawhiti.*

Right: *The house Tama-te-kapua, completed in 1872 at Ōhinemutu by Ngāti Whakaue. At this time many of the peoples that trace descent from ancestors who arrived in Te Arawa were forming themselves into a confederation, becoming known collectively as Te Arawa. Named as it is after the captain of Te Arawa, this great house became an important meeting place. When this photograph was taken in the 1890s, it was being used for Land Court sittings.*

## Te Atarahi

### The man who came back

This man died, and was buried. Then when summer came, and the month when the flax flowers open, he came up out of his grave and went around on the flax flowers drinking their nectar; he perched up there like a bird. All his hair had fallen out. There was only his head and his bones.

Some people came along, drinking from the flax flowers, and they saw the dead man. They were terrified and ran home. Then the others went to look, and asked who it could be. They visited the graves and saw that Te Atarahi's grave was empty.

They went back and found him still on the flax flowers. They chased him, and he jumped into some fern. Then the tohunga recited chants, and he slipped from the fern to the ground. They led him to the tūāhu, and his flesh returned; soon he again took on the appearance of a man. He was given food and he recovered.

He went on living there just as he had done before, but for a long time his hair did not grow back; it grew only about a year before his second death.

When he died the second time, that was the end.

## Te Awhiorangi

### The mana of all the adzes

The most ancient of the heirlooms brought from Hawaiki was an adze called Te Awhiorangi [The sky encircler]. It was the mana, the source of power, of all the adzes in the world, their spiritual prototype.

In the traditions of southern Taranaki, this adze was made by Ngahue and given to Tāne, who used it to cut the poles that he placed between his parents Rangi and Papa. From Tāne it passed down a line of eldest sons to Turi, captain of the *Aotea*. He took it with him to Aotearoa, and there, many generations later, it was hidden by one of his descendants in a forest near Waitōtara, in a

tapu burial place of the people of Ngā Rauru.

After this Te Awhiorangi was lost for seven generations. In 1887, a woman who was gathering fungus in the forest, and did not know the region, trespassed upon this place. Inside a hollow tree she saw something shining, and she was frightened and ran away crying. The spirits of the place sent a terrible thunderstorm, with lightning and snow, and one of the old men knew someone had trespassed there. He lifted up his chants and the storm ceased.

When they saw the adze the people recognised it at once. Te Awhiorangi was ceremonially taken from its hiding place and all of them wept over this sacred relic of their ancestors.

Among Ngāti Kahungunu on the east coast, it is asserted that Te Awhio-rangi was brought to Aotearoa by Tamatea, captain of the *Tākitimu*, and that on the ocean he used it to cut through the waves of a storm sent by enemies to bar the way.

## Te Hōkioi

### A great bird

The world's largest eagle, a bird weighing as much as thirteen kilograms, with a wingspan of up to three metres and talons wider than a tiger's claws, once inhabited the South Island and the southern half of the North Island. The New Zealand eagle preyed upon big, flightless birds

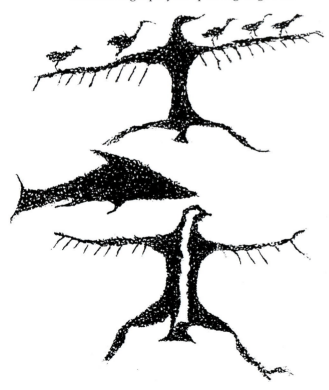

such as moa and takahē; it would perch high in a tree, then drop with great speed and force. It became extinct when its food supply dwindled, about five hundred years ago.

Stories in Māori tradition about a great bird named Te Hōkioi may be based partly upon information about this eagle which had been passed down and reinterpreted. One Māori authority wrote that Te Hōkioi was a very large hawk that lived on the tops of mountains, another that it stayed always in the sky and was a descendant of the star Rehua.

Some said it was seen only in flight, some that it was never seen because it always flew at night, and others that it was not visible to 'the multitude' but only to those of high birth. On rare occasions it could be heard loudly calling its name: 'Hōkioi, Hōkioi, hū!'

It was sometimes thought a bad omen to see or hear this bird, no doubt because of its association with warfare. When Te Rauparaha wanted military assistance from a people related to his own Ngāti Toa, his messenger sang a song about Te Hōkioi as a way of indicating the nature of his errand.

Because its home was in the sky, it was regarded as the ancestor of ceremonial kites, which generally took the form of birds.

It seems that there was only the one bird of this name, Te Hōkioi. According to one account it had red, black and white feathers, with some green and yellow, and a red crest. Some writers have thought this description to be a 'memory' of the New Zealand eagle, but it belongs rather to folklore.

In the far south, stories about Te Hokioi (or Te Hākawai) were shaped as well by encounters with another, actual bird that became extinct in the late 1950s. Until this time, people catching muttonbirds on the islands off Stewart Island claimed to hear at night the loud, startling cry of Te Hākawai. Ornithologists have established that the bird responsible for this call was the Stewart Island snipe. Sometimes on calm moonlit nights these birds would give aerial displays involving an eerie cry from a great height, a roaring whizzing noise as the bird descended, and occasionally a loud rattling sound.

Other names for Te Hōkioi are Te Hōkiwai, Te Hākawai and Te Hākuai. Another mythical bird,

*Early South Island rock drawings portraying 'bird-men', such as this from Frenchmans Gully near Timaru, probably relate to the great eagle that inhabited the region during the first five hundred or so years of Māori occupation. Myths about fierce birds known as Te Hōkioi and Te Pouākai probably also relate to this creature.*

Te Pouākai, may also have its origin in the early Māori experience of the New Zealand eagle.

## Te Hono-i-wairua

### The meeting-place of wairua

Orators and poets in many parts of the country trace their people's beginnings to Tawhiti-nui [Great-distance], Tawhiti-roa [Long distance], Tawhiti-pāmamao [Far distance] and Te Hono-i-wairua [The meeting of wairua]. The last of these is regarded as a land of origin to which the wairua return after death.

Some say Te Hono-i-wairua is in a land known as Irihia, which lies across the ocean. In the southern part of the North Island, there was a belief that at Irihia some wairua entered a house called Hawaiki-rangi [Sky Hawaiki] and from there rose up to the skies.

## Te Huhuti

### A love story

Near the end of the seventeenth century, a young rangatira named Te Whatuiāpiti was living on an island in Te Roto-a-Tara, a lake in southern Heretaunga (Hawke's Bay). While visiting a pā some distance away, he met Te Huhuti, the daughter of the rangatira there, and they fell in love.

Before leaving for his home, Te Whatuiāpiti told Te Huhuti to follow. She set out alone, and when she came at night to the shore of the lake she boldly swam across.

As she reached the island, she was found by Te Whatuiāpiti's mother. Some say the mother was angry at first because she had been told nothing of this, but that later there was a reconciliation. The lovers soon married, and had many descendants, who still recall the bravery with which their ancestor faced the dark waters to find the man she had made up her mind to marry.

## Te Ihi

### A powerful taniwha

Te Ihi began life as a man, then one day he dived from a waka into the waters of Lake Taupō and was lost to sight. He was thought drowned, but when he surfaced in Lake Rotorua it was seen that he had become a taniwha. In appearance he is like a giant reptile. Great waves are a sign of his presence.

A man named Tamamutu was carried off from Lake Tarawera by Te Ihi, and conveyed underground to the home of the taniwha in Lake Taupō.

There he was offered food, but he would not eat, knowing that if he did he would have to stay forever. After several days the taniwha returned him to the very place from which he had been taken, and his friends found him sleeping by the water. They were amazed to see that he had become quite bald. There was not a hair left on any part of his body.

## Te Kāhui Tipua

### A company of giants

These are tipua, beings with extraordinary powers; their name means 'The Supernatural Company'. They lived in a distant land known as Te Pātū-nui-o-Āio, then grew tired of their home and travelled to other islands. But they were not satisfied, and kept moving on. Even at Hawaiki the food did not please them, and they crossed over to Te Ika-a-Māui (the North Island). They got here by walking across the sea. Their guide was a large white bird named Komakahua.

Then they began quarrelling among themselves, fighting so hard they were in danger of extinction. To avoid this, Komakahua took three of the most dangerous tipua over to Te Wai Pounamu (the South Island). Those he chose were Te Kārara-huarau (or Te Ngārara-huarau), a reptile with a human head; Te Pouākai, a huge bird; and Kōpūwai, who had a man's body and the head of a dog.

In the south he found homes for them, well apart: Kārara-huarau in a cave near Takaka, Te Pouākai on Tawera (Mount Torlesse), and Kōpūwai near the Matau (Clutha) River. Since Kārara-huarau was the worst of the three, Komakahua made his own home near his cave so he could watch what he did.

Some say Te Kāhui Tipua were the first occupants of Te Wai Pounamu, and that they were a band of ogres who could stride from mountain range to mountain range, swallow rivers and transform themselves into anything animate or inanimate that they chose. In some accounts they arrive on the *Uruao*. In others they are introduced to the kūmara by Rongo-i-tua, who arrives one day from Hawaiki.

## Te Kahureremoa

### A journey to find husband

This woman was the daughter of Pāka, a rangatira living at Wharekawa by the Hauraki Gulf. She lived, it seems, in the early seventeenth century.

When she grew up her father wanted her to marry a neighbouring rangatira, but she would not agree. Later this suitor arrived with a gift of fish, and Te Kahureremoa ran to get one for herself. But Pāka angrily sent her away, saying that since she had refused the man she could not have any of his fish.

Te Kahureremoa was deeply shamed. She left the basket of fish, went inside her house and wept. Then she made up her mind that she would leave her father and her people, and would have Takakōpiri as her husband. This man was a rangatira of Waitaha, an Arawa people living at Te Puke. He was a distant relative, and she had seen him when he had visited Hauraki; she knew him to be a good-looking man of wealth and position.

She set off that night, running away with her slave. By the time her people found them gone, they were so far ahead they could not be caught. They made their way along the shore of the Hauraki Gulf as far as the Waihou River, then boarded a passing waka owned by people who had recognised her. She went upriver to Te Raupa, spent a night there, then climbed the Kaimai Ranges. Looking down, she saw Katikati and

*Wīrope Hotereni Taipari (1831–1897) of Ngāti Maru, one of several rangatira in the Hauraki region who gave written accounts of their traditions to Pākehā scholars.*

Tauranga, and far in the distance the lands of Takakōpiri.

After passing through Katikati and Te Wairoa, Te Kahureremoa and her attendant reached Te Puke. She found Takakōpiri, and she married him. Their marriage linked their two peoples and their daughter Tūparahaki became an important ancestor.

## Te Kai-whakaruaki
### A giant reptile

Te Kai-whakaruaki was a reptile living in the Te Parapara stream at Tai-tapu (Golden Bay). This monster used to devour the travellers who approached his home. Finally their fate was discovered and an army under the leadership of Pōtoru went to fight him.

Among them was a valiant warrior of Ngāi Tahu who used to kill seals with his fist as his only weapon. This man now boasted, 'One blow of my fist, and he dies! Is he more powerful than the seals I kill with a single blow? How can he survive me?'

Pōtoru had planned an ambush, but the seal-killing warrior insisted that he must first have the opportunity to fight Te Kai-whakaruaki. So when all was ready he went forward alone.

He waded into the river and the reptile approached at once. The man struck the monster on the nose, pushing it sideways and twisting his head, then Te Kai-whakaruaki came again, his mouth gaping wide. The warrior dealt another blow, and this time he missed the nose. His fist went straight into the reptile's mouth and he disappeared into its belly.

The army then attacked, and after a fierce battle Te Kai-whakaruaki was killed. Inside his body they found human bones, and weapons and garments of every kind. And the people of the region once more lived in safety.

## Te Māmaru
### A northern vessel

This ship was first named the *Tinana*. Under the command of Tūmoana it sailed from Hawaiki to Ahipara, then many years later Tūmoana returned to Hawaiki, leaving behind his daughter Kahutianui. The vessel was refitted and given a new name, *Te Māmaru*, then it sailed back under the captaincy of Tū-moana's nephew Te Parata.

At Tokerau (Doubtless Bay) *Te Māmaru* made landfall, according to some authorities, at Te Ikatiritiri (Taipā); others say it landed at Rangiaohia. After exploring the bay, Te Parata

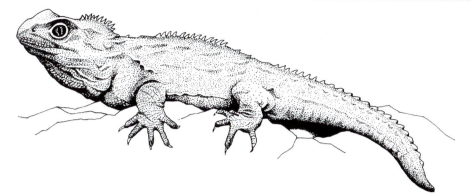

built his pā at Rangiaohia. He married Kahutianui and they became founding ancestors of Ngāti Kahu.

## Te Mangōroa
### The Milky Way

The Milky Way is often known as Te Mangōroa [The long shark]. Hamiora Pio of Ngāti Āwa writes that 'the biggest company of people in the sky is Te Mangōroa. All these people travel together, they do not scatter. The fathers, mothers, elder and younger brothers, grandchildren (male and female), children, old men and cousins, all keep together. Their great task is to foretell the coming of day. Such is the Māori sign of the coming dawn – those people in the sky.'

At the approach of dawn, Te Mangōroa swings around in the sky and awaits the sun with his head towards the east. Some explain that he loves the sun because the sun is his younger brother.

In a saying, Te Mangōroa represents good times that will come again:

E tūtaki ana ngā kapua o te rangi,
Kei runga Te Mangōroa e kōpae pū ana.

Banks of clouds cover the sky,
But Te Mangōroa lies stretched out above.

Other names for the Milky Way include Te Ikaroa [The long fish], Te Tuahiwi-nui-o-Rangi [The great ridge of sky], and Te Kupenga-o-Taramainuku [Taramainuku's net].

## Te Ngārara-huarau
### An enemy of humans

A favourite story tells how a giant reptile kidnaps a woman, makes her his wife, then is attacked and killed by her people.

One of the names given to this monster, especially in the south, is Te Ngārara-huarau [The reptile with many progeny].

*The word ngārara refers to reptiles, both gecko lizards and the tuatara (above), which for some sixty-five million years has been the sole surviving representative of an ancient order of reptiles. Giant ngārara in tradition may, it seems, be either geckos or tuatara, or perhaps a mixture. Taniwha also may have certain of the characteristics of ngārara, sometimes in combination with such features as shark teeth and bat wings. The male tuatara has a row of spines down its head and back which it erects when excited, as when hunting, and spines like these are mentioned in some stories about taniwha.*

The name may relate to an episode in which, in some versions, a couple of the creature's scales turn into ordinary-sized reptiles that become the parents of all reptiles. Since tuatara and geckos do not in fact possess scales, this is rather confusing; but reptiles were thought to be closely related to fish, and this kinship is emphasised in some of the stories about them.

Generally the reptile, having captured a human woman, tries to get accepted into human society. A woman living on Rangitoto (D'Urville Island) was kidnapped by Te Ngārara-huarau but eventually escaped; her brothers built a great house to hold the repulsive creature, invited him to their village, then burnt the house around him.

Usually the monster is male, but in the far south a female reptile named Te Ngārara-huarau pursued a human man, Ruru-teina, and was lured into a house and burnt to death.

Occasionally a reptile of this name does not show an interest in women but straightforwardly devours the humans he encounters. One such creature lived at Te Pukatea, near Te Whanganui (Port Underwood, near Blenheim). He was killed by a hero named Rongomai-papa, despite the scalding hot urine he directed against him.

In a story from the Wairarapa, Te Ngārara-huarau was a taniwha that looked rather like a reptile. This creature lived first at Waimārama, then deserted his cave, leaving behind scales that turned into tuatara, and found a new home in the Kōurarau Stream, in the headwaters of the

Ruamahanga. There he killed the travellers who passed his cave, swallowing them down along with the spears and loads they were carrying.

The Wairarapa people discovered what was happening and set a trap. In a forest nearby, they cut into the trunk of every tree so it would fall when the taniwha thrashed about. Two fast runners lured the creature from his cave, then sped towards the forest. The trees fell as planned, and Te Ngārara-huarau was crushed beneath them. His great head is there now, turned to stone.

In the South Island, where a rather different dialect is spoken, the reptile's name is often Te Kārara-huarau.

## Te Niniko
### A man with a fairy wife

When a fairy [patupaiarehe] woman saw this handsome man dancing, she loved him. Soon she visited him in his house, where he lived on his own. Every night she came, then disappeared before dawn.

Te Niniko was proud of his beautiful wife and wanted his people to know about her. She told him it was too soon: 'You must wait till my child is born, otherwise you will never see me again.'

But Te Niniko did tell his people, and they advised him to stop up the chinks in the house so the fairy woman would not know the dawn was coming. He did this, then next morning when the sun was high in the sky he pulled aside the door and bright light streamed into the house. The fairy woke and knew she had been betrayed. She ran outside and climbed to the top of the house, and in the sight of all she sang a song of farewell to her husband. A patch of mist came down and carried her off, and Te Niniko was left lamenting.

This is the story as told in 1905 by Rīria Te Kāhui of the Taranaki people. In another west coast version, Te Niniko is not a dancer but a highly tapu tohunga, and lives alone for this reason; until his seduction by the fairy, the only people he allows into his house are other tohunga. Another storyteller again, Wiremu Te Whēoro of Ngāti Mahuta, wrote in 1871 that Te Niniko was a Christian preacher who neglected his religious duties after meeting the fairy.

Her farewell song was widely known and is still sung today.

## Te Parata
### Origin of the tides

Te Parata, or Parata, is a giant sea-creature who lives in the deepest part of the ocean or, according

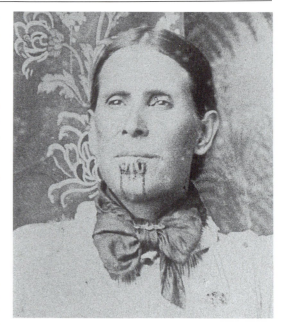

*Rīria Te Kāhui, wife of Te Kāhui Kararehe of Taranaki, in 1905 told the story of Te Niniko to Percy Smith, who later published it.*

to some, at the edge of the sky. The tides are caused by his breathing, which happens twice a day. He is often regarded as a son of Tangaroa, whose realm is the sea, though some say he is Tangaroa himself under a different name.

'Te Parata's mouth' is a proverbial expression referring to angry seas, or sometimes the steep descent where the world ends; some of the heroes who embark upon voyages to Aotearoa, such as those on board *Te Arawa* and the *Aotea*, narrowly escape death at this place. The expression is also used more generally in speaking of any dangerous circumstance that threatens destruction.

## Te Pouākai
### A giant bird

Often this is a single bird, Te Pouākai, though some writers tell of a pair of birds and their young. Sometimes the creature lives in Hawaiki, or a similar island, and is killed by two seafarers driven ashore in a storm. These men build a specially designed house and attack the bird from within it.

In other accounts Te Pouākai lives in Aotearoa. In the best known of these stories, one of the birds made its home on Tāwera (Mount Torlesse, highest peak in a mountain range bordering the Canterbury Plains). This bird carried off and devoured the people who gathered plant foods and snared weka and ducks on the plain below.

Soon the people were desperate, not daring to leave the safety of their village. Then Ruru, a brave man and a swift runner, devised a plan. One night he led forty warriors to a place near the mountain where there was a hollow in the ground. Over this they began to construct a house with a very strong framework but no thatch, just open spaces between the rafters. Every night they worked on this structure, and soon it was finished. The men went inside, while Ruru set off to lure Te Pouākai.

At dawn he saw the enormous bird flying towards him. He ran for his life, reaching the house just in time, and the door was pulled shut behind him. Te Pouākai clawed at the roof, thrusting its right foot between the rafters; some of the men were crushed in the talons, but the others managed to hack the leg off. The furious bird thrust in the other foot, and again killed some warriors before the foot was cut off. The right wing went in, and the same thing happened. Then the bird thrust in its left wing, and that too was cut off.

The surviving warriors, Ruru among them, unfastened the door and clubbed the now helpless Te Pouākai to death. Then they set out to find its nest and any young ones there might be. Halfway up the mountain they heard voices singing. It was the little birds mourning their parent.

The men stood and listened until they had committed the song to memory, then continued their climb. On the summit they discovered the nest and destroyed the two young birds inside.

Stories about Te Pouākai seem to have been told mostly in the South Island. A giant bird of prey, the New Zealand eagle, once inhabited the South Island and the lower part of the North Island; it lived upon moa and other flightless birds, and became extinct about the same time that they did, perhaps about five hundred years ago. These stories may be based upon information about this bird which had been passed down and reinterpreted. Traditions about another giant bird, Te Hōkioi, may have a similar origin.

In stories set in Hawaiki, Te Pouākai is sometimes the companion of another great man-eating bird, Matuku-tangotango.

## Te Pupū and Te Hoata
### Origin of volcanic fire

Two sisters are the origin and personification of the supernatural [tipua] fire that creates volcanoes and thermal activity. They are sometimes believed to be descended from Te Rā [The Sun] through Para-whenua-mea.

Their fire was introduced to the country by

*The White Terrace of Lake Rotomahana, formed by the thermal activity brought by Te Pupū and Te Hoata from Hawaiki. Along with the nearby Pink Terrace, it was destroyed in the Tarawera eruption of 1886.*

the powerful tohunga Ngātoro-i-rangi (their brother, or sometimes descendant). After arriving from Hawaiki on *Te Arawa*, this man set off with a slave to explore the country, and at Taupō he decided to climb Mount Tongariro. (This name then belonged to the volcanic peaks now known as Tongariro, Ruapehu and Ngāuruhoe.)

Ngātoro-i-rangi and his slave were attacked by wind and snow, and by the time they reached the summit they were in danger of freezing to death. So Ngātoro-i-rangi called with a voice like thunder to Te Pupū and Te Hoata, back in Hawaiki, and the sisters heard him and came at once.

On the way they rested on Whakaari (White Island, an active volcano), and there they lit a fire that is still burning. Afterwards they made their way underground to Tongariro, with sparks from their fire becoming hot springs, geysers and mudpools.

At Tongariro their fire warmed Ngātoro-i-rangi, though it came too late for his slave. Ngātoro-i-rangi seized the fire and hurled it into the crater, where it still burns. Then the sisters returned to their home, creating as they went the thermal activity at such places as Whaka-rewarewa, Ōhinemutu and Tikitere. Some say the fiery subterranean channels they formed are still in existence.

In some traditions, Ngātoro-i-rangi's sisters are Kuiwai and Haungaroa; when they hear him, they send the tipua Te Pupū and Te Hoata with fire to save him. Another belief is that Te Pupū and Te Hoata are two taniwha.

The name Te Pupū means 'The bubbling-up' or 'The steaming-up'. The meaning of Te Hoata is not known.

## Te Rangihouhiri
### Leader of a long migration

The people of Ngāi Te Rangi now belong to the Tauranga district. Their ancestors once lived near Ōpōtiki, far to the south, and like other peoples from that region they trace their origin to the arrival from Hawaiki of the *Mātaatua*.

After being defeated in battle they left the Ōpōtiki district for the east coast. Their subsequent history was eventful.

Initially they fled across the ranges to Whāngārā, where they sought shelter in a subordinate capacity with a section of Ngāti Porou. Eventually, when their numbers grew, the local people feared they were becoming too powerful and attacked them. Ngāti Houhiri (as they were then known) repulsed the attack but soon afterwards

left Whāngārā under the leadership of Te Rangihouhiri.

They migrated first to Ūawa (Tolaga Bay), then Te Kaha, then Tōrere. Next they returned to the Ōpōtiki district, but after another defeat they moved on, fighting their way northwards along the Bay of Plenty. Presently Ngāi Te Rangi, as they were now called, reached Maketū. This district was occupied by the Tapuika people, a section of Te Arawa.

Ngāi Te Rangi were offered land near Maketū and for a while lived there peacefully, but Te Rangihouhiri still coveted Maketū, and a series of battles followed. Although Te Rangihouhiri himself was killed in one of these engagements, it seemed at first that he had found his people a home. Ngāi Te Rangi were now strong enough to form alliances through marriage with Tapuika, and they appeared to be firmly established in the Maketū region.

But other branches of Te Arawa did not accept their presence, and Ngāi Te Rangi finally abandoned Maketū for Tauranga. There they stormed the great pā at Mount Maunganui and overcame the two peoples in the region, Ngāti Ranginui and Waitaha. The Tauranga district became their home, and as always the fighting was followed by marriages between the two sides.

## Te Rapuwai
### An early people

In the South Island, Te Rapuwai were sometimes regarded as very early human inhabitants. Some people believed they came up from the ground. Others said that they arrived from Hawaiki on the *Uruao*, and that soon after their arrival they fought and overcame monsters, such as Kōpūwai, who preyed upon them.

Others believed Te Rapuwai to have been giants, not humans, even when they agreed they had come on the *Uruao*. Some claimed they were more than two and a half metres tall; they could easily kill ordinary men by bashing their heads together, but they were unskilled in the use of weapons so were no match for Māori warriors.

## Te Rēinga
### The place of departure

The usual belief is that after death a person's wairua remains three days with the mourning relatives, then sets out for a destination known as Te Rēinga [The leaping place] and as Te Rerenga Wairua [The leaping place of the wairua]. This windswept barren promontory is in the far north-west of the North Island. Its English name is Cape Rēinga.

Some wairua make their way down the rivers, then travel by sea; others go by land. People in the far north were well aware of their presence, and built their food storehouses facing north so that the wairua in their passage through the air would not spoil their contents by entering or crossing them. Some people could hear on misty days the faint high singing of the wairua, and their chatter and laughter.

Since the wairua are passing through regions that are new to them, and they do not want to offend the unknown atua there, they leave at their resting-places twisted twigs or grass as offerings to the spirits [whakaū]. Such offerings were made by ordinary travellers, but these ones could be recognised by the fact that the leaves were of plants that belonged to districts in which the dead had lived, and did not grow in that locality.

The ascent begins at the northern end of Te One Roa a Tōhē (Ninety Mile Beach). On Haumu, the headland above the beach, wairua from the two coasts and from the inland districts meet, then set out together along ridges in the interior. On Maringi-noa [Keep pouring down] they gaze back and weep, farewelling their relatives and their land. Further along, in the valley of Wai-ngunguru [Murmuring waters], a stream can be heard mourning their passing. There is another hill, Herangi, then a stream, Te Werahi, with a waterfall that becomes silent as they go across. They climb the last ridge, which extends along the rocky cape; this place is tapu. They go up Hiriki Hill, then down a steep slope.

On the way down they pass two small, tapu streams which are known to some as Te Wai-o-raro-pō [The waters of night below] and Te Wai-o-rata [The waters of divination]; occasionally a wairua will refuse to drink from Te Wai-o-raro-pō or cross Te Wai-o-rata, and may perhaps return to this world. Others speak of a small stream at this point which bears the name Te Waiora-a-Tāne [Tāne's waters of life]; they say a guardian spirit ferries the wairua across this stream in his waka, or else that he puts a bridge in place for them, and that sometimes this guardian will send a person back to the world. Some believe that in this stream the wairua undergo a transformation that prepares them for their journey through the seas to Hawaiki.

The path ends at a precipitous cliff, and from this point there is no return. An ancient stunted pōhutukawa tree clings to a cleft in the rock below; the wairua make their way there, then down a

*Pōhutukawa trees are tolerant of salt spray and cling tenaciously to cliffs, their roots often exposed. From one such tree at Cape Rēinga the wairua are believed to leap to the entrance of the underworld.*

hanging root (some say a branch). From a platform of rock they watch the swirling seaweed that hides the watery cave beneath, and they leap down when the waves have swept it aside.

This cave is is known as Motatau, or Morianuku or Maurianuku. Some say its rocks have been stained by the red ochre [kōkōwai] worn by the generations who have passed through it, and that the fish are red as well. Others tell us that the waters are black and the fish of a kind found nowhere else.

The underworld itself, which lies beneath, is often known (like the approaches to it) as Te Rēinga; its other name is Night [Te Pō]. In one northern tradition, the wairua enters a series of regions, becoming weaker as it passes through them. On the first level there are Aotea to the west, Te Uranga-o-te-rā [The glowing of the sun] to the east, and Hikutōia to the north. Below lies another level and then, deepest of all, a region known as Toke [Earthworm]. There the wairua becomes a worm and returns to the world, and when a worm dies a person's existence is ended.

But many believe that the wairua only visit the underworld and that afterwards they go out over the ocean to the far homeland of Hawaiki. The strong currents around Te Rēinga take them to Manawa-tāwhi, largest of the islands known now as the Three Kings. The souls look back and weep once more, sending their greetings [mihi] for the last time to their relatives and the land, then they move on out towards Hawaiki.

These are the northern traditions, which naturally provide more geographical detail about this journey than those elsewhere. In most parts of the country the general idea of a journey north to Te Rēinga was accepted, and names such as Haumu and Morianuku are mentioned by poets. But in certain regions the beliefs were different. Sometimes it seems to have been thought that Te Rēinga, or Te Rerenga, lies close at hand and can be readily reached; sometimes there is a journey of a different sort.

Another leaping-place was Ōtiki (East Cape), in Ngāti Porou territory. This high promontory has few trees upon it, as the clays of which it is composed are constantly eroding. James Stack, son of a missionary, visited the area in 1846 and was told by Māori companions that this headland was Te Rerenga Wairua and that 'its bareness was caused by the trampling of feet of the dead belonging to their tribe, who took their final leap from it into the next world'. References in songs suggest that the wairua were thought to pass from there to Whanga-o-keno, a small tapu island offshore, then make their way towards the rising sun and Hawaiki.

Some peoples in the southern part of the North Island, such as Ngāti Kahungunu, believed that the wairua after death go down Tāheke-roa [long descent] to regions known as Te Muriwaihou and Rarohenga; in this case there was apparently no association with a specific locality. Another belief in this region was that some wairua were pulled down by currents in the southern ocean, but that others could enter a house called Hawaiki-rangi [Sky Hawaiki] and from there rise up to the sky. Indeed in all parts of the country, including the north, it was believed that the wairua of some persons of high rank did not go down below but were able to rise up to the sky. This belief was ancient; it was not a consequence of contact with Christianity.

During the second half of the nineteenth century, knowledge of these other traditions lessened and in some cases apparently disappeared. Te Rēinga in the far north became the place to which all the wairua make their way.

As for what happens below, the accounts differ in different parts of the country and from one story to another. Sometimes the wairua are represented as living in a way not too different from life above. When Hutu went down to rescue Pare, he found people playing games. When Mataora went down, the people tattooed him; later he brought this skill back up, and his wife Niwareka brought a knowledge of weaving. In Taranaki, much knowledge was gained from Miru, who lives in a house down below.

Some say the wairua possess an abundance of fine plant foods, kūmara and taro (probably because they are living in the earth, where these crops grow). Others think they live on flies and excrement, the reverse of what is acceptable in the world above.

*On the Three Kings Islands, some sixty kilometres off Cape Rēinga, the wairua are believed to gaze back a last time before moving on across the water towards Hawaiki.*

# Te Ririō
## Guardian of Tongariro

The windswept plateau around Mounts Ruapehu, Ngāuruhoe and Tongariro was ruled by Te Ririō and two other atua, Takaka and Taunapiki. With their followers they lived high on these mountains and the nearby Kaimanawa Ranges. They were sometimes spoken of as maero, being rather similar to humans but very hairy and with clawlike hands.

They punished infringements of the laws of tapu and constantly watched the actions of travellers passing through the intensely tapu uplands near their homes. Many people in this wild region heard them shouting and singing, though they were visible only to those they carried off.

People passing the mountains for the first time showed their respect for the spirits by shading their eyes with wreaths of leaves that prevented them from gazing at those sacred heights. Even the local people, who did not wear wreaths, were careful to recite the proper chants, avoid needless chatter, and never cook food while close to the mountains. Those who broke these rules were certain to meet with misfortune. Even if Te Ririō did not descend upon them, they would encounter a rainstorm, sleet or snow.

In the forests nearby, people hunting pigeons, kākā and tūī believed that the birds with white plumage which they occasionally saw (in fact, albino) were the property of Te Ririō. These birds were tapu. If a man killed one, even by accident, a spirit would swoop down and carry him off into the night. He might never come back, or he might return many days later, crazed and babbling about what he had seen.

# Te Rongorito
## An opponent of strife

This woman, an important ancestor in the upper Waikato, lived in the valley of the Waipā River. She named her home Te Marae o Hine [The daughter's (or woman's) marae], and it became the centre of an area that was set apart as tapu. No strife occurred there and no war parties were permitted to enter, so in times of war it became a place of refuge. Down through the generations this rule was strictly observed.

Te Rongorito was a daughter of Rereahu and his second, high-born wife, Hine-au-pounamu. One of her brothers was Maniapoto, founder of Ngāti Maniapoto. Another was Matakore, founding ancestor of Ngāti Matakore.

# Te Ruahine
## A source of fertility

Mythical voyagers cast upon the shores of Hawaiki, or some other strange island, often encounter an old woman living alone or with younger women as her companions. This woman's main role is to be in possession of fertility. Sometimes she is termed a ruahine, a word that is generally used of a woman who may be old and is certainly a person of rank, and who participates in rituals in which her female powers are required (as in the removal of tapu). Sometimes in these myths the woman's name is Te Ruahine or an extended version of this name.

Hawaiki itself is traditionally the source of fertility, the place where the kūmara grows without cultivation, and similar ideas are sometimes involved when the island is nameless or bears some other name. The presence only of women is again indicative of the island's potential for fertility – one that the voyager actualises.

The fantasy takes different forms. The mythical Tura lands on this island, tries to have sex with Te Ruahine, and is instead given one of her granddaughters as a wife. In due course he teaches the proper method of childbirth, which people have followed ever since.

In a tale of adventure, two brothers in their waka are blown in a storm to the distant shores of Hawaiki. They find a woman [te ruahine] who is eating whale meat (this being, along with kūmara, one of the favourite foods associated with Hawaiki), and she enlists their aid in destroying a great bird that has devoured her people. This they do, and afterwards (according to one storyteller) the younger brother, who has distinguished himself in the struggle, is given the woman's daughter as a wife.

Another tale, that of Pipit and Banded Dotterel, is apparently a comic variant on the theme. These two birds were once men, who went to steal kūmara from the Te Ruahine's storehouse. When she found them there, eating and defecating, and gave chase, they snatched up her (probably female) grandchild, then turned into birds and flew off. Later they cooked and ate the grandchild.

Māori mythology, like other mythologies, reflects in endless ways a male nervousness about women – who were an essential presence, greatly valued, yet potentially dangerous and, in some contexts, associated with death and Night [Te Pō]. The very fact that women have the power to give birth made for anxiety. Sometimes the woman in these stories provides a man with kūmara or a wife, but on other occasions she is

*In myth, Te Ruahine is a woman who lives in a distant island, sometimes Hawaiki, and is in possession of fertility. In ritual, a ruahine is a woman who participates in rituals where female powers are required. In this scene a ruahine, in about 1850, recites ritual chants on the roof of a new house as part of a ceremony to remove sufficient of the tapu of the house to allow people to live in it.*

menacing and her possessions must be taken by force.

The hero of another story, Paowa, visits Te Ruahine-mata-māori, who knows the rituals for growing kūmara, and is hospitably offered a meal of this food. Nevertheless he sends her off on a pretext, burns her home and flees in his waka. Revealing her demonic nature, the woman pursues him across the ocean in the guise of a shag, but Paowa kills her and seizes her precious red cloaks.

These myths about te ruahine or Te Ruahine (or a women with an extended version of this name) seem to belong mainly to the South Island and the far south of the North Island. Usually they are set in Hawaiki or a similar island, but Tāwhaki, in a South Island version of his myth, encounters Te Ruahine-mata-morari [The old blind woman] in the sky.

In this myth she is indeed blind, and Tāwhaki restores her sight, but in most of the other stories nothing apart from her name suggests blindness. She may have featured first in a story where she is in fact blind, then later moved to tales where this is not the case. Perhaps in response to this rather puzzling fact, she sometimes becomes Te Ruahine-mata-māori [The old woman with ordinary eyes].

In the myth where Te Ruahine-mata-morari meets Tāwhaki, she is equivalent to the northern figure of Whaitiri. The other old women in these southern stories have much in common with Whaitiri, in that like her they are powerful figures in possession of food and, often, marriageable grand-daughters. Often a visiting male acquires these possessions.

## Te Tahi-o-te-rangi
### The tohunga who rode a whale

This tohunga belonged to a section of Ngāti Awa who were living at Whakatāne. He could command the elements, and he often called up the rain, thunder and lightning. As a result his people's crops kept being destroyed by floods.

The people wanted to be rid of Te Tahi but

knew they could not shed the blood of a tohunga. Finally they decided to go fishing for sharks by Whakaari (White Island) and leave him there to die.

They took him to Whakaari, they ate some fish, and Te Tahi soon became thirsty. When he asked for water, they told him, 'It's all gone. But you know where it is here, won't you fetch some for us?'

Te Tahi took up his gourd and started off, and as soon as he passed behind a headland they set sail for Whakatāne. He ran to a lookout, gazed around, and saw the waka far out on the ocean.

He wept, then when he had finished weeping he climbed on to a rock and called to the taniwha. Before long they floated up. Te Tahi mounted their rangatira, Tūtara-kauika, and the great creatures swam towards the land. Soon they caught up with Ngāti Awa and the taniwha asked what they should do with them.

Te Tahi said, 'Let shame be their punishment.'

He reached the shore before his people and was walking along the beach as the waka came in. Ngāti Awa at first could not believe he was Te Tahi, then they saw to their shame that it really was so.

When Te Tahi died and was buried, his taniwha friends came to fetch him. They carried him off, and he is now a taniwha in the ocean. Sometimes he saves his descendants from drowning.

## Te Waka-a-Raki
### A cargo of stars

In South Island tradition, *Te Waka-a-Raki* [Raki's ship] is a very early waka that sailed to Aotearoa from an unknown land. Raki is the South Island equivalent of the northern name Rangi, so this man may be identified or associated with Rangi the sky father, but this is not known.

The crew were Te Tinitini-o-te-Para-rākau [The great multitudes of the Para-rākau]. Their ship made landfall at the northern end of the North Island, then its likeness was transferred to the sky. There it became Tama-rereti's ship.

*Te Waka-a-Raki* brought the stars, which now occupy their high positions as signs of the seasons: good seasons and bad, seasons of food or scarcity. Ever since this time they have sent down their messages to the people below.

## Te Wera
### A warrior who met his match

Te Wera, a famous warrior of Ngāi Tahu born in about 1730, won many battles in the far south. On one occasion he led an expedition to Rakiura (Stewart Island) and easily conquered the few people of Ngāti Mamoe who were living there. But then he was threatened on the shore by an angry sea lion. Although Te Wera had never fled from human enemies, he did run now from this ferocious beast.

A saying recalls that 'Te Wera's enemy was a bull sea lion' [Te hoa kakari o Te Wera, he whaka-hao]; there is also a version in which his adversary is a female sea lion. The implication of these sayings is that everyone meets their match sooner or later. They were quoted in the North Island as well as in the south, often by people who could not have known anything about Te Wera apart from the saying itself.

*Te Wera, who fled from a sea lion, may not have seen one before his expedition to Rakiura (Stewart Island). Bull sea lions are heavily built, grow to over two metres in length and can be very dangerous.*

## Te Whare Kura
### A great house in Hawaiki

In a Whanganui tradition, the peoples living in Hawaiki used to assemble to discuss matters relating to their gods and ancestors in a great house, painted with red ochre and very tapu, which was known as Te Whare Kura [The crimson house]. The carved posts supporting this building were their ancestors.

Around this house stood much smaller buildings, which together housed seventy tohunga. Each of these small buildings bore the name of one of the skies.

Inside Te Whare Kura the leaders of the different peoples were ranged in two great divisions, one on each side of the house. One

*Hoani Wiremu Hīpango (?1820–1865), a leading rangatira of Te Āti Haunui-a-Pāpārangi. An authority on Whanganui traditions, he passed on a great deal of information to an Anglican missionary, Richard Taylor, who published some of it. More remains in manuscript.*

division was led by the great rangatira Uenuku, famous for his oratory and wisdom; with him were a hundred and eighty high-ranking men. The other division was led by Maru, god of war. This dangerous company included the evil Whiro and his sons, also a group of reptile gods under the leadership of Tū-tangata-kino.

At first there was unity and accord, then the two sides quarrelled. Anarchy and confusion arose, sorcery was practised for the first time, and in the end they fought. The great warrior Whakatau-pōtiki set fire to the building, and a multitude perished in the flames.

From that early time in Hawaiki there has been no unity among human beings. Groups of people have ever since opposed each other.

Another writer says nothing about a struggle between two sides, claiming instead that Te Whare Kura was erected so that those inside could make offerings to Maru. And many people say that Whakatau-pōtiki burnt a different house, Te Tihi o Manōno.

These are mythical accounts. In reality, schools were held in tapu buildings for the instruction in

esoteric knowledge of high-ranking youths. In some parts of the country, including the west coast, the expression referring to such a house of learning was Te Whare Kura.

## Tia
### An early Arawa explorer

After arriving from Hawaiki on *Te Arawa*, Tia set out from Maketū with Māka and other companions to explore the interior and claim territory for his descendants. On the way he gave names to the places through which he passed.

He reached the Waikato River and followed it to its source in a great lake. At Pākā, on the eastern shore, he saw a high rocky cliff that resembled a cloak of the kind he was wearing, a black and yellow garment known as a taupō. At the foot of the cliff he erected a tūāhu to propitiate the unknown gods there and establish his claim to the district. He fastened his own taupō cloak to the tūāhu as an offering, and he called the region Taupō. (This name is given now to the entire lake. Its full name is Taupō-nui-a-Tia – Tia's great Taupō.)

Tia then walked along the shore, erecting other tūāhu at intervals. Meanwhile the powerful tohunga Ngātoro-i-rangi, who had also come on *Te Arawa*, had arrived in the region and was himself erecting tūāhu to propitiate the gods and establish his claim to the land. When he saw Tia's tūāhu by the rocky cliff, he cunningly constructed his own tūāhu from old materials so it would seem that he had the prior claim.

When the two men met, Tia was no match for Ngātoro-i-rangi. Persuaded by the sight of the shrine that looked much older than his own, he left this region for Ngātoro-i-rangi and continued on to Tokaanu, on the southern shore. There he settled with his people near the forested western ranges, with their abundance of birds. Later he made his way to Mount Tītīraupenga, in the north-west, and his bones now lie on the summit of this tapu mountain.

Tia's son Tapuika became the founding ancestor of the Tapuika people in the Te Puke area.

## Tieke-iti
### A dancing thief

There were once two brothers, Tieke-iti [Little Tieke] and Tieke-rahi [Big Tieke]. These brothers behaved quite differently. The elder brother, Tieke-rahi, would go out fishing, while the younger one would go stealing kūmara.

One day the owners of the kūmara lay in wait

for him, and when the thief was inside the storage pit they blocked the entrance and caught him. They were going to kill him, but Tieke-iti said, 'Wait, don't kill me till I've danced for you.'

Everyone agreed to this: 'Yes, yes!'

So he started to dance his haka. They admired his skill and allowed him to continue. All the time he danced further away, then he ran off and they couldn't catch him.

While this appears to be a simple anecdote, South Island versions of the tale suggest more complex origins. There the thief steals from a woman called Te Ruahine-mata-morari [The old blind woman] who, it is sometimes said, lives in Hawaiki. Her treasures are her kūmara and her daughter (which together represent fertility). A dancing thief – or sometimes a pair of them – tricks the old woman into parting with her kūmara and her daughter.

# Tiki

## Origin of sexuality

In some traditions, as on the east coast, the first human is a woman whom Tāne creates (usually she is Hine-ahu-one). In other traditions, the first human made by Tāne is a man named Tiki. Sometimes Tāne then makes a wife for Tiki.

In other accounts again, it is Tiki himself who creates the first person. And some authorities bring these ideas together by saying that Tiki is Tāne's penis.

When Tiki makes the first human, as often on the west coast Tiki is sometimes regarded as a son of the first parents, Rangi and Papa. His wife Mārikoriko was not born in the usual way but was formed from earth by the echo and the quivering heat of the sun.

The first human made by Tiki is usually, if not always, a male. On the west coast, one story is 'that Tiki took red clay and kneaded it with his own blood, and so formed the eyes and limbs, and then gave the image breath'. Others claim 'that man was formed of clay, and the red ochreous water of swamps, and that Tiki bestowed both his own form and name upon him, calling him Tiki-āhua, or Tiki's likeness'.

In another account we are told that 'Tiki, a son of Tū, made man, by kneading clay with his own blood; and forming it after his own image, he danced before it, then breathed on it, and it became a living being, whose name was Kauika. After this men began to multiply.'

As the maker of the first man, Tiki is as well the creator of all children born subsequently. In Hokianga, warriors returning from battle made offerings to Tiki because they had been killing people whom Tiki had made. Since Tiki was opposed to war, the kūmara, in this region, was sacred to him – it being a food plant associated with peace and festivity. As well, Tiki is mentioned in chants recited to heal broken bones (just as Tāne's name is used in such chants in other regions).

Always, though, it is Tiki who is the initiator of sexuality itself. Even when Tāne was believed to have made the first woman and had sex with her, love-making was Tiki's speciality. In songs, 'Tiki's activity' [te mahi a Tiki] is sex rather than the creation of a child. A woman poet in trouble for taking a lover might blame her predicament upon Tiki, since he had started it.

But that was not all, because Tiki's innovation had unexpected consequences. Sexuality and new life, it was found, led to death, a fact that Tiki had not mentioned. 'Tiki's many tricks' [ngā rau-hanga a Tiki] is an expression used by poets in two ways. Sometimes it refers to love-making, but in laments for the dead, Tiki is a trickster because his act of generation had an unlooked-for outcome in death.

*As an ordinary noun, the word tiki refers to free-standing wooden figures and figures of greenstone worn around the neck. Greenstone tiki are greatly valued for their beauty and rarity, and for the link they provide with earlier generations who have worn them.*

## Timu-whakairia
### A source of sacred knowledge

In the homeland of Hawaiki, Ruawhārō and his younger brother Tūpai insulted the great rangatira Uenuku by constantly taking for themselves the best fish in his men's net. After the angry fishermen retaliated by throwing the net over them, setting them free only when their skins had been lacerated by the spines of the fish, the brothers decided to ask their grandfather Timu-whakairia to teach them the ritual chants that would enable them to revenge this injury.

Since they planned a voyage to Aotearoa, the two men also wished to acquire the mauri of the whales, which Timu-whakairia possessed. These mauri took the form of two sacred pools and a great rock that held the life-force of all the whales in the ocean. The pools and the rock could not themselves be brought, but this was in any case unnecessary. All that had to be done was to take away their spiritual semblance [āhua] through the use of potent chants.

So Ruawhārō and Tūpai set out to visit Timu-whakairia, the most powerful tohunga in Hawaiki. On the way they came across the old man's beautiful wife Kapuarangi working on her own in her flax plantation. Forgetting their errand, the two men desired her and possessed her. Two pet birds belonging to Timu-whakairia saw this scene and flew at once to tell their master.

Since the men were his grandsons, Timu-whakairia did not destroy them but instead planned his revenge. When his visitors arrived he seated them upon fine mats and presented

*Timu-whakairia's house, with the two birds that flew to tell what Ruawhārō and Tūpai had done, and with the tapu pool that was the mauri of the whales. Alongside is Ruawhetuki, an important ancestor who was a grand-daughter of Rongo-whakaata. Carvings high on the porch wall of Te Mana o Tūranga, a house opened in 1882 at Manutūkē in the Tūranga (Gisborne) region.*

them with a large, delicious meal of a variety of pūpū [periwinkle] which has one drawback: this shellfish has an almost immediate purgative effect. Very soon disaster overcame the two men and the mats upon which they sat. Their shame was Timu-whakairia's revenge.

Further ordeals followed, then Timu-whakairia agreed to give Ruawhārō the ritual chants he desired. He would not consent to teach Tūpai, considering that only the elder brother with his higher status was worthy of instruction. But Tūpai eavesdropped outside the building, and according to one story he was able to repeat the chants when Ruawhārō at first failed to do so.

In the end Ruawhārō was able to transfer to Aotearoa the mauri of the two pools and the mauri of the whales. Some storytellers say that Timu-whakairia also gave Ruawhārō a tapu adze, named Hui-te-rangiora, which possessed miraculous powers.

## Tinirau
### Rangatira of the fish

This handsome man lived on Motu-tapu [Sacred island] or, it is sometimes said, in Hawaiki. He had power over all the fish in the ocean, especially the whales, and he had one particular pet whale named Tūtūnui. Generally in Tinirau's story there is an episode in which he has a visitor (usually named Kae) whom he permits to return home on the back of Tūtūnui.

Often Tinirau has a wife, Hine-te-iwaiwa (or Hina-uri). Having heard what a fine man he was, this woman swam through the ocean for many days to find and marry him. She became his wife, disposed of two jealous co-wives, and presently had his son Tūhuruhuru.

Kae, in these versions of the story, is a tohunga who visits the island to conduct the naming ceremony over the baby boy, or sometimes instead he is a rangatira present for the occasion. In versions where there is no wife or son, Kae may be cast up on the shore or may come as a tohunga to heal Tinirau's illness.

Whatever the circumstances, Tinirau lends Kae his pet whale, warning that when the creature is close to land he will shake himself and must then be allowed to return to the sea. But Kae abuses the trust placed in him. He remains seated on the whale's back until the tide ebbs and the great

*A carving in Te Mana o Tūranga, at Manutūkē, which probably represents Tinirau's whale Tūtūnui; the figure alongside must in this case be either Tinirau or Kae, who stole the whale and was killed in retaliation. Whales, the rangatira of the ocean, were symbolic of rich food.*

creature is stranded, then he and his people kill and eat him.

The appetising smell of the meat from the ovens is blown on the wind across the water, and Tinirau knows what has happened. Immediately he plans revenge. In some accounts he sends a war party, in others a party of women who must find Kae and bring him back. The war party recite a potent chant to make Kae sleep; the women have first to perform an erotic dance so that Kae will laugh and they can identify him by his uneven teeth. In both cases Kae is carried back to Hawaiki, sound asleep, and wakes unsuspecting in Tinirau's house. There he is killed by Tinirau in payment for the whale.

This myth provided a model for the avenging of a wrong. A meal that smelt good might in some circumstances be spoken of appreciatively as Tūtūnui; but when a rangatira had been killed by enemies, his relatives might signal their determination to avenge him by identifying his death with that of Tūtūnui. In ritual, Kae sometimes represented an enemy upon whom revenge was to be taken.

Among Ngāti Porou, Tinirau's treacherous friend is Ngae rather than Kae; among Tūhoe he is Kau-niho-hāhā [Kau with crooked teeth]. Related stories are known elsewhere in Polynesia. In Sāmoa, which the ancestors of the Māori left

some two thousand years ago, a similar story is told of Tinilau and 'Ae, with two turtles instead of a whale.

# Tipua
## Supernatural presences

Tipua, generally speaking, were beings with extraordinary powers that had mana and were tapu. Many were atua that had taken the material form [ariā, or kōhiwitanga] of a tree, a log, a rock or a pond. Travellers treated these sacred landmarks with great respect, as they would otherwise meet with disaster or at the very least encounter stormy weather.

Often these tipua were of great antiquity and were located in especially significant places. In the Whakatāne Valley and the Urewera Mountains, tipua in the form of rocks and trees (also dogs and a pond) were the children of Tāne-atua, who had arrived from Hawaiki on *Mātaatua*, and his wife Hine-mataroa. It was Tāne-atua who had placed these children in the landscape as guardian spirits of the land, the mountains and the forests. Their presence in these wild places must have been reassuring to the people to whom they belonged, and a warning to others.

To escape the bird-woman Kurangaituku, Hatupatu recited a chant that made a rock split open; he hid inside, and it closed upon him. Later, when Kurangaituku was gone, he came out and went on again. This tipua rock now stands beside the Ātiamuri highway. Offerings of twigs and fern are still made to it.

Sacred places were often guarded by tipua. One of Tāne-atua's sons is a tapu pond of great mana on the summit of Maungapōhatu; this pond, named Rongo-te-māuriuri, has within it a taniwha of the same name. This taniwha (that is, the waters of the pond) used to pursue any person who intruded upon it.

As well as placing tipua in the landscape, early ancestors might themselves become tipua after death. Haumapūhia, who formed Waikaremoana, placed in the lake a log with supernatural powers, Tūtaua, which is both a tipua and a taniwha. She herself then turned to stone and became a tipua.

Sometimes a more recent ancestor had recited chants over a stone or tree to give it the power to destroy anyone who should interfere with it. Such landmarks were, among other things, an assertion of the property rights of the people concerned.

People passing a tipua tree or rock would often perform a ritual known as uruuru-whenua or whakaū. They would place an offering of a green twig at its foot, and recite a ritual chant acknowledging the mana of the spirit within:

Ka ū ki Mata-nuku, ka ū ki Mata-rangi,
Ka ū ki tēnei whenua hei whenua.
He kai māu te ate o te tauhou.

Arrived at Point-of-earth, arrived at Point-of-sky,
Arrived in this land, as land.
The stranger's heart is food for you.

It was especially important for newcomers to recite this chant, but it seems that often everyone did so.

Other tipua took the form of animals, such as dogs and birds. Again some of these were ancestors. Hine-ruarangi, daughter of the early ancestor Toi, was drowned by a taniwha while poling her waka past a deep pool in the Whirinaki River. She then assumed the form of a shag, and still lives by this pool; there is never more than one shag at this place in the river. It was believed by Ngāti Whare at Te Whāiti and Ngāti Manawa at Galatea that when someone was ill and about to die, Hine-ruarangi always knew. Three days beforehand she would fly over the village, bringing a warning but surely also, in her concern for her descendant, giving some comfort.

Despite the dictionary definitions, in most instances it is misleading to describe tipua (or tupua, a dialectal variant) as goblins or demons. Generally a tipua seems to have been an entity that possesses supernatural (more than normal, magic) powers, so is not what it seems. A tipua rākau, or 'tree tipua', is a tree with special powers.

A teka tipua or 'tipua dart', such as Ngarue gave his son, is a dart with special powers.

Occasionally 'demon' is a possible translation, as in the case of the evil Whiro-te-tipua [Whiro-the-tipua], although here again the underlying idea may be that Whiro appeared to be an ordinary human but was not one in reality. Similarly, the word tipua is occasionally used of evil spirits who pretend to be human (Kametara unknowingly married one of these); though such imposters are more often described as atua.

The first Pākehā to visit the country were sometimes called tipua, again apparently because they were not what they seemed. They looked much like humans but (with their unfamiliar technology) possessed inexplicable powers.

## Tira-mākā
### Companies of spirits

Crowds of spirits known as Tira-mākā could be seen at times travelling high up in the air, moving through space. Only the tohunga and other matakite [people with second sight] could see them. Ordinary people did not have this power.

The word tira refers to a travelling party, while the adjective mākā describes them as elusive and formidably strong. They were sometimes thought to be wairua, souls of the dead, and sometimes to belong to a race of spirits that formerly inhabited these islands and were still visible to a seer [matakite]. The tohunga would perform rituals to disperse the spirits and prevent them from harming people.

## Tītapu
### Fine plumes

This name is associated with the plumes of the albatross, or sometimes those of the white heron or huia – these being the three most valued plumes worn in the hair by people of high rank. The name might be given to the plume itself, or Tītapu might be regarded as the original owner of such plumes or the place from which they could be obtained. One story was that an island known as Tītapu, frequented by albatrosses, once existed in Raukawa (Cook Strait) but has now sunk beneath the sea.

The expression 'Tītapu's plume' [te rau o Tītapu] was a term of praise for a high-ranking man.

In a Ngāti Kahungunu story, the name Tītapu belongs to a man who is killed by his brother-in-law. He returns in the shape of a white heron and stabs his murderer to death.

*The plumes of the white heron, along with those of the huia and albatross, were greatly valued because of their beauty and rarity.*

## Toa-rangatira
### Founder of Ngāti Toa

Toa-rangatira was born at Kāwhia, perhaps in the later years of the seventeenth century. He was a younger son, and his father Korokino at first showed little interest in him. But Toa-rangatira was skilful and industrious in all that he did, and as well he was bold and clever in outwitting his elder brother Koroau. Finally he won his father's approval and became his successor.

Toa-rangatira took part successfully in many battles. He lived a long life, and after his death in south Kāwhia his son Marangai-paroa became the leading rangatira in the region.

The people of Ngāti Toa trace their descent and take their name from Toa-rangatira. They

*Pū, a woman of Ngāti Toa, portrayed with her baby and her sons Roro and Toa at Porirua Pā in Pōneke (Wellington) in 1844. In the early 1820s her people had successfully undertaken a long migration south from Kāwhia.*

remained in the Kāwhia district until 1821, then under the command of Te Rauparaha they set out on a long journey that took them eventually to Kapiti Island in the southern part of the North Island.

# Tōhē
## A southward journey

A renowned ancestor of Te Aupōuri, the people living furthest to the north, Tōhē belonged to the fourth generation of descendants from Pō, who arrived from Hawaiki on the *Kurahaupō*. Tōhē's daughter Rānini-kura married a rangatira who lived far to the south, and in his old age Tōhē determined to visit her. Some say he had discovered in a dream that she was ill.

Tōhē's relatives begged him not to go, for it

was a long and hazardous journey. But Tōhē would not be turned from his purpose. He set out boldly along the western shore, taking with him a single companion, a faithful servant named Ariki. Their way lay along the immense stretch of sand that was later named Te One Roa a Tōhē [Tōhē's long beach]. (Its English name is Ninety Mile Beach.)

As they went, Tōhē named the places they passed after events that occurred there. When, for instance, they came to a stream too deep to wade, Tōhē saw shoals of mullet in the water and he recited a chant asking for their assistance. Two very large mullet at once swam to the bank, the men rode across on their backs, and Tōhē named the stream Wai-kanae [Mullet stream].

After travelling for many hours the men were exhausted, but Tōhē appealed to his atua, the guiding spirits of his ancestors, and their strength was renewed. At the end of the long beach they came to rocky headlands, then a place where someone had set a number of snares. Seeing that these were badly made, Tōhē named the district Herekino [Badly tied up].

They continued on, with Tōhē naming many places in this way. They swam across Hokianga Harbour, then walked right down the coast to the high rocky outcrop of Maunganui. There they paused for a meal.

But now Tōhē forgot that his atua, in taking him under their protection, had warned him never to look back. On Maunganui he wept for his home and gazed back towards it. So Tōhē was abandoned by his guardian spirits and he did not reach his daughter. He and his servant died there on Maunganui.

# Tohunga
## Guardians of sacred knowledge

In every section and sub-section of a people there were a number of tohunga, or priests, of differing powers and status. Always one man was recognised as the most powerful of all, and the most dreaded. Quite often this tohunga was an important rangatira, so the same person might be a leading political figure and a high priest.

At whatever level, the position of tohunga was generally hereditary, passing from father to son. Often the eldest son was chosen, but sometimes in a high-ranking family it would be a younger son instead.

The father would secretly teach the boy, perhaps at night when others were asleep, or under a tree where no-one would disturb them. Extensive learning of ritual chants [karakia], waiata, sacred history and genealogies was required.

As well as passing on their knowledge and role within their own family, some learned tohunga taught at houses of learning [whare wānanga]. These schools were attended, generally in the winter months, by boys of high rank who might travel considerable distances to do so.

An early missionary, Thomas Buddle, described Tāwhaki, a great tohunga of the people of Ngāti Maniapoto, as an 'old man apparently about eighty years of age, with a long flowing beard, white as snow, appearing as mysterious and singular in all his movements and converse as you might expect such a personage to be . . . [his son] Ngawhare told me his father was the oldest man in the country . . . he had been proof against all disease; and, though he had accompanied the tribe on many a war expedition, no spear could pierce him, and no gun had power to touch his sacred person.

'The secret of all this was, he had a whatu in his breast – a sacred red stone given him by his predecessor, which was his preserver; nor could he die while it remained within him

' "Bye and bye," said Ngawhare, "when I see my father so decrepit that he is really sinking beneath the weight of years, and life has become a burden, I shall request him to give the whatu to me – then he will die. I shall swallow it, and succeed him in the priesthood." '

Another early writer, John White, tells us it was believed that 'one of the principal gods resides within a seer, and that there are many others who attend him in all his movements'. If any remarkable event took place, 'it was the business of the priest to expound its import. He was the guide of the people in almost all their concerns; in his hands was the direction of the policy of the tribe; nothing, in fact, save the ordinary actions, could be done without him . . . he was seer, physician, and general, also sorcerer, as well as priest.

*Two northern tohunga. Tohitapu* (right below), *a powerful rangatira and tohunga of Te Roroa, portrayed in the 1820s or '30s by his opponent, the missionary Henry Williams; and Patuone* (left below), *who upon his death in 1872 was thought to be well over a hundred years old.*

*Patuone was the eldest son of Tapua, principal rangatira and tohunga of Ngāti Hao, a section of Ngā Puhi living at Hokianga. Chosen to succeed his father as tohunga as well as rangatira, Patuone received an intensive education in his people's religion and history.*

'As priests, they had to conduct all ceremonies; as seers, by dreams and divinations they foretold the issue of events, and held conversation with the spiritual world, in songs taught them by spirits, shadowing forth the future . . . as wizards, by their incantations they bewitched those who might have given them or others offence; as physicians, they cured the sick by incantations; as generals, they led and determined the movements of war.'

A tohunga was highly tapu, and so by extension were his house, his possessions, everything he touched. Being tapu, he had to keep most carefully away from situations that could threaten his tapu and thereby insult his atua [gods], who would vent their anger upon him. Uncontrolled contact with cooked food was especially destructive of tapu. After conducting an important ritual, a tohunga could sometimes eat and drink only when fed by an attendant.

In some parts of the country at least, it was believed that the mythical Tāwhaki had established in certain ways the role of the tohunga.

## Toi

### An early inhabitant

There are many different myths about Toi, all related. In Arawa tradition, Toi-te-hua-tahi [Toi the only child] is a rangatira who stays behind in Hawaiki when Te Arawa sets out for Aotearoa. In some west coast traditions, Toi is again an early ancestor in Hawaiki and Toi-te-hua-tahi is one of the taniwha that escort the Aotea during its voyage. In a Ngāti Kahungunu story, Toi sets out from Hawaiki to find his grandson Whātonga whose vessel has been swept out to sea; in the end Toi reaches Aotearoa and settles at Whakatāne, where Whātonga, after much searching, finds him.

But Toi is often the earliest ancestor living in this country, here before the waka arrive. In this role he is important especially to the peoples of the southern Bay of Plenty, the Urewera Mountains and the east coast. Sometimes he is a descendant of Māui, who fished up the land then remained upon it. But usually it is simply said that he was the first man in this land.

Another of his extended names is Toi-kai-rākau [Toi who ate trees] – a name he gained, it is explained, because he did not possess the kūmara, so was dependant upon wild plant foods such as fernroot and the mamaku tree-fern. He is regarded as the source of these plants, having left them in the land as sustenance for his descendants. Sometimes it is said that he did not possess fire

but ate his food raw. And some assert that he and his people never made war.

So Toi is often a transitional figure, one who lacks the normal human possessions of fire and the kūmara, and does not act as people do now. This is not surprising, since his role in such traditions is to be the first person living in the land.

The name Toi must be a personification, like so many others. The word toi, in mystical contexts especially, refers to the origin and source of human beings, and to the earliest persons living in a land. His name, then, must mean something like 'Original Inhabitant'.

Both Ngāti Porou and Ngāti Awa possess myths in which two seafarers arrive one day from Hawaiki and offer Toi a meal of preserved kūmara. Toi likes this unfamiliar food so much that with their assistance he organises an expedition to obtain it from Hawaiki. The stories differ from this point on; Ngāti Porou say that Toi's home was at Whitianga (Mercury Bay) and that the waka he sent was the Horouta, while Ngāti Awa have him living at Whakatāne and sending Te Ara Tāwhao. In each case this voyage leads to the introduction of the kūmara to Aotearoa.

Certain peoples claim a distinguished origin, tracing their descent to a supernatural visitor who one night came down from the sky and became the lover of Toi's wife – or in some accounts his daughter. Such things happened in the beginning.

In Rarotonga in the Cook Islands, the island's first inhabitant is similarly said to be a man named Toi. There must be a relationship between the Rarotongan traditions and those of Aotearoa, because each of these men called Toi has a son whose name is Rauru. It used to be thought that the two traditions referred to a single historical person, who was envisaged as travelling with his son from one land to the other, but it is now realised that the Rarotongans and the Māori possess differing versions of the same myth – and that this is further evidence of the close relationship between their cultures. Both peoples located their myth in the country in which they were living.

In Hawai'i a rather similar tradition tells of a man called 'Ai-la'au (in Māori this would be Kai-rākau). A very early inhabitant, he possessed power over the volcanic fires on the island of Hawai'i and gained his name, literally 'Eat trees', because these fires destroy the forests. Here we have another name related to that of Toi-kai-rākau, with a different explanation as to its origin.

## Tokomaru
### A west coast waka

The peoples of northern Taranaki, such as Te Āti Awa, Ngāti Mutunga and Ngāti Tama, often trace their origins to the *Tokomaru*, which brought their ancestors from the homeland of Hawaiki.

In a song sung by Te Āti Awa, the men in charge of this waka are named as Tama-ariki and Rākeiora. This song also records that the vessel landed at the Mohakatino River and that these men and their followers built a house there, named Marae-rotuhia. A boulder believed to be the anchor of the *Tokomaru* lay for many generations on a ridge near the Mohakatino; it is now in the Taranaki Museum.

The people of Ngāti Tama similarly regard Tama-ariki as their founding ancestor; they formerly believed that Rākeiora, the tohunga on board the vessel, became after his death a god who protected the fertility of the kūmara.

Peoples tracing descent from the crew of *Tokomaru* spread north as far as the Mōkau River, which forms the boundary with the Tainui peoples. The southern boundary of the Tokomaru peoples, at Ōnukutaipari (south of New Plymouth), is shared with the Taranaki people, who claim descent from the *Kurahaupō*.

A different tradition, not so widely known, was published by George Grey. According to this, the captain of the *Tokomaru* was Manaia, who left Hawaiki after being involved in a war there. The vessel made landfall on the east coast, sailed around Muriwhenua (North Cape) and landed at the Tongaporutu River. There the crew left the god Rākeiora, and their waka as well. Finally they settled at Waitara in northern Taranaki, having conquered the people they found there. They became, it is said, ancestors of Te Āti Awa.

As well, *Tokomaru* is sometimes claimed by Ngāti Ruanui in southern Taranaki and by the Whanganui peoples. In these regions Rākeiora is regarded as the captain of the vessel.

## Tongameha
### The spirit in control of eyes

It was believed that each part of the body was under the control of an atua. For the eyes, this spirit was Tongameha.

When the great Tāwhaki was preparing to attempt the difficult climb to the skies, he and his party approached a place where they had to pass the pā in which the dreaded Tongameha lived. Tāwhaki warned his companions not to look in that direction, but one of his slaves did look,

defying the tapu. Tongameha killed him at once and tore out one of his eyes.

## Tonganui
### Owner of a house under the sea

Some peoples, such as Te Arawa and Ngā Puhi, say that when Māui was fishing for land, his fishhook caught the gableboard (some maintain, the doorway) of a house under the ocean which was owned by an old man named Tonganui. Māui slowly pulled up the house, and with it the fish on which people were to live. As he did so he recited a hiki, a lifting chant, which begins, 'Tonganui, why are you holding on so stubbornly down below' [He aha tāu, e Tonganui, e ngau whakatuturi ake i raro?].

In poetic metaphor, someone said to have fished up Tonganui is understood as having made an important 'catch' of some kind.

## Tū
### Origin of warfare

This fierce warrior is always an early ancestor, often one of the sons of the first parents, Rangi and Papa. In the best-known version of the myth, from the Arawa peoples, the wind, Tāwhirimātea, attacks the earth, and only Tū is brave enough to withstand him. Afterwards Tū turns upon his other brothers, angry that they did not come to his assistance in the struggle with Tāwhirimātea. He kills these brothers, who are Tāne, Tangaroa, Rongo and Haumia (and who represent, respectively, birds and trees, fish, kūmara, and fernroot).

In this way Tū sets the pattern for the future, for he represents human beings and the brothers he kills are the creatures and plants upon which humans depend for their survival. Because Tū attacked them in the beginning, human beings now, when they have performed the proper rituals, can safely kill and eat their relatives Tāne, Tangaroa, Rongo and Haumia, and they can cut down the trees, which are Tāne.

This episode also sets the pattern for warfare: men make war now because Tū did so in the beginning. When a baby boy was dedicated to a future life as a warrior, and again when rituals were performed over men about to go into battle, Tū was spoken of as the source and representative of the duty and honour they were accepting. Similarly, the chant performed by warriors girding themselves for battle was sometimes said to have been composed and sung for the first time by Tū (or Tū-tawake) as he made ready for

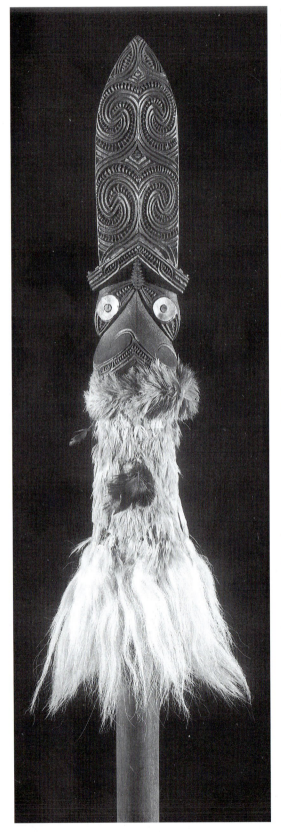

war. Repeating his actions, these men identified themselves with Tū, taking upon themselves his bravery and prowess.

While it was mainly as a role model that he offered his assistance, offerings were made to him by those who were entering his realm. The body of the first enemy warrior killed was often offered to Tū.

Since Tū was primarily the originator of warfare in general, every people possessed as well a powerful god such as Kahukura, Uenuku or Maru, who was presented with offerings and asked for assistance in times of war.

In numerous ways the warlike Tū was opposed to peaceable figures such as Tahu and Rongo. We are told by one authority that Tū was associated with the right (male) side of the body and Rongo with the left (female) side. Orators and poets might recall the saying, 'Tū has his men, but so has Rongo – you have forgotten this' [He tāngata tō Tū, he tāngata anō tō Rongo; ko koe i wareware]. This was as much as to say, 'Don't forget that while Tū is a force, Rongo is also to be reckoned with.'

The name Tū is a personification associated with assertive, aggressive action, since the word tū means 'stand, standing, upright'. He was honoured with many extended names, among them Tū-mata-uenga, Tū-tawake, Tū-ka-riri [Tū who fights], and Tū-mata-whāura [Tū with a flushed face].

While it is usually Tāne or Tiki who makes the first person from soil, this role is occasionally assigned to Tū. This is apparently because he took the form of a human being.

## Tūāhu

### Sacred, ritual centres

Every settlement had at least one tūāhu, a shrine where the tohunga performed rituals of many kinds. It was the main site where atua were approached and offerings were made to them.

The word tūāhu derives from ahu, which refers to a heap or mound, and most tūāhu consisted essentially of such a mound. Often the mound was of earth, either a natural feature or, it seems, one specially constructed. Sometimes there were stones, which apparently might replace the hillock; a tohunga might select a place where

*High-ranking warriors often carried a taiaha, a long staff of hard tough wood. A wide blade at one end was employed for striking; a thrusting point at the other takes the form of a stylised head with outstretched tongue. This head is adorned with red kākā feathers and dog hair.*

there was a naturally occurring rock, or he might pile up a heap of unworked stones, or set one or more such stones upright in the ground. Occasionally a wooden pillar was employed.

Tūāhu seem to have varied considerably in form and location, even within a single region. Often they were at some distance from a settlement, hidden among tapu trees or flax bushes in a sacred place [wāhi tapu] where the dead were laid to rest – and which served also as a repository for discarded garments and baskets of leftover food that had belonged to tohunga and other high-ranking people and were now too dangerously tapu to be left anywhere else. Ordinary people kept well away, approaching only in the company of the tohunga when they were to participate in a ritual.

Many communities must have had more than one tūāhu, since there are accounts of several kinds used for different purposes. A pā, for example, would have a tūāhu inside its walls as well as outside, so that access to the atua would be possible when the people were under siege.

In the Taranaki region, the tūāhu within a pā took the form of a small enclosure fenced about with high posts, with a tapu pillar inside. In this sacred enclosure the tohunga performed rituals, and from there he addressed the people to make known the will of the gods. It was located by the tohunga's house, or sometimes by the main gateway, where there also stood the small carved box, on a high pole, which contained the emblem of the god under whose protection the pā was placed.

In an emergency a tūāhu could be improvised; a tohunga could even cup his hand and use this

*Tūāhu were small, as tapu things so often were in Māori life and ritual. In this early drawing the tohunga is communicating with an atua that has entered the small figure [taumata atua or tiki wānanga] which, ritually bound and with a fillet of red kākā feathers below the head, is upright on the ground before him. As the tohunga recites his ritual chants, in a quick singing tone, he tugs upon a string tied around this figure. On the left, an ancestor stands under a small shelter.*

*A tūāhu at Hauraki, near the ancient Puhirua Pā in the Rotorua region. The small unworked stones represent the principal atua of the Arawa peoples: Maru-te-whare-aitu, Rongomai, Ihungaru and Itupawa. When this photograph was taken in 1907, the workmen who cleared away the bracken were very careful to remove most of their clothing before entering the tapu ground and to leave behind all food, knives, tobacco, pipes and matches.*

as his shrine. But long-established tūāhu had great mana, and continuity was very important. When a tūāhu was to be moved, earth from the old site was taken to the new one.

Several tūāhu with extraordinary powers were established by the first ancestors to make the voyage from the homeland of Hawaiki. The tohunga Raka-taura, who was associated with the *Tainui*, established a tūāhu in the form of a raised mound on the summit of Puketutu Island in the Manukau Harbour, and this was used by the people of Tainui down through the ages; it was there that the tohunga of the Manukau peoples recited the chant that led the taniwha Ureia to his death.

Raka-taura established other tūāhu further to the south, among them a famous one on a hilltop at Te Ahurei, at Maketū in the Kāwhia Harbour. Other tūāhu established by the first immigrants include one at Whakatāne, beside a tapu mānuka tree, where the mauri of *Mātaatua* was deposited, and another that Turi, captain of the *Aotea*, established at Pātea. In all such traditions the making and sanctifying of a tūāhu is the first serious task these peoples undertake.

## Tūheitia
### A Waikato ancestor

In the sixteenth century, Tūheitia was the leading rangatira in the lands to the south of the mouth of the Waikato River. After his death he became a taniwha.

His wife was Te Ata, sister of a man named Tahinga. When the two brothers-in-law went fishing one day, Tahinga became angry when Tūheitia caught many fish and he got none. He pretended the anchor stone was caught on the bottom and persuaded Tūheitia to dive for it, then as soon as Tūheitia was in the water he cut the anchor rope and paddled off.

In vain Tūheitia called to his brother-in-law; Tahinga only mocked him. And so Tūheitia sank down into the ocean and died.

Meanwhile Tūheitia's wife Te Ata was waiting. Tahinga came back and told her Tūheitia was on the shore, but after a while she became frightened and went searching for him by the beach. As she gazed out to sea, Tūheitia's arm thrust up through the ocean as a sign that he had become a taniwha. The arm was far out over the water, but the woman recognised it by a tattoo that was on it.

She knew then that her husband was dead. She wept, then returned home, and later Tūheitia, longing for his wife, thrust his arm up once more, this time through the land. The arm came right up through the earth, with the tattoo upon it.

Te Ata was pregnant when Tūheitia died, and she later gave birth to a son, Māhanga, who became the founder of Ngāti Māhanga.

Tūheitia lives in the Waipā River. Just before the Europeans fought with the Tainui peoples, many people saw him swimming along and knew it was a bad omen. They said he was as long and wide as a whale.

This is the story as told by Wiremu Te Whēoro. Other authorities say that Tūheitia was killed by a visiting rangatira, Kōkako.

Others again tell a similar story of Te Atai-o-rongo, saying that he married Rangi-waea of Te Ākau, was killed by his brother-in-law Hoeta and became a taniwha. Afterwards his hand came as a sign to his wife in the house at night, and his wairua told her what she must do. When the hand returned, going out by the ridgepole, sea water dripped into the house.

His wife later had his son, Kaihu, who in time avenged his murder.

## Tuhirangi
### A taniwha guardian

This taniwha guided and protected Kupe's ship during his voyage from Hawaiki. Afterwards he was placed by Kupe in Raukawa (Cook Strait), in the dangerous waters at Te Au-miti (French Pass), a narrow passage with seething currents which separates Rangitoto (D'Urville Island) from the mainland of the South Island. There he welcomes and protects the crews of waka venturing into that region. He lives in a cave known as Kai-kaiawaro (or Taitawaro).

In the late nineteenth century, Tuhirangi became associated with a dolphin that was famous at the time. For more than twenty years, from 1888 onwards, a white dolphin inhabited a stretch of water off Pelorus Sound, north of French Pass. He regularly met and accompanied passing ships, leaping and riding in the bow-wave, and people formed such an attachment to the creature that the Government gave him legal protection. While Pākehā called this dolphin Pelorus Jack, Māori people naturally recognised him as Tuhirangi.

## Tūhoe-pōtiki
### Founding ancestor of Tūhoe

The Tūhoe people of the Urewera Mountains acknowledge two main lines of descent, one indigenous and the other stemming from the people who arrived from Hawaiki in the *Mātaatua*

# Tapu

F1

Tapu restrictions were imposed to mark the importance of a situation, person or possession. Tasks requiring special skills and concentration, such as carving and the weaving of fine garments, involved the observance of restrictions in the preparation of materials and in the work itself.
*Above:* Weavers inside a house at Porirua.
*Below:* A fine kahu huruhuru [feather cloak].

F2

*Above:* While small waka were not normally tapu, restrictions were observed in the case of large, finely decorated vessels. These rules of conduct were all the more strict when a dangerous voyage was to be undertaken. Near Kororareka in 1828, a military expedition awaits a favourable wind.

Only a few restrictions, such as a ban on eating inside, were imposed on small, ordinary houses, but the carved houses of rangatira, being identified with the mana of their owners, were under more rigorous restriction. *Below:* Kaitangata, on Māna Island, owned by the great rangatira Te Rangihaeata and probably built in the 1820s.

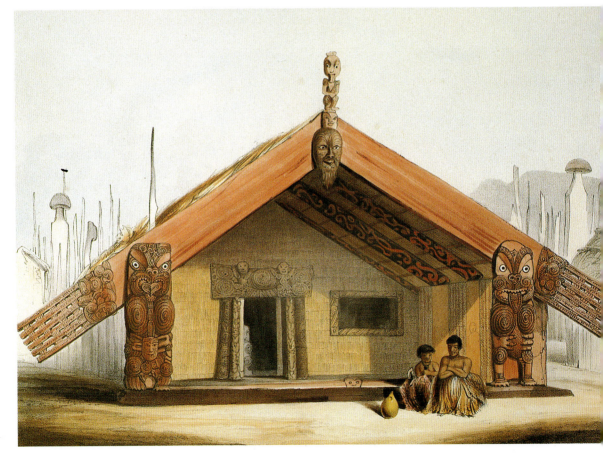

*No Horua, Ngatitoa*

Tohunga and their wives led a highly tapu existence. Nohorua, elder half-brother of Te Rauparaha and the tohunga of their family, with his wife Te Wainokenoke and their son Tuarau at Porirua in 1844. Having recently been ill, Te Wai had to stay for a time in an especially tapu state. During this period everything she touched became tapu as well, and remained so for three days. To warn others, places where she had sat were fenced off with circles of twigs.

The expression wāhi tapu [sacred place] referred often to a place where things that had become tapu, such as food left from a meal eaten by a tapu person, were placed for safety. *Above:* On a hill overlooking Taupō Pā at Porirua, a wāhi tapu in the form of a storage platform held property (dried fish, household utensils, a fine garment) that had become tapu, would remain so for a certain period, and in the meantime could be approached only by the tohunga. However, a wāhi tapu might also be an intensely tapu mortuary monument that held the body of a relative until the time came for the bones to be ritually lifted and taken to their final resting place. *Below:* In Queen Charlotte Sound, the tomb of Huriwhenua, a rangatira of Ngāti Toa. Two rows of palings, painted with red ochre and adorned with albatross feathers, surround an inner enclosure that contains an upright monument formed from part of a waka.

F8

Since the head of a man of rank was extremely tapu, anything that came into
contact with the head was also tapu and had to be treated with great care.
*Above:* A heru [ornamental comb], worn in a topknot on ceremonial occasions.

*Below:* Finely carved boxes held by small figures indicated the high value
and the tapu of their contents. They might contain articles such as
greenstone pendants, teeth of the mako shark or tattooing chisels,
or hold tinder employed when kindling tapu fire for ritual purposes.
A box carved in a traditional style by Jacob Heberley (1849–1906).

This ancient figure of Matuatonga, who ensured the fertility of the kūmara crop on Mokoia Island and the lands around Lake Rotorua, is now in the Auckland Museum Te Papa Whakahiku. However, another stone figure of this name remains on Mokoia.

Greenstone tiki gain much of their mana and tapu from their association
with the successive generations that have owned them.

Tattooing was a highly tapu art because of the pain and danger involved,
because of the blood that was shed, and because the head was in any case
tapu. Asked in 1899 to carve a panel illustrating male and female moko
[tattoo], the innovative Arawa artist Tene Waitere produced a work that
represents a woman dreaming of two rangatira.

and settled in the Whakatāne region. Of their Mātaatua ancestors, the most important is Tūhoe-pōtiki, from whom they take their name.

Tūhoe-pōtiki was a grandson of Wairaka, who was a daughter of Tōroa, captain of the *Mātaatua*. As well he was descended from the local people, because the ship's crew had soon formed alliances through marriage with the peoples already in the region. Because of this relationship with the local people, Tūhoe-pōtiki first settled at Rūātoki. After a quarrel with his brothers he went north to relatives in the Rotorua district, then later moved to the Waikato. His death occurred through drowning, at Kāwhia. His children, however, remained in the south.

Tūhoe-pōtiki should not be confused with Pōtiki, an indigenous ancestor of the Tūhoe people who lived much earlier. In the beginning, Te Maunga [The mountain] came down from the skies and took to wife Hine-pūkohu-rangi [Sky mist woman], who bore him a son, Pōtiki. (In the

Right: *Two leading rangatira of Tūhoe in 1898, Tūtakangā-hau of Maungapōhatu (left) and Numia Kererū of Rūātoki. Tūtakangāhau was a learned man who gave the writer Elsdon Best a great deal of information about Tūhoe life and thought. Much was published; much more remains in manuscript.*

*A white dolphin that regularly met ships in the French Pass (Te Au-miti) region became known to Pākehā as Pelorus Jack, but was recognised by Māori people as Tuhirangi.*

PELORUS JACK.
The only fish in the world protected by Act of Parliament.

This remarkable white fish accompanies for several miles all steamers passing through the French Pass, on the Nelson-Picton run, New Zealand. "Jack" is estimated to be from 12 to 14 feet in length, and always alone.

region where this happened, mountains and mist are very often found together.)

Pōtiki's descendants became known as Ngā Pōtiki. Many generations later, they and another indigenous people, Te Tini o Toi [Toi's multitude], intermarried with the Mātaatua immigrants and produced the Tūhoe people.

But while these people are mainly of indigenous descent, and Pōtiki is very important to them, they also value the Mātaatua ancestry which they trace through Tūhoe-pōtiki (or Tūhoe, as he is often known). They speak of their origins as follows:

Nō Toi rāua ko Pōtiki te whenua,
Nō Tūhoe te mana me te rangatiratanga.

The land comes from Toi and Pōtiki,
The mana and the nobility come from Tūhoe.

Tūhoe-pōtiki's descent goes back, through his great-grandfather Tōroa, to the powerful woman Whaitiri [Thunder] who lived in the sky but visited the earth to marry a human man. So while the people of Tūhoe trace their ownership of the land to Toi and Pōtiki, through Tūhoe-pōtiki they trace their mana to Whaitiri, and the sky that is her home.

## Tū-horopunga
### A menacing figure

In songs, sayings and myths, Tū-horopunga is a man who swallows things down. People spoke of him when talking about greed: 'Tū-horopunga is at his work again' was a comment on someone eating more than a fair share. Occasionally, too, he was thought to swallow human beings. A poet in the far north spoke of someone who had died as having been swallowed by Tū-horopunga – so he could, with others, be blamed for death.

The association with death (though not with swallowing) is present in an ancient lament, sung in Taranaki and the southern Waikato, which has Tū-horopunga as an associate of Miru, owner of a house down below which is known as Te Tatau o Te Pō [The Door to Night]. A Kāwhia storyteller associates this song with a story about a high-ranking woman, Hine-kōrangi, who was visited one night by a handsome man wearing fine garments. This man was Tū-horopunga. He became Hine-kōrangi's lover, then was accepted as her husband.

When Tū-horopunga told his father-in-law that his home was down below, the old man asked to visit him. Tū-horopunga agreed, but warned that the travellers must bring their own

food, because if they ate the food down there they could never return. So presently an expedition set out; though the father must have had his doubts, because he left Hine-kōrangi behind in the upper world.

Some of the travellers died on the way, but the others reached Miru's house and stayed there for a month. Then when the father wished to return, his son-in-law insisted that he should first be given another daughter, Hine-kōrangi's younger sister. In vain the father pleaded and wept. He had no choice but to sing his lament and leave her there.

After a perilous journey they returned to the world above. When Hine-kōrangi saw that her sister was missing, her tears ran down like water. And the song that the father sang in the underworld has ever since been sung over those who, like the younger sister, have been taken by Tū-horopunga into his house.

In related myths in the Tuamotu atolls, Tū-horopu[n]ga rules the ocean and, in one story, a realm known as Havaiki-the-below. We are told he is a prodigious eater. Among both Māori and Tuamotuans this idea must derive, in part at least, from the fact that his name was thought to comprise the word horo, 'swallow'.

## Tūhourangi
### A very tall man

An early ancestor descended from people who arrived on *Te Arawa*, Tūhourangi was one of the eight children of Rangitihi. He had two sons, Uenuku-kōpako and Taketake-hiku-roa, and was founder of the Tūhourangi people (many of whom, until the eruption of 1886, lived by Lake Tarawera).

According to tradition Tūhourangi was enormously tall, some say about three metres in height. He was such a powerful man that while standing on the shore of Lake Rotorua he used to shout across to Mokoia Island telling his slaves to prepare him a meal.

His bones were buried at Pukurahi Pā on Mokoia. Every spring they were disinterred, and to promote the fertility of the kūmara crop they were placed beside the cultivations while the tohunga were performing the planting rituals.

## Tūkete

### A precursor

Some South Island writers say that this man arrived there from Hawaiki before anyone else, when the seas were still very rough. So that later

*Pāora Tūhaere (c.1825–1892), principal rangatira of the Tāmaki section of Ngāti Whātua, recorded the early history of his people.*

voyagers could reach the country safely, he recited ritual chants to calm the waves.

When he came ashore he found that the land was tapu and inhabited by fairies [tūrehu], and that it was still soft and shaking. To prepare it for human habitation, he destroyed the tapu and dispelled the fairies by lighting ritual ovens.

His ship is said by some to have been named *Huruhuru-manu* [Bird's feather]. Others claim that it was the *Tairea*, or the *Mātāhourua*.

Another man called Tūkete, a rangatira of Ngāti Mamoe, is said to have possessed a taniwha guardian (see the next entry). This taniwha may originally have been associated with this earlier, mythical explorer.

## Tūkete's guardian
### A taniwha down south

A taniwha in the form of a great shark, as long as a house and spotted red and black, used to inhabit the Raggedy Passage, a channel between Codfish and Stewart Islands (as they are now known).

This taniwha was at first the guardian of Tūkete, a Ngāti Mamoe rangatira who lived nearby. When Tūkete was killed in battle, the taniwha continued to haunt the coast where his master had lived and died.

In the whaling days Tūkete's taniwha always appeared when Pākehā ships sailed through the channel. In 1888, when a dolphin took up residence in Raukawa (and became known to Pākehā as Pelorus Jack), some people said that this was Tūkete's taniwha, and that he was now spending the winter by Stewart Island then going north in the summer.

## Tumutumu-whenua
### An ancestor from the ground

The people of Ngāti Whātua lived originally in the North Cape region. Later they moved to the Kaitaia and Hokianga districts, then further south to Kaipara and Tāmaki.

They believed that their first ancestor, Tumu-tumu-whenua, was not of this world but came up from the ground. However, his wife Repo did belong to this world, because her people were the fairies [patupaiarehe].

Traditions about Tumutumu-whenua must be related to those concerning another early inhabitant, Tuputupu-whenua, who went down into the ground.

## Tuna
### The phallic eel

The word tuna is the ordinary term for an eel, and Tuna is the personification of the eel. In South Island tradition, Tuna came down from the sky because the upper regions were too dry. Another belief, there and elsewhere, was that he was killed for having seduced Māui's wife Hina (or Hine) while she was bathing. Māui revenged himself by digging a trench (and also, it is sometimes said, placing ten skids inside it). When Tuna made his way along this watercourse he was chopped to bits by Māui.

This episode is reminiscent of one of the many ways of catching eels. In some places such as Wairewa (Lake Forsyth), where a shingle bank separates a lake from the ocean, trenches are cut towards the sea and the eels are trapped within them.

Wairewa's rich eeling grounds were under the care of a mauri, an eel god that served also as a boundary mark. This god, Tiki Tuna, took the form of a carved image with a man's head but the body of an eel. A good catch was ensured by ritual chants addressed to him by the tohunga, who received on his behalf the first eel caught. It was Tiki Tuna, the people at Wairewa believed, who had come from the sky and seduced Hina.

When Tuna (or Tiki Tuna) was chopped up by Māui, the pieces turned into other life forms. Tuna's head went to the rivers and became freshwater eels, his tail reached the ocean and became the conger eel, the long, hair-like nostrils on the tip of his upper jaw turned into vines and certain other plants, and his blood coloured the rimu, the tōtara and other trees that now have reddish wood.

This myth was based on an older one that is still told in many other parts of Polynesia. There, Tuna's chopped-off tail sometimes turns into the conger eel but his head is planted and grows into the first coconut palm – the most treasured of

*An eeling party at Wairewa (Lake Forsyth) in 1948. The men are splitting the eels and hanging them up to dry, while the women make the kete that will transport them.*

plants. The three holes in the coconut are the eel's eyes and mouth.

The climate of Aotearoa is too cold for the coconut palm, so in the Māori story the head has become the origin of freshwater eels. These were much more important in Aotearoa, which has longer rivers and more swamps than other Polynesian islands.

The story keeps the association with trees, since Tuna's blood was now thought to have coloured the wood of certain trees.

## Tū-nui-o-te-ika
### A powerful atua

In several regions Tū-nui-o-te-ika was a powerful war god. Among Ngāti Kahungunu on the east coast, he was believed to have come from Hawaiki in the *Tākitimu*; some said he had preceded it as a ball of fire. His appearance as a comet foretokened disaster.

Among Tūhoe he was usually known as Tū-

nui-a-te-ika. There he was one of the main stars, though the identity of this star is not now known. A tohunga was his medium, and offerings of first fruits were made to him.

## Tuoro
### Giant eels

These monsters live in swamps and lakes and occasionally come up out of the water to feed on plants by the shore. A tuoro will chase and kill anyone it sees, unless the person is able to escape by setting fire to the vegetation – because the eel cannot pass over ground that has been burnt.

Tuoro have large lumps on their tails with which they kill their victims. They howl like dogs and can make their way underground. On the summit of Mount Maungapōhatu in the Urewera Mountains, in a pond known as Ōtara, there lives a tuoro that long ago formed the deep valley of the Waikare Stream.

They are sometimes known as tuna tuoro [eel tuoro] and as hore.

## Tuputupu-whenua
### An ancestor beneath

In the far north, the people of Ngā Puhi at Hokianga believed that Tuputupu-whenua [Sprung from the ground] was an early ancestor who now lived under the ground with his wife Kūī. These two were the original inhabitants of the country.

The navigator Kupe came from Hawaiki in search of Tuputupu-whenua, and found him at last in Hokianga. On his return Kupe spoke to Nuku-tawhiti, who had decided to sail to Aotearoa, and told him where he would find Tuputupu-whenua. But when Nuku, in the *Māmari*, reached the mouth of the Hokianga Harbour, Tuputupu-whenua went down into the ground, and there remained.

If someone dreamt that Tuputupu-whenua came up from the ground, it was a warning that warfare or illness lay ahead.

Traditions about this man must be related to those about another northern ancestor, Tumu-tumu-whenua, who also came up from the ground.

## Tura
### Originator of childbirth

In this myth Tura sets out on a voyage with the evil Whiro, then discovers that their waka is going down to death. Just then they pass an island (sometimes it is Hawaiki), so Tura leaves the vessel and Whiro continues on without him.

Tura lives on the island with the people he finds there, who are Nuku-mai-tore's Descendants; in some versions of the story they are all women, in others there are men as well. These people are not fully human and they make no use of fire. However, Tura teaches them how to kindle fire, and they are delighted with the food he cooks.

The people give him a wife, named Hine-kura, then when she is pregnant they come to cut her open and remove the child, because that is the only way they know. Tura chases them away and erects a pole for his wife to press on during childbirth; he recites a ritual chant to ease the birth, and the child is born. So then the people see that there is a pathway along which a child should go.

Tura continues to live there, but one day his wife sees grey hairs on his head, asks about them, and discovers that he will grow old and die. Afterwards Tura becomes homesick and longs for his former wife, Rakura-matua, and his son, Ira-tū-roto. He sets out to find them, and on the way he becomes ill. His son learns of this in a dream, comes seeking him, and cares for him until he recovers.

Kindling fire and cooking in earth ovens were closely linked in traditional Māori thought with sexual intercourse and pregnancy, so Tura's innovations belong together. In both respects he sets the pattern for the future. But by introducing the proper methods of childbirth, he inevitably brings into existence the human experience of growth and decay. Human birth necessarily brings human death, so Tura's hair becomes grey and he suffers from illness. That is why the saying 'the afflictions of Tura' [ngā taru o Tura] refers to grey hair and illness.

Tura's story also teaches, however, that it is a filial duty to care for parents who are ageing and ill.

## Tūrongo and Māhina-ā-rangi
### An important marriage

Tūrongo grew up at Te Whaanga, just north of the Aotea Harbour, perhaps in the early sixteenth century. He was of distinguished descent, being a son of Tāwhao, a leading rangatira, and Pūnui-a-te-kore, Tāwhao's principal wife. Yet his circumstances were difficult, because Tāwhao's secondary wife, Maru-te-hiakina, had given birth to a son shortly before he was born. Since this boy, Whatihua, was the elder of the two brothers,

he was regarded as superior in rank despite his mother's inferior status. Inevitably these men grew up as rivals.

In this situation Tūrongo's marriage was crucial. At first it seemed that he would marry Ruapūtahanga, a high-ranking woman of Ngāti Ruanui in southern Taranaki, but Whatihua cunningly put an end to this arrangement. When Ruapūtahanga arrived with her retinue, Whati-hua managed to impress her so much that she married him instead.

Tūrongo in his grief abandoned the house he had built for Ruapūtahanga. He left his home and set out on a long journey to Heretaunga (Hawke's Bay). There at Kahotea he stayed with a leading rangatira, Angiangi, who was building a large carved house. Tūrongo joined the work-men and won praise for his skill and industry. Meanwhile he had fallen in love with Angia-ngi's beautiful daughter, Māhina-ā-rangi.

Angiangi willingly accepted Tūrongo as a son-in-law, and Tūrongo and Māhina-ā-rangi were married. Tūrongo lived for a time with Angiangi, then returned to prepare a home for Māhina-a-rangi.

At this point Tāwhao wisely called his two sons together and divided his lands between them. Whatihau was given the coastal lands around Kāwhia Harbour and to the north, and Tūrongo inherited the lands to the south. In accord with his father's wishes, Tūrongo moved inland and built a pā on a hill, Rangiātea, in the central basin of the Waipā River (east of the present town of Ōtorohanga). Soon afterwards Māhina-ā-rangi arrived with their newborn son Raukawa.

Left above: *Māhina-ā-rangi and Tūrongo (at the back) stand by the pou-toko-manawa [central pillars] of Te Toka-nganui-a-Noho at Te Kūiti in the southern Waikato. This famous house was presented to King Tāwhiao in 1873 by the prophetic leader Te Kooti, who at this time was sheltering from Government forces with Tāwhiao and Ngāti Maniapoto. Te Kooti and many of his followers belonged to the east coast. By placing Māhina-ā-rangi and Tūrongo in these positions, Te Kooti was recalling the ties between the peoples of the east coast and those of the Waikato which had been initiated by the marriage of these two early ancestors.*

Left: *In fulfilment of a prophecy made by King Tāwhiao, the King Movement, under the leadership of Te Puea, established the Tūrangawaewae Marae at Ngāruawāhia in 1920. When a large meeting house for the reception of visitors was completed in 1929 with the assistance of Apirana Ngata and others on the east coast, the early genealogical links between the peoples of the east coast and the Waikato were recalled on both sides and the house was named Māhina-ā-rangi. Nine years later, a residence for King Koroki built alongside was named Tūrongo.*

Tūrongo spent the rest of a long life at Rangiātea. His father Tāwhao lived with him and established a house of learning, also known as Rangiātea, which became an important cultural centre.

Tūrongo's marriage to Māhina-ā-rangi was of much importance in joining the descent lines of the peoples of the east coast and those of the Waikato. Their son Raukawa married a woman of Te Arawa and had many distinguished des-cendants.

*Wiremu Kauika of Ngā Rauru, who lived at Waitōtara, in 1904 wrote an account of Aokehu's conquest of the taniwha Tūtaeporoporo. He also gave a genealogy [whakapapa] showing that he was a descendant of Aokehu, who had lived seventeen generations previously.*

## Tūtaeporoporo
### Revenge for a master's death

In the Rangitīkei district a couple of generations after the arrival of the *Aotea*, a man named Tūariki made a pet of a young shark he had caught. He placed him in a tributary of the Rangitīkei River, fed him regularly, and performed rituals to turn him into a taniwha. The creature grew big, and soon became a taniwha the size of a whale. His name was Tūtaeporoporo.

Some time later, warriors from the Whanganui region visited Rangitīkei and killed Tūariki, then took his body back home and cooked it. And when Tūtaeporoporo went in search of his master, the scent from the oven reached him on the wind.

So then the taniwha swam up the Whanganui

River to seek revenge for his master's death. He made his home in a deep pool beneath a high ridge called Taumaha-aute (now known also as Shakespeare Cliff), and there he attacked and devoured all the men and women who travelled up and down the river.

When the people realised the cause of their relatives' disappearance, they left their homes and fled inland. Then one of their number, Tama-āhua, told them about a famous killer of taniwha, a warrior named Aokehu who was living at Waitōtara. They begged him to ask for Aokehu's assistance, and he flew to do this – for he possessed the power of flight.

Aokehu agreed to help Tama-āhua, because the two men were related by marriage. So Tama-āhua flew back, and next day Aokehu and his men reached the Whanganui River and were shown the taniwha's home.

Aokehu told the people to make a wooden chest the same size as himself, with a close-fitting lid. He entered the chest, taking with him two tapu shark-tooth knives, and instructed them to fasten the lid and set him afloat.

The chest with this brave warrior floated along and approached the taniwha's lair. Tūtae-poroporo smelt the good smell of food, and he rushed out and swallowed the chest down into his belly. So then Aokehu, inside the monster, began to recite ritual chants, one to put him to sleep and another to make him rise up and float to the surface. The chants did their work, and the now helpless taniwha drifted ashore. He was killed at once, and the lashings were cut from Aokehu's chest.

Aokehu cut open the creature's body with his shark-tooth knives and found inside the bodies of men, women and children. These they buried in their pā. Tūtaeporoporo was left as food for the birds of the air and the fish of the sea, and the people returned rejoicing to their homes.

## Tū-tāmure
### An ugly warrior

Tū-tāmure, a great-grandson of the famous Tamatea, spent his youth at Ōpōtiki. When he became a man, he and his elder brother Taipū-noa set out on an expedition of war. At Te Māhia (Māhia Peninsula), their men lay siege to the strong Maunga-a-kahia pā to the north of Nuku-taurua.

Tū-tāmure did not know that this pā was under the command of Kahungunu, a relative of his who was now an old man. Nor did Kahungunu know the identity of this formidable young rangatira who was leading the attack upon his people. So Kahungunu sent a man to call from the palisades and ask for this information, and Tū-tāmure himself, in proud metaphorical language, divulged his name.

It was Kahungunu who long ago had given him that name. So the old man knew now that his people would survive. To make peace between them, he asked his daughter Tauhei-kurī to go into the midst of that company and sit beside Tū-tāmure in token of her willingness to be his wife. Tauhei-kurī did so, but when Tū-tāmure made overtures to her that night, she would have nothing to do with him.

In the morning a storm came up, it rained, and Tū-tāmure saw his reflection in a pool of water. He looked closely, and he saw that he was ugly. He said, 'Was it for nothing that this woman wouldn't have me? No, it's because I'm really ugly.'

*The snapper, a common and much-appreciated fish. When Kahungunu was a young man he had quarrelled with his half-brother Whāene, who slapped him on the face with a snapper. Tū-tāmure [Hit by snapper], born soon afterwards, was given his name by Kahungunu to ensure that this insult would not be forgotten.*

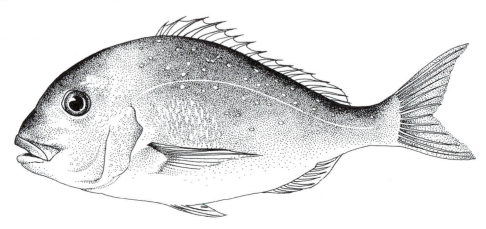

As for the woman, she married his brother Taipū-noa instead. The people in the pā were saved, and the war party returned to their own homes.

## Tū-tangata-kino
### A reptile or a taniwha

In some parts of the west coast of the North Island, this atua, whose name means Tū-the-evil-man, took the form of an especially powerful reptile. It was thought that spirits in the form of reptiles could crawl through people's mouths while they were asleep and gnaw their stomachs, producing illness, and Tū-tangata-kino was sometimes the reptile responsible for this.

But such powers worked both ways. Because he was so dangerous, Tū-tangata-kino was a highly effective guardian when the proper ceremonies were performed. A man about to go on a journey might ensure his wife's faithfulness by reciting a chant naming Tū-tangata-kino, with Maru, as the guardians of her virtue in his absence. The wife's knowledge that she would be punished by Tū-tangata-kino for any transgression no doubt helped to ensure the effectiveness of this chant.

Tū-tangata-kino was a guardian in other situations too, often in association with a reptile named Moko-hiku-waru. Sometimes these two were guardians of the house of Miru, ruler of the underworld.

On the Whanganui River, a different story is told. In this tradition, Tū-tangata-kino is a taniwha who guided the *Aotea* during its voyage from Hawaiki and afterwards settled at Pātea with its captain, Turi. There he remained until the time of Turi's grandson, a tohunga named Tūhaepō who possessed extraordinary powers.

Tūhaepō used to fly through the air on the back of Tū-tangata-kino, travelling with great speed between Pātea and his home on the upper Whanganui. On the river there, at a place known as Te Ohu which is midway between Te Maire and Maraekōwhai, he kept his taniwha by a flat rock, some forty metres long, called Petipeti-ā-urangi. He would stand on this rock to summon him.

The rock therefore became tapu. Down through the ages it has been guarded by Tū-tangata-kino, and people passing in waka were always careful to place an offering of a twig or small branch upon it, reciting the proper chant. This was done with many taniwha on the river but was especially important with Tū-tangata-kino; while the others might punish neglectful

travellers with a thunderstorm, Tū-tangata-kino would overturn their vessels and drown them. Only Tūtae-poroporo was as dreaded as Tū-tangata-kino, but he was killed many generations ago, while Tū-tangata-kino has survived into modern times.

Although the rock is no longer tapu, the tradition continues, more through respect than fear. The pilots of the first Pākehā river boats were usually Māori, and they taught this ritual to their passengers. At the Taniwha Rock, as it is now generally known, people going down the river in canoes and jet boats still make offerings of willow twigs to avoid trouble in the rapids ahead.

## Tūtara-kauika
### A guardian taniwha

Tūtara-kauika is an ocean taniwha, in the form of a whale, who protects the people with whom he is associated. In one tradition he accompanied the *Tākitimu* to Aotearoa, then remained in the sea by Wairoa as the guardian of his people. In another tradition he escorted Pou-rangahua's waka, a frail craft constructed of bark and albatross skin, on its voyage to Hawaiki.

Tūtara-kauika sometimes saves people in danger of drowning out at sea. He may be accompanied by a companion, a taniwha named Te Wehenga-kauika. Occasionally he leads a group of such taniwha, all in the form of whales.

## Tūtaua
### A singing log

When Haumapūhia created Lake Waikaremoana in the Urewera Mountains, she placed upon its waters a tōtara log known as Tūtaua. For many generations this log drifted around the lake, singing in an eerie whistling voice. He was a taniwha, and was also spoken of as a tipua – an entity with an uncanny life of its own.

From time to time Tūtaua drifted ashore. If anyone cut a piece of wood from him, he would be gone next morning.

## Tū-tawake
### A fierce warrior

Sometimes Tū-tawake is an extended name for Tū, who initiated warfare. In other traditions, Tū (or Tū-mata-uenga) is the primary figure and comes very early in the genealogies, while Tū-tawake comes later and has a separate existence as a warrior.

This is the case in some parts of the east coast and in the South Island, where Tū-tawake is the son of an evil woman named Houmea. According to Ngāti Porou and some other peoples, the first war in history was conducted by the great rangatira Uenuku. As the warriors were about to invade the pā of their enemies, Tū-tawake came forward and recited a ritual chant over his spear. He then distinguished himself in the battle that followed.

In reality, Tū-tawake's chant must have been recited over their weapons before battle by warriors who were identifying with his role and wished to acquire his powers.

## Tūtekohe
### A rangatira and his dog

This powerful man lived in the Tūranga (Gisborne) district. He was of such high rank that he commanded tribute from everyone in the region.

Tūtekohe was very fond of his pet dog Kauere-huanui, and overfed him so that he became very fat. When visitors came to his home, he would allow the dog to lick the fat from the tops of the gourds of preserved birds which stood ready to be presented to his guests. He was so powerful that his visitors were forced to ignore this insult.

However, when a rangatira named Rākaipākā visited Tūtekohe's pā with some companions, Tūtekohe did worse than this. The two rangatira were apparently far from friendly. The story is that Tūtekohe's potted birds were presented to his dog rather than his guest. Rākaipākā received only the bones the dog did not eat.

Rākai-pākā returned to his home showing no signs of anger, but that night someone came to Tūtekohe's pā and lured his dog outside. The creature was killed, taken away and eaten.

When the dog failed to answer his call next morning, Tūtekohe knew what had happened. His warriors attacked Rākaipākā's people and drove them south to the Māhia Peninsula and Nūhaka, where their descendants, Ngāti Rākaipākā, still live today.

Tūtekohe's name is sometimes given as Tūtekohi.

## Tū-te-koropanga
### Originator of plant obstructions

Tū-te-koropanga's main obstructions are prickly plants. In myth and rhetoric, these represent insuperable obstacles, or sometimes obstacles that can be overcome only with great difficulty. For this reason they were spoken of by poets and orators throughout the country.

In the north there is no explanatory myth, but in the South Island the story is that Tū-te-koropaka (as he is usually called there) ran away with Rukutia, wife of Tama-nui-a-Raki. He fled

*Tūtekohe, his dog Kauere-hua-nui, and one of the gourds containing potted birds from which he allowed the animal to eat. A poupou in the porch of Te Mana o Tūranga at Manutūkē, near Gisborne.*

*The ongaonga or tree nettle, a common plant that grows up to three metres high. Its leaves, branchlets and branches all bear stout hairs that can inflict an extremely painful and toxic sting.*

with her to Aotearoa and built a house, then to prevent Tama from reaching them he planted around it the tree nettle (ongaonga), the clinging bush lawyer and the spiky matagouri. These plants were his obstructions. Some say he had brought them with him for this purpose.

Tama, however, overcame the obstructions. He armed himself with a taiaha and a sharp flint, he recited a ritual chant, and he bent the plants with his taiaha, cut them with his flint and forced his way through. Later he overcame other obstacles that Tū-te-koropaka had placed in the ocean. He was still angry with his wife and killed her, but next spring she came back to life.

Some people in the south say that Tū-te-koropaka is the ancestor of the Waitaha people there and that he arrived from Hawaiki on the *Matiti*.

## Tū-te-nganahau
### The source of trouble

On the west coast of the North Island, the fierce Tū-te-nganahau is sometimes a son of the first parents, Rangi and Papa, and it is he who cuts the sinews that join these two in the beginning. Tū-te-nganahau seems here to be an extended name for Tū, who in most parts of the country initiates strife and the practice of warfare. Sometimes, however, Tū-te-nganahau is a figure with a separate existence who may act in association with Tū (or Tū-mata-uenga).

## Tutumaiao
### Spirits on the beaches

If you are walking along a beach and see, far ahead, misty forms like people that retreat as you advance, these are the Tutumaiao. Some say they visit the beaches from their homes in the sea.

In parts of the far north, the Tutumaiao were regarded as one of three peoples (the others were the Tūrehu and Kūī) who lived here in the beginning, before the arrival of human beings.

In the far south, where the Aurora Australis, or Southern Lights, can sometimes be seen, one of the names for this phenomenon was Tutumaiao.

## Tū-whakairi-ora
### A great warrior

In the mid-sixteenth century, a rangatira named Pouroumātā was killed at Whareponga by the people of Ngāti Ruanuku among whom he had been living. Most of his relatives chose to ignore this, but his daughter Te Ataākura mourned her father and planned her revenge.

To raise a son to avenge the murder, she at once married Ngātihau of Ūawa (Tolaga Bay). She and her husband then went to live at Ōpōtiki, where he had relatives. Their first child was a girl, and she wept for her hopes. But the second was a boy, Tū-whakairi-ora.

As he grew up, Tū-whakairi-ora was constantly reminded by his mother and his people that he was the one who would avenge his grandfather. Strengthening rituals were performed by tohunga, he was carefully trained, and in time he fought his first battle and killed his first man. When he had won fame as a warrior, he set out to achieve his destiny.

From Ōpōtiki he made his way around the coast to the mouth of the Wharekāhika River (at Hicks Bay), where his relative Te Aotaki was the leading rangatira. Te Aotaki received Tū-whakairi-ora with honour and gave him his daughter Ruataupare as his wife.

Tū-whakairi-ora lived at Wharekāhika with Ruataupare on land given her as a marriage settlement, then some years later, when he was sufficiently established in the region, he summoned allies from his wife's people and from his own people at Ōpōtiki. He led an army in a fleet of waka to Whareponga, the home of Ngāti Ruanuku, and there gained a great victory, avenging the death of his grandfather.

Afterwards Tū-whakairi-ora continued to live at Wharekāhika. His descendants, who are known as Te Whānau-a-Tū-whakairi-ora, became one of the strongest sections of Ngāti Porou, occupying territory from a point just east of Tikirau (Cape Runaway) to what is now East Cape.

Ruataupare eventually quarrelled with Tū-whakairi-ora and set out with her followers to found a people of her own. She conquered Te Wahine-iti, an ancient people at Tokomaru Bay, and her descendants, Te Whānau-a-Ruataupare, are living there still.

*Mohi Tūrei (c.1830–1914) of Ngāti Porou, a great orator and authority on tradition, published much in Māori-language newspapers and the* Journal of the Polynesian Society. *Among his writings is a classic account of the life of Tū-whakairi-ora.*

## Tū-whakararo
### A murdered relative

One of the main avengers in Māori tradition is the warrior Whakatau. The man whose death he avenges is usually Tū-whakararo, an elder brother (or sometimes father) who has been murdered by people living in a great house known as Te Tihi-o-Manōno. Setting out with a small band of chosen warriors, Whakatau burns this house and kills all those within.

In some versions of the myth, Tū-whakararo dies while visiting a brother-in-law. In others he visits his mother's brothers, and the trouble begins when he falls in love with a chief's daughter, Maurea (or Hakiri-maurea or Mouria-kura), and she returns his love. Another suitor challenges Tū-whakararo to a wrestling match. Tū-whakararo twice defeats this jealous rival, then goes to put on his cloak. Having been unable to beat him in a fair fight, the rival seizes this opportunity. He blinds Tu-whakararo by throwing sand in his eyes, then kills him.

## Tūwharetoa
### Founder of Ngāti Tūwharetoa

This powerful rangatira lived at Kawerau in the Bay of Plenty in the sixteenth century. His mother Haahuru belonged to the earliest peoples in the region, those descended from Toi, Te Hapū-oneone and Kawerau, while his father Mawa-ke-taupō belonged to the Arawa and Mātaatua peoples and was a seventh-generation descendant of the great tohunga Ngātoro-i-rangi. Tūwharetoa therefore obtained his right to land from his mother's ancestors and his mana from his father's ancestors.

Tūwharetoa was a handsome man, attractive to women. With Pae-ki-tawhiti, his high-ranking first wife, he had a daughter, Manaia-wharepū, and a son, Rongomai-te-ngangana. Soon afterwards, while visiting Rongomai-uru-rangi, the leading rangatira of Ngāi Tai by the Mōtū River, Tūwharetoa fell in love with this man's daughter Hine-mōtū. Since she was already promised to a local man, the girl did not ask her father's permission but ran away with Tūwharetoa. She lived with him at Kawerau and bore him eight children. Some years later Tūwharetoa took a third wife, Te Uira-roa, with whom he had five children.

Tūwharetoa also had a famous liaison with Rangiuru, wife of the Arawa rangatira Whaka-ue-kaipapa. This happened when Tūwharetoa visited Mokoia Island during Whakaue's absence. When Rangiuru bore Tūwharetoa's son Tū-tānekai, Whakaue accepted the boy and brought him up as his own.

As well as being a valiant warrior and a wise leader, Tūwharetoa was an expert carver and organised the building of finely carved and ornamental houses throughout his people's lands. He lived to a great age.

His descendants later conquered Ngāti Hotu, an early people who were in possession of the Taupō region, and intermarried with them.

# Uenuku

## A great rangatira in Hawaiki

Uenuku, in many myths, is a great man who lives in Hawaiki in the early times. When he engages in battle he is always triumphant.

In the traditions of both the *Aotea* and *Te Arawa*, people threatened by Uenuku are forced to migrate from Hawaiki to Aotearoa. In an east coast myth, Māia comes for the same reason. In the traditions of the *Tākitimu*, Ruawhārō and Tūpai manage to revenge themselves before their departure by comandeering the vessel, but it is nevertheless their quarrel with Uenuku that leads to their departure.

In another east coast tradition, Uenuku is indirectly responsible for Paikea's journey from Hawaiki on the back of a whale. After Uenuku discovers his wife's adultery and kills her, the wife's brother Wheta (or sometimes Tāwheta or Whena) avenges her death by killing nearly all of Uenuku's many sons. In the ensuing war, Uenuku and his son Whatiua overcome Wheta in a series of great battles. (By so doing they set the pattern for the future, becoming role models for actual warriors faced with the sacred task of avenging a relative's death.)

After this victory, Wheta's relative Pai-māhu-tanga is taken as a slave wife by Uenuku. Their son Ruatapu inherits her low status, and on a crucial occasion is deeply shamed when Uenuku reminds him of this. In revenge he takes Uenuku's sons out to sea in a ship and drowns them all – except for Paikea, who rides a whale to Aotearoa and becomes an important ancestor.

In stories such as these, Uenuku is a man rather than a god [atua]. Some peoples, however, know Uenuku as a powerful atua who protected his people and was appealed to in times of war. This is his significance to the Tainui peoples.

He was often believed to take the form of a rainbow and to convey warnings to people by the manner in which he manifested himself. Some authorities identified him with Kahukura, another god revealed as a rainbow, while others associated each of these two gods with a particular kind of rainbow. One early account says that as well as inhabiting the rainbow, Uenuku lives 'in the red clouds which sometimes adorn the eastern and western sky'. In Tūhoe belief, he was a man who after death became the rainbow.

It is not known whether Uenuku ever occupied both of these roles in a single region: whether, that is, he was ever considered to be both a protective god and a victorious rangatira in Hawaiki.

*The Tainui peoples accept this ancient sculpture as the symbol of their traditional god Uenuku. Discovered in Lake Ngaroto in 1906, it is over two and a half metres high.*

## Uenuku-tuwhatu
### A life-giving rock

This man, the elder son of Whatihua and Ruapūtahanga, lived at Kāwhia and Taranaki in the sixteenth century. One of his sons, Hotunui, spent his later years in Hauraki. A daughter, Hine-au-pounamu, married Rereahu and bore eight children who became famous ancestors in the southern Waikato.

Later, Uenuku-tuwhatu turned to stone. He is now a sacred rock, a tipua that stands near the mouth of the Awaroa Stream in the Kāwhia Harbour. In this form he was believed to possess the power of making childless women conceive, and many women visited him for this reason. Children born to them afterwards were known as the sons and daughters of Uenuku-tuwhatu.

His name is sometimes given as Uenuku-tuhatu.

## Ureia
### A taniwha at Hauraki

Ureia was the taniwha guardian of the people of Ngāti Tamaterā at Hauraki. His den, a deep pool at the mouth of the river at Te Kirikiri, was a dangerous place where swirling currents often capsized waka.

Ureia himself was a quiet creature, who left his den only when he sensed that his people were about to experience misfortune. His presence then was recognised as a warning. Those who saw him reported that he resembled an average-sized whale.

One day he was visited by Haumia, the taniwha guardian of a different section of the Tainui people who were living by the Manukau Harbour. Haumia stayed a while, then invited Ureia to pay a return visit to the Manukau. Ureia agreed, and the two set off.

But this was a plot. Haumia had promised his tohunga to lure Ureia to the Manukau, and at this very moment they were before their tūāhu on the peak of Puketutu Island reciting potent chants to ensure his capture. According to one story, Ureia was caught in a baited trap; porpoise meat was put in a minature house on a tiny raft, which was floated out on the water then pulled back on a cord after the taniwha had entered it. (Here it seems to have been Ureia's wairua that was captured.)

Others say that Haumia led Ureia into a snare that had been placed at the entrance to the harbour, and that Ureia fought for four low tides and four high tides before he died.

## Uru and Ngangana
### Ancient names

In different traditions these names are differently associated. Sometimes they appear in genealogies as early ancestors, with no associated stories (in a Tūranga song, Uru and Ngangana are a husband and wife in the early times; in a related Ngāti Porou tradition, Uru is the parent of Ngana).

In Taranaki, Uru and Ngangana are usually the owners of two waka, the *Rangi-totohu* and the *Rangi-kekero*, which convey people to death and destruction and are mentioned for this reason by poets. However, in a lament belonging to Ngāti Maru in the Waitara district, Uru-ngangana is apparently a single individual; he owns a house, named Punga-tatara, which is the source of waka of ill omen.

In Ngāti Kahungunu traditions concerning the high god Io, an atua named Uru-te-ngangana is the first-born of the seventy sons of Rangi and Papa. Because of his high rank he is angry when Tāne, a younger son, presumes to separate their parents, and he associates himself with another brother, the evil Whiro-te-tipua, in his opposition to Tāne.

In these traditions from Taranaki and Ngāti Kahungunu, the menacing nature of this figure (or figures) probably follows from the fact that the word ngangana can mean 'rage, bluster, make a disturbance'.

In Hawaiian tradition, Ulu and Nana-ulu are very early ancestors, the two sons of Ki'i (who is the equivalent of the Māori Tiki).

## *Uruao*
### A southern waka

This vessel set out for Aotearoa from distant islands known as Te Pātū-nui-o-āio [The great boundary of calm] and Tāepataka-o-te-raki [Place where the sky hangs down]. Its captain was Rākaihautū (sometimes Rākaihaitū).

*Uruao* made landfall in the northernmost part of the North Island, but the crew saw that this region was occupied. They sailed down the west coast, again discovering peoples in possession, then crossed to the South Island and landed at Whakatū (Nelson). They found this land to be uninhabited. Rākaihautū was the first man to light a fire there.

So the crew of the *Uruao* remained in the south. The waka had brought the ancestors of the Waitaha people, also (according to some accounts) two kinds of beings with extraordinary powers, Te Kāhui Tipua and Te Rapuwai. Some say that

*One of the learned men of Ngāi Tahu in the South Island,
Hōne Tāre Tikao (c.1850–1927). Much of his knowledge of
history and tradition was recorded and published.*

all of these were giants. They now found themselves places to live.

Meanwhile the humans divided into two groups and set out southward to explore the land. Rākaihautū led a party through the interior, while his son Te Rakihouia sailed along the east coast with another group.

Rākaihautū took with him his wooden digging stick, named Tū-whakarōria, and thinking that the country needed lakes, he dug them out at intervals: first Lakes Rotoroa and Rotoiti, then Hokakura (Lake Sumner), Whakamātau (Lake Coleridge), Ōtūroto (Lake Heron), Takapō (Lake Tekapō), Pūkakī, Ōhau, Hāwea, Wānaka, Whakatipu, Te Anāu and others.

After exploring the far south, the party walked back along the coast. Rākaihautū continued to dig out lakes as he went; the last were Waihora (Lake Ellesmere) and Wairewa (Lake Forsyth). Still today in poetry and oratory the collective name given the great lakes of the South Island is Ka Puna-karikari-a-Rākaihautū [The springs dug by Rākaihautū]. Sometimes the whole island is referred to by this name.

At this point Rākaihautū's work was ended. He had already met up with his son Te Rakihouia

and his companions. Now he thrust his digging stick into the ground by Wairewa, and it became the peak known as Tuhiraki (Mount Bossu). He then settled at nearby Akaroa.

The son's task, as he and his party had coasted south, had been to investigate the rich seafood resources in the region. On the high cliffs at Kaikōura he had discovered an abundance of seagull eggs (so that these cliffs later became known as Ka Whata-kai-a-Te Rakihouia [Te Rakihouia's foodstores]). Further on he had studied the migratory habits of eel and lamprey, and built weirs at the river mouths.

Most of the lakes believed to have been dug out by Rākaihautū were in fact created by glaciers. Since they had clearly been excavated by some agency, it was quite logical to think they had been dug by the first man to arrive from Hawaiki.

## Waihuka and Tū-te-amoamo
### A murderous brother

Two brothers once lived alone together, with no mother, no kinsmen and no home village. The younger was Waihuka and the elder Tūte-amoamo. Then Waihuka married a beautiful woman, Hine-i-te-kakara [Sweet-scented woman], and Tū-te-amoamo wanted her for himself.

So he asked his brother to go fishing, and Waihuka agreed. When their waka was full of fish they decided to return. But Tū-te-amoamo still wanted to kill his brother, so he called, 'Pull up the anchor.'

Waihuka said, 'I can't manage it.'

His elder brother insisted, so Waihuka dived down to free the anchor. At once Tū-te-amoamo cut the rope and hoisted the sail, leaving him there to die.

So the younger brother floated about in the water, wondering how he could save himself. He recited chants to the atua, then called, 'Albatross, carry me to land!' But the albatross paid no attention.

He called like this to all the birds, then all the fish, but none of them listened. Then the whale, his ancestor, heard his call and straightaway took him to the land.

Meanwhile Tū-te-amoamo had gone ashore. When Hine-i-te-kakara saw him, she thought her husband must be dead. She went into her house and wept for him.

That evening Tū-te-amoamo came and called to her, but she would not answer. Inside the house she was digging a hole by the wall; she at last escaped, and walked along the beach looking for her husband's body. The whale told her where to go, and she found Waihuka alive.

They wept together, then planned their revenge. That evening Tū-te-amoamo came to the house again and called to his brother's wife, 'Hine-i-te-kakara, open the door!'

Hine-i-te-kakara told him, 'Yes, come in, Tū-te-amoamo.'

The moment he entered, Waihuka leapt forward with his taiaha and struck his head from his shoulders.

This occurred at Marokopa, near Kāwhia. Hine-i-te-kakara and Waihuka had many children, who became renowned warriors and ancestors of Ngāti Apakura.

## Wairaka
### The woman who acted like a man

When *Mātaatua* landed at a river mouth after its voyage from Hawaiki, the men on board neglected their vessel, securing only its stern. Then they went off to climb a hill and view their new land.

Next morning the waves were breaking over *Mātaatua*. The captain's daughter Wairaka, realising their ship was in danger, called, 'The ship will be broken!'

But the men did not listen. They were distracted by the discoveries they were making.

So Wairaka called, 'Oh, I must turn myself into a man!'

She said this to shame the men, and she succeeded – though some say she still had to secure *Mātaatua* herself. Her words were remembered, and the name Whakatāne [Turn into a man] was given to the region and its river in memory of this occurrence (although there are some who claim it was her aunt Muriwai who did this).

Later, a party of travellers from Tāmaki (the Auckland region) came to Whakatāne. Wairaka fell in love with one of them, a handsome man who was a fine dancer, and made up her mind to marry him. When everyone was asleep, she went over to the place in the house where he had been lying. And to show he was her lover, she scratched his face before she left him.

Next morning she told her father what had happened and sent him to fetch the man whose face she had scratched. Then she found that she had been deceived. Someone else among the visitors, an ugly man named Mai, had noticed her interest and managed to change places with the man she loved. It was Mai who bore the scratch, and Mai whom she now married.

Her horrified exclamation became a saying: 'Oh what could I do, in the darkness that confused Wairaka?' [Ā, me aha koa e au, i te pō i raru ai Wairaka?].

## Wairua
### The soul that travels

Within a person there were believed to be two presences, a wairua and a hau, which can be termed souls. Both were implanted at conception by the father. The hau, which was associated with the breath, remained with the body until death, then disappeared. The other soul, the wairua, left the body during sleep and travelled around.

This belief explained the experience of sleep and of dreaming. If someone dreamt of a distant place, their wairua was visiting that place. If they dreamt of a person, their wairua was greeting that person's wairua. If they dreamt of the dead, their wairua had visited the underworld. During their travels the wairua were watchful and would convey a warning if necessary.

While the hau disappeared at death, the wairua continued to exist. After remaining with the body for three days, it set out for the underworld, home of the dead. It might, however, come back to visit the living, perhaps as a spider, a butterfly or moth, or a small bird. Except on such occasions, wairua were normally invisible, but tohunga and other persons with special powers could sometimes glimpse them hovering in the air or reflected in a stream.

The wairua of the dead might visit living relatives to warn of an approaching war party or some other evil. If someone had been murdered, tohunga might summon the person's wairua to tell him who had done it. He might also, at night, attempt to summon the wairua of the murderer in order to destroy him through sorcery.

## Waiwaia
### A taniwha in the Waipā

This taniwha was once a tōtara tree on the slopes of the Rangitoto Range, near the headwaters of the Waipā. For many years an old tohunga used to sit under this tree, and it became very tapu. But despite the tapu his grandchildren climbed the tree one day and began eating the berries.

This angered the old man's atua, because the children should have offered them some of the berries before eating any themselves. So the spirits sent the tree down into the earth and it disappeared from sight. The children heard the earth roaring like thunder and they knew they would die, so they called to their grandfather. He pacified the spirits and brought them back up.

As for the tree, he allowed it to go on its way. Its branches broke off and it sank further and further into the interior – it disappeared into the earth and the water. That tree had become a taniwha. It is Waiwaia, a taniwha of Ngāti Maniapoto.

Afterwards it was seen drifting along the Waipā; it was red in colour, and there were berries growing upon it. At Ngāruawāhia it reached the Waikato River. It went on out into the ocean, lay for a while by the shore, then afterwards came back again.

What Waiwaia does is to go floating along, then strand itself in a place; if it is recognised, it will soon leave for somewhere else. It keeps visiting places like this, lying there for a while then moving on.

There is a saying, 'The many stranding-places of Waiwaia' [Ko rau paenga o Waiwaia]. If someone in a party of travellers asked where they would spend the night, another person might reply, 'Oh, at the many stranding-places of Waiwaia.'

*Wiremu Te Whēoro (c.1825–1895) of Ngāti Mahuta, a leading rangatira who was an important writer on Waikato tradition. Along with much else, he recorded the stories of Waiwaia and several other taniwha.*

# Wehi-nui-a-mamao
## Source of the stars

In some regions, such as Heretaunga (Hawke's Bay) and the South Island, Wehi-nui-a-mamao is the man from whom the stars were acquired in the beginning. After Tāne had created the world by pushing Rangi the sky upwards, he wanted to make his father beautiful. He acquired the stars from Wehi-nui-a-mamao, he threw them up, and Rangi shone brightly.

Wehi-nui-a-mamao's stars were sometimes said to be the fastenings, the toggles, on his four dogskin cloaks – these being apparently equivalent to the expanse of the sky. There are other stories, though. One authority has him covering the stars with floor mats, apparently to protect them.

Dogskin cloaks were the most treasured of garments, worn only by high-ranking men. They were fastened on the right shoulder by a cluster of toggles of marine ivory, bone or greenstone.

# Whaitiri
## A powerful woman in the sky

The name Whaitiri means 'Thunder'. This woman lived in the sky with her husband and children. She was a cannibal and craved human flesh, so when she heard about a man down below called Kai-tangata she visited him, thinking his name must mean 'Eat-people'. Soon she married him, but afterwards she waited in vain to be offered a meal of human flesh. Kai-tangata was not a cannibal but a peaceful fisherman.

Presently Whaitiri and Kai-tangata had a son, Hemā. By this time she had become tired of waiting for human meat. In her anger she recited a ritual chant to make the fish swim away, and Kai-tangata caught nothing when he went out each day.

Then Whaitiri made up her mind to return to the sky. She decided she would first make the fish plentiful once more, so she recited another chant and performed its accompanying ritual. She taught this chant and ritual to her co-wife, so that people would know in future how to ensure an abundant supply of fish. She predicted that much later one of her grandsons would mount up to visit her. Then a cloud came down and took her to the sky.

In time Hemā had two sons, Tāwhaki and Karihi. When they grew up, these young men determined to visit their grandmother. Karihi failed in this difficult undertaking, but Tāwhaki succeeded and found Whaitiri at her home. She was blind, and was sitting counting out ten taro for her grand-daughters. Tāwhaki stole her taro one by one, then he healed her eyes and she could see. Afterwards she helped Tāwhaki to win one of her grand-daughters as his wife.

This is the story told by Ngāti Porou on the east coast and Ngāi Tahu in the South Island. Elsewhere there are differences. On the west coast of the North Island, Whaitiri had an especially important position. In an one early account it is said that she was the first old goddess of the ages of darkness [te atua kuia tuatahi o ngā pō], and that it was she (rather than Tāne) who recited the

chant that led to the separation of the earth and sky.

In west coast tradition, Whaitiri married Kai-tangata and had three sons. When Kai-tangata complained that the children were dirty, Whaitiri was offended and went back to the sky, but first she built for Kai-tangata the first heketua [latrine]. This was an event of consequence, because these structures had ritual significance. Whaitiri's heketua is still to be seen among the stars.

On the west coast as elsewhere, Hemā's son Tāwhaki succeeds in climbing to the sky. He encounters Whaitiri there, and restores her sight.

Sayings relating to Whaitiri are mostly concerned with her power to withhold food. If birds or fish became scarce just as visitors arrived at a village, the local people might say, 'It seems as though the offspring of Whaitiri are here.' This face-saving remark complimented the visitors by implying that it was their mana that had driven away the birds and fish, and that they must owe this power to their distinguished descent from Whaitiri.

Because taro was a favourite food that was never abundant, a careful cook would count her taro just as Whaitiri had done, taking from her

In the Urewera Mountains in about 1905, at a time when his people were suffering from severe economic and political difficulties, Rua Kēnana (above) became accepted as a prophetic leader by many sections of Tūhoe and other Mātaatua peoples (Ngāti Awa and Whakatōhea) after he and his wife Pinepine, instructed by the angel Gabriel, climbed tapu Maungapōhatu (a tipua mountain identified with the mana of Rua's people). It is believed that they were led up through the cold mists by Whaitiri, an ancestor of the Mātaatua peoples who was now revealed as Rua's sister, and that on the summit of the mountain she showed them the mauri that holds and preserves the mana of the people and the land. This mauri takes the form of a diamond, lying under water, that had been placed there by Rua's predecessor, the prophet Te Kooti. As well, Rua met Christ upon the mountain, and knowledge was communicated to him. Some say he was brother to Christ.

During the years that Rua spent after this as the visionary and millenarian leader of a community in the remote Maungapōhatu Valley (at the foot of the mountain), he made extensive use of both ancestral and Christian tradition. Left: On Christmas Day 1908, the lowest of Rua's four flags bears the name of his ancestor Te Tahi-o-te-rangi, whose extraordinary powers as a tohunga he was believed to have inherited.

storage pit exactly as many as her visitors. For this reason, taro could be spoken of as 'Whaitiri's counted food'. In some stories, though, it is seed kūmara that she is counting.

Whaitiri's special association with fish appears in a number of ways. Sometimes she sends down from the sky a great shower of fish as food for her grandson, Tāwhaki. In the far south, her 'fish' are two men whom she devours when her husband is not able to catch any fish for her. Among the people of Tūhoe, her 'fish' were frost and snow – presumably because the shortage of food experienced in the harsh Urewera winters was associated with Whaitiri.

Her residence in the sky, her association with thunder and her control over the supply of fish make Whaitiri a highly tapu and powerful figure. As well she is in possession of fertility, in the form of food and grand-daughters.

Why should such a powerful figure be initially blind? Her blindness makes it possible for the male hero to steal her food, a natural ambition given the symbolism involved. Also, a person who is blind is one who sits in darkness, and in Māori (and other Polynesian) thought there is a close link between females and darkness. When Tāwhaki heals her blindness, an underlying idea may be that males with special powers, being associated with light, can bring light to those persons (typically women) who sit in darkness.

As well, however, Whaitiri is sometimes associated with the ages of darkness that occurred before the world took shape, and one account has her taking an active role in the separation of sky and earth. Tāwhaki's grandmother is older than the world, and her darkness is also the darkness of the ages that preceded the world.

It is not surprising, then, that while Whaitiri could be dangerous, even demonic, she was a most prestigious ancestor. Tūhoe people trace their descent from Whaitiri through Tōroa, captain of the Mātaatua, claiming this as an important line of ancestry [aho ariki] because she was a celestial being.

Whaitiri is also known as Whatitiri and Whaitiri-mātakataka. In some ways she resembles Te Ruahine, who in southern myths is an old woman who lives in Hawaiki or a similar island and is in possession of food and, often, grand-daughters.

## Whakaahu
### Star of spring growth

Whakaahu is a star that brings the spring, the time when plants and foods of all kinds are

stimulated to growth (this being the meaning of the word whakaahu). It rises at dawn in early August and is probably Castor, though some have thought it may be Pollux.

Whakaahu and Puanga (Rigel) are sometimes regarded as the two sons of a person named Tai-ngaruē. They were thrown up above to be signs for human beings.

## Whakaotirangi
### A far-sighted woman

In the traditions of both the *Tainui* and *Te Arawa*, Whakaotirangi is the wife of the man who captains the ship on its voyage from Hawaiki. In each case she is responsible for ensuring that the kūmara arrives safely in Aotearoa.

According to the Tainui story, Whakaotirangi was the principal wife of Hoturoa. When the rest of the crew ate their seed kūmara on the way, she prudently kept hers tied up in a corner of her basket. Afterwards she planted them in soil brought from the homeland, in a place the crew named Hawaiki. They flourished exceedingly, along with her gourds and her paper mulberry tree.

The Arawa peoples, on the other hand, say that Whakaotirangi was the wife of Tama-te-kapua (who had stolen her from Ruaeo). When Ngātoro-i-rangi sent the vessel down towards Te Parata, the monster at the edge of the sky, most of the crew lost their seed kūmara, but Whaka-otirangi saved some of hers in a tightly fastened corner of her basket. Later she planted them and they grew prolifically.

An Arawa saying, 'Te kete rokiroki a Whaka-otirangi' [Whakaotirangi's tied-up basket], recalls this event. In Tainui tradition a slightly different proverb, 'Te kete rukuruku a Whaka-otirangi', has the same meaning.

These sayings celebrate Whakaotirangi's care and foresight. Since she could only retain a few of her kūmara, they are also used as an apology when limited food is available.

## Whakatau
### The warrior who gains revenge

It was the sacred duty of a warrior to avenge the killing of a relative. One of the most important of the avenging warriors in Māori tradition is Whakatau.

*In this Arawa carving from the early twentieth century, Whakaotirangi holds the basket of kūmara which she carefully preserved during the voyage from Hawaiki.*

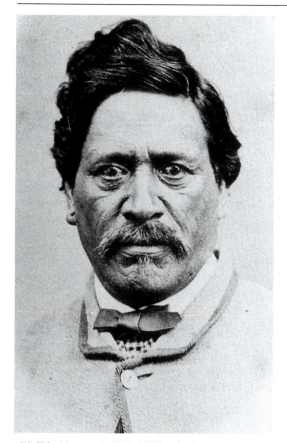

*Wī Tako Ngātata (c.1810–1887), a leading rangatira of Te Āti Awa, wrote an account of the myth of Whakatau, with other material, for the Governor, George Grey.*

He is very small, so small, some say, that he could be hidden under a fingernail. When he sails off to seek revenge, at the bow of the waka he is hidden like a spider.

He is a youngest son, and sometimes known as Whakatau-pōtiki [Whakatau the youngest]. All his brothers are tall, yet he is the one chosen to revenge the death of Tū-whakararo. With a few carefully chosen companions he sets out to do this.

In one version of the myth, from Ngāti Ruanui in southern Taranaki, when Whakatau enters the house of his enemies the bones of the murdered Tū-whakararo cry and wail in recognition. Whakatau recites a ritual chant, then runs from the house and jumps on to the roof. He throws a noose down through the smoke-hole, and catches one then another of the enemy warriors. Lastly he sets fire to the house. It burns to the ground, with the people inside.

Far away, Whakatau's mother, seated upon the roof of her house, sees the sky aflame and knows her enemies are destroyed.

There are numerous variations, though Whakatau's main deed is always much the same. Usually he avenges the death of Tū-whakararo, his father (or elder brother), and it is Apakura, his mother (or occasionally sister) who asks him to undertake this task. Usually the enemy, who live over the sea, are the people of Te Āti Hāpai, and their leading man is Poporokewa. The great house in which they live is Te Tihi-o-Manōno (or Te Uru-o-Manōno). Sometimes there is a scene within the house where Whakatau, having entered in disguise, reveals himself to the enemy before attacking them.

Occasionally it is another young man, Tūhuruhuru, whose death has to be revenged. He is the son of Tinirau and Hine-te-iwaiwa, so in this story it is Hine-te-iwaiwa who asks for Whakatau's assistance.

Sometimes the hero's birth is miraculous. When his mother Apakura throws her girdle into the sea, Whakatau is fashioned from the girdle, then nourished and taught by his ancestor Rongotākāwhiu. At the bottom of the ocean the boy flies kites, so that to those on shore only the kite and its string are visible above the water.

Brave warriors could be praised as 'the descendants of Whakatau-pōtiki', and poets often speak of him when they lament a death and urge revenge. The Ngāti Porou story includes a ritual chant that Whakatau recited as he girded himself for battle; it is safe to assume that warriors in real life recited this chant while putting on their war-belts, identifying themselves with Whakatau and acquiring his powers.

Related myths are known in other parts of Polynesia, including Sāmoa, which the ancestors of the Māori left behind some two thousand years ago. However, the enemies' house seems to occur only in the Māori versions.

## Whakaue
### A Rotorua ancestor

The western shores of Lake Rotorua, from Awahou to Ōhinemutu in the south, and Mokoia Island as well, are the traditional territory of Ngāti Whakaue. These people take their name from Whakaue-kaipapa, son of Uenuku-kōpako.

With his principal wife Rangiuru, Whakaue had six children. The three eldest sons were Tawakeheimoa, Ngārara-nui and Tuteaiti, the younger sons were Tūtānekai and Kōpako, and their daughter, the youngest, was Tupaharanui. The famous Tūtānekai was in fact a stepson, being the son of Rangiuru and a visiting rangatira, Tūwharetoa.

*Ōhinemutu with Mokoia Island in the distance, as sketched in 1845. Along with some other areas beside Lake Rotorua, these constitute the traditional territory of Ngāti Whakaue, who take their name from their ancestor Whakaue.*

# Whānau-moana
## A winged man

On the west coast of the North Island, Whānau-moana [Born of the sea] was the progenitor of a winged race of human beings. He owed his name to his miraculous birth.

It happened after Turi, captain of the *Aotea*, arrived from the homeland of Hawaiki. When his third son was born, the afterbirth was thrown into the sea. Later, it was washed up on the shore and found to be alive. Some people cared for the winged boy who grew from it, and he became a man.

At Waitōtara, Whānau-moana became the father of winged men who flew around quite openly during the day. At first they had no real home but flew from one place to another, alighting upon mountains and islands; later they lived in villages. The last of them, Te Kāhui-rere, lost his wings when a woman pressed down on them as he lay sleeping. But there are still people now who are descended from Te Kāhui-rere.

# Whāngai-mokopuna
## Origin of the Manawatū Gorge

This taniwha used to live at Motuiti (near the present town of Foxton). He was the pet of the Rangitāne people there, who used to bring him basketfuls of eels, but one day some children gave him only the heads of eels. Infuriated, Whāngai-mokopuna ate one of the children instead, then fled from the child's relatives.

He swam up the Manawatū River, then at its junction with the Tāmaki River he avoided a long detour by cutting straight through the hills, forming the steep-sided Manawatū Gorge. Afterwards he went up the Mangapuaka Stream, another of the Manawatū's many tributaries, and made his home in its headwaters.

The Mangapuaka is near Dannevirke. When Rangitāne people from Foxton visit the Dannevirke district a fog descends on Mount Raekatia, and the local people say that Whāngai-mokopuna is weeping over his old friends.

# Whānui
## The harvest star

Whānui is Vega, fifth brightest of the visible stars. When he appeared before dawn in late February he was thought to be coming from Hawaiki, and his presence was a sign that the kūmara crop had matured and could soon be harvested. If he moved slowly, it would be a good season; if he went fast, a poor season would follow.

Whānui was regarded as the father of the kūmara. His younger brother Rongo-māui once visited him in the sky, wanting to obtain the kūmara for human beings. When Whānui refused his request he stole the plant and brought it down, and ever since this time the kūmara has been cultivated upon the earth.

It is still necessary for Whānui each autumn to

send the mana of the kūmara, its vitality and productiveness, down to the people of this world. Every harvest-time he does this. But since he has not forgotten his brother's theft, he sends as well the three kinds of caterpillar which attack the kūmara.

## Whare-matangi
### A search for a father

A man named Ngarue left his wife and moved south from Kāwhia to Waitara. Since his wife was pregnant at the time, he left with her a magic dart [teka tipua] that would enable their son, when he grew up, to find his father. (Darts of this kind were light rods about a metre in length.)

So the boy was born, and was named Whare-matangi. When he became a man he followed his father's instructions. With his mother's assistance he cast the dart, reciting the chant he had been taught, and it flew far away. Whare found it and threw it once more; this time a rainbow showed where it lay. Again he threw it, and again, then on the fifth throw the dart landed on the marae of the house at Waitara where Ngarue was living. His father recognised him as his son and performed over him the tohi ritual that dedicated him to his future life.

## Whātonga
### Toi's grandson

An early ancestor named Toi occurs in the genealogies of many different peoples. Sometimes this man lives in Aotearoa in the beginning, and sometimes his home is in Hawaiki. Often his son is Rauru and his grandson is Whātonga.

While there are many stories about Toi and some about Rauru, in most places little is said about Whātonga. He is, however, regarded as the founding ancestor of the Rangitāne people, in the region of the Manawatū River. They regard Whātonga as a son of Rongoueroa, who lived some twenty-seven generations ago, and a grandson of Toi.

Their authorities say that Whātonga captained *Kurahaupō* on its voyage from Hawaiki, and that the other leading men on board were the navigator Ruatea and Popoto. They settled first at Nuku-taurua, on the northern shore of Te Māhia (the Māhia Peninsula), where their waka became a reef.

Whātonga later moved south to what is now the Hastings district, settling among people already there. Ruatea apparently also went south, for his son (some say grandson) Apa-hāpai-

taketake became the founding ancestor of Ngāti Apa in the Rangitīkei district. Popoto, who seems to have remained at Te Māhia, became an ancestor of Ngāti Kahungunu.

There is a story that Whātonga's voyage to Aotearoa occurred after he captained a vessel that was blown out to sea during a race between waka in Hawaiki. His grief-stricken grandfather Toi sailed in search of him, visiting many islands, while Whātonga meanwhile returned home safely. Whātonga then went searching for Toi; in Aotearoa he first visited Tongapōrutu, then found him at last at Whakatāne. Afterwards he sailed to Nukutaurua.

This tradition has been thought suspect, having been recorded in late accounts, but a song attributed to Whātonga's wife Hotuwaipara must refer to it. Addressing her grandson Wakanui, whose death she is lamenting, she speaks of Toi's voyage from Hawaiki:

Koia tō tipuna, a Toi-te-huatahi,
I kōhau ai i Tiritiri-o-te-moana nei.
Nāna tāua i makere mai ai i Hawaiki i
  runga i a *Kurahaupō* –
Ka tau ana Tongapōrutu, ka tau ana tāua
  Whakatāne,
Ka tangi te mapu toiora i a tāua, e tama ei!

And your grandfather, Toi-te-huatahi,
Came questing across Vast-expanse-of-
  ocean.
Because of him we left Hawaiki on
  *Kurahaupō* –
We anchored at Tongapōrutu, we anchored
  at Whakatāne,
And a shout went up, we were safe, my son!

While the poet does not say why Toi put to sea, and the song may not be as ancient as has been claimed, Whātonga's search for Toi seems to be well established in the traditions of this region.

## Whatu kura
### Stones of great mana

Smooth, highly tapu pebbles known as whatu, or whatu kura, were important in Māori religion. This word whatu means 'stone', not an ordinary stone but a special one employed in this way. It is also used of something that forms a centre, or core, such as the stone in a fruit and the pupil in an eye, and this idea was present too in the use of the sacred whatu. The adjective kura means 'precious' and sometimes 'crimson'.

Whatu kura were often red or reddish, sometimes white. Usually they were a couple of centimetres or less in length. Articles employed in ritual were often small in size, since this distinguished them from the mass of ordinary, common objects.

Whatu were also set apart by their sacred origins. They were believed to have been brought from Hawaiki by the tohunga on the ancestral waka, or else to have been acquired by early ancestors from the heights of the sky.

In South Island tradition, the hero Tāwhaki gains the first whatu from Tama-i-waho in the highest of the skies. In the southern part of the North Island, Tāne and Tangaroa each receive a whatu kura from the highest sky to enable them to create order in their respective realms, Tāne on the land and Tāngaroa in the sea. When a belief in a high god, Io, developed in the second half of the nineteenth century, this deity became the person who gave these whatu kura to Tāne and Tangaroa.

But it was not only in the beginning that whatu kura were acquired from Hawaiki or from the

*It was thought that the noisy, lively kākā flew across the ocean to Hawaiki and brought back whatu kura, small sacred stones employed by tohunga in ritual. In this way they provided renewed access to the sacred powers of which Hawaiki was the source.*

sky. It was thought that they were still being brought from Hawaiki, by kākā. These noisy, sociable parrots, regarded as the rangatira of all the birds, used to move around the country in large screeching flocks. It was believed that they flew to Hawaiki and back, and that on the return journey their leader carried with him a smooth, reddish stone upon which the other birds sharpened their beaks. This was sometimes termed 'parrot food' [ōkākā].

Others said that the stone was carried inside the bird's gizzard. There were those, too, who asserted that the birds brought the whatu kura from the heavens rather than from Hawaiki.

When a tohunga took such a stone from the leader of the flock, he gained its powers. The precedent set by Tāwhaki, or by Tāne and Tangaroa – ancestors who in different myths had gained whatu kura from the skies – gave mana to the proceedings.

Whatu kura were employed in many rituals, including those surrounding the teaching of esoteric knowledge. A young man about to receive instruction in a house of learning might be presented with a tapu stone to hold in his mouth while memorising traditions and ritual chants. Sometimes a student would be required to swallow a stone, which would remain in his chest throughout his life. We are told that when a tohunga had communicated sacred knowledge to his son, who later would succeed to his powers, he would before his death pass on to his son the stone he had carried within him.

Among the Taranaki and Whanganui peoples, whatu kura were stored in stone receptacles, also known as whatu, which were hollowed right through. On occasions of great moment the tohunga spoke through these hollow whatu. They might do this when addressing an army on the eve of battle, or reciting chants before a highly tapu god.

## Whiro
### Source of evil

This man performed many evil deeds, introducing into the world such practices as murder, cannibalism, adultery, theft and lying. Because he established precedents for behaviour like this, he can be held responsible for the actions of those who have imitated him. As well he carries people off to death, so he can be blamed for death. A poet speaks of 'Whiro, who brought evils upon us' [Whiro, nāna i hōmai ngā mate ki a tātou].

In the best-known story, told on the east coast and in other places, Whiro sets out on a sinister voyage that ends down below. He is accompanied by Tura, who at first does not realise where they are going. His waka is the *Hotu-te-ihi*, or *Hotu-te-ihi-rangi* or *Whatu-te-ihi*.

First, Whiro constructs the waka along with a companion (either Tura, an elder brother called Hua or Hourangi, or an unnamed nephew). Always he behaves badly. In some versions of the myth he takes for himself the log from which the waka will be constructed. Often, when the vessel is finished and the topstrakes are being lashed in place, he kills a boy (or man) who is helping with the lashing. He does this by pulling around his neck the rope that they have been using. He then buries the body in a pile of chips left from the adzing of the waka, but the body is found and the murder revealed. Sometimes it is the son of his elder brother whom he has killed, and this leads to fighting and the introduction by Whiro of the practice of cannibalism.

Instead of a murder, some versions have at this point an episode where it is discovered that Whiro has been having a liaison with his own nephew's wife.

After these dreadful deeds Whiro sets out on his voyage. Tura joins him, but becomes suspicious. When they pass an island (sometimes it is Hawaiki), Tura takes the opportunity to disembark. Whiro continues on, and his vessel goes down below.

Tura escapes from Whiro's waka because he belongs with life, not death. His main mythic role is to initiate the proper method of childbirth, and this he now does.

As for Whiro, he is a thief of people, whom he takes down to the underworld in his ship. On this occasion his victim is the boy (or man) whom he had noosed in the rope when lashing the topstrakes (this rope associates the boy with the waka and therefore its voyage; so does his burial in the chips left from the ship's construction). But Whiro's voyage is repeated whenever people die. Some poets explicitly identify the person whose death they are mourning with the boy murdered by Whiro.

For the singers of laments, Whiro's existence at least provided a reason for what had happened. And he did after all provide a means of transport for the wairua of the person who had died.

At a funeral and afterwards, the body was often placed in a small waka, and a little model of a waka might be put in the cave where the bones were finally laid to rest. It is not known whether these vessels were ever identified specifically with Whiro's waka, but they were certainly intended as a conveyance for the wairua.

On the west coast of the North Island, a different story was told (see the entries for Te Whare Kura and Monoa). But the myth of the waka's voyage was known as well in this region, although perhaps not in detail, because it is mentioned in a Taranaki song.

Another myth, from Ngāti Kahungunu, has the evil Whiro jealous of his younger brother Tāne, and in conflict with him (see the entry for Io).

Offerings were made to Whiro to placate him and escape his wrath. When someone obtained a supply of food, such as birds or fish, he would put a small amount aside and say, 'That's for you, Whiro' [Ki a koe, e Whiro]. In times of war it became necessary to act like Whiro, so people sought help again with offerings. He might predict the outcome of a battle to a tohunga who approached him, and he was often of assistance when enemies attempted sorcery.

Whiro is listed as an early ancestor in genealogies in different parts of the country; the name of the East Cape ancestor Whiro-nui [Great Whiro] may also derive from traditions concerning him. Whiro's extended name, Whiro-te-tipua [Whiro the tipua], conveys his nature.

In some other parts of Polynesia, including the Cook Islands and the Society Islands, a man with an equivalent name (such as Hiro or Iro) is a patron of thieves and a famous voyager. Since long ocean voyages were no longer possible in Aotearoa, the myth changed. Whiro now became a thief of men and women, and his voyage ended in the underworld.

## Whiro-nui

### Captain of the *Nukutere*

There is apparently no detailed account of the voyage of the *Nukutere* from Hawaiki. We are told that among the crew were the captain Whiro-nui, his wife Ārai-ara, and two tohunga, Mārere-o-tonga and Takataka-pū-tonga. The waka landed just south of East Cape and the people settled in that region.

Some years later, the early ancestor Paikea was making his way southward along the coast, having travelled from Hawaiki on the back of a whale. At Te Kautuku he encountered a woman bathing in a pool. She was Huturangi, daughter of Whiro-nui and Ārai-ara. When she took Paikea to her parents' house, the people there were performing a kūmara-planting ritual. They were doing it incorrectly, so Paikea showed them the proper way.

Paikea married Huturangi and lived for a while

with his father-in-law. But he wanted to explore the country to the south, for he was still searching for his home, Whāngārā, which he thought lay in that direction. So he set out along the coast, taking his wife and her parents. He also carried in a gourd his tame eel Tangotango-rau.

When the travellers reached Lake Roto-o-tahe (or Rototahi), near Anaura Bay, Paikea released his eel into its waters. As well, he left Whiro-nui and Ārai-ara in that locality. Whiro-nui became a taniwha and lived for many generations in the lake.

*Whāngārā, where Paikea and his wife Huturangi settled, remains a place of great significance to their Ngāti Porou descendants. Whāngārā Island, according to some, was originally the whale on which Paikea rode to Aotearoa.*

When Paikea and Huturangi finally reached Whāngārā, Paikea discovered that this place was not after all his former home in Hawaiki, although it was very similar. He and his wife lived there for the rest of their lives, and from their union came the most important lines of descent in Ngāti Porou genealogies.

# Notes on Sources

The list below provides some information on works consulted. It is far from comprehensive, often because of a superabundance of material and sometimes because the fragmentary and scattered nature of the information has made it difficult to give all sources. I have tried, however, to list fragmentary sources where significant use has been made of them.

Subtitles of entries are given only where there might otherwise be confusion.

**Introduction** Davidson 1984; Johansen 1954; Johansen 1958: 83; Jones 1994; Neich 1994; Orbell 1965: 17; Prickett 1982; Trotter & McCulloch 1989; Wilson 1987.

**Aituā** Te Rangi Hiroa 1950: 61, 415.

**Ancestors** Te Rangi Hiroa 1950: 500; Johansen 1954: 147–84; Orbell 1985: 167–68.

**Aoraki** Beattie 1949: 7–10.

*Aotea* Hammond 1924; Orbell 1985a: 35–37, 47, 52; Tautahi 1900; Taylor 1855: 117–20, 123–24, 139, 141.

**Aotearoa** Best 1917: 146.

**Apakura** Johansen 1958: 155–60.

**Apanui-waipapa** Fowler 1958; Stirling & Salmond 1980: 38–43.

**Āraiteuru: a taniwha at Hokianga** Polack 1838: I, 62, 118; White 1874: frontispiece, 1–5.

**Āraiteuru: a petrified cargo and crew** Beattie 1994: 426–27; Orbell 1985: 62–63; Te Maihāroa 1957: 25–27.

**Atua** Best 1897a; Best 1900–01: I, 199, Best 1924: 157–59; Dieffenbach 1843: II, 117–18; Johansen 1954: 5; Orbell 1985: 181; Shortland 1851: 30–31; Taylor 1870a: 57.

**Atua kahukahu** Shortland 1856: 292.

**Atutahi** Best 1925: I, 813–14, 850–51; Best 1922: 33, 42–43; White 1887–91: I, 45.

**Awa-nui-ā-rangi** Best 1925: I, 52–63, 918; Grey 1857: 62–63; Phillipps & Wadmore 1974: 20.

**Birds** Best 1942; Orbell 1985: 148–57, 180–213.

**Birth** Best 1905–07; Best 1929a; Makereti 1938: 112–33.

**Death** Oppenheim 1973.

**Dogs** Orbell 1985: see index.

**Fairies** Cowan 1930; Elvy 1957: 47–52; Orbell 1982; Orbell 1985: 131.

**Fernroot** Orbell 1985: 38–40.

**Fish** Best 1929.

**Gourds** Best 1925c: 129–34.

**Greenstone** Davidson 1984: see index; Orbell 1985: see index; Prickett 1982: see index; Wilson 1987: see index.

**Hakawau** Grace 1907: 61–71 (freely retold, but apparently based on a version otherwise unrecorded); Grey 1928: 147–49; Grey 1956: 215–20.

**Hākirirangi** Fowler 1974: 21.

**Hākuturi** Best 1925: I, 999–1000; Best 1982: 548; Reedy 1993:136–37, 198; Taylor 1855: 115.

**Hani and Puna** Cowan 1982: 112–13; Kelly 1949: 60–61; Phillips 1989: 10–11; Te Hurinui 1960: 246–52, 269.

**Hape** Best 1925: I, 59–60, 948–56; Davis 1990: 31, 35–36.

**Hāpōpō** Reedy 1993: 199.

**Hatupatu** Grey 1928: 81–89; Grey 1956: 143–57; Shortland 1856: 14–15; Taylor 1855: 47–49.

**Hau** Best 1900–01: I, 189–94; Taylor 1855: 78; Williams 1971: 38–39.

**Hau and Wairaka** Best 1982: 212–17; Cowan 1930: 119–27; Grey 1853: 89; McEwen 1986: 12–13, 16–17; Taylor 1855: 139–40.

**Hauāuru** Diamond & Hayward 1979: 31–32.

**Haumapūhia** Best 1925: I, 898, 971–72, 978–80.

**Haumia: origin of fernroot** Best 1902a: 50; Best 1925: I, 777–78; Grey 1928: 1–5; Grey 1956: 1–11; Orbell 1985: 38–40; Taylor 1855: 18.

**Haumia: a taniwha at Manukau** Graham 1946: 32–35; Orbell 1968: 28–29.

**Haumia-whakatere-taniwha** Orbell 1968: xx–xxi; Pomare & Cowan 1930–34: II, 26–27.

**Hautapu** Cowan 1930: 153–64.

**Hawaiki** Orbell 1985a.

**Hawaiki-rangi** Ngata 1990: 2–3; Smith 1913–15: I, 112–13; Ngata & Te Hurinui 1970: 4–5, 346–47.

**Hei** Salmond 1991: 190–92.

**Hikurangi** Johansen 1958: 31–36; Orbell 1985a: 87–89.

**Hina** Best 1925: I, 817, 835,1137; Best 1982: 364–67; Grey 1928: 24–28; Grey 1956: 62–68; Henry 1928: 620; White 1987–91: II, 121–25; Wohlers 1874: 14, 40–41.

**Hine-ahu-one** Reedy 1993: 118, 189–90; White 1887–91: I, 144–64.

**Hine-hopu** Stafford 1967: 174–78.

**Hine-i-tapeka** Best 1921: 5.

**Hine-kōrako: the pale rainbow** Best 1982: 303, 395–97; Makereti 1938: 119.

**Hine-kōrako: a female taniwha** Lambert 1925: 109–10.

**Hinemoa and Tūtānekai** Grey 1956: 183–91; Grey 1928: 106–13; Makereti 1938: 92–99.

**Hine-mokemoke** Best 1982: 575.

**Hine-nui-te-pō** Best 1925: I, 768, 833, 944–48; Reedy 1993: 126, 193–94; Taylor MS; Taylor 1855: 15–16, 30–31.

**Hine-poupou** Orbell 1968: xvii–xviii, 90–103; Pomare & Cowan 1930–34: I, 150–51.

**Hine-pūkohu-rangi** Best 1925: I, 864–67.

**Hine-rauāmoa** Best 1898: 635, 646; Best 1899: 95–96.

**Hine-rau-whārangi** Best 1924: 77–78; Best 1982: 312; Shortland 1882: 29, 109–10.

**Hine-rehia** Simmons 1987: 21–23.

**Hine-ruru** Schwimmer 1963.

**Hine-te-iwaiwa** Best 1902a: 50; Best 1925: I, 762, 774, 783–84, 802, 1087; Grey 1928: 50; Grey 1956: 93; Shortland 1882: 29, 109–10; Taylor 1855: 107–12; White 1887–91: II, 134–8, 141–44; Wohlers 1874: 25–26.

**Hine-tītama** Best 1924: 80.

**Hine-tua-hōanga** Best 1912: 106–7.

**Hine-waiapu** Best 1912: 56, 197; Best 1982: 526; Reedy 1993: 135–36.

**Hingānga-roa** Colenso 1880: 45–46; Fowler 1974: 32.

**Horoirangi** Cowan 1930a: 222–29; Stafford 1994: 123.

**Horo-matangi** Grace 1959: 76; Gudgeon 1885: 19–21; Gudgeon 1905a: 188–91; von Hochstetter 1867: 381–82; Kerry-Nicholls 1884: 167.

**Horouta** Johansen 1958: see index; Kapiti 1912; Kapiti 1913; Reedy 1993: 150–51, 181–82; White 1880: 12–13, 25–28; White 1887–91: III, 93–104.

**Hotumauea** Te Whēoro MS 1871; Te Hurinui 1960: 25–26, 29.

**Hotupuku** Grey 1928: 126–29.

**Houmea** Orbell 1992: 102–10; Reedy 1993: 49–52, 111–14, 152–55, 217–20.

**Houses of learning** Best 1923, Reedy 1993.

**Humuhumu** Graham 1946: 36–37.

**Īhenga** Shortland 1882; Stafford 1967: 24–42.

**Io** Johansen 1958: 190–93; Ngata & Te Hurinui 1961: 60–61; Smith 1982: 66–156; Te Rangi Hiroa 1950: see index.

**Ioio-whenua** Best 1902a: 50; Best 1925: I, 755–56, 777, 781.

**Irakau** Gudgeon 1906: 38–42.

**Irākewa** Best 1925: I, 716–18, 967; Best 1900–01: I, 180; Gudgeon 1892: 219; Orbell 1985a: 32–33.

**Irawaru** Grey 1928: 19–20; Grey 1956: 38–40; Reedy 1993: 124–25, 186–87.

**Iwi-katere** Best 1942: 368–70, 477–79.

**Kahukura: the discovery of net-making** Keene 1963: 91; Orbell 1992: 15–18.

**Kahukura: a powerful god** Te Hurinui 1960: 252–56.

**Kahukura: a sorcerer** Reedy 1993: 159–60, 205.

**Kahu-mata-momoe** Grey 1956: 121; Stafford 1967: 24–39.

**Kahungunu** Anon. 1932: 13; Gudgeon 1896; Gudgeon 1897; Mitchell 1944; Te Whare-auahi 1905.

**Kaiwhare** Grey 1928: 136–37; Orbell 1985: 127–29.

**Kametara** Te Whetū 1897.

**Kapu-manawa-whiti** Taylor 1855: 130; White 1887–91: V, 61–66.

**Karitehe** Tregear 1926: 526–27.

**Kataore** Best 1902: 30; Cowan 1930: 129–43; Grey 1928: 131–36; Massy 1900: 52–53; Stafford 1967: 66.

**Kaukau-matua** Davis 1855: 19; Fletcher 1913.

**Kawharu** Keene 1975: 46–47; Kelly 1949: 217–33; Pomare & Cowan 1930–34: I, 89; Smith 1897: 66–69; White 1880: 16, 30.

**Kēhua** Orbell 1990.

**Kiharoa** Phillips 1989: 90–92.

**Kiki and Tāmure** Grey 1928: 145–46; Grey 1956: 211–14; Ngata 1959: 288–91.

**Kiwa: an early Tūranga ancestor** Fowler 1974: 24; Pere 1898; White 1887–91: II, 191.

**Kiwa: guardian of the ocean** Best 1929: 1–2, 71–74.

**Kiwi** Best 1912: 216; Graham 1922; Smith 1897: 77–83.

**Kōhine-mataroa** Motuiti Community Trust 1987: 66–69.

**Kōkako** Kelly 1949: 89–98.

**Kōpū** Best 1922: 50–51; Williams 1971: kōpū.

**Kōpūwai** Cowan 1930: 168–70; Te Maihāroa: 1957: 16–20.

**Korotangi** Ngata & Te Hurinui 1961: 188–91.

**Kūī** Best 1982: 388, 435; White 1880: 15, 28; White 1887–91: III, 188, 191.

**Kūmara** Best 1925c: 47–119; Johansen 1958: 112–88; Walsh 1903.

**Kupe** Orbell 1985a: 26–32; Taylor 1855: 116–17, 123–25.

*Kurahaupō* Keene 1975: 2–3; McEwen 1986: 10–14; Shortland 1856: 24; Kararehe 1893; Te Rangi Hiroa 1950: 54.

**Lightning and thunder** Best 1924: 227; Best 1982: 421–22.

**Maero** Best 1982: 551–52; Cowan 1930: 170–73; Taylor 1855: 49.

**Māhaki** Best 1925: I, 920; Fowler 1974: 21, 33; Ngata & Te Hurinui 1961: 158–59; Ngata & Te Hurinui 1970: 116–17.

**Māhaki-rau** Fowler 1974: 11, 21, plate 32.

**Māhanga** Best 1925: I, 237; Grey 1857: 89; White 1887–91: IV, 59–60.

**Mahina** Kelly 1949: 48–49; Shortland 1856: 13; Stafford 1967: 474.

**Māhu** Best 1925: I, 978–980; Best 1897: 41–57.

**Māhu and Taewa** Tarakawa & Ropiha 1899.

*Māhuhu* Keene 1975: 44–45; Shortland 1856: 25; Smith 1896: 2–3.

**Mahuika** Grey 1928: 17–19, 186; Grey 1956: 34–38; Reedy 1993: 121–22, 185–86; Taylor 1855: 29–30.

*Māhunui* Pomare & Cowan 1930–34: I, 41.

**Māhutonga** Best 1921: 7; Best 1982: 412–13; Taylor 1855: 90.

**Māia** Fowler 1974: 21–23, plate 37.

**Makawe** Stafford 1994: 44.

*Māmari* Keene 1975: 52–56; Kereama 1968: 1–2; Orbell 1985: 109, White 1874: 5–6; White 1885: 106–8.

**Mana** Best 1924a: I, 386–90; Johansen 1954: 84–99; Mair 1923: 7, 43; Wilson 1907: 60.

**Manaia: an enemy three times defeated** Grey 1928: 71–80; Grey 1956: 128–42.

**Manaia: a family turned to rocks** Orbell 1985: 130–31; Piripi 1961.

**Mangamangai–atua** Best 1922: 20; Williams 1971: mangamangaiatua.

**Mangapuera** Downes 1915: 25–27.

*Mangarara* Orbell 1985: 49–50; Turei 1876.

**Mango-huruhuru** Smith 1908a: 69–75.

**Maniapoto** Kelly 1949: 85–88.

**Marakihau** Best 1925: I, 968; Stimson & Marshall 1964: 286.

**Mārere-o-tonga** Best 1902b: 35–38; Best 1925: I, 771–72, 815, 841; Shortland 1882: 18.

**Maru** Best 1922: 70; Cowan 1930a: 225–29; Smith 1905: 145–50; Taylor 1855: 33, 35, 67, 40–41, 85; White 1885: 115–16.

**Maruiwi** Best 1925: I, 63–79, Grey 1857: 58.

**Maru-tūahu** Grey 1956: 192–201, Kelly 1949: 99–108.

**Mataaho** Best 1982: 249, 373, 401–2; Grey 1857: 85; Grey 1928: 37; Grey 1956: 47.

*Mātaatua* Orbell 1985a: 32–33; Tarakawa 1894.

**Matakauri** Beattie 1945: 33–34.

**Matamata** Elvy 1949: 65–66.

**Mataoho** Graham 1980: 5; 14–15.

**Mataora and Niwareka** Best 1925: I, 938–39; Best 1982: 226–37; White 1887–91: II, 4–7.

**Matariki** Best 1902a: 109; Best 1925: I, 811–13; Best 1925c: 52–55; Dansey 1968; Grey 1857: 65; Orbell 1978: 78–79, 100–1.

**Mataterā and Waerotā** Johansen 1958: 121, 149, 176–77, Smith 1896: 3–8; Stimson & Marshall 1964: vaerotā, Ngata & Te Hurinui 1961: 92–93, Williams 1971: torohaki.

**Matuatonga** Best 1925: I, 929; Cowan 1930a: 191; Fowler 1974: 22; Ngata & Te Hurinui 1961: 158–59; Walsh 1903: 18.

**Matuku-tangotango** Grey 1928: 46–47; Grey 1956: 85–86; Orbell 1985: 109–10; Reedy 1993: 137–38; Taylor 1855: 115–16.

**Māui** Grey 1928: 6–23; Grey 1956:12–44; Reedy 1993: 119–26, 183–89, 193–94; Shortland 1856: 61–64; Taylor 1855: 23–31; Te Rangikāheke 1992.

**Mauri** Best 1900–01: II, 2–7; Best 1924a: I, see index; Best 1925a: 108–10; Best 1927: 109–14.

**Miru** Cowan 1930: 23–31; Kararehe 1898; White 1887–91: I, appendix.

**Moa** Best 1942: 229–30, 469; Orbell 1985: 88–89.

**Moeahu** Pōhūhū 1930a: 121.

**Moko-hiku-waru** Tautahi 1900: 230.

**Moko-ika-hiku-waru** Graham 1946: 37–38.

**Moko's Great Dog** Pomare & Cowan 1930–34: I, 109.

**Monoa** Taylor 1855: 69–71.

**Moon** Best 1899: 100–1; Best 1922: 21–28.

**Motu-tapu** Graham 1980: 19; Johansen 1958: 161.

**Mountains** Orbell 1985: 84–95.

**Mumuhau and Takeretou** Best 1925: I, 720, 974; Orbell 1985: 197; Shortland 1856: 14.

**Muturangi's Octopus** Elvy 1957: 12–13.

**Ngahue** Best 1912: 200; Grey 1928: 58; Grey 1956: 106–8; Reedy 1993: 135–36.

**Ngāi-te-heke-o-te-rangi** Gudgeon 1905a: 191.

**Ngake** Best 1917: 146–7.

**Ngake and Whātaitai** Adkin 1959: 45; Best 1917: 143–49.

**Ngātokowaru** Kelly 1949: 217–18, 248–49.

**Ngātoro-i-rangi** Davies & Darling 1851: 45; Grey 1928: see index; Grey 1956: 128–42; Orbell 1985a: 38, 53–56, 60.

**Night** Orbell 1985: 77–83.

**Nukumaitore's Descendants** Best 1982: 553; Orbell 1968: 82–83.

**Nuku-tawhiti and Rūānui** Hongi 1910: 92; Keene 1975: 52–56; Kereama 1968: 1–2; Smith 1896: 18–21; White 1874: 5–6; White 1880: 15–16, 28–29; White 1885: 106–8.

**Ocean** Best 1929: 72–73; Best 1982: 116, 252–58, 309, 410.

**Owheao** Grace 1959: 131; Neich 1994: 258.

**Pahiko** Orbell 1966.

**Paia** Best 1925: I, 747, 752; Johansen 1958: 87–88; Shortland 1856: 56; Tiramōrehu 1987: 2–5, 23–26; White 1887–91: I, 122–24.

**Paikea** Reedy 1993: 142–46, 200–4.

**Pane-iraira** Best 1982: 484; Graham 1946: 27; Kelly 1949: 55.

**Pani** Best 1925c: 48–53, 154–55; Cowan 1910: 117;
Johansen 1958: 119 ff., 185–87; Reedy 1993: 179,
Stack 1893: 25, Taylor 1870a: 67; White 1887–91:
III, 114–16.

**Pānia** Parsons 1994: 20; Tareha 1954: 20.

**Pāoa** Grey 1928: 156–73.

**Papa** Best 1982: 36, 278, 299–300; Best 1924: 232;
Best 1925a: 36.

**Papa-kauri** Graham 1946: 28; Gudgeon 1906: 29–31.

**Para-whenua-mea** Beckwith 1970: 179; Best 1921: 5,
Best 1925: I, 793.

**Pare and Hutu** Beckwith 1970: 147–49; Orbell 1992:
66–71.

**Pare-ārau** Best 1925: I, 810; Best 1922: 43–44;
Williams 1971: pareārau.

**Parikoritawa** Downes 1921: 38–39.

**Patito** Pomare & Cowan 1930–34: I: 55; White 1885:
105–6.

**Pāwa** Fowler 1974: 23–24; Kohere 1951: 34; Reedy
1993: 150–51, 181–82.

**Pekehaua** Grey 1928: 129–31; Pomare & Cowan
1930–34: I, 235–37.

**Peketahi** Orbell 1992: 47–52.

**Peketua** Best 1982: 263, 319.

**Pikiao** Stafford 1967: 82.

**Pikopiko-i-whiti** Beattie 1994: 391, 399, 402; Ngata
& Te Hurinui 1961: 98–101, Stafford 1994: 84.

**Pokopoko** Cowan 1930a: 219–20.

**Ponaturi** Grey 1956: 46–51, 88–90.

**Porourangi** Gudgeon 1895: 17–18; Reedy 1993: 147.

**Pōtaka-tawhiti** Grey 1928: 54, 67, 89; Grey 1956: 99,
157.

**Pou** Best 1925: I, 918–32; Fowler 1974: 20–21; Rimini
1901; Tregear 1926: 506; Waititi 1901, 1902, 1902a.

**Poutini** Best 1902a: 101; Best 1925: I, 841–44.

**Poutū-te-rangi** Best 1922: 59; Best 1925: I, 823;
Johansen 1958: 115, 173.

**Puanga** Best 1922: 47–49; Best 1925: I, 836–37; Hongi
1913: 196; Taylor 1870: 362.

**Pūhaorangi** Best 1925: I, 63, 905–9; Pomare & Cowan
1930–34: I, 21; Stafford 1967: 1.

**Puha-o-te-rangi** Grace 1959: 362–429.

**Puhi** Keene 1975: 57–61; Smith 1896: 18; Smith 1897:
27–29.

**Punga** Grey 1857: 44, 52, 61, 67; Taylor 1855: 33, 36.

**Pururau** Gudgeon 1906: 28.

**Pū-tē-hue** Best 1899: 95–96; Best 1925: I, 755–56, 771,
782–83.

**Rāhiri** Motuiti Community Trust 1987, Keene 1975:
60–61.

**Rakahore** Best 1924: 104–5; Shortland 1882: 21;
White 1887–91: I, appendix.

**Raka-maomao** Best 1925: I, 886–88, 896.

**Raka-taura** Orbell 1985a: 52–53; Pomare & Cowan
1930–34: I, 43 ff.

**Rākeiao** Phillipps & McEwen 1946–48: 2, 94; Stafford

1967: 59.

**Rangi** Grey 1928: 1–5; Grey 1956: 1–11; Shortland
1856: 55–61; Taylor 1855: 14–23.

**Rangiātea** Best 1918: 113–14; Kohere 1951a: 22;
Smith 1913–15: I, 81; Taylor 1855: 147; Te Hurinui
1960: 33.

**Rangiriri** Gudgeon 1906: 40; Taylor 1855: 95.

**Rangitāne** McEwen 1986.

**Rangitihi** Stafford 1967: 57–60.

**Rarotonga** Williams 1971: tāmore; Grey 1928: 59;
Grey 1853: 229, 430; Grey 1857: 4.

**Rata** Reedy 1993: 136–38; Shortland 1856: 4–7;
Taylor 1855: 115–16.

**Rats** Best 1942: 416 ff.

**Raukata-ura** Henry 1928: 374; White 1885: 153–56;
172–73. (White gives the name sometimes as
Raukata-ura and sometimes as Rakata-ura. The
latter name is either a misprint or a variant
form.)

**Raukata-uri and Raukata-mea** Best 1928; Grey 1853:
291; Henry 1928: 374; Johansen 1958: 156–58;
Pomare & Cowan 1930–34: I, 69; Reedy 1993:
207–8; White 1887–91: I, appendix; Williams
1971: hue, raukatauri, whiri.

**Raukawa** Kelly 1949: 85; Orbell 1985a: 1–2.

**Rauru** Grey 1857: 75; Smith 1907: 175–88.

**Rehua** Best 1925: I, 816–23; White 1887–91: I, 5.

**Rei-tū and Rei-pae** Keene 1975: 34–36; Kelly 1949:
139–43; Kereama 1968: 3–4.

**Reptiles** Orbell 1985: 157–63.

**Rona** Best 1925: I, 803, 958; Best 1982: 35, 386–95;
Grey 1857: 50; Orbell 1968: 18–19; Taylor 1855: 95;
Tregear 1891: Rona.

**Rongo** Best 1902a: 50; Best 1925: I, 770 ff.; Makereti
1938: 175–202; Ngata & Te Hurinui 1961: 60–63.

**Rongokako** Best 1925: I, 929, 990; Fowler 1974: 24;
Lambert 1925: 231–33, 258.

**Rongomai** Cowan 1910: 109–10 ; Taylor 1855: 33–34,
41–42.

**Rongo-tākāwhiu** Best 1982: 155–56; Best 1925: I, 896;
Ngata & Te Hurinui 1961: 248–49; Grey 1928: 49,
Grey 1956: 91–92.

**Rongo-whakaata** Fowler 1974: 11; Phillipps &
Wadmore 1956: 17.

**Ruaeo** Grey 1956: 109–10, 117–19; Orbell 1985: 47.

**Rua-ki-pōuri** Ngata & Te Hurinui 1970: 4–5, 250–51,
434–35; Ngata 1990: 2–3; Smith 1913–15: I,
123–34.

**Ruamano** Elder 1934: 255; Best 1925: I, 963–65;
Phillipps & Wadmore 1956: 7.

**Ruapūtahanga** Kelly 1949: 71–79.

**Ruarangi and Tāwhaitū** Cowan 1930: 55–64;
Orbell 1968: 8–11; Shortland 1882: 47–50.

**Ruatāne and Tarapikau** Cowan 1930: 65–70.

**Ruatapu** Reedy 1993: 142–46, 200–2.

**Rua-taranaki** Smith 1907: 144–51.

**Rua-te-pupuke** Best 1928a; Best 1929: 80, 238; Best 1982: 259, 313; Reedy 1993: 55–56, 158–59.

**Rūaumoko** Best 1925: I, 778, 884; Henry 1928: 459–62; McLean & Orbell 1975: 104–5, 200; Taylor 1855: 32, 146.

**Rukutia** Beckwith 1970: 352–62; Grey 1853: 93; Ngata 1959: 220–21; Williams 1971: rukutia; Wohlers 1875: 110–15.

**Ruru-teina** Orbell 1992: 32–39; Te Maihāroa 1957: 6–12.

**Sky** Orbell 1965: 16–17; Orbell 1985: 67–72.

**Stars** Best 1925: I, 806–54; Best 1899; Best 1922.

**Sun** Best 1925: I, 786–92; Best 1925a: 50.

**Taha-rākau** Hera 1970; Orbell 1992: 140–46.

**Tahu** Best 1899: 118; Best 1982: 275, 312; Grey 1857: 85; Orbell 1965: 18–19; Taylor 1855: 18, 33.

**Tahu-pōtiki** Reedy 1993: 156.

**Tahurangi** Smith 1907: 219.

**Taiāmai** Keene 1975: 65–66.

**Taiau** Fowler 1974: 23, 25.

**Taikehu** Orbell 1985a: 57.

*Tainui* Aoterangi 1923: 4; Graham 1951; Kelly 1949; Orbell 1985a; Shortland 1856: 4–10; Simmons 1976: 165–76; Tauwhare 1905; White 1880: 6, 20; White 1887–1891: V, 5–16.

**Taipō** Elvy 1957: 7.

**Takarangi and Rau-mahora** Orbell 1992: 147–50.

**Takere-piripiri** Cowan 1930: 77–87; Taylor 1855: 51.

*Tākitimu* Fowler 1974: 13–14; Mitchell 1944: 60–61; Nihoniho 1907–8.

**Takurua** Best 1922: 60–61.

**Tama** Beattie 1994: 405; Best 1912: 206–7.

**Tama-āhua** Downes 1915: 15–16; Taylor 1855: 33–34.

**Tama-i-rēia** Diamond & Hayward 1979: 33.

**Tama-i-waho** Best 1925: I, 904–9; Best 1982: 399–401; White 1887–91: I, 125–30.

**Tama-nui-a-Raki** White 1887–91: II, 34–47.

**Tama-o-hoi** Cowan 1930: 146–48.

**Tama-rereti** Best 1925: I, 839; Taylor 1870: 363.

**Tamatea** Orbell 1985a: 59–60.

**Tama-te-kapua** Grey 1928: see index; Grey 1956: 99–105, 109–21; Orbell 1985a: 46–47.

**Tāminamina** Graham 1946: 29.

**Tāne** Orbell 1985: 167; Orbell 1991: 12–13, 43–46; Reedy 1993: 118, 178; White 1887–91: I, 130–64.

**Tāne-atua** Best 1925: I, 56, 210, 234–36, 712–13, 895, 967, 973; Gudgeon 1892: 231–32.

**Tangaroa** Grey 1928: 1–5; Grey 1956: 1–11; Orbell 1985: see index; Reedy 1993: 158–59, 190.

**Tangaroa-piri-whare** Grey 1857: 58, 84; Te Whēoro MS 1971.

**Tangaroa's whatu kura** Best 1929: 3–4, 58; Downes 1910: 218; Gudgeon 1906: 33–36; Tikao 1939: 38.

**Tangotango** Best 1898: 646; Best 1925: I, 748–51, 762–63, 781–82; Reedy 1993: 84, 189.

**Taniwha** Elder 1934: 255; Graham 1946; Shortland 1856: 75; Tikao 1939: 78; White: 1874: 28. See also sources for entries on individual taniwha.

**Tapu and noa** Grey 1853: lxxviii; Pomare & Cowan 1930–34: I, 259–71; Shortland 1836: 101–13; Taylor 1855: 55–64.

**Tāpui-kākahu** Orbell 1992: 118–21.

**Tara** Adkin 1959: see index; Best 1917; McEwen 1986.

**Tara-ao and Karewa** Pomare & Cowan 1930–34: I, 125–32; White 1887–91: IV, 187–91.

**Tara-i-whenua-kura** Reedy 1993: 131, 177; Taylor 1855: 69–71.

**Tara-ki-uta and Tara-ki-tai** Fowler 1974: 18–19; Phillipps & Wadmore 1974: 9; White 1887–91: III, 118–22.

**Taramainuku** Orbell 1985a: 57.

**Taranga** Grey 1928: 6 ff.; Grey 1956: 12 ff.; Reedy 1993: 119–23, 183–86.

**Tarawhata** Best 1925: I, 711; Cowan 1910: 198–99; Orbell 1985a: 49-57; Taylor 1870: 266.

**Taro** Best 1925c: 123–28; Hammond 1894.

**Tautini-awhitia** Orbell 1992: 82–88.

**Tautoru** Best 1925: I, 823–24; Best 1922: 47–49; Williams 1971: tautoru, kakau, tuke.

**Tāwera** Best 1922: 50; McGregor 1898: 62.

**Tāwhaki** Best 1899: 95; Best 1925: I, 777; Orbell 1965: 17–18; Reedy 1993: 189–90; Taylor 1870a: 64–65.

**Tāwhirimātea** Grey 1928: 1–4; Grey 1956: 3–8; Phillipps 1955: 21.

**Te Akē** Pomare & Cowan 1930–34: I, 95–105.

**Te Aoputaputa** Anon. 1926; Gudgeon 1906: 51–52; Mair 1923: 23–26; Kohere 1951: 20–22; Porter 1925.

*Te Ara Tāwhao* Best 1904; Best 1925: I, 702 ff.

**Te Ara-tukutuku** Best 1982: 486.

*Te Arawa* Grey 1928: 59–70, 180–81; Grey 1956: 99–142; Orbell 1985a: 38–65; Shortland 1856: 12–15; Tarakawa 1893.

**Te Atarahi** Orbell 1992: 63–65; Shortland 1882: 45–47.

**Te Awhiorangi** Best 1912: 240–45; Tautahi 1900: 229–33.

**Te Hōkioi** Best 1908: 256; Best 1982: 563; Grey 1872; Miskelly 1987; White 1887–91: VI, 3.

**Te Huhuti** Orbell 1992: 151–55.

**Te Ihi** Taylor 1855: 50.

**Te Kāhui Tipua** Stack 1998: 15; Te Maihāroa 1957.

**Te Kahureremoa** Orbell 1992: 166–77.

**Te Kai-whakaruaki** Te Whetu 1894: 16–19.

*Te Māmaru* Keene 1975: 24; Salmond 1991: 317–21.

**Te Mangōroa** Best 1899: 109–10; Best 1922: 44-46; Hongi 1913: 204–5; Williams 1971: Māngōroa.

**Te Ngārara-huarau** Makitanara 1983; Te Aro 1894; Tūnuiarangi 1905; Te Whetū 1893.

**Te Niniko** Smith 1908: 22–23; Te Whēoro MS 1871.

**Te Parata** Best 1982: 254; Colenso 1889; Orbell 1985:

38; Tregear 1891: parata; White 1885:1, 19.

**Te Pouākai** Orbell 1968: 80–104; Taylor 1855: 398; Te
Maihāroa 1957: 12–15.

**Te Pupū and Te Hoata** Best 1925: I, 793, 977; Cowan
1927: 25–27; Kerry-Nicholls 1884: 181–83.

**Te Rangihouhiri** Lyall 1979: 98–105; Phillipps &
Wadmore 1956: 25–26.

**Te Rapuwai** Elvy 1957: 8; Stack 1898: 20; Beattie
1915–22: part II, 130–1.

**Te Rēinga** Keene 1963: 182; Mitcalfe 1961; Pangu
1905; Shortland 1856: 150–55; Stack 1937: 124–25;
Taylor 1855: 103–6; White 1885: 117.

**Te Ririō** Best 1982: 535–36; Cowan 1927: 110–12;
Gudgeon 1906: 46–47.

**Te Rongorito** Kelly 1949: 85; Te Hurinui 1960: 34.

**Te Ruahine** Orbell 1968: xviii–xix, 72–75, 90–104;
Te Maihāroa 1957: 21–22; White 1887–91: I, 62.

**Te Tahi-o-te-rangi** Orbell 1973.

**Te Waka-a-Raki** Beattie 1915–22: part VIII, 139–40,
154 (1918).

**Te Wera** Beattie 1915–22: part IV, 55–56 (1916);
Pomare & Cowan 1930–34: I, 213; Taylor 1855:
395–96; Williams 1971: hao, kake.

**Te Whare Kura** Taylor 1855: 65–71; White 1885:
115–16.

**Tia** Davis 1990: 30–37; Grace 1959: 58–62

**Tieke-iti** Orbell 1968: xviii–xix, 52–53.

**Tiki** Grey 1853: 357, 377; Gudgeon 1905: 125;
McLean & Orbell 1975: 200; Orbell MS 1977: I,
208–13; Reedy 1993: 118, 180, 190; Taylor 1855:
18–19, 23, 33; White 1885: 101, 181; White 1887–
91: I, 151 ff.

**Timu-whakairia** Best 1925: 1, 771–72; Fowler 1974:
13–14; Nihoniho 1907–08.

**Tinirau** Best 1925: I, 773; Grey 1928: 24–31; Grey
1956: 62–76; Reedy 1993: 168–69, 206–8;
Shortland 1856: 64–67; Taylor 1855: 107–14.

**Tipua** Best 1982: 521–32; Graham 1946, Gudgeon
1906.

**Tira-mākā** Best 1925: I, 996; Williams 1971: tiramākā.

**Tītapu** Ngata & Te Hurinui 1961: 134–35; Orbell
1968: 36; Smith 1900: 167; Williams 1971: tītapu.

**Toa-rangatira** Kelly 1949: 225; Pomare & Cowan
1930–34: II, 49–66.

**Tōhē** Davis 1990: 18–23; Keene 1963: 45–52; Keene
1975: 9.

**Tohunga** Buddle 1851: 22; White 1885: 132–83.

**Toi** Beckwith 1970: 178–79; Orbell 1985a: 25–31, 54.

*Tokomaru* Grey 1956: 173–82; Simmons 1976:
182–88; Te Rangi Hiroa 1950: 52–54.

**Tongameha** Grey 1928: 40; Grey 1956: 53; White
1887–91: I, appendix.

**Tonganui** Grey 1928: 16; Grey 1956: 31–32; Ngata
1959; Stimson 1937: 36; Taylor 1870: 129–30.

**Tū** Best 1925: I, 770–71; Grey 1857: 39, 60, 73;
Gudgeon 1905: 125; Taylor 1855: 75–81; Taylor

1870a: 65.

**Tūāhu** Johansen 1958: 63–91.

**Tūheitia** Te Whēoro MS 1871; White 1887–91: IV,
58–59.

**Tuhirangi** Best 1925a: 107; 124, Downes 1914.

**Tūhoe-pōtiki** Best 1925.

**Tū-horopunga** Grey 1853: 291; Grey 1857: 40; Ngata
& Te Hurinui 1961: 92–93; Orbell 1992: 72–82;
Stimson 1937: 93–95.

**Tūhourangi** Pomare & Cowan 1930–34: I, 238–39.

**Tūkete** Beattie 1915–22: [part I], 107–8.

**Tukete's guardian** Beattie 1915–22: part XII, 135–36
(1920).

**Tumutumu-whenua** White 1880: 16, 29–30.

**Tuna** Taylor 1944: 18; White 1887–91: II, 76–85.

**Tū-nui-o-te-ika** Best 1982: 116, 906.

**Tuoro** Best 1925: I, 967, Best 1982: 519–21.

**Tuputupu-whenua** White 1880: 15–16, 28–29.

**Tura** White 1887–91: II, 6–19.

**Tūrongo and Māhina-ā-rangi** Kelly 1949: 69–76;
Phillips 1989: 21–22; Te Hurinui 1960: 26–30,
33–34.

**Tūtaeporoporo** Downes 1915: 12–16; Pomare &
Cowan 1930–34: I, 99–100; Orbell 1992: 52–62;
Taylor 1855: 52.

**Tū-tāmure** Reedy 1993: 151–52; 194–95.

**Tū-tangata-kino** Best 1982: 74; Downes 1915: 102–4;
Taylor 1855: 34, 165; White 1887–91: I, 96.

**Tūtara-kauika** Fowler 1974: 15; Best 1925: I, 923;
Ngata & Te Hurinui 1961: 72–73.

**Tūtaua** Best 1897: 94.

**Tū–tawake** Reedy 1993: 141–42, 152–55, 190, 217–20;
Orbell 1968: xvi, 64–71.

**Tūtekohe** Fowler 1974: 17–18; Ngata & Te Hurinui
1970: 286–91.

**Tū-te-koropanga** Orbell 1985: 179–80; White 1887–
91: II, 35–47; Wohlers 1875: 110–15.

**Tū-te-nganahau** Ngata & Te Hurinui 1961: 252,
Orbell 1965: 18; Taylor 1855: 18–20, 33.

**Tutumaiao** Best 1982: 550–51; Beattie 1994: 400;
White 1887–91: III, 188–89.

**Tū-whakairi-ora** Gudgeon 1895: 29–32; Turei 1911;
Wilson 1907: 233–50.

**Tū-whakararo** Grey 1928: 32–36, 48; Grey 1956:
77–83, 90.

**Tūwharetoa** Grace 1959: 103–8.

**Uenuku** Best 1925: I, 864–67; Davis 1855: 227; Grey
1857: 62, 118; Reedy 1993: 138–46, 196–205; Taylor
1855: 117; White 1887–91: III, 1–60.

**Uenuku-tuwhatu** Gudgeon, 1906: 29; Kelly 1949: 99,
448, 450; White 1887–91: IV, 110.

**Ureia** Graham 1946: 30; Orbell 1968: xix–xx, 28–29,
109.

*Uruao* Davis 1990: 86–91; Orbell 1985: 60–61;
Pomare & Cowan 1930–34: I, 42. See also Tama-
rereti, Te Kāhui Tipua, Te Rapuwai.

**Uru and Ngangana** Ngata & Te Hurinui 1961: 154–57; Ngata & Te Hurinui 1970: 258–61, 434–39; Smith 1913–15: I, 118–23.

**Waihuka and Tū-te-amoamo** Orbell 1968: 20–27, 108–9.

**Wairaka** Tarakawa 1894.

**Wairua** Best 1900–01: I, 177–89; Best 1982: 124; Orbell 1985: 78–83.

**Waiwaia** Orbell 1970; Te Whēoro MS 1871.

**Wehi-nui-a-mamao** Best 1922: 44; Tiramōrehu 1987: 24, 30; White 1887–91: I, 52.

**Whaitiri** Beckwith 1970: 238–58; Best 1925: I, 909–18; Best 1922: 33; Johansen 1958: 99–107; Kohere 1951: 31–32; White 1887–91: I, 44; Wohlers 1874: 15–18, 41–42.

**Whakaahu** Best 1922: 62–63; Hongi 1913: 201.

**Whakaotirangi** Grey 1857: 86, Orbell 1985a: 45–46.

**Whakatau** Grey 1928: 32–36, 46–49, 174; Grey 1956: see index; Johansen 1954: 132–8; Johansen 1958: 155–60; Shortland 1856: 67–71; White 1887–91: II, 147–54.

**Whakaue** Stafford 1967: 84; Stafford 1994: 92.

**Whānau-moana** Cowan 1930: 21–22; Smith 1908: 41, Taylor 1855: 33–34.

**Whāngai-mokopuna** McEwen 1946: 17.

**Whānui** Best 1925: I, 824–28; Best 1922: 63–64.

**Whare-matangi** Best 1982: 133–35.

**Whātonga** McEwen 1986: 3–14; Nēpia Pōhūhū 1930.

**Whatu kura** Downes 1910; Hammond 1924: 214.

**Whiro** Best 1924: 107; White 1887–1891: II, 6–19; Williams 1867: 237.

**Whiro-nui** White 1880: 14–15, 28.

# References

The following abbreviations are used:
*JPS Journal of the Polynesian Society*
*TPNZI Transactions and Proceedings of the New Zealand Institute*

Adkin, G. Leslie 1959. *The great harbour of Tara*. Christchurch.

Anon. 1926. 'White magic of the Maori.' *JPS* 35: 315–27.

Anon. 1932. *Echoes of the pa*. Gisborne.

Aoterangi, Wirihana 1923. *Fragments of ancient Maori history*. Collected by John McGregor, translated by George Graham. Auckland.

Beattie, Herries 1915–22. 'Traditions and legends collected from the natives of Murihiku.' 14 parts. *JPS*, passim.

Beattie, Herries 1939. See Tikao, Teone Taare.

Beattie, Herries 1945. *Maori lore of lake, alp and fiord*. Dunedin.

Beattie, Herries 1949. *The Maoris and Fiordland*. Dunedin.

Beattie, Herries 1957. See Te Maihāroa, Taare.

Beattie, Herries 1994. *Traditional lifeways of the southern Maori*. Ed. Atholl Anderson. Dunedin.

Beckwith, Martha 1970. *Hawaiian mythology*. Honolulu. (1st edn 1940).

Best, Elsdon 1897. *Waikaremoana: the sea of the rippling waters*. Government Printer, Wellington.

Best, Elsdon 1897a. 'Te Rehu-o-Tainui.' *JPS* 7: 41–66.

Best, Elsdon 1898. 'The art of the whare pora . . .' *TPNZI* 31: 625–58.

Best, Elsdon 1899. 'Notes on Maori mythology.' *JPS* 8: 93–121.

Best, Elson 1900–01. 'Spiritual concepts of the Maori.' 2 parts. *JPS* 9: 173–99, JPS 10: 1–20.

Best, Elsdon 1902. 'Notes on the art of war . . .' part 1. *JPS* 11: 11–41.

Best, Elsdon 1902a. 'Food products of Tuhoeland.' *TPNZI* 35: 45–111.

Best, Elsdon 1902b. 'The diversions of the whare tapere . . .' *TPNZI* 34: 34-69.

Best, Elsdon 1904. 'Te Aratawhao.' *TPNZI* 37: 130-38.

Best, Elsdon 1905–07. 'The lore of the whare-kohanga.' *JPS* 14, 15, 16, passim.

Best, Elsdon 1908. 'Maori forest lore: being some account of native forest lore and woodcraft . . . of the Tuhoe . . .' Part 2 *TPNZI* 41: 231–85.

Best, Elsdon 1912. *The stone implements of the Maori*. Government Printer, Wellington.

Best, Elsdon 1917. 'The land of Tara and they who settled it.' Part I. *JPS* 26: 143–69.

Best, Elsdon 1918. 'The land of Tara and they who settled it.' Part V. *JPS* 27: 165–77.

Best, Elsdon 1921. 'The Maori genius for personification . . .' *TPNZI* 1–13.

Best, Elsdon 1922. *Astronomical knowledge of the Maori*. Wellington.

Best, Elsdon 1923. *The Maori school of learning*. Wellington.

Best, Elsdon 1924. *Maori religion and mythology*. Part 1. Wellington.

Best, Elsdon 1924a. *The Maori*. 2 vols. Wellington.

Best, Elsdon 1925. *Tuhoe: the children of the mist*. 2 vols. New Plymouth.

Best, Elsdon 1925a. *Games and pastimes of the Maori*. Wellington.

Best, Elsdon 1925b. *The Maori canoe*. Wellington.

Best, Elsdon 1925c. *Maori agriculture . . .* Wellington.

Best, Elsdon 1927. *The pa Maori*. Wellington.

Best, Elsdon 1928. 'The story of Ngae and Tutununui.' *JPS* 37: 261–70.

Best, Elsdon 1928a. 'The story of Rua and Tangaroa . . .' *JPS* 37: 257–60.

Best, Elsdon 1929. Fishing methods and *devices of the Maori*. Wellington.

Best, Elsdon 1929a. *The whare kohanga and its lore*. Wellington.

Best, Elsdon 1942. *Forest lore of the Maori*. New Plymouth.

Best, Elsdon 1982. *Maori religion and mythology*. Part 2. Wellington.

Buddle, T. 1851. *The aborigines of New Zealand*. Auckland.

Colenso, William 1880. 'Historical incidents and

traditions of the olden times . . .' *TPNZI* 13: 38–57.

Colenso, William 1889. *Ancient tide-lore and tales of the sea* . . . Napier.

Cowan, James 1910. *The Maoris of New Zealand.* Christchurch.

Cowan, James 1927. *The Tongariro National Park.* Wellington.

Cowan, James 1930. *Fairy folk tales of the Maori.* 2nd edn. Auckland.

Cowan, James 1930a. *The Maori yesterday and today.* Auckland.

Cowan, James 1982. *Tales of the Maori* . Wellington.

Dansey, Harry 1968. 'Matariki.' *Te Ao Hou* 61: 15-16.

Davidson, Janet 1984. *The prehistory of New Zealand.* Auckland.

Davies, John and D. Darling 1851. *A Tahitian and English dictionary* . . . Papeete.

Davis, C. O. B. 1855. *Maori mementos.* Auckland.

Davis, Te Aue 1990. *He kōrero pūrākau mo ngā taunahanahatanga a ngā tūpuna: place names of the ancestors. A Maori oral history atlas.* Wellington.

Diamond, J. T. and B. W. Hayward 1979. *The Maori history and legends of the Waitakere Ranges.* Auckland.

Dieffenbach, Ernst 1843. *Travels in New Zealand.* 2 vols. London.

Downes, T. W. 1910. 'On the Whatu-Kura.' *JPS* 19: 218–21.

Downes, T. W. 1914 .'Pelorus Jack. Tuhi-rangi.' *JPS* 23: 176–80.

Downes, T.W. 1915. *Old Whanganui.* Hawera.

Downes, T. W. 1921. *History of and guide to the Wanganui River.* Wanganui.

Elder, J. R. 1934. *Marsden's lieutenants.* Dunedin.

Elvy, W. J. 1949. *Kaikoura coast: Maori history, traditions and place-names.* Christchurch.

Elvy, W. J. 1957. *Kei puta te Wairau: a history of Marlborough in Maori times.* Christchurch.

Fletcher, H. J. 1913. 'Ngahue's ear-drop.' *JPS* 22: 228–29.

Fowler, Leo 1958. 'The knight errantry of Tamahae.' *Te Ao Hou* 24: 11–16.

Fowler, Leo. 1974. *Te Mana o Turanga.* Gisborne.

Grace, A. A. 1907. *Folk-tales of the Maori.* Wellington.

Grace, John Te H. 1959. *Tuwharetoa: a history of the Maori people of the Taupo district.* Wellington.

Graham, George 1922. 'A Maori history of the Auckland isthmus.' In *The city of Auckland,* John Barr. Auckland.

Graham, George 1946. 'Some taniwha and tupua.' *JPS* 55: 26–39.

Graham, George 1951. 'Tainui: Maihi te Kapua te

Hinaki narration.' *JPS* 60: 80–92.

Graham, George 1980. *Maori place names of Auckland: their meaning and history.* Ed. D. R. Simmons. Auckland.

Grey, George 1853: *Ko nga moteatea* . . . Wellington.

Grey, George 1857. *Ko nga whakapepeha me nga whakaahuareka a nga tipuna o Aotea-Roa.* Cape Town.

Grey, George 1872. 'Description of the extinct gigantic bird of prey Hokioi.' *TPNZI* V: 435.

Grey, George 1928. *Nga mahi a nga tupuna.* 3rd edn., ed. H. W. Williams. Wellington.

Grey, George 1956. *Polynesian mythology.* 3rd edn. Christchurch. (1st edn. 1855).

Gudgeon, T. W. 1885. *'History and doings of the Maoris . . .'* Auckland.

Gudgeon, W. E. 1892. 'Maori migrations to New Zealand.' *JPS* 1: 212–32.

Gudgeon, W. E. 1895. 'The Maori tribes of the east coast of New Zealand.' Part 2. *JPS* 4: 17–32.

Gudgeon, W. E. 1896. 'The Maori tribes of the east coast of New Zealand.' Part 4. *JPS* 5: 2–12.

Gudgeon, W. E. 1897. 'The Maori tribes of the east coast of New Zealand.' Part 5. *JPS* 6: 177–86.

Gudgeon, W. E. 1905. 'Maori religion.' *JPS* 14: 107–30.

Gudgeon, W. E. 1905a. 'Maori superstition.' *JPS* 14: 167–92.

Gudgeon, W. E. 1906. 'The Tipua-kura, and other manifestations of the spirit world.' *JPS* 15: 27–57.

Hammond, T. G. 1894: 'The taro . . .' *JPS* 3: 105–6.

Hammond, T. G. 1924. *The story of Aotea.* Christchurch.

Henry, Teuira 1928. *Ancient Tahiti.* Honolulu.

Hera 1970. 'Taharākau.' *Te Ao Hou* 69: 6–7.

Hongi, Hare 1910. 'Ruatapu, son of Uenuku.' *JPS* 19: 89–93.

Hongi, Hare 1913. *Maori-English tutor and vade-mecum.* Christchurch.

Johansen, J. Prytz 1954. *The Maori and his religion in its non-ritualistic aspects.* Copenhagen.

Johansen, J. Prytz 1958. *Studies in Maori rites and myths.* Copenhagen.

Jones, Kevin L. 1994. *Ngā tohuwhenua mai te rangi: a New Zealand archaeology in aerial photographs.* Wellington.

Kāpiti, Pita 1912. 'The history of Horouta canoe.' *JPS* 21: 152–63.

Kāpiti, Pita 1913. 'Kumara lore.' *JPS* 22: 36–41.

Kararehe, Te Kāhui 1893. 'The Kurahoupo canoe.' *JPS* 2: 186–91.

Kararehe, Te Kāhui 1898 'Te tatau-o-te-po.' *JPS* 7: 55–63.

Keene, Florence 1963. *O te Raki.* Auckland.

Keene, Florence 1975. *Tai Tokerau.* Whangarei.

Kelly, L. G. 1949. *Tainui.* Wellington.

Kereama, Matire 1967. *The tail of the fish: Maori memories of the far north.* Auckland.

Kerry-Nicholls, J. H. 1884. *The King Country.* London.

Kohere, Reweti 1951. *The autobiography of a Maori.* Wellington.

Kohere, Reweti 1951a. *He konae aronui.* Wellington.

Lambert, Thomas 1925. *The story of old Wairoa . . .* Dunedin.

Lyall, A. C. 1979. *Whakatohea of Opotiki.* Wellington.

McEwen, J. 1946. 'Historical notes from Tamaki-nui-a-rua (Dannevirke).' *JPS* 55: 15–25.

McEwen, J. 1986. *Rangitāne: a tribal history.* Auckland.

McGregor, John 1898. *Popular Maori songs . . .* Supplement 1. Auckland.

McLean, Mervyn and Margaret Orbell 1975. *Traditional songs of the Maori.* Wellington.

Mair, Gilbert. 1923. *Reminiscences and Maori stories.* Auckland.

Makereti 1938. *The old-time Maori.* London.

Makitanara, Tuiti 1983. *Two Maori stories from Marlborough.* Ed. Melodie Watson and Margaret Orbell. Canterbury Maori Studies 1. Christchurch.

Massy, E. I. 1903. *The Tarawera eruption: 1886 and some Maori legends* London.

Miskelly, C. M. 1987. 'The identity of the hakawai.' *Notornis* 34: 95–116.

Mitcalfe, Barry 1961. 'Te Rerenga Wairua: leaping place of the spirits.' *Te Ao Hou* 35: 38–44.

Mitchell, J. H. 1944. *Takitimu: a history of the Ngati Kahungunu people.* Wellington.

Motuiti Community Trust 1987. *Tamatea Motuti.* North Hokianga.

Neich, Roger 1994. *Painted histories: early Maori figurative painting.* Auckland.

Ngata, A. T. 1959. *Nga moteatea.* Vol. 1. Wellington.

Ngata, A. T. and Pei Te Hurinui 1961. *Nga moteatea,* vol. 2. Wellington.

Ngata, A. T. and Pei Te Hurinui 1970. *Nga moteatea,* vol. 3. Wellington.

Ngata, A. T. 1990. *Nga moteatea,* vol. 4. Wellington.

Nihoniho, Tuta 1907–08. 'The story of the "Takitimu."' *JPS* 16: 220–25, 17: 93–107.

Oppenheim, R. S. 1973. *Maori death customs.* Wellington.

[Orbell, Margaret] 1965. 'The gods of the ancient Maori world.' *Te Ao Hou* 52: 16–20.

Orbell, Margaret 1966. 'Three old stories.' *Te Ao Hou* 56: 18–22.

Orbell, Margaret 1968. *Maori folktales.* Auckland.

Orbell, Margaret 1970. 'Two letters from Hari Hemara Wahanui to Elsdon Best: June 1917.' *Dominion Museum Records in Ethnology* 2: 5.

Orbell, Margaret 1973. 'Two versions of the Maori story of Te Tahi o te Rangi.' *JPS* 82: 127–40.

Orbell, Margaret MS 1977. 'Themes and images in Maori love poetry.' 2 vols. PhD thesis in Auckland University Library.

Orbell, Margaret 1978. *Maori poetry: an introductory anthology.* Auckland.

Orbell, Margaret 1982. 'The other people: Maori beliefs about fairies.' In *Oral and traditional literatures,* ed. N. Simms, *Pacific Quarterly Moana.* Hamilton (pp. 83–92).

Orbell, Margaret 1985. *The natural world of the Maori.* Auckland.

Orbell, Margaret 1985a. *Hawaiki: a new approach to Maori tradition.* Christchurch.

Orbell, Margaret 1990. 'He Kōrero Kēhua.' *Te Karanga* 6: 2: 12–22.

Orbell, Margaret 1991. *Waiata: Maori songs in history.* Auckland.

Orbell, Margaret 1992. *Traditional Māori stories.* Auckland.

Pangu, W. T. H. 1905. 'Te Rerenga Wairua.' *Te Pīpīwharauroa* 90: 7–8.

Parsons, Patrick 1994. 'A harbour lost.' *New Zealand Historic Places* 45: 19–23.

Pere, Wī 1898. 'Kiwa, the navigator.' *JPS* 7: 111–13.

Phillipps, W. J. and J. M. McEwen 1946–48. *Carved houses of Te Arawa.* 2 vols. Dominion Museum, Wellington.

Phillipps, W. J. 1955. *Maori carving illustrated.* Wellington.

Phillipps, W. J. and J. C. Wadmore 1956. *The great carved house Mataatua of Whakatane.* Wellington.

Phillips, F. L. 1989. *Nga tohu a Tainui: landmarks of Tainui.* Otorohanga.

Piripi, Morore 1961. 'Ko te timatanga mai o Ngatiwai: history of Ngatiwai.' *Te Ao Hou* 37:18–21. (See also *Te Ao Hou* vols. 38, 39, 54.)

Pōhūhū, Nepia 1930. 'Nepia Pohuhu.' 1st instalment. *Te Wananga,* vol. 1, no. 2.

Pōhūhū, Nepia 1930a. '[Nepia Pohuhu].' 2nd instalment. *Te Wananga,* vol. 2, no. 1.

Polack 1838. *New Zealand . . .* 2 vols. London.

Polack 1840. *Manners and customs of the New Zealanders.* 2 vols. London.

Pomare, Maui and James Cowan 1930–34. *Legends of the Maori.* 2 vols. Wellington.

Porter, T. W. 1925. *Legends of the Maori and personal reminiscences . . .* Christchurch.

Prickett, Nigel (ed.) 1982. *The first thousand years.* Palmerston North.

Reedy, Anaru 1993. *Ngā kōrero a Mohi Ruatapu, tohunga rongonui o Ngāti Porou: the writings of Mohi Ruatapu.* Christchurch.

Rimini, T. W. 1901. 'Te puna kahawai i Mōtū.' *JPS* 10: 183–88.

Salmond, Anne 1991. *Two worlds: first meetings between Maori and Europeans 1642–1772.* Auckland.

Schultz, E. 1909. 'The Samoan version of the story of Apakura.' *JPS* 18: 139–42.

Schwimmer, E. G. 1963. 'Guardian animals of the Maori.' *JPS* 72: 397–410.

Shortland, Edward 1851. *The southern districts of New Zealand.* London.

Shortland, Edward 1856. *Traditions and superstitions of the New Zealanders.* 2nd edn. London.

Shortland, Edward 1882. *Maori religion and mythology.* London.

Simmons, D. R. 1976. *The great New Zealand myth.* Wellington.

Simmons, D. R. 1987. *Maori Auckland.* Auckland.

Smith, Jonathan Z. 1982. *Imagining religion: from Babylon to Jonestown.* University of Chicago Press, Chicago.

Smith, S. Percy 1900. 'Wars of the northern against the southern tribes of New Zealand in the nineteenth century, part V.' Supplement to *JPS* 9.

Smith, S. Percy 1896. 'The peopling of the north.' 1st instalment, supplement to *JPS* 5.

Smith, S. Percy 1897. 'The peopling of the north.' 2nd instalment, supplement to *JPS* 6.

Smith, S. Percy 1905: 'Some Whanganui historical notes.' *JPS* 14: 131–58.

Smith, S. Percy 1907. 'History and traditions of the Taranaki coast.' Chapters 1–6. *JPS* 16: 120–219.

Smith, S. Percy 1908. 'History and traditions of the Taranaki coast.' Chapter 7. *JPS* 17: 1–47.

Smith, S. Percy 1908a. 'History and traditions of the Taranaki coast.' Chapter 8. *JPS* 17: 52–78.

Smith, S. Percy 1913–15. *The lore of the whare wananga.* 2 vols. New Plymouth.

Stack, J. W. 1893. *Kaiapohia, the story of a siege.* Christchurch.

Stack, J. W. 1898. *South Island Maoris: a sketch of their history and legendary lore.* Christchurch.

Stack, J. W. 1937. *Early Maoriland adventures.* 2nd edn. London.

Stafford, D. M. 1967. *Te Arawa.* Wellington.

Stafford, D. M. 1994. *Landmarks of Te Arawa. Volume 1: Rotorua.* Auckland.

Stimson, J. F. 1937. *Tuamotuan legends (Island of Anaa).* Bishop Museum, Bulletin 148. Honolulu.

Stimson, J. F. and D. S. Marshall 1964. *A dictionary of some Tuamotuan dialects of the Polynesian language.* The Hague.

Stirling, Eruera and Anne Salmond 1980. *Eruera . . .* Wellington.

Tarakawa, Takaanui 1893. 'Ko te hoenga mai o Te Arawa, raua ko Tainui i Hawaiki.' *JPS* 2: 220–52.

Tarakawa, Takaanui 1894. 'The coming of Mata-atua, Kurahaupo, and other canoes . . .' *JPS* 3: 65–71.

Tarakawa, Takaanui and Paora Ropiha 1899. 'Mahu rāua ko Taewa.' *JPS* 8: 122–34.

Tarakawa, Takaanui 1909. 'Te korero mo Kataore.' *JPS* 18: 205–215.

Tareha, Tuiri 1954. 'Ko Pania.' *Te Ao Hou* 10: 20.

Tautahi, Hetaraka 1900. 'Ko "Aotea" waka.' *JPS* 9: 200–33.

Tauwhare, Rihari 1905. 'The coming of Tainui.' *JPS* 14: 96–99.

Taylor, Richard MS. In Auckland Public Library: Taylor MS 297/18, item 5 [p.1]. (The author is indebted to the Librarian of the Auckland Public Library for permission to use this manuscript.)

Taylor, Richard 1855. *Te Ika a Maui . . .* London.

Taylor, Richard 1870. *Te ika a Maui . . .* 2nd edn. London.

Taylor, Richard 1870a. *Maori and English dictionary.* 2nd edn. Auckland.

Taylor, W. A. 1944. *Waihora: Maori associations of Lake Ellesmere.* Leeston.

Te Aro 1894. 'Te patunga o Mokonui.' *JPS* 3: 165–67.

Te Hata, Hoeta 1916. 'The Ngati-Tuwharetoa occupation of Taupo-nui-a-Tia.' *JPS* 25: 104–16.

Te Hurinui, Pei 1960. *King Potatau.* Wellington.

Te Maihāroa, Taare 1957. *Folklore and fairy tales of the Canterbury Maoris.* Told by Taare Te Maiharoa to Maud Goodenough Hayter, ed. Herries Beattie. Dunedin.

Te Rangi Hiroa 1950. *The coming of the Maori.* 2nd edn. Wellington.

Te Rangikāheke 1992. *The story of Māui by Te Rangikāheke.* Ed. Agathe Thornton. Canterbury Maori Studies 5. Christchurch.

Te Whare-auahi, Pango 1905. 'Te hekenga a Kahuhunu.' *JPS* 14: 67–95.

Te Whēoro, Wiremu MS 1871. 'The ancient history of the Tainui tribes.' NZ MS 712. In Auckland Public Library. (The author is indebted to the Librarian of the Auckland Public Library for permission to use this manuscript.)

Te Whetū 1897. 'Kame-tara and his ogre wife.' *JPS* 6: 97–106.

Thornton, Agathe. See Te Rangikāheke.

Tikao, Teone Taare 1939. *Tikao talks: traditions and tales told by Teone Taare Tikao to Herries Beattie.* Recorded by Beattie. Dunedin.

Tiramōrehu, Matiaha 1987. *Te waiatatanga mai o te atua.* Ed. Manu van Ballekom and Ray Harlow. Canterbury Māori Studies 4. Christchurch.

Tregear, Edward 1891. *Maori-Polynesian comparative dictionary.* Christchurch.

Tregear, Edward 1926. *The Maori race.* Wanganui.

Trotter, Michael and Beverley McCulloch 1989. *Unearthing New Zealand.* Wellington.

Tūnuiarangi, H. P. 1905. 'Te kōrero mo Ngarara-huarau.' *JPS* 200–4.

Turei, Mohi 1876. A Maori legend. *Te Waka Maori o Niu Tirani* 22 August 1876: 201–3.

Turei, Mohi 1913. 'Taharakau.' *JPS* 22: 62-66.

van Ballekom, Manu and Ray Harlow. See Tiramōrehu, Matiaha.

von Hochstetter, F. R. 1867. *New Zealand* Stuttgart.

Waititi, Manihera 1901. 'Te kura-pae-a-Māhia.' *Te Pīpīwharauroa* 45: 7.

Waititi, Manihera 1902. 'Te kura-pae-a-Māhia.' *Te Pīpīwharauroa* 48: 9.

Waititi, Manihera 1902a. 'Te kura-pae-a-Mahina.' *Te Pīpīwharauroa* 57: 6.

Walsh, P. 1903. 'The cultivation and treatment of the kumara . . . *TPNZI* 35: 12–24.

White, John 1874. *Te Rou; or, the Maori at home.* London.

White, John 1880. 'Legendary history of the Maoris.' *Appendices to the House of Representatives* G–8.

White, John 1885. *Maori customs and superstitions.* Auckland.

White, John 1887–91. *The ancient history of the Maori.* 6 vols. and a vol. of plates. Wellington. (References are to English-language sections of these volumes.)

Williams, Herbert W. 1971. *Dictionary of the Maori language.* Wellington.

Williams, William 1867. *Christianity among the New Zealanders.* London.

Wilson, John (ed.) 1987. *From the beginning: the archaeology of the Maori.* Auckland.

Wilson, J. A. 1907. *The story of Te Waharoa.* Christchurch.

Wohlers, J. F. H. 1874. 'The mythology and traditions of the Maori in New Zealand.' Parts 1 and 2. *TPNZI* 7: 3–53.

Wohlers, J. F. H. 1875. 'The mythology and traditions of the Maori in New Zealand.' Parts 1 and 2. *TPNZI* 8: 108–23.

# Illustration Credits

For permission to reproduce photographs in their collections, I am indebted to the directors of the following institutions. Black and white photographs are identified by page number, and colour photographs by letter and number; thus A1 is the first photograph in the first colour section. Alexander Turnbull Library, Wellington: pages 17, 19 above, 19 below left, 35, 49 (copy by John Barr Clarke of sketch of Lake Waikaremoana by J. C. Hoyte), 53, 62 above, 128, 151, 173, 177, 228, 243, 246 (John Guise Mitford, watercolour, 1845). Auckland City Art Gallery: 39 (Trevor Lloyd, 'Rangitoto,' drypoint, 65 × 263 mm, presented by Connie and Olive Lloyd, 1973), D1 (watercolour by John Kinder, 'Manaia, Whangarei,' 205 × 338 mm, presented by H. A. Kinder, 1937). Auckland Museum Te Papa Whakahiku: 19 below right, 35 left, 42 above (sketch by Richard Taylor), 78, 87 below, 107, 170, 182, 187, 202, 205, 242, 245, A10, F10, F11. Auckland Public Library: 112, 164, 185, 219 right, 227. Canterbury Museum: 131, 239. Gisborne Herald: 99. Gisborne Museum and Arts Centre Te Whare Taonga o Tairawhiti: 139, 236. Hocken Library, University of Otago: 18 left (watercolour by William Fox, 'Matthias, native missionary at Moeraki,' 250 × 176 mm), 111 below. Institute of Geological and Nuclear Sciences: 51 below, 93 below, 127, 208, D6, D7, D8, D9, D12 (photos Lloyd Homer). Meteorological Service of New Zealand Limited: E 3. Museum of New Zealand Te Papa Tongarewa: 14, 23, 25, 32, 41 above, 58, 61 below, 62 below, 66 left, 80, 84, 91 above, 93 above, 102, 104, 108, 109, 117, 118, 119, 123, 140, 151 below, 153 above, 153 below, 161, 177 below, 178, 192, 222, 223 below, 225 above, 230 above, 231, 244, E1, E2, F2, F8, F9, F12. New Zealand Post: E6, E7, E8, E9, E10. Otago Museum: 191. Rotorua Museum of Art and History Te Whare Taonga o Te Arawa: 66 right, 69, 71, 138, 197, 199, 216 (photo Andrew Warner). Te Awamutu District Museum: 237 (with the kind permission of Te Arikinui Dame Te Atairangikaahu). Wellington Marine Museum: 225 below. Whanganui Regional Museum: 180, 212. Whangarei Museum: 18 right, 72, 73.

For permission to take photographs for publication, I am indebted to the directors of the following institutions. Auckland Museum Te Papa Whakahiku: 65, 152, A9 (photos M. Orbell). Canterbury Museum: 37 below (photo University of Canterbury), 195 (photo Theo Schoon). Museum of New Zealand Te Papa Tongarewa: 57 (photo M. Orbell), 188 (photo Brian Turner), A7 (photo M. Orbell). Otago Museum: A3 (photo Michael de Hamel). Whanganui Regional Museum: 68, 91 below, 111 above, 213 (photos M. Orbell).

For permission to take photographs for publication, I am indebted also to the owners of the following meeting houses. Rangitihi, Rotoiti: 149 (photo Gordon Walters). Rongopai, Waituhi: 81, 167, A8 (photos M. Orbell). Te Mana o Tūranga, Manutūkē: 95, 214, 215, 234 (photos M. Orbell). Te Tatau-o-Hape-ki-tuarangi, Waimana: 45 (photo Gordon Walters). Uruika, Lake Rotoiti: A2 (photo Gordon Walters). Whitireia, Whāngārā: 130 (photo M. Orbell).

The portrait of Rīria Te Kāhui (204) was kindly lent by her descendant Ailsa Smith. Father Henare Tate kindly gave permission for the photograph of Kōhine-mataroa (89) to be reproduced from the book *Tamatea Motuti* (Motuti Community Trust, North Hokianga 1987). I am grateful to the Vestry of the Rangiātea Rohe for permission to publish a photograph taken by myself inside Rangiātea (A5).

Other photographs have been provided by the following. Lawrence Aberhart: 168. Jill Carlyle: 175, 250. Geoffrey Cox: B4, B5. June Northcroft Grant: front cover, A6, E4, E5. Peter Hallett: A4. Jos of Jos's Photography: D3, D4. Dawn E. Kendall: 31. B. J. Mason: D5. Graeme Matthews: D10. Geoff Moon: B1, B2, B3, C2. M. Orbell: 56, 198. Craig Potton: C1, C3. Theo Schoon: 47 left, 47 right, 83. B. W. Thomas: C5. Photographs on 106, 145, 155 below, 157, 219 left, 230 below and 241 are from the author's collection.

Sandra Parkkali has specially done the drawings on pages 27, 29, 33, 41, 63, 125, 144, 161, 203, 211, 232, 235 and 248, and the map (20).

Other illustrations have been provided by Betty Brownlie (34 and 77, from *The secrets of natural New Zealand* by Betty Brownlie and Ronald Lockley, Auckland, 1987); Piers Hayman (51 above, 57 below and 103, from his book *Discovering the birds of New Zealand*, Auckland, 1984); *New Zealand Geographic* (painting by Dave Gunson) D6; F. L. Phillips (88 and 159, from his book *Nga tohu a Tainui: landmarks of Tainui*, vol. 2, Otorohanga, 1995); and Dennis Turner (36, from his book *Tangi*, Wellington, 1963, by permission of Reed Publishing, Auckland).

The drawings by Vivian Ward on 86 and 207 are from Mike Bradstock's book *Between the tides* (Auckland, 1989), and are published with his permission. The drawings by Russell Clark (43, 101, 124, 194) are from an edition of George Grey's *Polynesian mythology* published in 1956 by Whitcombe and Tombs, Christchurch, and are published by permission of Penguin Books, Auckland. The drawings by Wilhelm Dittmer (38, 116, 147) are from his book *Te Tohunga* (London, 1907). The drawings by Theo Schoon (37 above, 97, 141, 200) are reproduced from photographs in the collection of Gordon Walters.

Artworks in publications in the Canterbury University Library and the Macmillan Brown Library were photographed by Duncan Shaw-Brown, Merilyn Hooper and Barbara Cottrell of the University's Audio-Visual Aids Department; I am grateful also to the librarians who helped. The works are as follows:

George French Angas, *The New Zealanders illustrated*. London, 1847. Pages 9 above and below, 35 right, 61 above, 87 above, 135, 218, A1, B7, D11, F1, F4, F5, F6, F7.

T. Bell, 1843, 'Reptiles,' in Charles Darwin's *The zoology of the voyages of H.M.S. Beagle . . .* London (facsimile edn, Nova Pacifica, Wellington, 1980). Page 120.

W. L. Buller, *A history of the birds of New Zealand*. London, 1888. Pages 136, 143, 217, B6.

Barnet Burns, *A brief narrative of a New Zealand chief*. London, 1844. Page 60.

Augustus Earle, *Narrative of a residence in New Zealand*. London, 1832. Pages 13, 15.

Augustus Earle, *Sketches illustrative of the native inhabitants of New Zealand*. London, 1838. F3.

George Grey, *Polynesian Mythology . . .* London, 1855. Page 210.

J. Hawkesworth, *An account of voyages undertaken by the order of his present majesty*. London, 1773. Pages 42 below, 76.

J. S. Polack, *New Zealand . . .* London, 1838. D2.

J. S. Polack, *Manners and customs of the New Zealanders*. London, 1840. Pages 70, 162 below.

Taylor, Richard, *Te Ika a Maui . . .* London, 1855. Pages 186, 223 above.

*Te Puke ki Hikurangi*. Page 53.

W. T. L. Travers, *The stirring times of Te Rauparaha . . .* Christchurch, 1906. Page 83.

Dumont d'Urville, *Voyage pittoresque autour du monde*. Paris, 1839. Pages 92, 166, 189.

F. R. von Hochstetter, *New Zealand*. Stuttgart, 1867. Page 40.

E. R. Waite, 'Pisces,' part II. In *Records of the Canterbury Museum*, vol. 1, no. 3, June 1911. Pages 51, 162.

# Index